An Ethics of Personality

An Ethics of Personality

Agnes Heller

BLACKWELL
Oxford UK & Cambridge USA

First published 1996

Blackwell Publishers Ltd
108 Cowley Road
Oxford OX4 1JF
UK

Blackwell Publishers Inc.
238 Main Street
Cambridge, Massachusetts 02142
USA

British Library Cataloguing in Publication Data

A CIP catalogue record for this book is available from the British Library.

Library of Congress Cataloging-in-Publication Data

Heller, Agnes.
An ethics of personality / Agnes Heller.
p.   cm.
Includes index.
ISBN 0-631-19889-X (alk. paper). – ISBN 0-631-19891-1 (pbk.: alk. paper)
1. Ethics.   2. Personality.   I. Title.
BJ1031.H45   1995
171'.3 – dc20
Typeset in 10 on 11½ pt Sabon
by Best-set Typesetter Ltd., Hong Kong
Printed in Great Britain by Hartnolls Ltd, Bodmin, Cornwall

This book is printed on acid-free paper.

In memory of
Ferenc Fehér

Contents

Acknowledgements   viii

Introduction   1

Part I   Nietzsche and *Parsifal*   9
(Prolegomena to an Ethics of Personality)

Lecture One   11
Lecture Two   23
Lecture Three   38
Lecture Four   50
Lecture Five   69

Part II   Vera, or Is an Ethics of Personality Possible?   93

Dialogue One: Is There an Ethics of Personality?   95
Dialogue Two: If There Is, How Can We Describe It?   139
Dialogue Three: If There Is, How Can We Practise It?   190

**Part III   Letters Concerning Moral Aesthetics:
On the Beautiful and the Sublime Character,
on Happiness and Love**   221
(Samples of the Correspondence between Mrs Sophie Meller
and her Granddaughter, Fifi)

Notes   298

Index   309

Acknowledgements

I am grateful to David Taffel, John Krummel and Mary Dortch for the editing of the manuscript. I thank John Krummel for preparing the index, and also all the students of my Nietzsche class for engaging me in many good discussions.

Introduction

It was ten years ago that I set myself the task of writing a comprehensive yet modern moral philosophy. I called the project *A Theory of Morals*. Given that the project was meant to be comprehensive, it had to encompass all three approaches of traditional moral philosophies: the interpretative, the normative and the therapeutic-educational. But because it was meant to be a modern moral philosophy, it was impossible to combine the three approaches into one. I had to address the issues of morals three times, each time from the viewpoint of one of the three different aspects of moral philosophy. In the introduction of the first volume, *General Ethics* (Blackwell, 1988) I wrote,

> general ethics, moral philosophy, and theory of conduct are the three aspects of the same project. A project can be referred to as one and the same if, and only if, one and the same decisive question is raised and answered throughout the entire inquiry ... There is indeed *one* decisive question I raise and try to answer throughout the whole inquiry ... The fundamental question addressed is: 'Good persons exist – how are they possible?' This question will be answered in the first part from the position of theoretical reason (that of the participant observer), in the second part from the position of practical reason (that of the participant member of the contemporary world), and in the third part from the position of the human person as a whole (that of the individual who seeks good life).

In the introduction to the second volume of my theory of morals, *A Philosophy of Morals* (Blackwell, 1990), written immediately after the first, I reconfirmed my commitment to the third: 'The working title of the completing volume is *A Theory of Proper Conduct*, but I would rather term it a theory of moral wisdom, for this is exactly what the book is meant to be.' Having said this, I wanted to go on immediately with the work on the third volume, but this time – unexpectedly – the subject-matter itself began to resist my efforts. It was as if the 'spirit of our age'

spoke to me and warned me against deadly dangers such as being
untimely, too rhetorical, boring, and what is worst, assuming the authority of a judge without having been authorized. As a result I began to
wonder whether there was something fundamentally wrong with my
philosophical ideas. After facing this impasse I put aside the work on the
third volume of my *Theory of Morals* to find out first what the 'spirit of
our times' actually requires. The fruit of this inquiry is my book *Philosophy of History in Fragments* (Blackwell, 1993). I came to the conclusion
that, although there is nothing essentially wrong with my preliminary
ideas concerning the essential message of the third volume, there is a
serious problem with the genre. One cannot write nowadays about the
'good life' of single individuals in a traditional philosophical style. Both
the argumentative prose and the narrative prose require the philosopher
to assume a position of authority and speak for others and in the name
of others. But if 'good life' is custom-made – as it is in modern times – the
philosopher cannot assume the position of authority without telling lies,
and sometimes even boring lies. And in philosophy one should not lie.
There was already a shift in style between the first and second volume of
my *Theory of Morals*. Here, however, the shift had to be more dramatic.
In order to remain true to the message, I had to seek new forms of
communication.

I re-baptized the third volume *An Ethics of Personality*. The new title
emphasizes my commitment to a specific modern tradition in ethics one
which a few philosophers (among them Lukács) termed the 'ethics of
personality'. Although I choose this title to emphasize that we (all of us
who are committed to a serious and authentically modern ethics) are
sailing in the same boat, my relation to the ethics of personality is by no
means uncritical. *An Ethics of Personality* is the third volume of my
theory of morals. It does not invalidate the first two volumes, but
reinforces them in its own way. At the end of this book someone quotes
Wittgenstein's *Tractatus* (6.54–7), the passage about throwing away the
ladder. One has to climb the ladder first to be able finally to throw it
away. General ethics and philosophy of morals can also be understood as
such rungs of the ladder; one must climb up finally to arrive at an ethics
of personality that can be legitimately called an *ethics*, and not just a
theory of personality. Yet I prefer to speak of crutches rather than of
ladders. The simile of the ladder suggests the image of 'ascent', the simile
of the crutch does not. And if we believe (as I do) that there is a new
beginning in an ethics of personality all the time, the metaphor of ascent
can be misleading. Furthermore, if one throws the ladder away, one is
entirely on one's own. A crutch can be put down but can also be picked
up if one needs it again. And most of us need it, some rarely, some more
frequently, but we all can need it when the chips are down; crutches must
be kept just in case. But whether one speaks of a ladder or of crutches, my
story ends here just as Wittgenstein's *Tractatus* ends with the throwing

away of the ladder. No further volume is possible. The project that I entitled ten years ago *A Theory of Morals* is now accomplished.

The traditional ethics of personality has no use of the ladder. It begins with the experience of contingency. Influenced by the once proud dream of the deification of man, it gambles on the single individual as the sole and complete carrier of ethics. Ethics of personality is, in this sense, an ethics without norms, rules, ideals, without anything that is, or remains, merely 'external' to the person. There are as many ethics of personality as authors; e.g. Goethe, Marx, Nietzsche, Lukács represent entirely different versions of the common enterprise. But three types of approach can still be distinguished. The first assumes the universal viability of an ethics of personality. If only all external constraints put on the single individual were removed, every human person would be fully moral on his or her own way, and each and every individual would become a many-sided, universally developed personality. The classicistic ideal is based on this optimistic version of an ethics of personality. The second type (of an ethics of personality) does not doubt that external constraints must remain in place for the common man, but puts its money on the exceptional specimen of the human species: the exceptional person will be perfect in his or her own way and also absolutely free. No one else is worthy of theoretical interest. The third type encompasses philosophers who do not share even the limited illusions concerning an ethical elite, and also those who disapprove of such an approach. Still, they do not care for the 'ladder' or for 'crutches'; they just care for the single individual in his or her predicament of taking responsibility.

The last position is assumed recently by Jacques Derrida, particularly in his 'Force of law: the "mystical" foundation of authority' and in *The Spectres of Marx*. I will now enumerate a few important aspects of this ethics, with no aspiration to criticism or a comprehensive interpretation; my remarks will be preliminary.

Derrida says that ethics is an answer to the claim of the Other. The Other does not make his or her claims from the outside, but from the inside (he calls, summons, makes demands on us, frequently violent demands). We (alone) decide. Every decision is a leap. No decision can be based on knowledge. Consequences cannot be known; there is no rational choice. (But certainly, the leap is not irrational either.) Ethics is about personal responsibility, the responsibility taken for the Other. Personal responsibility is the single central category of ethics.

Everything that Derrida says in this context on ethics fits into the general framework of the third type of ethics of personality. The first type dismisses repsonsibility (for if everyone is fully ethical one does not need it), the second version emphasizes responsibility to ourselves, but not for the Other. The third type, however, can centre on the sense of an augmented (or even unconditional) responsibility. I agree with Derrida in everything he says. My problems are not with what he says but what he leaves (for the time being) unsaid. His is an ethics of personality without a ladder or crutches. To avoid misunderstanding: for Derrida it is imperative that one have crutches; he emphasizes this point very strongly, for example in 'Force of law: the "mystical" foundation of authority': without law there is no justice, even if justice is not based on the law. Derrida assumes that crutches (laws, norms, virtues, principles) exist, it is just that he is not theoretically interested in critically surveying them. Yet since we need those crutches, moral philosophy also needs to be theoretically interested in them.

Let me also canvass the central moral issues that are strongly emphasized in Derrida's latest works and lectures. I prefer to 'typify' these issues, no longer speaking exclusively about Derrida's intuitions but about the third tendency of a contemporary ethics of personality in general.

The Question of Responsibility

Morality is the answer to the Other's summons, or claim. The Other calls, makes demands on you from within. Which others? All the others: those who ever lived, those who are now living, and all those yet unborn. The question is, whether a person can (in practice) answer the call of all others. If not, which others should one prefer to other others? Moreover, if there are calls which ask me to do something and an Other calls for me to do the opposite, to which of the calls should I listen? There exists an answer to all these questions: Kant's categorical imperative. The categorical imperative is the claim of *all* others within you, since 'humankind in us' includes all those who ever lived, who are now living, as well the yet unborn. But even this absolute law cannot orient us fully. For it is in the choice of our maxims and not in our actions that we ought and also can answer the summons of all possible others; in actions we can not.

It was one of Max Weber's greatest blunders to juxtapose the 'ethics of responsibility' with the Kantian ethics. For if there is an ethics of absolute responsibility, it is exactly the Kantian ethics. Still, Weber's intuition was sound when he assumed that if the others make claims upon you from the outside, so that you have to answer the call of a few, and very specific, others, a different kind of responsibility is to be assumed. If you decide to live up to this specific kind of responsibility, you need crutches. Which are the best crutches? How can one employ them? Weber believes that the consequences of the action should first be considered, that foreknowledge can serve as the best crutch. But this is a very unreliable one.

Neither the Kantian nor the Weberian solution can satisfy a pure ethics of personality. In a pure ethics of personality one cannot subject one's action or decision to any norm whatsoever, not even to the universal moral law. As a consequence, the call of the Other from the inside cannot constitute a 'law', and it cannot be universal. Actually the others as *single others* make claim upon you, summon you; and *every* single other does so – those who ever lived, those who are living and the yet unborn. How can a single person take responsibility for all individual others? To this question Derrida answered (in a recent debate) that the one who does so will immediately die. The discovery of this connection leads straight to the tradition of the imitation of Christ. But there is no imitation of Christ without a 'minimum' of Christianity. Christian ethics, however, cannot serve as the yardstick to the ethics of personality; even if only the bare minimum of the Christian ethical norms is accepted, the ethics of personality loses its 'purity'. Dostoevsky too faced the momentous question of the all-inclusive personified responsibility. He said that every person is responsible for every other person; if only every person knew this, there would be paradise on earth at once. Redemption is, however, beyond the pale of an ethics of responsibility.

Finally, all absolute solutions lead us back to the consciousness of our finitude. Finite beings have to limit themselves. Finite beings are responsible for *some* others – or at least, they are responsible for some others more than to other others. So we return to the initial questions, Why do we listen to the call of these others and not to the call of other others? How do we decide the priority? Randomly?

These are the questions of finite beings, and finite beings do not know absolute answers. The ethics of responsibility is the ethics of the consciousness of human finitude and of contingency. It is the springing off point of this ethics that we never know anything for sure, that every decision is risky, and that we must take the risk. No crutch (law, norm, orientative principle) eliminates contingency and the risk. But they can illuminate – up to a point – the way to show the character, if not the amount, of the risk. 'Crutches' do not determine action. For example, there are people who prefer a more risky course of action to a less risky one. And anyway, we leap with our legs not with our crutches. Moreover, the use of crutches is not obligatory. But if there are crutches, one can use them, provided that one feels the need to use them. This is why moral philosophy needs to provide some orientative principles for the actors who seek moral advice. Philosophy does not invent such principles; it just brings them to the attention of modern (contingent) actors, and offers them for employment in need.

The Question of the Leap

It is true that every decision, every action is a leap. We never know ahead what waits us on the other shore. Yet not every leap is equally risky, and we do not leap all the time over the same abyss. Although knowledge does not play a significant role in our decisions, thinking sometimes does. So also do orientative moral principles and norms of virtue frequently help us to decide whether we should leap or not, or leap in this direction rather than in another one. If an ethics just reaffirms and reconfirms the truth *that* we leap, it falls short of being a helpful one. It needs to advise us about many other things: which kind of leap is morally more significant than other ones, what circumstances we might consider morally decisive for taking an action, which of our observable motivations should we rather keep in check, and so on and so forth. Let me compare two choices. One can be confronted with the choice to betray one's friend or to get a job, or to remain truthful to one's friend or lose the job. One can also have the choice to grade a student paper 'A' or 'B'. In both cases we leap either in one or in the other direction, and we also take a risk. It is possible that the student will commit suicide if he gets a 'B'. But the moral risk is remote in the second case, whereas it shows itself absolutely and unconditionally in the first. One could say that it is precisely because of the manifest presence of the moral content of the choice that a decent person does not need advice in the first case, whereas in the second case, where the devastating result of the act is just a remote possibility, no advice can – or need – be given in matters of choice. In the examples under scrutiny one does not need a crutch. But frequently, and particularly in a concrete context, choices present themselves less clearly. If one tries to diminish – although not eliminate – moral risks, one had better consult regulative ideas, orientative principles, not in order to follow imperatives, but in order to listen to an advice drawn from accumulated experience, without feeling the obligation to follow it.

No philosopher of an ethics of personality (third version) will deny the relevance of such and similar considerations (Derrida certainly not). The question still remains whether philosophy should address itself to these matters and considerations. My conclusion (in this book) is that this cannot be avoided. All modern ethics culminates in an ethics of personality. An ethics of personality tells us that we are morally responsible for ourselves and our fellow creatures and that we should leap – yet it provides no crutches. This is why modern men and women still need a general ethics and a philosophy of morals; an ethics of personality alone does not suffice.

An ethics of personality cannot address, on its own, the crucial question, Why do we listen to the claims, the voices, the summons of others at all? This is why I have constantly to take recourse in this book to the central insight of my philosophy of morals: there is a fundamental leap, the leap that renders moral meaning to all consecutive leaps, and this is the (existential) choice of ourselves as decent (good, honest) persons. For only after this leap has been accomplished will men and women ask the question, What is the right thing for me to do? The fundamental leap has no 'reason' and no traceable cause. For such a fundamental choice no norms can be provided, no advice given, no orientative principles presented. If it is founded, the foundation is transcendent.

This volume consists of three parts.

Since my greatest difficulties in conceiving an ethics of personality arose from the task of finding the proper philosophical genre I had to be careful in adjusting the genre to the task. It soon turned out that I had to choose three different philosophical genres for each of the three parts. First of all, I had to say certain things that I could not say directly. Expressing them directly would have destroyed the message I wanted to convey. Thus I needed to employ the trick of indirect communication as many other philosophers have before me, among them Kierkegaard, the philosopher who inspired me in more than one way. I had to put on masks, not in order to hide myself behind them but in order to assume the position of others. I had to make the others speak. Without letting others speak their own language and develop their positions, moreover, without letting others act and interact on their own, criticize each other and also me (or one of my other masks), I would have hardly been able to live up to the requirements of an authentic ethics of personality.

The first part of the book is written in the style of university lectures, the second as a dialogue, and the third takes the form of a correspondence. In spite of the change of genre all the three parts are thoroughly connected; the second is the continuation of the first, and the third that of the second. The students who conduct the philosophical dialogue of the second part have together attended the lectures on Nietzsche (described in the first part), and they continue to discuss the problems raised in those lectures. The young girl in the correspondence of the third part has attended the Nietzsche lectures, and she has also read the dialogue (the second part); she reflects upon both in her letters to her grandmother.

Each of the three parts of this book is guided by one of the representative stars of the philosophical constellation. The first part stands under the star of Destiny, the second under the star of Truth, the third under the star of Wisdom. Walter Benjamin called these stars, these 'ideas', 'deified names'. One can speak or write under a philosophical star, under the guidance of the 'deified name', without writing or speaking about the star itself. The first part of the book stands under the star of Destiny, because it is inspired by the love of Destiny (*amor fati*); the second part stands under the star of Truth, because it is inspired by the love of Truth. But in the third part, which stands under the star of Wisdom, the signs become reversed. It is not Wisdom that men and women seek here, but it is Wisdom that seeks its own life-sources: the Sublime, the Beautiful, and Love.

All three parts tell a story of the summons, or claim, that is laid on a person by an Other, and it tells the story of the responsibility assumed by this person. And every person's answer to this summons, to this voice, will be unique. This is why the second part of this volume had to be a dialogue and the third part had to take the form of a correspondence.

The later Heidegger believed that philosophy is a sort of poetry. I doubt it. But when I let my characters speak their minds and interact in their own way, I had to make use of a little fiction.

With one exception, none of the characters of the dialogue and of the correspondence is modelled entirely on real persons, living or dead; they are admixtures of real-life figures, literary figures and of philosophers. The one exception is Sophie Meller, the grandmother of the correspondence. In her character I tried to draw a real-life portrait of my own grandmother, née Sophie Meller (1858–1944). My inferior ability in characterization cannot do her justice. I would have needed Goethe's genius to show her as she really was.

Part I
Nietzsche and *Parsifal*

Prolegomena to
an Ethics of Personality

Lecture One

You may wonder why I am starting to discuss the ethics of personality with an illustration, for Nietzsche's ethics does seem to serve us as an illustration of this kind of ethics. Nietzsche is not even my proxy: he does not speak in my name (at least not entirely). I let him speak for himself. I treat Nietzsche the way he has treated so many other philosophers: I neglect many features, or rather masks, of his 'immoralist moralism', and put into the foreground those of his ideas which serve the purpose of my topic best, or those of his masks behind which I can also occasionally hide myself.

The ethics of personality is always *an* ethics of personality. Since it defies generalization, it cannot be approached in the same way as general ethics can. It is impossible to write a treatise on the ethics of personality. One must illustrate it in order to speak about it. or rather, one must take a paradigmatic case, a single person, a single life to exemplify its essence and its meaning. True, all kinds of ethics scrutinize a practice. But general ethics addresses itself to the discussion of the general features of this practice, together with the universal and particular conditions of such practice. General ethics speaks about ethics in general, and it considers the ethics of X or of Y, i.e. of single individuals, only in so far as they are specimens of the human species, the members of a group, or the denizens of a particular historical world and epoch.

Moral philosophy – or philosophy of morals – on the other hand, addresses itself directly to contemporaries. A modern moral philosophy turns to the modern (contingent) persons who seek an answer to the burning question 'What is the right thing for me to do?' Modern men and women are contingent and can live and be successful, without ever having asked the moral question proper. They need first to choose themselves as moral persons before assuming the moral position. To choose oneself as a moral person is an existential choice. An existential choice is a leap in so far as it is not determined. This means in practical terms that the person who has chosen himelf as a decent person existentially will never raise questions like 'Why should I be good rather than bad?' In other words, he will not seek to find or to establish causes or reasons for his determination to be a decent person. He will just be one. More precisely, he will become what he already is, namely a decent, upright person.

I admit that up to this point a modern philosophy of morals closely resembles an ethics of personality. After all, every decent person chooses herself, and herself alone, as a decent person; she chooses her own character and she is the one who will remain true to herself as a 'projection' in becoming what she is. The movement she develops is identical with the movement undertaken by a repository of an ethics of personality. The subtitle of Nietzsche's *Ecce Homo*[1] reads, 'How one becomes what one is' ('Wie man wird, was man ist'). But here the similarity abruptly ends. The representative repository of an ethics of personality will not turn to you (to us, to anyone) with the question 'what is the right thing for me to do?', for no one could possibly advise him, neither would he seek advice. It is always the Other who advises, and turning towards the Other for advice means assuming the position of intersubjectivity, which includes the position of others, their needs, desires, values, norms, in sum, their expectations.[2] When it comes to answering the moral question, a person assumes her position for herself, out of her own character, yet it is still a position with an aspect of generality. In the terms of an existential moral philosophy, one must repeat with Kierkegaard's Judge William that 'the individual is the universal'.[3] Yet in the terms of an ethics of personality the individual is never 'the universal' when she becomes what she is, she becomes a unique personality, an individual unlike any other: 'Hoert mich! denn ich bin der und der . . . Verwechselt mich vor Allem nicht!'[4] (Listen to me! I am this and this . Above all, don't mistake me for someone else!')

A philosophy of morals must accompany decent persons on their life's way – but it can accompany any decent modern person, and which philosophy we choose to serve as our model will not matter. This is so because every decent person can illustrate the existential position of decency; we can pick as our model the decent person whom we know best, even if he is known to no one else but ourselves. For the existential choice of decency (goodness) is not the choice of uniqueness, but the choice of the individual as the universal. This becomes impossible from the position of an ethics of personality. The person who serves as the paradigm of an ethics of personality has not chosen himself as a decent person, but as something else, e.g. as a politician, a general, a philosopher or a poet, eventually also just as a genius of self-creation. I have termed this latter kind of existential choice the choice under the category of the particular (in contrast to the moral choice under the category of the universal). I have also pointed out the tremendous risk of such a choice, as well as the indescribable felicity should the 'project' come off successfully. True, a single person can choose himself both under the category of the universal and the category of difference, yet even then one and only one of the two will be the fundamental choice.[5] If one chooses oneself under the category of the universal, many other choices still remain, essential ones among them. If one chooses oneself under the category of difference, there are no choices left anymore. As Nietzsche writes, 'Ich hab nie eine Wahl gehabt.'[6] ('I never had a choice'.) One is (becomes) one's own destiny not by tolerating one's own fate, but by loving it while suffering under its burden; this is what Nietzsche means by *amor fati*.

The existential choice under the category of difference is also a leap, but not everyone can make such a leap. The man who can do so is called by Nietzsche the 'lucky throw of the dice'.[7] The term 'throw of the dice' alludes to contingency: luck in the exceptional case. The 'lucky throw' is the aristocrat among the contingent existences. His possibilities also include a probability. Whereas an average contingent person (provided that she chooses herself as a decent person under the category of universality) can gain practically infinite possibilities, so that in her case possibility will stand higher than actuality, this is not so in case of a 'lucky throw'. For him, possibilities are excluded, and the one and only probability is translated into destiny. There is only one track to follow, one passion to live for; there is no second possibility left. This is why *amor fati* is the freedom of the man of destiny. Nothing less than the love of fate, the self-abandonment to one's destiny can make a 'lucky throw' which has no second choice left.

An ethics of personality is an ethics of such a 'lucky throw of the dice'. This is why it cannot be illustrated or exemplified by one of our close personal acquaintances. It must be exemplified by precisely such a 'lucky throw'. Beside numerous fictional ones, there are a few outstanding 'real life persons' who lend themselves easily to such an exemplification. Nietzsche constantly refers to the two most obvious ones: Napoleon and Goethe.

George Bernard Shaw, who had a predilection for an ethics of personality and who, like Dostoevsky and Ibsen before him, created several fictional characters to exemplify both the grandeur and the internal problematic of this ethics, portrayed Napoleon in *Man of Destiny* as its prototype.[8] But in fact, Napoleon is too extreme a case to be a representative illustration of a decisive modern ethical position.

Nietzsche was never tired of stressing that the most formidable epitomizers of the ethics of personality were also the most formidable seducers.[9] Among other things, they seduce by their very existence. Ethical models, if they are traditional, call for emulation, imitation. The *kalogathos* of Plato or the *megalopsychos* of Aristotle were presented as models to be imitated by all noble persons. An ethics of personality is, however, an ethics of inimitability. One becomes oneself, one cannot become like someone else. If Napoleon serves as a model of an ethics of personality, Napoleon is conceived of in his inimitability. The seductiveness lies in the charisma of the great personality that calls for the imitation of the inimitable. A paradigmatic case of an authentic ethics of personality proves itself in the accomplished work and in the truthfulness invested in this work. Still, the seductive aura that induces imitation haunts all representative real-life heroes of the ethics of personality. There is only a single case in which the imitation of the inimitable can be morally unproblematic and, moreover, exemplary: the case of the 'lucky throw' *qua* the moral genius and his charisma *qua* moral. It does not matter here how far the imitator lags behind the original, for no transgression will follow from it. Still, even the imitation of goodness (the imitation of Christ) can demonize the recipients of this goodness. Dostoevsky's hero, Count Mishkin, the 'Idiot', is a representative case in point. But if the achievement to be imitated falls beyond the pale of ethics, be it in the field of aesthetic, political, military, or any similar accomplishment, or just the perfect aesthetic formation of one's own life, the imitators of the 'lucky throw' will always end up as failures or as criminals, perhaps both. The young Lukács pondered in his diary the question of the difference between Novalis and Hjalmar Ekdal.[10] And he came up with an answer typically in keeping with the standards of an ethics of personality. While Novalis accomplished his work, Hjalmar Ekdal (the imitator of romantic genius) was a failure and also made himself guilty of the death of his daughter. Not all the petty imitators of Novalis or Goethe were morally guilty, but all of them proved to be failures.

The Napoleon paradigm differs from the Beethoven or the Goethe paradigm in the sense that Napoleon was a man of arms and politics. His imitators did not claim to be great discoverers or authors, but sincerely pretended to be revolutionary historical actors and conquerors of a kind. This is why the representative Napoleon imitators were all guilty of wronging others, sometimes even on a grand scale. Several of Dostoevsky's heroes exemplify this pattern, first and foremost Raskolnikov. Hence, to take the 'case of Napoleon' as the exemplification of an ethics of personality would carry us too far, beyond the realm of ethics, and even within the confine of ethics, beyond our limited purpose.

It seems as if Goethe could serve as the best 'master model'. Goethe designed the ethics of personality, he practised it himself during his long life, and so did many of his favourite heroes, particularly the main characters in *Wilhelm Meister's Lehrjahre*. Goethe was an enormous success story in work and life alike, Though he said emphatically that the actors are always guilty and only the spectators are innocent;[11] the scrupulously moralist-religious author Franz Rosenzweig gave him credit for being guiltless According to Rosenzweig[12] Goethe was the only person who succeeded in actualizing an ethics of personality without becoming guilty, who nimbly walked the tightrope stretched over the abyss between birth and death. His counter-example was Nietzsche. Yet Nietzsche himself said once that he modelled his Dionysus on Goethe.[13] And when Lukács experimented with the idea of returning to an 'ethics of personality', he planned to write a book entitled *Goethe's Lebensfuehrung (Goethe's Conduct of Life)*.[14]

Had I had it in mind to present you with an unproblematic apology of an ethics of personality, I would have chosen Goethe instead of Nietzsche as my paradigmatic case. Although Goethe portrayed, from Werther to Tasso, the pitfalls of this ethics, he still believed that it could ultimately work. He rejected all its alternatives on the grounds of his conviction that the ethics of personality was within our reach. To opt for Goethe rather that for Nietzsche would perhaps have better suited our democratic age. Although Goethe's conduct of life was highly exceptional, he was convinced that every man and women can become 'complete' in a similar fashion. Every person, great or small, can be creative in something and thus can become exceptional. Goethe would have subscribed to Kierkegaard's dictum that every person is an exception, but only under the condition that he or she actualizes all his or her unique potentialities, whatever they might be.

To speak of the case of Nietzsche (*Der Fall Nietzsche*), rather than the case of Goethe, is a choice, but not one based on my personal taste. Had I listened to my personal taste, I would have discussed Goethe instead. Like Nietzsche himself, and Lukács, Rosenzweig and so many others, I too am fascinated by the conduct of life of a person who danced nimbly on the rope that had been stretched over the abyss of his life, between birth and death. But it is not personal taste that matters. We are soon closing the most horrible century known in human history. The chickens of the nineteenth century have come home to roost in the twentieth. All kinds of nihilism joined forces in it to bring hell on earth. A few lessons have to be learned. Among other things, it is prohibited to continue cherishing the uplifting illusion that an ethics befitting free and beautiful creative personalities, one that makes all external norms, values, commandments, or prohibitions superfluous, and painful decisions, repressions, and self-censorship obsolete, will or could replace *Sittlichkeit* on the one hand and morality on the other. More precisely: the model of an entirely autonomous, well-balanced, many-sided, beautiful personality remains a relevant Utopia; it has also remained mine. But a Utopia is a regulative idea. And no regulative idea can sweep under the carpet the moral problems and dilemmas that ensue from our actual possibilities. And it is by those possibilities that we remain enframed. This is why I chose Nietzsche rather than Goethe as my paradigmatic case.

This sounds unconvincing. After all, it would be absurd to hold

Goethe, the great universalist, the renaissance-type humanist and cosmo-
politan, responsible for paving the way for totalitarian barbarism.[15] By
contrast, several radical philosophers of the nineteenth century, Marx
and Nietzsche the most representatives of them, were not entirely innocent victims of their retrospective ideological exploitation by some cheap
propagandists of totalitarian powers. They exposed themselves to such
an appropriation. Radical philosophers, after all, programmatically
broke with the philosophical tradition (particularly with the metaphysical one). They divided philosophy into 'philosophy hitherto' and the new
philosophy, the 'new enlightenment', and they designed a philosophy of
practice, philosophy becoming practice.[16] They constantly 'unmasked'
their adversaries, were committed to desublimation, and preferred speaking the language of 'power', force' and the like. They despised both
capitalism and democracy; they yearned for 'grandeur', war, final decisions: for the great show-down. They combined biting criticism with
prophetic or even apocalyptic language. This is precisely why they are
perhaps better suited to be representative figures in an inquiry that
addresses itself to the paradoxes of an ethics of personality, and not just
to its (unkept) promises.

Of the four representative radical philosophers (Marx, Kierkegaard,
Nietzsche and Freud) only two – Marx and Nietzsche – shared all the
above-mentioned features of radical philosophy. In addition, both were
committed to an ethics of personality. But the issue of ethics remained
in general peripheral in Marx's *œuvre*. Marx concentrated on the
desublimation of 'social consciousness' by pointing at its dependency on
social being. Traditional ethics, as one aspect of social consciousness,
was dealt with by him within the framework of all other superstructural
manifestations of 'social being'. The total transformation of 'social being'
in the direction of the end of alienation, was meant to provide the full
and perfect conditions for the ethics of personality. Because, in the
process of de-alienation every single person will merge with humankind,
the ethics of personality will remain the sole ethics.[17] Yet for Marx the
move towards an ethics of personality is not a personal task, for the total
transformation of social being is eminently the matter of revolutionary
class action. Lukács injected a modicum of Nietzsche into Marx in his
papers of 1918–19. It was not a Marxian element, but still not an entirely
alien substance.[18] Without a Nietzschean stream the Marxian ethics of
personality would remain empty and merely rhetorical.

This leaves us with Nietzsche. He is the radical philosopher of the
nineteenth century who perfectly suits our intellectual purpose.

First, the ethics of personality was personal to Nietzsche: whenever he
discusses the ethics of personality, he also discusses himself. 'Also', I said,
not solely. For every ethics of personality is that of a unique personality;
one can write a report about an ethics of personality in telling the story
of one's life. Inserted between the preface and the first chapter of

Nietzsche's *Ecce Homo*, we read, 'Wie sollte ich nicht meinem ganzen Leben dankbar sein? Und so erzähle ich mir mein Leben,'[19] ('How could I not be grateful for my whole life? Thus I narrate my life to myself.') Nietzsche begins to tell the story of his life to himself. This is his, and no one else's story. Yet already this brief reference indicates that there are important shared features between one ethics of personality and another. The first feature is gratitude towards one's own life inherent in *amor fati*, a prominent characteristic of an ethics of personality. A person who conducts his life in the spirit of an ethics of personality will always say 'yes' to his own life, irrespective of his suffering, his solitude, his marginalization, or his bad luck in all matters that are external to his personality. A 'lucky throw of the dice' says 'yes' to his own life (and thus to life in general), not because he is lucky in life, but because it is his life, his fate, because he became what he has (always) been. Here we arrive at the deepest layer of Nietzsche's vision of the eternal recurrence of the same. To accept the mythological image of the eternal recurrence of the same with gratitude and gaiety is tantamount to wishing to live one's own life again and again, and never another life, never in another place (for example in the other world) or in another time (past or future). The repetiton of the same as a gesture of resolve is a critical feature of an ethics of personality.[20] He who shies away from the acceptance of the eternal recurrence of the same or does not embrace it passionately proves (to Nietzsche) thereby that he is alien to the ethics of personality or has failed in practising it.

I have already pointed out that to live according to an ethics of personality is tantamout to accomplishing one's work. One accomplishes one's work, one becomes what one is, one says 'yes' to life simultaneously, if one constantly affirms one's own work. At the end of each day during the six days of creation God tells himself with satisfaction that whatever he has done was 'good'. Similarly, the repositories of an ethics of personality know their own work as 'good'. 'Good' stands not just for successful but also for authentic (a failure in something can also be authentic and thus a success). A person is authentic[21] in Nietzsche's view if he never lies in or with his work. Truthfulness is embodied in the work. The work must be truthful, for if it is not truthful, it is not the manifestation of an ethics of personality. A man who lies in his work is – according to the standards of this ethics – a base creature, that is, a scoundrel. Let me refer back to the sensitive reception to Nietzsche by Shaw. In his drama *The Doctor's Dilemma*, the dying painter, who is far from being ethical if measured by the common standards of his time, proudly says that he has never lied with colour or pencil. Whatever else he may have done, he still has never corrupted the centre of his life.

Since truthfulness in one's work is so decisive a constituent of all ethics of personality, Nietzsche constantly experiments with a typology

of this ethics, assigning different modes of uprightness to different kinds
of works (*Werk*). In general, the Nietzschean types are heuristic devices,
ideal-types in the sense that Weber later introduced them into social
theory. One does not subsume cases under an ideal-type but rather
understands all single unique cases by following the guidance of such
types. For example, when Nietzsche enumerates the various types of
nihilism (and not always exactly the same ones), [22] he draws distinctions
from his heuristic perspective in order to illuminate why he regards
nihilism, in spite of the self-complacency of a positivistic age, as the
representative feature of modernity. But let me return to the typology
that directly concerns the ethics of personality. In Nietzsche, different
kinds of creative practices require different kinds of ethics. The ethics of
a philosopher-personality differs from the ethics of an artist-personality.
Among others, a philosopher becomes what he is if he (also) practises a
kind of asceticism; but the artist can afford to be sensual. Moreover – and
this is the decisive difference – there is a deep connection between a
philosopher's life and his philosophy, because a philosopher's life is
almost entirely embodied in his philosophy. It is questionable whether a
philosopher 'lives' in any other way at all. In *Ecce Homo*, where
Nietzsche tells the story of his life to himself, he tells the story of his
books; and after leaving behind childhood and early youth experiences,
he speaks about himself exclusively through the self-interpretation of his
writings. According to Nietzsche, his life is – in the last instance –
identical with his philosophy, and he presupposes that this is the case
with all philosophers. In his early paper on the philosophy of the
Greeks,[23] Nietzsche pointed out that he was not primarily interested in
the philosophic message of the pre-Socratic sages, but rather in their
personalities, for it was their personalities first and foremost that embodied their philosophies.[24] Nietzsche frequently ponders the characters
of Socrates and Plato, for he was convinced (and so am I) that a fairly
good insight into a philosopher's character can be gained from his
philosophy. That Plato must have struggled with extremely strong sensual impulses sounds obvious to me, even if I do not expect much
theoretical benefit from this kind of innocent 'unmasking'. All in all,
Nietzsche, true to himself, personifies philosophy. But when it comes to
art, he no longer personifies. In contrast to the philosopher – philosophy
relationship, in Nietzsche's opinion the artist is absent from his work. He
can create works of entirely different kinds, and none of them will
manifest or express his personality.[25] Yet although the artist's personality
does not manifest itself in his work, if an artist lives according to an
ethics of personality, this will also show in his work: he will never lie in
it. This will be a sensitive point for Nietzsche in the Wagner case. Since
an artist is unlike his heroes, unlike his works, Wagner's baseness and
inauthenticity does not disturb Nietzsche as long as he believes that his
works remain authentic. The greatest accusation Nietzsche ever mounted

against Wagner was that he lied in his music: 'der Musiker wird ein Schauspieler, seine Kunst entwickelt sich immer mehr als ein Talent zu luegen', sounds the verdict against decadent artists in general, and Wagner in particular.[26] But Nietzsche does not accept historical conditions as mitigating circumstances. An artist remains free to create an untimely work that has nothing to do with his character; Wagner was free to choose a real (Zarathustrian) hero for portrayal, but he failed pathetically. To create the character of Parsifal was not a must for Wagner – it was a crime, or a joke, or a choice in bad taste (depending on Nietzsche's momentary mood and the context of the accusation). I shall return to this issue in Lecture Four.

In addition to the philosopher and the artist, a few other types are incidentally mentioned by Nietzsche, among them that of the scientist. However, from the perspective of an ethics of personality, we can ignore them.

We shall discuss Nietzsche's conception of an ethics of personality in greater detail later. But this – still preliminary – discussion was necessary in order to clarify matters and eliminate misunderstanding. Nietzsche was a self-professed immoralist, or rather an 'immoralist moralist'.[27] Simultaneously, he conducted a lifelong crusade against traditional (metaphysically founded) moral philosophy, against morality in general, and against Christian morals in particular. This same immoralist Nietzsche is committed to an ethics of personality. Thus, in spite of his transvaluation of all values, Nietzsche's ethics embraces several traditional moral concepts. After all, the juxtaposition of good and bad, the virtues of truthfulness and courage, the centrality of responsibility are concepts that are shared by moral philosophy, ethics and the ethics of personality. Of course, all those traditional values, virtues and moral concepts are radically reinterpreted and even reversed by him, but even so, they do not cease to belong in the family of moral words.

Nietzsche's ethics of personality (as all typical ethics of personality) says 'no' to moralism and to moral philosophy. Although a few moral words are shared by the language of moral philosophy, of moralism and of the ethics of personality, the respective intellectual grammars of those three are entirely different.

But there are more things in common between Nietzsche and some ancient moralists than just some moral words; certain aspects of their attitudes are also strikingly similar. Moralists are sceptics, and Nietzsche describes himself (as well as Zarathustra) as a sceptic. Moralists are not metaphysicians; nor is Nietzsche. Moralists do not systematize; nor does Nietzsche.[28] Moralists ridicule the human race (particularly the mores of their times) and they unmask hypocrisy; so does Nietzsche. Moralists prefer laughter to crying; so does Nietzsche. Moralists scrutinize the unwholesome moral habits of their contemporaries from an up-side-down perspective, with greater or lesser contempt; so does Nietzsche.

Moralists are 'unpleasant' fellows, so is their truth – such is similarly the case with Nietzsche. There are a few moralists whom Nietzsche highly appreciates (especially Montaigne and Lichtenberg), there are some others whom he dislikes (for example Larouchefoucauld),[29] but he shares some of the above features with them all.

Prior to 1887, Nietzsche frequently used one of the favourite terms of abuse of moralists: 'hypocrisy' (or *tartufferie*). Nietzsche, like all other moralists, despised hypocrisy; the essential difference between moralists in general and a unique 'immoralist moralist' specimen like Nietzsche in particular, lies in their interpretations of hypocrisy. In the book of the moralists a hypocrite pretends to act morally, although he is not moral; in the book of the 'immoralist moralist' morality itself is hypocrisy. In the book of the moralists, morality is the standard; it is not morals that they ridicule but self-righteousness, pretentiousness, double talk, false pretences, the misuse of moral language for doing immoral things. In Nietzsche's book Life is the standard, that is, saying 'Yes' to life: such as growing, developing one's own forces, talents, powers, relying on one's affects, letting oneself *become*. Morals (the standard of moralists) are hypocritical by the standard of Life (the standard of an immoralist moralist). Whether or not one believes in the moral ideals that one confesses, whether one lives according to them or just pays them lip service, is to Nietzsche's mind of secondary importance, for the moral standards themselves are a kind of *tartufferie*. In this sense both Saint Paul and Tartuffe are guilty of *tartufferie*, although they are – *qua* personalities – not to be placed on the same level.[30]

Yet there is a tendency in the early, but especially in the middle Nietzsche (perhaps up until *Beyond Good and Evil*), to practise a moralist's critique in reverse: whereas moralists ridicule man's petty vices, Nietzsche instead ridicules their petty virtues. For the grand virtues are not the Christian ones, but the kinds of *virtu* portrayed in Machiavelli's *Prince*.[31] In his latest writings, however, when Nietzsche became almost fanatically obsessed by the urgency to crush Christian morality and all of its successor morals (*écraser l'infâme!*) and when he frequently adopts a prophetic, self-irony-lacking stance, the similarity between 'moralist moralism' and 'immoralist moralism' begins to fade. In this period, Nietzsche uses terms such as *'tartufferie'* less frequently, and his rage and despair get the upper hand over his scepticism and sense of humour.

However, Nietzsche's crusade is conducted not against moralists, but against moral philosophers, against the promoters of Jewish-Christian ethics and their 'hypocritical' descendants. Every moral philosopher is an enemy, but Plato and Kant are the most formidable of all enemies (if one excludes Saint Paul, who was no philosopher). Could we say that Nietzsche was an anti-moral-philosophy-oriented moral philosopher in the same fashion as he was, indeed, and claimed to be, an 'immoralist' moralist?

I think that we cannot make this statement. Had Nietzsche been a metaphysician, had he selected an *arché* (a foundational principle) and had he built on it, or around it, an edifice of real truth about morals, had the revaluation of moral values refuted the truth of traditional values, we would have good reason to call him an anti-moral-philosophy-oriented moral philosopher. But Nietzsche did not conceive an alternative (anti-moral) moral philosophy. His ethics of personality would not qualify it. This is not just because moral philosophy (that is, the victorious morality of the western world and of many eastern cultures in addition) is far superior in might to an ethics of personality (not just). Because moral philosophy is the 'rule', whereas an ethics of personality remains a rare exception, but also for a deeper reason. Moral philosophy and the ethics of personality never meet, they can never fight an ultimate struggle, for they do not enter the same ring, they do not play the same game.

The story I am going to tell in my forthcoming lectures is the story of Nietzsche, the tragic philosopher who mobilized his best intellectual powers in support of a new morality and a new moral philosophy, just to arrive, again and again, and increasingly forcefully, at the self-defeating conclusion that there is no alternative moral philosophy in sight with which replace the old one. Think it over: I revalue the house of my fathers. This house they perceived as a most beautiful one and they valued it as priceless. I have now gathered the courage to show it to be a filthy hole, a prison, a gloomy abode. But I do not build a new house while I am 'unmasking' the old one. The old one still remains, although it now stands devalued.

Along with other philosophers, Nietzsche practised that kind of reversal of signs which would later be termed by Sartre the 'radicalization' of evil. The evil is already here, we suffer under it. But suffering is passive, whereas freedom is active. We gain, or rather regain, our freedom by turning around the causes (reasons) of our suffering as well as the perspective we take towards our suffering. All that which before had been branded 'evil' will now become good. We (the evil ones, the determined ones, the externally constituted ones) will constitute ourselves, and from our own perspective we throw back the evil into the faces of the men and their values, which have previously determined us.

In Nietzsche's narratives the radicalization of evil is one aspect of the transvaluation of all values. According to one of his fictions, there was once a successfully executed radicalization of evil: this happened during the so-called 'slave revolt' in morals, during the slave revolts of Jews and of Christians. In the present, the transvaluation of all values must lead to another radicalization of evil: the radicalization in reverse. Now the free spirits have to say what once the slaves said: we, the 'evil' ones, the immoralists, are really the good, the noble ones. In spite of the many-sided stories of this historical mythology, where Nietzsche delineates some of his dreams about a new cultural aristocracy – a future redivision of modern society into 'high' and 'low' castes, with the overmen, the total nihilists, becoming the historical repositories of the new reversal of values that overcomes nihilism – Nietzsche does not really believe in such a change to come.[32] To reiterate, although it is the ethics of personality alone that can be contrasted (opposed) to the old moral philosophy, the two mortal enemies never meet. They are perhaps not even enemies, for the latter is not interested in the first; it simply ignores it, at least in practice, though not necessarily also in philosophy.

God is dead, the old Christian God has died. He died of old age, of pity, or he was killed – just to mention a few variations on the theme.[33] 'God is dead' is not Nietzsche's 'word', it is, rather, a quotation referring to one of the cultural commonplaces of the nineteenth century.[34] This is why the crusade against morals and Christianity becomes the centrepoint of the practice called the 'radicalization of evil'. God is dead, he cannot be resurrected. The world has been already desublimated, there is no spirit left in it. Utilitarianism, this most primitive version of 'unmasking', indicates the advanced disenchantment of the world.[35] Nothing has been left for radicals but to radicalize this evil, to unmask the lies of decadence, of pessimism, of the modern natural sciences, of the philosophy of nihilism. The mask has been torn off, the ugly face appears. Another mask waits to be torn off, and an even uglier face will appear behind it. Radical philosophy does not make compromises. But Nietzsche faces the paradox.

Kierkegaard appealed to us to face the paradox; this is why he, as an 'ethicist' (which is one of his masks) could address single individuals *qua* single individuals. The single individual is, after all, the universal. Conversely, Nietzsche did not begin with a paradox.[36] He was not ready to resign his prophetic appeal, his dreams about new supermen, although he was aware of the impossibility of such an eventuality. Nietzsche did not begin, yet he ended up with a paradox, for he created a paradox for himself, an unwilled and unacknowledged one, when he found the only efficient anti-poison and remedy (*pharmakon*) in the individual who is not also the universal. Perhaps this is why he, unlike Kierkegaard, never addressed just one single individual, but rather always a group of followers: the free spirits, men who were unlike himself, but still close enough to listen, if not to understand. Finally, his ethics of personality peaks in *Ecce Homo* where the philosopher tells his own story to himself. This exercise is certainly no match for the 'ascetic ideal'.

Lecture Two

Now we arrive at our central topic: we are going to discuss the significance of Nietzsche's increasing obsession with Wagner.

The young Nietzsche loved Wagner but he was not obsessed by him. He put Wagner on a pedestal in *The Birth of Tragedy*, where he also used him as his mouthpiece.[37] In the *Untimely Meditations* ('Richard Wagner in Bayreuth') he began to distance himself from his composer friend, but with tact, step by step. After the break with Wagner there was not yet a 'case of Wagner', and even less was there a 'Nietzsche contra Wagner'. Nietzsche's obsession with Wagner began to develop when his project of writing a book with the preliminary title *Will to Power* got bogged down. It was then that Nietzsche began to evoke memories from his past which tied Wagner mystically, or rather providentially, to the turning points of his own life, as both unforgettable friend and most formidable foe. Nietzsche backdates his obsession. Surely, his memories are authentic, like everything about Nietzsche, yet providential significance came to be attached to those memories far later, in the period after *On the Genealogy of Morals* and before darkness clouded Nietzsche's mind.

Personal memories of the friendship with Wagner may have remained warm, but it is the break with Wagner that assumed public significance. Nietzsche kills the beloved and respected brother who had never harmed him, yet whom he hates. He kills him not for what he is, but for that which he had done. In contradistinction to the biblical myth, Nietzsche kills his brother, not because his brother was more loved by the Father, but because he loved the Father more than his brother did. Nietzsche kills the prodigal son, not because he left his father's hearth, but because he returned there. In building up the myth of his fateful Wagner-relationship, Nietzsche in fact transvalues traditional values in so far as he reverses both the myth of Cain and Abel and the myth of the prodigal son. Thereby he creates a new model, or rather a representative *leitmotif*, for the modernist avant-garde he thus anticipated.[38]

Let me quote two representative passages, both from *Ecce Homo*, the first from the chapter on *Menschliches, Allzumenschliches*, paragraph 5.

Before turning to the first quotation, a few things still need to be said. It deserves to be mentioned that the entirety of Nietzsche's later interpretation of this (relatively early) book is impregnated through-and-through with Wagner reminiscences. The book *Menschliches, Allzumenschliches* is now (at the very end of Nietzsche's rational life) recalled by the author as the offspring of the 'crisis' in his life and work: and this crisis, again, is associated with his break with Wagner. As always in the case of Nietzsche, personal life and philosophical life merge. As always, his ethics of personality emerges as the guiding spirit.

> Was ich damals entschied, war nicht etwa in Bruch mit Wagner – ich empfand eine Gesammt-Abirrung meines Instinkts, von der der einzige Fehlgriff, heisse er nur Wagner oder Basler Professur, bloss ein Zeichen war. Eine Ungeduld mit mir uberfiel mich; ich sah ein, dass es die höchste zeit war, mich auf mich zurückbesinnen.[39] (What I then decided was not just the break with Wagner. I realized there was a general lapse of my instincts, and single false steps, whether they were Wagner or the Basel professorship, were simply signs of it. Impatience overcame me; I realized that it was high time for me to return to myself.)

Be true to yourself; this is the first, or perhaps the only maxim of the ethics of personality. The good instinct (good also in an ethical sense) turns you back towards the right path, your own path, the path of your maxim. Wagner is just a 'symptom', a symptom of an ethical shortcoming, for he became a stumbling block on the path of becoming Nietzsche. The break with Wagner results from the good instinct that brings one back to oneself.

Being true to ourselves is, of course, a tricky thing. First, one can ask the question, 'To which self?' Nietzsche says that one has to liberate one's 'unterste Selbst' (the self 'deepest down') from behind or beneath many other 'selves'.[40] But which is the 'unterste Selbst'? The very self that turns out to be the most significant in retrospect? But if so, then it depends on the person's instinct at the time of retrospection which of his selves he will (again retrospectively) describe as the most significant self at this time of crisis. On a philosophical level, no bad circularity results from the above. Nietzsche was the most significant pioneer of the now widespread idea that pure facts do not exist, since all facts are interpretations from various perspectives. But is the elimination of theoretical difficulties tantamount to the elimination of the practical ones? How can one then separate the maxim 'Be yourself!' from the other maxim, 'Be yourself enough!'? Is the second not the maxim of an ethics of personality to the same extent as the first? In Ibsen's *Peer Gynt* it is the Trolls, fairy-tale versions of the complacent bourgeoisie, who subscribe to the maxim, 'Troll, be yourself enough!' But Nietzsche's practice is just Nietzsche's practice. Nietzsche's life, future, and instinct, his deepest self, demanded that he broke with Wagner – and so he did. Yet, is this increasing obsession with Wagner, particularly in light of his break with him, not the sign of the opposite? If you leave someone behind, do you still harp on the break, or on the other? Do you still justify yourself on every occasion? Do you daily curse someone whom you left so far behind? Wouldn't it be more reasonable to presume that the Wagner – Nietzsche relationship turned into a Wagner–Nietzsche symbiosis after Wagner's death and that this uncanny development had something to do with Nietzsche's abandonment of the project of *The Will to Power*?

After this detour I must now return to the first of the above-mentioned quotations. Nietzsche dictated the texts of his *Menschliches, Allzumenschliches* to Peter Gast. He was in a state of constant suffering. When the book was ready, he sent two copies 'to Bayreuth'. Then, 'Durch ein Wunder von Sinn im Zufall' ('through the miracle of sense in contingency'), a beautiful copy of the *Parsifal* arrived with Wagner's dedication to Nietzsche: 'seinem theuren Freunde Friedrich Nietzsche, Richard Wagner, Kirchenrat' ('to his faithful friend Friedrich Nietzsche, Richard Wagner, church counsellor'). Nietzsche continues, 'Diese Kreuzung der zwei Buecher – mir war's als ob ich einen ominoesen Ton dabei hoerte. Klang es nicht, als ob sich Degen kreuzten? . . . Jedenfalls empfanden wir es beide so: denn wir schwiegen beide . . .'[41] ('This crossing of two books – I seemed to hear an ominous sound. Didn't it sound just like the crossing of two sabres? At any rate, we both perceived it so; then we both remained silent.'). Wagner's signing himself as 'Kirchenrat' was an ambiguous gesture: self-ironical, but provocative and awkward.[42] The crossing of the book-gifts assumed a symbolic-mythological dimension; this is why Nietzsche uses a modified metaphor of the lucky throw of the dice (the miracle of sense in the accidental). The crossing of books made a sound; how does the crossing of the books sound? Like the crossing of sabres: with a sharp, metallic tone. He who has a musical ear can hear it. This was the first crossing of sabres between Nietzsche and Wagner – the rest was silence. But how can we speak about the *first* crossing of the sabres, if the first is not followed by a second and a third? The rest was silence, because shortly afterwards Wagner died.

But Wagner's shadow, more formidable than the living Wagner himself, continued to fight the duel. It was Parsifal, not Wagner, who carried the holy spear. Parsifal fought with sharper weapons than Wagner ever could have. For Wagner, as an artist – we have learned this from Nietzsche – was unlike the creatures of his imagination. The heroes whom he created began to live an independent life; sometimes they were everything Wagner himself was not. In his crusade against Wagner, Nietzsche fought in fact not against Wagner, but against Parsifal, and it was Parsifal (not Wagner) whom he could never defeat. About this we shall speak a little later.

I now turn to the second quotation. Nietzsche begins to tell the story of *Zarathustra*.

> Die Grundkonzeption des Werks, der Ewige-Wiederkunftgedanke, diese hoechste Formel der Bejahung, die ueberhaupt erreicht werden kann – gehoert in den August 1881 . . . Rechne ich . . . von jenem Tage an vorwaerts, bis zur ploetzlichen . . . eintretenden Niederkunft im Feburar 1883 – die Schlusspartie, dieselbe, aus der ich im Vorwort ein paar Saetze citiert habe,[43] wurde genau in der heiligen Stunde fertig gemacht, in der Richard Wagner in Venedig starb – so ergeben sich achtzehn Monate fuer die Schwangerschaft.[44] (The fundamental conception of the work, the thought of the eternal recurrence of the same, this highest formula of affirmation that can absolutely be achieved – belongs to August 1881. It is from this date that I reckon, till the sudden delivery in February 1883 – the final part, the same part from which I quoted a few passages in the preface, that had been accomplished the same sacred hour when Richard Wagner died in Venice – so I had eighteen months of pregnancy.)

The months of Wagner's illness are the months of Nietzsche's spiritual pregnancy. The delivery of the child (the book/prophet, the son Zarathustra) takes place exactly at the hour of Wagner's death. We should listen to the music of the sentence. The solemnity of the announcement of Wagner's death (Nietzsche speaks about the 'sacred hour' of both the birth of his 'son' Zarathustra and the death of the father of Parsifal) is surrounded by the picturesque and verbose description of the author's 'pregnancy'. And at the beginning of it all, at the very beginning of the paragraph, stands the thought of the eternal recurrence of the same, the thought that arose in him suddenly, yet not without a preliminary signal (*Vorzeichen*). Nietzsche speaks about a total and abrupt change in his taste, particularly in his musical taste and adds, 'Man darf vielleicht den ganzen Zarathustra unter die Musik rechnen . . .'[45] 'Perhaps one can put the whole Zarathustra under the reading of music'.). To sum up: on the day of Wagner's death, another, anti-Wagnerian, kind of music was born. This new music (Nietzsche's *Zarathustra*) is centred on the thought of 'the eternal recurrence'. The thought of the eternal recurrence is the litmus paper: he who is strong enough to see himself and the world from this perspective has proven himself noble. He is a lucky throw of the dice and he stands for an ethics of (his) personality.

The mythologization of the Nietzsche–Wagner relationship in *Ecce Homo* is a symbol of Nietzsche's growing obsession with Wagner, and especially with *Parsifal*.[46] The story goes back to the *On the Genealogy of Morals*, or rather to the first entry concerning this project in Nietzsche's notebooks. The entry reads as follows:

> Zur Genealogie der Moral Erste Abhandlung von Friedrich Nietzsche (first treatise).

2. das asketische Ideal (the ascetic ideal)
3. Verantwortlichkeit (responsibility)
4. 'ich' und 'er'[47] ('I' and 'he')

The next entry reads as follows:

Vorspiel des P[arsifal], groesste Wohltat, die mir seit langem erwiesen ist. Die Macht und Strenge des Gefuehls, unbeschreiblich, ich kenne nichts, was das Christentum so in die Tiefe naehme und so scharf zum Mitgefuehl braechte. Ganz erhoben und ergriffen . . . das groesste Meisterstueck des Erhabenen, das ich kenne, die Macht und Strenge im Erfassen einer furchtbaren Gewiss-heit, ein unbeschreiblicher Ausdruck von Groesse im Mitleiden darueber . . .[48] The overture of *Parsifal*, the greatest blessing to be granted me for a long time. The power and strength of feelings, inde-scribable, I know of nothing that grasped Christianity so profoundly and brought it to such a level of empathy. Completely subtle and moving . . . the greatest masterpiece of the sublime that I know, the power and strength in grasping a fruitful certainty, an indescribable expression of greatness of empathy about it . . .

In retrospect, Nietzsche interpreted his Zarathustra as the new music of a new taste, the mystically born anti-work to Wagner, but *On the Genealogy of Morals* was perceived, from the time of its inception, as the paradigmatic anti-Wagnerian work, or rather, as the Anti-Parsifal. 'Ich' and 'er' should be read as 'Nietzsche' and 'Wagner', or rather as 'my son Zarathustra' and 'his son Parsifal'. There are several other additional readings, but finally, they all boil down to the simplest formula: Nietzsche and Wagner.

'I' and 'he', but not 'I' or 'he'. Nietzsche, the man of shades and nuances, did not like absolute alternatives. Furthermore, opposites are not necessarily also alternatives. In addition, the project began with the essay on the ascetic ideal (which became the third essay in the final version) – and the ascetic ideal is best presented by Wagner's Parsifal. At least that is what Nietzsche suggests in the next journal entry, which we have just quoted.

The modernist composer Adrian Leverkuehn (in Thomas Mann's novel, *Doktor Faustus*) composes (in despair and disgust) his fictitious masterwork (*The Lamentation of Doktor Faustus*) as a counter to Beethoven's Ninth Symphony. In his words he is 'taking back' the Ninth Symphony. Something similar can be said about Nietzsche and his *On the Genealogy of Morals*. The book was conceived as the gesture of 'taking back' Wagner's *Parsifal* – this masterwork of empathy, this indescribable expression of greatness through compassion. Nietzsche says that compassion should not be, empathy should not be: they must be 'taken back'; Christianity must be 'taken back'. Wagner gave us 'die groesste Wohltat', but it must be taken back. Sincerity, authenticity, life (and my personality) demand that they be taken back.

The first entry in Nietzsche's philosophical diary on the project of *On the Genealogy of Morals* illuminates the message of the book, though it is also the case that one can clearly catch the message from the final version without knowing this entry. The structure, or rather the composition, of *On the Genealogy of Morals* is unlike that of all other books by Nietzsche. Three essays treat three subject-matters, and they are properly introduced by a preface (*Vorrede*, not *Vorwort*). Anglo-Saxon philosophers regard this structure as scholarly and solid, all the more so since they detect a straightforward line of argumentation in each and every essay. This is a grave simplification, which does disservice to Nietzsche's work and gives rise to a host of pointless polemics. But let us sidestep this issue. I read Nietzsche's *On the Genealogy of Morals* as an opera (or rather, as a music-drama) in three acts preceded by the overture. Nietzsche's music-drama follows Wagner's music-drama (*Parsifal*) quite closely, yet with a twist: namely the former 'takes back' the latter. Nietzsche transvalues the values of *Parsifal*, and thus transvalues the *Parsifal*. The problem (an insurmountable problem for Nietzsche, but not for us) is that he does not finally succeed in entirely 'taking back' *Parsifal*, just as the fictitious Adrian Leverkuhn does not finally succeed in entirely 'taking back' the Ninth Symphony. 'Taking back' is not refutation, it is not falsification; it means simply 'this should not now (or any more) be.' But what should be, or can be, instead? Can redemption from the Redeemer be a match for the redemption of the Redeemer?

The proposal to read *On the Genealogy of Morals* as a music-drama (opera) in three acts (and an overture), sounds so obvious to me that I am surprised that the idea has not occurred to anyone of whom I know. In fact, I am sure that it *has* occurred to many people before me (with whom I am not familiar, for it is impossible to know the whole corpus of Nietzsche literature). I may have missed a very important discussion conducted on the topic along these same lines. But since I do not know about it, I continue on my own.

The literary form of *On the Genealogy of Morals* could suggest a drama (a tragedy perhaps), rather than a music-drama. To buttress my interpretation, I can use Nietzsche's own already-quoted remark, suggesting that *Zarathustra* should be read as a piece of music. After all, Nietzsche was also a composer. But we do not need to use the testimony of an authority. It is enough to read all the notebooks of Nietzsche once through in their historical sequence: it is like reading music. A theme emerges in the notebooks, first in pianissimo. Perhaps it does not return for a while. Then it reappears, interwoven with other themes. The same theme resounds in many variations and rhythms. The variations on the theme begin to dominate all entries. There are more crescendos than diminuendos. Then the main theme appears in forte. Having dominated the scene, the theme (and some of its variations) begin to assume the form of a book. Afterwards, the same theme (and its variations) begin to fade;

eventually, they entirely disappear. This also happens if no book results
from the fortissimo-dominated stage of the theme's evolvement – as in
the case of the *The Will to Power*. After dozens of entirely different
variations on the topics, the titles, and the chapters, the main theme and
its variations reappear only sporadically, in piano, and then disappear.
Other themes and variations take their place.

That which we can hear if we listen to the flow of Nietzsche's whole
œuvre, we can also hear if we read his single, well-shaped works. The
literary form of these works varies, only the musical – composition-like
– handling of the themes, the forming of the dominants and the subdomi-
nants, preserves the same pattern. I speak of dominants and subdomi-
nants in order to underline that, in musical terms, Nietzsche's works are
rather traditional. Nietzsche had a classicistic taste (in music), although
he was avant-guarde *avant la lettre* in aesthetic theory. Whether he had
original talent as a composer cannot be established. What can be decided
is that this combination (classicistic taste in musical techniques and
modernist-avant-garde ideas of composition in aesthetic matters) could
not possibly be brought together in a musical composition proper. But
philosophy conceived of as musical composition proved to be the perfect
way for Nietzsche to reconcile taste and thought. To speak with Kant's
vocabulary, Nietzsche could become a genius with taste because he
exercised his genius as a philosopher and brought his taste into the
bargain with a musical way of speculating about philosophical themes.
This was, indeed, a lucky throw of the dice.

The musical composition of philosophical thoughts resulted in a
unique mixture of consistency and inconsistency. If one reads a work of
Nietzsche as a chain of philosophical argumentations, one will soon
detect unnecessary leaps, logical contradictions and the like. Once an
interpreter takes great pains to eliminate those 'apparent' contradictions,
he does a disservice to Nietzsche, who had a very low opinion of logical
consistency.[49] Or, if one reads for example the first essay of *On the
Genealogy of Morals* and then sums up what Nietzsche had to say about
good and bad or good and evil, one will end up with a half-baked half-
truth. For the definitions (*Bestimmungen*), descriptions, formulations
and paradoxes of Nietzsche are either naked statements of a theme or
variations on that theme. The same theme (e.g. good, evil, guilt, conscience) appears in the book in many variations and in different rhythms.
None of them is 'the one' that could be referred to as 'what Nietzsche
said about *X*'. They are not the same, they do not even complement each
other without fail, because they are just what they are: variations on a
theme. They are the same, they are also different, but there is no 'identity
in difference' here, for no single theme (be it its first or last appearance)
can be described as the identity of the variations (difference), although all
variations are the variations of this 'identity'. And yet there is consistency
in Nietzsche just as there is consistency in a Beethoven symphony or in a

Mozart opera. If one listened to a few works of Beethoven repeatedly, one could later recognize a Beethoven work immediately, and one has a kind of presentiment (or pre-knowledge) of the next tone, of the following musical sentence, or of the finale of a work one has never before heard. Similarly, those who read some Nietzsche will know what Nietzsche could or would have said about an author, a moral sentence, or a philosophical proposition, even if Nietzsche did not say anything about them as far as the reader knows. This is so because the cachet of Nietzsche's personality is distinctly present in all of his works. His personality is the common (consistent) theme in all his masks or selves, in all the variations of his personality that constitute his works.

After this detour let me return to *On the Genealogy of Morals*. It is an opera (or rather, a music-drama proper) and it follows in the footsteps (or rather in the musical steps) of the music-drama that Nietzsche is going to 'take back' (but which in fact he cannot entirely take back). This is the only inconsistency of Nietzsche; or rather, his personality is split on this issue. Two 'selves' of Nietzsche, neither higher than the other, are interlocked, and their conflict is not resolved. This is why Nietzsche might have felt 'the sense of the uncanny' looming over this book. In fact, Nietzsche says about *Genealogy* (in *Ecce Homo*) that it is the uncanniest (*das Unheimlichste*). '*Unheimlich*' means uncanny, but it also means: being without a home, an absence of familiarity, strange, frightening, disquieting. *Genealogy* is disquieting not just for the reader (for whom it is meant to be) but also for the author.

I suppose that Nietzsche became obsessed by Wagner because the great challenge to 'take back' the *Parsifal* did not come off. It is at that juncture that the battle with Wagner-Parsifal begins, a battle for life and death. Now the sabres are crossing. 'I' and 'he' now becomes 'Nietzsche contra Wagner'. Yet Nietzsche's affects, his drive (his will-to-power), his sincerity, his nobility, his horror at false words, his own individual categorical imperative (to describe him in his own ethical terms) make him stop short of 'taking back' *Parsifal*. Yet, *Parsifal* must (should) be taken back. Finally, Nietzsche escapes – into madness.[50]

Let me repeat: prior to *Genealogy*, Nietzsche was not yet obsessed by Wagner. Numerous things are said about Wagner in many of Nietzsche's works, both approvingly and disapprovingly. For example, in *Beyond Good and Evil*, Wagner's turn towards Schopenhauer is treated with disapproval, whereas the overture of *Meistersinger* gets the highest praise.[51] But it suffices to cast a cursory glance at just the titles of the works by Nietzsche after *Genealogy* in order to see the overwhelming importance of this final spiritual battle.

The next title is *The Case of Wagner*. It is a declaration of war against the seducer. 'Ach, dieser alte Zauberer! Dieser Klingsor aller Klingsore! Wie er uns damit dem Krieg macht! uns, den freien Geistern! ... Wohlan, alter Verfuehrer! Der Cyniker warnt dich – cave canem.'[52]

('Ah, the old sorcerer! This Klingsor of all the Klingsors! How he wages war against us all! Us, free spirits! All right, old seducer! The cynic warns you: cave canem.') We have to note that here, as in many other places, Nietzsche uses the Wagnerian mythology against Wagner.[53] Yet in the same work he integrates Wagner into a (reversed) Christian mythology. 'Was wunder, dass gerade in unsern Zeiten die Falschheit selber Fleisch und sogar Genie wurde? dass Wagner 'unter uns wohnte'. Nicht ohne Grund nannte ich Wagner den Cagliostro der Modernitaet . . .'[54] ('Is it any wonder that falsity became flesh, even genius, precisely in our time, and that Wagner has dwelt among us? Not without reason have I called Wagner the Cagliostro of modernity.')

The Case of Wagner is followed by *Götzendämmerung* (*The Twilight of the Idols*), a work which was perceived by the author as his first attempt in book form at a transvaluation of all values (it was then, Nietzsche says, that he began to philosophize with a hammer). The title is an obvious echo of *Götterdämmerung*. The preface declares 'Diese kleine Schrift ist eine grosse Kriegserklarung'.[55] ('This little piece of writing is a great declaration of war.') In spite of the Wagnerian allusion in the title, there is very little on Wagner in the book. A war is declared on Christianity, metaphysical tradition, (moral) morality; thus the war is conducted against the values of *Parsifal*. *Parsifal*'s God, morality and metaphysics – these are the idols. They stand now destroyed (not just deconstructed as before) by the hammer. *Cave canem . . .*

Then comes (among the works that were no longer published by Nietzsche) *Der Antichrist*. From the perspective of our problem (and from the perspective of other vital issues which we cannot discuss here) the Christ/Antichrist dichotomy is not as simple as it first seems. At first sight Nietzsche's identification is clear. *He* is the Antichrist or the sworn enemy of Christianity (since in German the word Christian is 'Christ', 'Antichrist' also means 'Anti-Christian'), whereas Wagner, who 'became pious',[56] fights for and in the colours of Christ and Christianity. But if we recall the above-quoted passages from *The Case of Wagner*, this first approach to the interpretation of the 'Antichrist' cannot satisfy us. It is one variation on the Antichrist theme, it may even be the most frequently returning variation, yet it is not the only one.

After all, Nietzsche identifies Wagner with Klingsor (the arch-enemy in Wagner's *Parsifal*) and he adds that it is no wonder that in times of falsity it is Wagner 'who has dwelled among us'. Wagner, not Nietzsche, is the demonic seducer: he is the one who fits into the image of Antichrist. And who fits into the image of Christ? Sometimes Parsifal, the 'enemy', yet at other times Nietzsche himself, although he never fits entirely. The best way to decipher this play of identifications, shifts and reversals is to think about the text in musical terms.

Nietzsche's interpretations of Jesus vary so frequently that it would be an oversimplification to present an even relatively consistent version. But in the text of the *Antichrist* (and from the perspective of Nietzsche's Wagner complex) one particular passage deserves closer attention.[57] Here, and on other occasions too, he speaks of Jesus's 'childishness':[58]

> Er beweist sich nicht, weder durch Wunder, noch durch Lohn und Verheissung . . . er selbst ist jeden Augenblick sein Wunder, sein Lohn, sein Beweis, sein 'Reich Gottes' . . . Man koennte, mit einiger Toleranz im Ausdruck, Jesus einen 'freien Geist' nennen . . . Er redet bloss vom Innersten: 'Leben' oder 'Wahrheit' oder 'Licht' ist sein Wort fuer das Innerste . . . Eine solche Symbolik par excellence steht ausserhalb der Religion . . . sein 'Wissen' ist eben die reine Thorheit darueber. (He does not prove himself through either miracle, reward, or mission. He is at every moment his own miracle, his reward, his proof, his 'Kingdom of God' . . . One could, if tolerating the expression, call Jesus a 'free spirit' . . . He speaks only from within: 'life' of 'truth' or 'light' are his words for what is innermost . . . Such a symbol *par excellence* stands outside religion . . . his knowledge of it is just pure foolishness.)

Here Jesus of Nazareth is described as a 'lucky throw of the dice' who is (almost) a free spirit, a man who knows no other ethics but the ethics of (his) personality. The association with 'free spirits' links Jesus to Nietzsche rather than to Wagner, yet Jesus was a *reiner Thor*, and this links him, not with Nietzsche, but with Parsifal, albeit the pre-Christian Parsifal prior to redemption. However, is it not precisely *der reine Thor* who is promised to be the 'Erlöser'? Who is who? Who is the enemy of whom? Who is the Enemy? Who is the Redeemer? Is the cynic (*cave canem!*) merely playing around with mythological figures? Is this a joke? Once Nietzsche asks whether *Parsifal* was meant by Wagner as a joke.[59] Was this question meant as a joke? But Nietzsche is serious. And if these shifts and reversals of roles are jokes, the jokes themselves are serious.

The Antichrist is followed by *Ecce Homo*. The title is dense and pregnant with multiple possibilities for interpretation. 'Ecce homo' is the solution of Oedipus to the riddle of the sphinx (and much later Adorno and Horkheimer will trace the birth of a man-centred world, of a pernicious 'humanism', back to this exclamation).[60] 'Ecce homo' – thus Pilate points at Jesus. 'Ecce homo' (*voilà, un homme!*) – so Napoleon reflects upon Goethe. The exclamation 'ecce homo!', this 'pointing at', characterizes not only the person who is pointed at, but also the one who does the pointing. Oedipus cannot be pointed at (then), he is the one who points at (something else), just like Pilate or Napoleon. The figure of Oedipus accompanies Nietzsche throughout almost his whole life. He writes a school essay on Oedipus Rex.[61] The identification of Oedipus (from *Oedipus Rex*)[62] and Dionysus in *The Birth of Tragedy* is well known. Later, the Dionysus theme reappears in many and in significantly different variations. But in all his (later) interpretations Dionysus will be associated with the ethics of personality (regardless of whether Goethe or

Nietzsche himself will be identified with Dionysus). Pilate occupies an interesting place in Nietzsche's mythology. His (in-)famous question ('What is truth?') is hailed as the greatest wisdom to be found in an otherwise boring and tasteless book (The New Testament).[63] Nietzsche's special respect for Napoleon has already been mentioned. What is the common feature in Oedipus, Jesus, Pilate, Napoleon and Goethe? The ethics of personality. *Ecce Homo* is not just a book about Nietzsche's ethics of personality, it also defines the content of his personality.

The content of a personality is that personality's destiny. Yet this destiny cannot be fully conscious, it cannot be translated into the language of an external goal, a project, an end; for if it is translated, the personality collapses. Yet Nietzsche does something in this book that transcends the limits of an ethics of personality: he renames his destiny, he redefines it, he raises his project, he makes himself the vehicle of an external project. The content is defined, in the last instance, as the final and radical 'unmasking' and destruction of Christianity: 'Wer über sie aufklärt, ist eine *force majeure*, ein Schicksal – er bricht diese Geschichte der Menschheit in zwei Stücke. Man lebt vor ihm, man lebt nach ihm.' ('The man who enlightens us about it is a *force majeure*, a destiny; he breaks the history of humankind into two parts.') The ethics of personality is reversed here: the task defines the personality *qua* 'destiny', and not vice versa.

In *Ecce Homo*, the direct fight against Wagner seems to lose momentum. At one point, Nietzsche mentions his self-restraint: as an old artillerist, he could have sent against Wagner the heavy artillery, but 'ich hielt alles Entscheidende in dieser Sache bei mir zurück, ich habe Wagner geliebt'[64] ('I kept everything decisive in this ease to myself; I loved Wagner'). This confession only reflects Nietzsche's momentary state of mind, for in his last booklet, *Nietzsche contra Wagner*, he returns to the battlefield. The last moments of Nietzsche's rational life are actually dedicated to the collection of a few of his writings against Wagner to show the world that 'wir sind Antipoden'[65] ('we are antipodes'). The obsession with *Parsifal* re-emerges at the highest pitch: 'Denn Parsifal ist ein Werk der Tücke, der Rachsucht, der heimlichen Giftmischerei gegen die Voraussetzungen des Lebens, ein schlechtes Werk.' ('For *Parsifal* is a work of mischief, lust for revenge, of secret poisoning of the conditions of life, a bad work.') If we recall Nietzsche's report on his feelings on the occasion of his first encounter with the music of *Parsifal*, it becomes obvious that his insistence that *Parsifal* must be 'taken back' got the upper hand against his own musical experience: he did not hear any more what he was hearing. And then (in the sub-chapter 'Wie ich von Wagner loskam' ('How I got rid of Wagner')) two dominant motifs, that of *amor fati* on the one hand, and the motif of Nietzsche contra Wagner on the other hand, merge into one. Wagner and Nietzsche's lives again become intertwined; this time, however, not in a mystical, mythological manner, as in *Ecce Homo*, but in a simple, human, all too in human manner. For 'ich hatte Niemanden gehabt als Richard Wagner' ('I had had no one else but Richard Wagner') writes Nietzsche,[66] but he could not become himself without abandoning him.

Neither Nietzsche's break with Wagner nor his obsession with Wagner and *Parsifal* during the last years of his sanity can be addressed, let alone explained, in a meaningful way merely by scrutinizing Nietzsche's objections against Wagner one by one, or even all together. Let us reiterate briefly a few suggestions from the immense corpus of Nietzsche literature.

First come the psychological explanations. Let me briefly give two examples: Nietzsche allegedly resented the fact that Wagner could not hide his low opinion of Nietzsche's musical compositions.

This is a very insensitive explanation. Not only did Nietzsche write books against *ressentiment*, he also personally despised it and never practised it (he presumably never even felt it). Furthermore, although Wagner could not praise works of music he considered of little or no artistic value, even when they were produced by a beloved friend, he certainly expressed genuine respect and adoration for Nietzsche's young genius. This otherwise banausic, rude and vain man overcame all his odious character traits whenever he encountered a true man of genius, and he was willing to raise such a man above himself. Whether he was younger or older, much or little known, did not matter to him. It was actually Nietzsche who made this observation. When he read a letter from Wagner to Baudelaire, many years Wagner's junior, written in a tone of awe, adoration and humility, Nietzsche compared it to those written by Wagner to himself.

Let us turn to another version of explanation: Nietzsche was allegedly in love with Cosima Wagner; he was jealous of Wagner; or, alternatively, he could not forgive Wagner his debauchery and his rudeness to Cosima.

Nietzsche might have been in love with Cosima, but then he was also in love with Wagner. Cosima might have been identified with Ariadne, but other women also served as models for Ariadne. Furthermore, as a fine and sensitive man, he was certainly disgusted with Wagner's debauchery, and generally, with his lack of self-control when it came to matters of 'sensuality'. But 'disapproval' is a moral term, and Nietzsche, as an immoralist moralist, never 'disapproved' in a moral sense, but only in terms of an ethics of personality (for example, in denouncing Wagner's insincerity in his music). Otherwise he merely expressed his disgust. Certainly, he would have never lived like Wagner, but after all, he *was not* Wagner.

Now we come to several objections which Nietzsche himself frequently mounted against Wagner: Wagner was a rabid anti-Semite, while Nietzsche despised anti-Semitism. For him, anti-Semites were men of *ressentiment*, specimens of the species *Herdentier* (animals of the herd).

But anti-Semitism could not have been the reason for Nietzsche's break with Wagner, even less for his obsessive attacks on Wagner. Wagner was already an anti-Semite when Nietzsche used to be his friend, and Nietzsche never entirely broke all relations with his sister, who was an equally rabid anti-Semite.

Wagner was a German nationalist, whereas Nietzsche held German (and all other kinds of) nationalism in contempt. This is true. Yet Nietzsche attacks not only Wagner's character, but also his music, and in (the later) Nietzsche's mind Wagner's music is not German at all, but French. Furthermore, whatever bad features are attributed to Wagner's character by Nietzsche, none of them according to Nietzsche's own theory – had anything to do with the ethical and aesthetic value of Wagner's work.

Nietzsche may have, then, attacked Wagner because of his 'French' music. To be 'French' was understood as having artistic commitment to the French decadence of the mid-nineteenth century. It was with great acerbity that Nietzsche explicated the similarity between Madame Bovary and the Wagnerian (pseudo-mythological) heroines. At this point we encounter a genuine aesthetic problem. Nietzsche dreamt of a healthy avant-garde music that would overcome decadence (although his own taste was rather conservative), and from this perspective Wagner was part of the problem, not the solution. But, at least in his last years, Nietzsche discussed decadence as as subcase of nihilism, or rather as a side-branch of the latter; and as far as nihilism was concerned, both the Germans (Luther) and the Russians were treated as more formidable and more dangerous enemies than Flaubert, George Sand, or the Goncourt brothers.[67]

Next: *Parsifal* was accused of being 'Catholic'. Yet being a Lutheran is no praise from Nietzsche's mouth either.

Further: let us consider the issue of supposed betrayal by Wagner. He had (allegedly) betrayed Feuerbach (and his own revolutionary youth), he had betrayed Siegfried (by changing the project of the opera).[68] A philosopher of an ethics of personality can speak of 'betrayal' by an artist if, in betraying someone else (Feuerbach, Siegfried) the artist betrayed himself. After all, Nietzsche himself 'betrayed' Schopenhauer and also Wagner. The argument of 'betrayal' is valid under the condition that Nietzsche can demonstrate Wagner's self-betrayal. But this one can show only if one proves that the Wagnerian works themselves are bad (and that Wagner could have composed something different had he remained true to himself). But what if Wagner was, in fact, true to himself (his work and vocation) while betraying Feuerbach and joining Schopenhauer? What if Schopenhauer had proved wholesome for the artist's work, while harmful for the philosopher's? However, Nietzsche could not make allowances for this (very Nietzschean) interpretation for the simple reason that he considered Wagner's *œuvre* decadent, with the sole possible exception of the *Meistersinger* overture, and as dangerous and fraudulent.

I have left the trump card to the end: Wagner became a traitor (to freedom, to knowledge, to thinking) by composing a religious work. True enough, Wagner had also composed works with a religious tinge previously (for example, *Tannhäuser*), and his *Götterdämmerung* made a case for the deepest pessimism.[69] Yet *Parsifal* is the ultimate betrayal.

Since Nietzsche befriended Wagner after he had composed *Tannhäuser* and the *Ring*, the religious 'tinge' in Wagner's work could not have been the reason for the break. Moreover, it is not far-fetched to say that exactly those elements in Wagner's music which first attracted Nietzsche are also those which he abused most vehemently at the end of his (rational) life. For example, in a letter to Rohde, as he tried to explain what attracted him so much to Wagner, the young Nietzsche writes (with some self-irony): 'die ethische Luft, der faustische Duft, Kreuz, Tod und Gruft'[70] ('the ethical air, the Faustian odour, the cross, death and hell'). This is actually what he gets in *Parsifal*, too. But let me advance a thought, or rather a suspicion. Nietzsche wanted to 'take back' *Parsifal* so vehemently, not because it was religious or nihilistic and decadent, but because it was not pessimistic. Or, to reformulate this statement in Nietzsche's own terms, *Parsifal* is (beside the *Meistersinger*), Wagner's only work in which the author is a decadent, and yet his hero overcomes decadence. Parsifal, the hero, is far more similar to Nietzsche than to any other of Wagner's heroes. In addition, and this makes it worse for Nietzsche, the ethically superior hero in the *Parsifal* is not Parsifal himself but the 'good man', Gurnemanz, in whom there is no trace of decadence or pessimism. But in Nietzsche's mind the 'good man' is the scandal of ethics. From whatever angle we discuss it, *Parsifal* is a work that (in Nietzsche's mind) should not be.

Let me return (I hope for the last time) to Nietzsche's obsession with Wagner after *on the Genealogy of Morals*. All Nietzsche's paradigmatic relationships, his personal or historical mythologies, are subsequently rewritten or rethought under its spell. I have mentioned earlier the shifts and the reversals in his presentations of Jesus and the Antichrist. It is no wonder that the already mentally sick Nietzsche signs one of his letters 'Dionysus' and the other 'The Crucified'. Now I come to speak briefly of the representative myth for philosophers: the Socrates–Plato relationship.

Nietzsche tells many stories about Socrates and Plato. We encounter here, as usual, several variations on the same theme. Some variations disappear, others become more forceful, and new variations emerge. In his earliest and middle creative period, the variations are simpler (fox example, Socrates: the rationalist, who destroys the tragedy; or Plato who was not Greek, but a Semite). A little later Nietzsche suggests that some of his remarks on philosophers (particularly on Plato) should be read as caricature.[71] In his most deeply philosophical works, such as *Beyond Good and Evil, On the Genealogy of Morals* and *Götzendämmerung*,[72] Nietzsche's approach to Socrates and Plato becomes, to speak a musical language, polyphonic. There are many shifts, reversals, ambiguities, switches of roles. But, to cut a long story short (from our limited perspective), the Socrates–Plato relationship increasingly resembles the Wagner–Nietzsche relationship. In other words, Nietzsche reflects upon his relationship to Wagner through his reflection upon Plato's relationship to Socrates.

It was first Socrates, and then 'the dangerous philosopher' in general, who was described by Nietzsche as 'Cagliostro und Rattenfaenger der Geister, kurz . . . Verführer'[73] ('Cagliostro and rat-catcher of minds, in short – seducer'). You may recall, since we have recently quoted it, that these were exactly the words which Nietzsche employed to denounce Wagner.

Let me put together one story out of several variations. Socrates was a plebian, a man from the street, vulgar, comic, ugly, erotic, as well as decadent and sick. He was a sick son of a sick culture (the gods were already dead). In order to overcome the anarchy of feelings, he invented the ascetic ideal, and thus seduced the noble youth of his city in the mask of the Healer, the Redeemer. This was a total misunderstanding. One could ask: is this the image of Socrates or of Wagner? It is certainly meant to be Socrates, but Socrates is understood here via Wagner. Plato is also understood via Nietzsche, yet Plato is not Nietzsche. Plato should have been a Nietzsche but he was not; when Nietzsche at one point ran the risk of becoming a Plato, he escaped.

Plato was a noble man. He used the vulgar folksongs of the banausic Socrates and adjusted them to his refined taste.[74] He was like a free spirit, but alas, he could never entirely get rid of Socrates. He associated moral rectitude with happiness, and he perfected the ascetic ideal instead of abandoning it. The danger that looms over all Platos in the history of philosophy is that they remain under the spell of their own Socrates. Nietzsche resisted the temptation to remain so when he got rid of his Socrates/Wagner ('Wie ich von Wagner loskam'): 'How I got rid of Wagner'. The break with Wagner was his turning-point; Nietzsche/Plato, in getting rid of Socrates/Wagner, catapulted himself into loneliness and lovelessness, but also into the 'thin mountain air' of his own fate.

Still, one wonders whether the banausic, ugly, erotic, plebian actor and joker (the 'Kirchenrat') or whether the redeemer-Parsifal, or the 'good man' Gurnemanz, each on his own, would tell the same story.

Lecture Three

Yesterday, we all attended the performance of *Parsifal*. As you saw, the stage direction was traditional and unobtrusive. To have experienced something more exciting, you should have watched Szyberberg's movie version of *Parsifal* instead. I would have discouraged you from doing so, for Szyberberg would have imposed a very strong interpretation upon you. The other alternative would have been to listen to one of several excellent recordings. But *Parsifal* is a music-drama, not a symphony; even if one listens to a record, one needs to have the *mise-en-scène* at least in one's imagination. One of Nietzsche's famous objections to the late Wagnerian opera, namely that it is oriented toward theatrical effect[75] and that it has a pictorial *valeur*, advises us to engage two of our senses (hearing and seeing) in our attempt to interpret *Parsifal*. True, Nietzsche also accuses the later Wagner of becoming the advocate of pure music and of abandoning his great idea of the fusion of tragedy and music.[76] But he was supposed to have done so mainly in his aesthetic writings.

You heard and saw the Wagnerian text simultaneously, but you certainly could not have immersed yourself in it. I can now ask you to revive the music by memory, so far as possible, and to experiment with alternative *mise-en-scènes* at all stages. What I can add to your recollection is only the text. In presenting (and interpreting) some select parts of the text, and in treating *Parsifal* as a drama, I am simply complementing your experience of its music as far as is possible. This is a deficient kind of interpretation. Yet the purpose of these lectures is not the interpretation of *Parsifal*, but the interpretation of Nietzsche's relation to *Parsifal*, of Nietzsche's obsession with the work and with Wagner in the last few rational years of his life. This, again, is important because it might shed some light on Nietzsche's ethics of personality, and Nietzsche's ethics of personality might in turn shed light upon the paradoxes of the ethics of personality in general. For this purpose even our deficient interpretation will suffice.

Near the end of my previous lecture I indicated that the usual explanations of Nietzsche's break with Wagner are irrelevant, regardless of whether or not they are borrowed from Nietzsche's self-interpretations. Even if all those statements were true (that, for example, Wagner betrayed his youth, that he turned from paganism to religion, from atheism to Catholicism and the 'supper'), they would still not explain Nietzsche's break with Wagner. We did, however, catch a glimpse into the only relevant (because unspecific) self-interpretation: Nietzsche had to break with Wagner because he had to follow his own star, his own luck, his own fate, his own affect, his own instinct, his own 'will to power' – and so he did. Nietzsche's last musical composition (before the break) bore the title 'Hymnus an die Freundschaft' (Hymn to friendship). This title was later changed to 'Hymnus an das Leben' (Hymn to life). *Amor fati . . .*[77]

But, under close scrutiny, even the statements just enumerated are not true, or at least not entirely true. Let us cast a cursory glance at the prehistory of *Parsifal*. In 1843 Wagner composed an oratorio: 'Das Liebesmahl der Apostel'. His preoccupation with the *Parsifal* project began in 1845, in his 'Feuerbachian' period. It was in 1865 that he wrote the first prose sketch of *Parsifal*. This had happened before he met Nietzsche. True, it was in 1877 – two years after the break initiated by Nietzsche – that Wagner completed the text. The break either preceded the alleged cause of the break (*Parsifal*), that is, Nietzsche reacted to a Wagner who then did not yet exist, or Wagner reacted to the break with a challenge that Nietzsche would take up in a work (*On the Genealogy of Morals*) that was to be written long after Wagner's death; in a similar vein, Wagner is supposed to have reacted to a Nietzsche who at the time of the composition of *Parsifal* did not yet exist. Nietzsche broke off relations with the author of *Parsifal*, because he had known about *Parsifal* before it had been composed; and Wagner challenged Nietzsche to a duel because he had known all about Nietzsche's works from *Morgenröthe* up to *Nietzsche contra Wagner*, much before the time of their conception. Two paradigmatic, and in this sense historical, spiritual children are attacked while still in the minds of their fathers. What is this? The story of Romulus and Remus? Or visitation in reverse?

But let us return to the work that we saw and heard just yesterday. Who is Parsifal?

No matter what kind of morality (pagan, Christian, sceptical, secular-humanist or other) motivates the characters of a drama, the chief heroes of a tragedy stand always for an ethics of personality. It is their fundamental affects that drive them towards the fulfilment of their destiny. What Hegel termed 'pathos'[78] is also a kind of the Nietzschean *amor fati*. Tragic heroes are always self-propelled; although the task that they are fated to fulfil is normally presented by the world – by the 'situation' – and is not, at least not entirely, self-created. In creating a modern, that is, a contingent, tragic character, the artist has to face an (almost) insur-mountable difficulty. The task that such a character is destined to fulfil must be entirely self-created, yet the person's fate must remain paradig-matic for the world. In Nietzsche's mind romantic drama could not cope with this predicament; that is why the romantic playwrights do not let their heroes 'be', why they constantly and forcibly interfere with their fate. The prototype of romantic dramatist is Schiller, and Nietzsche believes Wagner (particularly in *Parsifal*) to be yet another Schiller.[79] Nietzsche refers to Siegfried as the really 'free' hero of Wagner (where 'freedom' also stands for contingency and the ethics of personality) because Siegfried remains entirely self-propelled; in contrast Wagner (just like Schiller) imposed on Parsifal a commitment to an idea that originates outside the hero, thereby violating sincerity and modernity.

Who then is Parsifal? Since he is a dramatic hero who stands for an ethics of personality, he must be understood backwards, from his end: from the fulfilment of his destiny. If he is a contingent person (which he is), and a symbol of the ethics of personality (which he is, in spite of Nietzsche's frequent disagreement), his task, destiny and fate must be self-created.

Let us cast a preliminary glance at the moment where Parsifal's destiny is fulfilled: 'Parsifal: . . . No more shall it be hidden: uncover the Grail, open the shrine!' The shrine is uncovered: this is aletheia, unconcealment, the moment of Truth, the light of Truth. And then, 'Parsifal mounts the altar steps, takes the Grail from the shrine already opened . . . falls to his knees before it in silent contemplation'. Boys, youths and knights sing together: 'Miracle of Supreme Salvation – our Redeemer redeemed!' (in German: 'Höchsten Heiles Wunder! Erlösung dem Erlöser!')[80]

Parsifal's destiny is thus fulfilled in two moments. First, by uncovering (unconcealing) the Grail: this is the moment of Truth. He is the one who uncovers the Truth. If we could isolate the first moment from the follow-ing two, Parsifal could still be seen to embody the perfect image of a contingent (modern) man. The gesture of unconcealment could have meant: 'Here is my Truth, I show you my Truth.' But the second moment of Parsifal's fulfilment cancels this possibility, for our hero falls to his knees before the Grail in silent prayer and contemplation. For the time being we do not need to think in terms of Christianity or in the spirit of the myth of Good Friday. Consider only this: Parsifal, the contingent person, reaches his own destination by falling to his knees before Truth. It is *his* Truth (he was the one, and no one else, who un-covered the Grail); but this truth does not originate in him, it stands above him, it is higher than him. Parsifal arrives at his destiny when he uncovers some-thing that is higher than himself and when he humiliates himself before this 'higher' something. In Nietzsche's terms Parsifal is unlike Siegfried. He is not a free man (a free man cannot fall to his knees before anything); and since Wagner made him unfree, he did not let Parsifal run his own course; he violated his own hero's instincts by forcing him to humiliate himself before the Light of Truth. The chorus of boys, youths and knights does not add to Parsifal's destiny but hails it: they sing about the Redeemer who had been redeemed. This last sentence is ambivalent in the highest degree. It can mean: our redeemer (Parsifal) is, or should be, redeemed by the holy Grail (Christ), yet it can also mean: our redeemer (Christ) is, or should be, redeemed by Parsifal, a man. The appropriate part of the text in the second act supports the second interpretation. Still, neither of these two interpretations alone does justice to the music-drama. For only if we think both interpretations together in their am-bivalence, and if we remain standing (listening, watching, contemplating) at the very juncture – along the seam of naïve religiosity and of blas-phemy (for here it is man who redeems God), it is possible that Parsifal's destiny will appear to us in a clear light.

Nietzsche certainly does not tolerate ambivalence on this issue. He very rarely speaks in terms of 'either/or', but here he does: humility, genuflection, falling on one's knees before anything is an act of unfreedom, capitulation of the ugliest kind. Either – or. Either one is a free person or one is not. And in the modern world one cannot embody an ethics of personality unless one is entirely free.

But if this is so, why did Nietzsche develop such a keen interest in *Parsifal*? Why the effort to 'take back' *Parsifal* (in the same way as Adrian Leverkuehn 'took back' Beethoven's Ninth Symphony)? One of the reasons is this: Parsifal's destiny is ambiguous. He is not less contin-gent a person than Siegfried, perhaps he is more so; and he is certainly more sophisticated. The orphan Siegfried at least inherited pieces of the miraculous sword, called Notung, from his father, whereas Parsifal won the sacred spear entirely by his own effort and through his own ability for absolute empathy.

Had Parsifal not been a contingent person, driven by the love of his fate, we would hardly need to understand him 'backwards', from the perspective of the fulfilment of his destiny. But since he is contingent, the 'end' – Truth (unconcealment), Parsifal's falling to his knees before the truth through which the Redeemer is to be (has been, will be) redeemed – must remain prominent in the discussion. Starting from the end, we can now return to the beginning.

The first act begins without Parsifal. We find ourselves in a sick world where, as Gurnemanz complains, 'the liege lord of a conquering race [*Geschlecht*] in the pride and flower of his manhood fell a slave to his sickness!' Nothing is as it was before; the holy spear of might, self-confidence and faith was lost to the enemy. Amfortas uncovers the Grail rarely and with great difficulty; Truth disappears from the world. In one word: we encounter a decadent culture in Nietzschean terms. The deca-dent culture turns to phoney (and luxurious) remedies like the soothing bath or the spices of Arabia. Amfortas desires death: only death will be his redeemer. But this decadent culture has received a holy vision, a message: 'Enlightened through compassion – the innocent fool – wait for him, the appointed one.'

During his work on the opera *Tristan*, Wagner associated the suffering Tristan of Act Three with Amfortas in Walter von Eschenbachs's epic poem, *Parzifal*. At that time he wrote (in a letter to Mathilde Wesendonck) that Amfortas is really the central figure of *Parzifal*. After fiddling with the idea of composing his own *Parzival*, He concludes, 'Das mag Geibel machen und Liszt mag's komponieren!'[81] ('Geibel could do it and Liszt might set it to music!'). Amfortas is a man of decadence who challenges the old order just like Tristan. Both are afflicted by a deadly wound; they desire nothing but death and covet death as their redemption, but they cannot die. Tristan is redeemed by Isolde's love as Tannhäuser is redeemed by Elizabeth's love. But the redeemers die too. Decadence and pessimism (in Nietzsche's sense) merge in both operas.[82] But they do not merge in *Parsifal*. Amfortas is no more the central figure, although he remains a kind of a Tristan, the decadent who cannot live and cannot die. Had he remained the central figure, Wagner's *Parsifal* would have become a work like the previous ones, entirely inspired by the philosophy of Schopenhauer. But this is the work in which Wagner leaves Schopenhauer behind, as once did Nietzsche, but in a way unlike Nietzsche's. *Parsifal* portrays a world of decadence – but it is not a pessimistic work – for decadence has been overcome at the end of Act Three by Truth; the Grail is saved, the redeemer redeemed. Yes, if a work of art could be described by an 'idea' (as it cannot), one could say that the 'idea' of Wagner's *Parsifal* is provocatively Nietzschean (please, recall the ironical dedication of the 'beautiful' copy of *Parsifal* sent to Nietzsche), since it is about overcoming decadence. Decadence is overcome by the triumphant Parsifal's gesture of uncovering the Grail (Truth). Amfortas dies just as Tristan, Tannhäuser and Siegfried do, but there is no *Götterdämmerung* here. Decadence is overcome, the world of Truth restored. Amfortas could not be the central figure of the *Parsifal* that Wagner finally composed. His suffering from the deadly wound (sin and also decadence) becomes the condition of redemption. Yet the last sentences and sounds of the work (about the redemption of the redeemer) do not refer to Amfortas. Not death, but Truth (and the promise of resurrection) is redemption.

Emphasis is on the word 'triumph': Parsifal is triumphant just as Hans Sachs is triumphant. But Parsifal, the virtuoso of religiosity, is not a Hans Sachs; Gurnemanz, rather, is the brother of Hans Sachs. Since *Parsifal* is neither an artist's tragedy (like *Tannhäuser*) nor an artist's comedy (like *Meistersinger*), but instead a mystery-play, Gurnemanz cannot be an artist. He is just the good man, the decent man, the upright man. Instead of Amfortas, Gurnemanz became the central character in Wagner's *Parsifal*.

It would be an attractive idea to start a discussion on *Parsifal* as the greatest modern achievement in the genre of the non-tragic drama,[83] but here we need to restrict ourselves to an inquiry into the possibility of an ethics of personality. Amfortas cannot be the central figure in Wagner's last work, because he is not the carrier of an ethics of personality. Originally, when Wagner associated Amfortas with Tristan, he must have conceived a different Amfortas (although he felt that in the framework of Eschenbach's story such a plan could not be realized). Tristan embodies an ethics of personality: he is fated to love Isolde and he follows his affect, his passion *qua* his destiny (symbolized by the potion), to the end. He becomes what he was: Isolde's lover true to the grave. But Amfortas is different. He is stricken by destiny (the sinful love of Kundry) after having already been destined to the service of the Grail; he is left empty between two fates: one of them he does not want to fulfil, the other he cannot. But Gurnemanz is one of the purest embodiments of an ethics of personality, just as he is. He is upright in a very everyday sense; there is nothing 'royal' about him. He simply loves people and helps them, he helps even Kundry too: he disapproves of cruelty (the killing of the swan), of *ressentiment* and of prejudice (the squires' abuse of Kundry). After returning from his long journey, Parsifal addresses him with the only word befitting him: 'good man' (*dich, guten Greisen, zu begrüssen*). In a way Gurnemanz too arrives at the peak of his life when, having recognized Parsifal as the redeemer, he leads him into the shrine of the Grail. But the triumph of Gurnemanz's life is not the fulfilment of his fate. His fate is just 'to be' what he has always been: a good man. Here he stands and cannot stand otherwise. He is the only good man in *Parsifal*. For the virtuoso of religiosity (namely Parsifal) becomes better than good, but he is never just good. Gurnemanz is good, for it is always the Other (never himself) that occupies the centrepoint of his life. Gurnemanz is good in a way other than Sentha or Elizabeth are good: unlike those saviour women, he is not a saviour man. Even less does he 'save' someone he loves. He just loves; he loves people, the beasts, the flowers and the trees. Gurnemanz loves life for life's own sake.

Both Gurnemanz and Parsifal were disturbing puzzles for Nietzsche; Gurnemanz because he was just the opposite of his own hero, Zarathustra, and Parsifal because he too much resembled Zarathustra in one (essential) thing, though not in all others.

In Nietzsche's Christian panopticum, the 'good man' is the prototype of nihilism, decadence and pessimism. There are four distinct features of this 'good man'. First, he subjects himself to external regulations (Nietzsche accuses all good men of *tartufferie*). Second, he is too weak to fight and to conquer; this is why he preaches pity, forgiveness and the like. Third, *ressentiment* grows big in his soul. Fourth, he hates life.[84] Few of these constituents of the 'good man' apply to Gurnemanz. Still, he is in Wagner's mystery-play the model of the good man and this is how the redeemer will address him.

I said that Gurnemanz, modelled on the ideal of Saint Francis, loves life and says 'yes' to life. The little controversy between him and Parsifal (who by that time has already assumed the stature of an ascetic priest) takes place in Act Three, after Gurnemanz has sprinkled water on Parsifal's head. Parsifal turns to the wood and meadow with rapture: 'How fair seem the meadows today! ... never did I see so fresh and charming the grass, the blossoms and flowers, nor did they smell so sweetly of youth or speak with such tender love to me.' Listen to the music! It is so obvious: the man who fulfils his fate rejoices and nature rejoices with him. Then Gurnemanz replies, 'That is ... the magic of Good Friday, my lord!' Now Parsifal is taken aback; the 'ascetic priest' that he has become prefers sorrow and gloom: 'Alas for that day of utmost grief! Now, I feel, should all that blossoms, that breathes, lives and lives anew only mourn and weep.' But Gurnemanz disagrees: 'You see that is not so.' Then follows the most charming praise of life (especially in song, for the text, beautiful as it is, cannot do justice to Gurnemanz's enthusiasm): the tears of repentant sinners besprinkle field and meadow ... 'now all creation rejoices at the Saviour's sign of love', and so on. Parsifal does not answer Gurnemanz directly, he turns rather to Kundry who, yearning for redemption, now sheds her first tears: 'Your tears too are a dew of blessing: you weep – and see, the meadow smiles.' Thus the redeemer takes over the motif of the 'good man', but transforms it in the spirit of his own *amor fati*.

Nietzsche's Zarathustra is a healer; so is Parsifal. Zarathustra teaches the 'overman', the redeemer. Yet no prophet (or philosopher) 'teaches' the redeemer in *Parsifal*; there is nothing to invent or to teach here. The healer's coming was announced by transcendent voices. The promise was made prior to the opening of the play; it is only repeated in the play. If you wish, Parsifal resembles the overman and Zarathustra in one person. He can be both in one, precisely because no man can here make the promise. Man can only repeat the promise of those transcendent voices. Parsifal is a Zarathustra/overman whose destiny (fate) is metaphysically grounded. But how can the destiny of a contingent man be metaphysically (transcendentally) grounded? How can the fate of a contingent man, of a man of an ethics of personality, be announced by divine voices? Is not Nietzsche right when he says that *Parsifal* is a 'joke'?

The gist of the matter is that Parsifal remains unaware of those divine voices; he does not understand anything of the goings-on in the realm of mysteries (of Truth, metaphysics, Holy Grail, and the like) before becoming what he is. Gurnemanz is right when he commands him to leave the holy spot at the finale of Act One. God (or the angels) may have had foreknowledge of Parsifal's future but they did not guide Parsifal on his way. Least of all did they predetermine it: Parsifal had been and remained a self-made man through and through. The 'function' (if I may use this terrible word) of the divine voices is not the guidance of Parsifal's destiny, but the announcing of the source, or rather the centre, of this destiny: enlightenment through compassion (sympathy, empathy). Put bluntly, the virtue of the redeemer, as well as the value from which such a virtue springs, is announced. It is this value and virtue that is transcendent (or metaphysical) in the *Parsifal*: *Mitleid* (compassion).[85] *Mitleid* is neither chosen nor unchosen; *Mitleid* is simply felt. Without *Mitleid* there is no Redeemer.[86] Zarathustra and his overman, these Nietzschean healers or redeemers, hailed cruelty and despised empathy. In this respect, Parsifal though he resembles Zarathustra, is the anti-Zarathustra (before Zarathustra existed). Here we must note that redemption cannot be willed. If redemption (of others) could be willed, Parsifal could not be interpreted as the embodiment of an ethics of personality; he would have received his goal (as promised) from above. But Parsifal does not 'will' to redeem, for he does not even know what 'redemption' means. He became a redeemer through something he felt; through his own affect, his own 'will-to-power' (in Nietzsche's sense). In the *Parsifal* story compassion (*Mitleid*) is the only (yes, the only!) affect, feeling or emotion which, provided it becomes the main driving pathos and the centre of a personality, can redeem. this is so because compassion is the sole feeling that includes the Other. The value and virtue of *Mitleid* come from 'above'; it is transcendent in the sense that we can reason against it (as Nietzshe brilliantly did), as much as for it. Yet Parsifal's *Mitleid* comes entirely from within. The transcendent becomes immanent here. We will come back to this story soon.

Before I associated Parsifal with Zarathustra and his overman, I had associated him with Napoleon. A country bumpkin (*der Naturbursch Parsifal*, as Nietzsche says) happened to be 'thrown' by sheer accident into a decadent (exhausted, sick) world of a high and sophisticated culture, just like the young Bonaparte (similarly a country boy) happened to be 'thrown' from the remote Corsica into the exhausted and refined world of a dying old regime. Both 'marginals' became, finally, the anointed kings of the kingdom from whence they had been first driven. I do not want to compare their fates; I merely want to point out once again that Parsifal is a contingent modern individual in Wagner's portrayal.

After his adventure with decadent culture, Parsifal arrives – entirely by accident as far as he is concerned – at an equally decadent, yet also demonic, counter-culture. The demonic world cannot be described by the simple word 'evil', it is also 'base' in a very Nietzschean sense. We learn that Klingsor did his best to become holy, to belong to the high spiritual culture of truth, and that he failed. Thus he built his castle and his kingdom out of mere *ressentiment*. Because he failed, others should fail also; where he did not succeed, no one should. He belongs to the (modern) men of whom Goethe wrote,

> Was klagst du ueber Feinde,
> sollten die werden Freunde,
> denen ein Wesen wie Du bist
> im Stillen ein ewiger Vorwurf ist.[87]

Klingsor is demonic, because he uses all possible means to achieve his only goal: the one who enters Klingsor's territory should lose himself. We have to notice here that Wagner (and not only in *Parsifal*) attributed *ressentiment* to the base-evil, and not to the good. And, although he does not transvalue the traditional values, his perception of *ressentiment* resembles that of Nietzsche. *Ressentiment* is linked by Wagner, if not as radically as by Nietzsche, to 'equality'; it is also associated with the attitude of slaves (though the slave could also be a king, like Klingsor). Wagner's men of *ressentiment* (Alberich, Hagen or Beckmesser) pride themselves on being equals to the spiritually 'blessed' ones, the nobles, the refined, the talented, the successful; it is an attitude, a claim, a conviction which constantly justifies itself and is not simply identical with the feeling of envy.

Let me return to the evil that Klingsor is spreading and to the means he applies to afflict his victims. Klingsor mobilizes the whole paraphernalia of seduction for one purpose: making his victims lose themselves. Amfortas not only lost his chastity, he also lost his spear in the embrace of Kundry. The loss of the spear can also stand for the loss of masculinity.[88] Masculinity means here power, force, potency and purpose; its loss means decadence, powerlessness, decay. One should not misunderstand Klingsor: he himself is decadence incarnate. What Nietzsche remarks about Wagner's heroes in general marvellously fits Klingsor in particular: 'Mit Muskeln aus Vorzeiten und mit Nerven von Uebermorgen'[89] ('with the muscles of prehistory and the nerves of the day after tomorrow'). He became what he became, because he did not succeed in becoming what he had wanted to be. And he still wants to become something else than what he is: 'unredeemed shall the guardian of the holy treasure languish; and soon – I know it – I myself will guard the Grail' (Act Two). If everyone contracted the disease at Monsalvat, and if all hope for the uncovering of the Truth were lost, Klingsor would have won his final victory. But how? By occupying the dead place, by guarding a Grail that has lost its meaning and by lacking the slightest chance of uncovering the Truth.

The temptation set up by Klingor is sexual. There are men and women (in Wagner) who do not lose, but rather find, themselves in sensual love, and who through love fulfil their destiny, such as Tristan and Isolde.

Sensual love, like love in general, is the principle, and the pathos, of their life. Yet sensuality is a temptation to 'lose oneself' for those men and women whose pathos and destiny is vested in something else. This is the case with Amfortas and Parsifal. Despite the story of the potion, it is Tristan and Isolde who commit themselves to their own love. They are not 'tempted' by a third party, they are not manipulated into something, they are not playthings of an external power. The temptation by Kundry, however, is set up: it is manipulated; it has a strategic character (all means are used to achieve the end: seduction). To succumb to such a temptation means to lose one's freedom, autonomy, personality. This is what Tannhäuser is telling Venus in her cave; he has lost his freedom, he wants to get back his freedom in the 'real' world. And what is the 'real' world? It is the world where there is suffering. Tannhäuser is afraid that he will no longer be able to see the reality of things if he continues to dwell with Venus. This is not spelled out in *Parsifal*, yet Klingsor's palace is very much like Venus's cave. And Parsifal is an extremely sensual youth; Nietzsche once compared him to Cherubino.[90] You may remember that I mentioned Ibsen's Peer Gynt and the race of Trolls. Peer Gynt accepts all conditions of the Trolls just in order to be happy, except one: he is reluctant to let his eye be cut. If his eye is cut he will see the world just like a Troll, and not like a man. The cave of Venus (in *Tannhäuser*) is presented by Wagner as the kingdom of the Trolls. Living in constant delight, in the dark or under artificial illumination, one loses one's 'normal' eyesight, one's ability to judge. This is so also in Klingsor's world. It is artificial; there are no meadows here, no forests; all flowers are just make-believe; there is no nature. There are no tears in this world either. Kundry cannot weep; she can only laugh. She sheds her first tears at the moment when her sins are forgiven.

If one listens to *Parsifal* with the ears of Nietzsche, one can understand his reasons for scorn. Let me mention a seemingly insignificant issue: Wagner associates laughter, more precisely laughter in solitude, with evil. But Nietzsche's Zarathustra is constantly laughing, and frequently also in solitude. Laughter in Nietzsche is the manifestation, or rather the symptom, of superiority. Wagner's 'evil' had to be radicalized, his values had to be transvalued, reversed. But is this possible? Could Klingsor, a decadent himself, the king of an artificial, lifeless world, win? And if he won, if Truth would never again to be uncovered, if the fraudulent sanctity, as well as the value of compassion (*Mitleid*) of the symbolic Monsalvat were gone, if after the death of God all resurrection were to be cancelled, who would save us from Klingsor? Is there another saviour in sight, any other 'midday' but the ascendance of Parsifal to the throne where he uncovers again the (old) Truth, the Truth that we have lived by (and for) in our western, European, Jewish-Christian civilization? Where are those 'Roman' values Nietzsche covets, except in his own imagination? Klingsor is a sick dictator who has no other means of temptation than manipulation and force; to use a modern expression, his domination is not legitimated by one single idea or belief. He forces others (the epitome of which is his main asset, Kundry) to obey; he holds them on the strings of their weaknesses and transgressions. He is a modern tyrant, an epitome of modern evil; there is no grandeur in him, unless naked force can be so termed.

Let us return to Act Three of Wagner's mystery-play. Parsifal arrives at Monsalvat on Good Friday. Just as Napoleon Bonaparte, he had to fight his way through many countries and had to win many victories before he could find his way back to Monsalvat and be crowned the king of the Grail. He arrives, I repeat, on Good Friday. God is dead. God is dead also in a modern (and Nietzschean) sense. As Gurnemanz tells Parsifal, 'the Grail has long lain enclosed within the shrine . . . The divine bread is now denied us . . . Never more do messages come here . . . our dispirited and leaderless knighthood wander about, pale and woeful . . .' Parsifal, the self-made man, arrives on Good Friday; he brings back the spear, he heals the wound and then . . . he uncovers the Grail. It is still Good Friday (not yet Easter), when a white dove descends upon Parsifal's head. 'Our Redeemer redeemed.' God is dead, but he can or will be resurrected by a man who is enlightened by *Mitleid*, and who fights his way back to the ancient (old European) Truth and holds fast to it. In lieu of the transvaluation of all old values, *Parsifal* (and Parsifal himself) stands for the hope that those old values, which no one now upholds, can still be reconquered and redeemed by men; true, only by such men as also embody an ethics of personality. We can perhaps reproach Wagner for the latter restriction, but Nietzsche was in no position to do so.

If there was someone who understood this message, it was Nietzsche. Among the countless denunciations of *Parsifal* we find a remark that I consider both odd and telling. Nietzsche remarked, and not only once, that he would never forgive Wagner his *Parsifal*. In other words, Nietzsche rejected *Parsifal* as a moral failure, a transgression, a crime committed by its author. This in itself is not yet odd; after all, Nietzsche dismissed the concept of *l'art pour l'art*, and particularly the norm of *impassibilité*. Nevertheless, it is odd that in Nietzsche's mind an opera could be an unforgivable transgression. It is absolutely unforgivable because it is about forgiveness; and it is precisely the insincere defence of forgiveness (Nietzsche mentions the lack of *Redlichkeit*) which is absolutely unforgivable.

Wer zeigt mir noch etwas Widerlegteres, etwas von allen höheren Wertgefühlen so endgültig Gerichtetes als das Christentum? In ihm die Verführung als Verführung erkannt zu haben, in ihm die grosse Gefahr, den Weg zum Nichts, der sich als Weg zum Gottheit zu geben wusste – diese ewigen Werte als Verleumder-Werte erkannt zu haben – was anderes macht unseren Stolz, unsere Auszeichnung vor zwei Jahrtausenden aus?[91] (Who shows the thing that had been so refuted, the thing so severely judged by values higher than Christianity? To recognize in it seduction *as* seduction, the road that leads to nothingness while pretending to lead to God – to see in eternal values the fraudulent ones of betrayal – what else makes us proud, what else has made us proud, and given us honour, over two thousand years?)

Parsifal is the seducer; the seduction to Christendom through the apotheosis of forgiveness is unforgivable. Nietzsche does not forgive Wagner – he composes his own (anti) Parsifal instead.

Lecture Four

We can now return to our starting-point. Nietzsche's work, *On the Genealogy of Morals*, is composed as an opera, or rather as a music-drama, in three acts with one overture. It is in his musically composed prose-opera that Nietzsche 'takes back' Wagner's *Parsifal*. It is for Nietzsche a matter of 'Redlichkeit' to unmask the seducer; yet it is also a matter of 'Redlichkeit' to face the paradoxical nature of his own position.

On the Genealogy of Morals 'takes back' *Parsifal*, yet it does not follow the story of *Parsifal* slavishly. It has its own story to tell. Still, the two stories are synchronized to an astonishing degree. In what follows, I do not do justice to the complexity of Nietzsche's work. We are still interested in the topic 'Nietzsche and *Parsifal*' mainly from the perspective of an ethics of personality.

Anti-Parsifal viewed from the perspective of *Parsifal*: Synopsis

Overture

This is the composition of a philosopher. A book of philosophy is a memoir. Writing (composing) about the philosopher-Parsifal, we (philosophers) also write about ourselves. Thus the Parsifal-motif must appear in the first sentence. And it does. 'We are unknown to ourselves, we men of knowledge [*wir Erkennenden*] ... We have never sought ourselves – how could it happen that we should ever find ourselves?' As in a proper overture, the theme anticipates the whole. Philosophers are described as honey-gatherers who care only about 'bringing something home' (*etwas heimzubringen*). (The inverted commas indicate a direct reference by Nietzsche to Parsifal's spear.) But, unlike Parsifal, they do not experience life, they cannot prove themselves in action; so when the twelve beats of noon suddenly starts up (as in Act Three), they do not understand their own experience. Yet they ask, 'Who are we really?' and 'afterwards . . . count the twelve trembling bell-strokes of our experience, our life, our being – and alas! miscount them.'[92] This Parsifal remains a stranger in the kingdom of Monsalvat.

The second paragraph first states the topic of the music-drama (the origin of moral prejudices), the theme of *Anti-Parsifal*. The complexity of the variations on the theme is prefigured. Then the metaphor of the tree appears (it too will be varied many times). This is the metaphor of the philosopher as the carrier of an ethics of personality: 'Rather do our ideas, our values . . . grow out of us with the necessity with which a tree bears fruits . . . *one* will, *one* health, *one* soil, *one* sun.'[93]

Immediately afterwards Nietzsche speaks about himself, about his immoral or immoralistic 'a priori', and about his anti-Kantian 'categorical imperative'. The whole book (the opera) is now prefigured as Nietzsche's own world and truth, 'a country of my own, a soil of my own, an entire discrete, thriving, flourishing world, like a secret garden . . .'[94]

Does not the philosopher, with his 'secret garden' resemble Klingsor? Perhaps, because the magic garden is erected by the philosopher himself, yet also not, because he has not conjured up this garden out of *ressentiment*, but by following the voice of his own categorical imperative, his 'a priori'. The work (the garden) is his fate, his personality through and through.

Then the musical motif of the story (genealogy of morals) re-emerges, and from there the main theme develops *forte* (with reference to Schopenhauer, not Wagner, of course): 'I understood the ever spreading morality of pity . . . as the most sinister symptom of the sickness (nihilism) of our European culture.'[95] The *pharmakon* of pity is verily poisonous. Parsifal's remedy kills. And then follows the attack on the 'good man': 'What if a symptom of regression were inherent in the 'good', likewise a danger, a seduction, a poison, a narcotic, through which the present was possibly living *at the expense of the future*?'[96] The virtue of compassion and the 'good man' are treated here as symptoms – the symptoms of decay and of pessimism. Here Nietzsche simply reverses Wagner's signs. In *Parsifal* Gurnemanz is not portrayed as 'symptomatic' but, in Kierkegarrd's terms as exceptional (the individual exister, the exception, is the universal). Nietzsche challenges this presentation as unreflecting and unthinking.

Nietzsche now promises us that he will discover the land of morals for the first time: 'onwards! our old morality too is part *of the comedy*!'[97] No mystery-play should be expected. After all, seriousness will be rewarded by cheerfulness. But listen please: 'Cheerfulness . . . is a reward:

the reward of a long, brave, industrious, and subterranean seriousness, of which, to be sure, not everyone is capable.'[98] Is it not Parsifal, the philosopher who is speaking? Is cheerfulness not the symptom of the fulfilment of our destiny that grew out of 'our tree', our 'a priori', as the reward for our blind courage and good craftsmanship?

Act One: 'Good and evil', 'good and bad'

I skip here, with regrets, Nietzsche's polemics against Rée and utilitarianism, his story concerning the origin of good and bad, and many of his otherwise fascinating (and controversial) etymological and philosophical speculations. We have to follow our narrow path to shed some light on the Nietzsche–*Parsifal* controversy and on the relevance of this controversy (or rather obsession, fascination) to an ethics of personality.

The issue good–bad, good–evil is not incidental to the first act of Wagner's *Parsifal* either. We can read *Parsifal* also as a 'novel of education' (*Bildungsroman*) and recognize in the character of our Parsifal a younger brother of Wilhelm Meister or of *Der Grüne Heinrich*.[99] And if we do so, we shall soon realize that the education of our hero begins with his killing of the swan. The actor (Parsifal) remains ignorant of the meaning of his deed, and still he becomes the central figure of a minidrama where the spectators make sense of something that he cannot grasp. Let us follow the script loosely.

> *Gurnemanz:*   Unprecedented act! Here – look – here you struck him
> . . . the eyes glazed – do you see his look?

In other words, Gurnemanz confronts Parsifal with the result of his deed. The confrontation is simple and dramatic; the perpetrator should face murdered innocence. The face-to-face situation has several dimensions. Parsifal faces his victim, the dead swan, and he also faces his accusers, the knights of the Grail. Wagner's 'genealogy' does not differ here substantially from the genealogy of Nietzsche. Since Parsifal has not yet developed conscience, he cannot react with 'bad conscience' to the sight of murdered innocence. The face-to-face confrontation does not elicit the feeling of guilt, but rather the affect of shame.

Gurnemanz, as a sensitive moral person, does not just tell young Parsifal: you have violated the sacred order, shame on you; but he also tries to explain what the sacred order is, and why exactly this is the sacred order, and what the violation of this order implies. Gurnemanz, the good man, is a man of enlightenment, a kind of ethical rationalist, for he believes that the youth will understand the obvious (and what is the sacred order if not the obvious?), particularly if it is so vividly explained. What is Parsifal's first reaction? He breaks his bow. This indicates clearly that he misunderstood the relation between himself and his deed, that he has no idea about the causal relation, that he blames the bow (the thing) and not himself for the death of the swan. But Gurnemanz insists: 'Now do you appreciate your misdeed?' In a wordless answer, Parsifal passes his hand over his eyes. This is the gesture of shame. He does not want to see the swan (the victim of his cruelty), and he does not want to be seen by Gurnemanz and all of his accusers. Yet Gurnemanz insists again: 'Say, boy, do you realize your great guilt? How could you commit this crime?' Parsifal is then supposed to give an account of his motivations. And he answers, 'I didn't know.' Here we seemingly arrive at a dead end. Yet the contingent person's moral education begins in fact at the point of 'I do not know.'

The face-to-face confrontation with the victim (not with the accusers) has an emotional effect on Parsifal, but no knowledge (*Erkenntnis*) of good and bad or good and evil results therefrom. The enlightenment rationality in Gurnemanz's appeal remains ineffective. And here comes the most concise and the most touching account on the human condition of contingency. 'Who is your father? I don't know. Who sent you this way? I don't know. Your name, then? I had many, but I know none of them any more.' *Stunde Null* (zero hour).

After Gurnemanz's failure, another person takes over Parsifal's moral education: Kundry.[100] She reminds Parsifal that robbers and wild beasts feared him. This is a Siegfried motif.

Parsifal: Who fears me? Say!
Kundry: The wicked!
Parsifal: They who threatened me, were they wicked [*böse*]? ... Who is good?

Here we arrive – in the wake of Parsifal's moral education – at the question of good and evil.

Nietzsche too begins his *Genealogy* at the zero hour. As we all know, he begins his story with the concept 'good', the self-identification of the noble, the aristocratic (*vornehm*) caste. The 'bad' is the 'other', the socially lowly, the cowardly, the base one deserving of contempt. The distinction of good–evil is the first transvaluation of values. It happens in a slave revolt carried out by the Jews and finalized by Christianity. As a result, the noble, the good ones, the 'others' will be constituted as the 'wicked'; whereas those who determine them as wicked will identify themselves as good. The tree-comparison returns here; Christianity could grow only as a branch of the trunk of Jewish hatred: 'This Jesus of Nazareth, the incarnate gospel of love, this "Redeemer" ... was he not this seduction in its most uncanny and irresistible form, a seduction and bypath to precisely those *Jewish* values and new ideals?'[101] You will notice that Nietzsche describes Jesus Christ and Parsifal in exactly the same terms, and not only here. Let me paraphrase Nietzsche: have you understood him? Nietzsche accuses the anti-Semite Wagner of nothing else but of having conceived (through his hero, Parsifal) the most sophisticated and sublime (and also the most seductive and the most dangerous) defence – of what? Of Jerusalem, of Judaism – against Rome. In the 'eternal battle' between Rome and Jerusalem, Wagner allegedly took sides with Jerusalem and Nietzsche with Rome. This is how (and why) their sabres crossed on the world stage.[102]

Let us now return to Parsifal. He asks the question: 'Who is good?' And Gurnemanz answers, 'Your mother whom you deserted . . .' This sounds obviously fraudulent to Nietzsche. For at Monsalvat, in the shrine of the Redeemer, 'the good' should be identified with ourselves. The real (authentic, sincere) Jewish-Christian answer (according to Nietzsche) would have been, 'we are the good ones' or 'you – whom the wicked ones pursued – you are good.' But none of this happens here. Good and evil are constituted in a very different way. The youth is pursued by the wicked, but because he deserted his mother he is not good – rather she is good. And there are other surprises in store. Kundry announces that Parsifal's mother is dead, and Parsifal reacts by furiously seizing Kundry by her throat. Gurnemanz exclaims, 'Insane youth! Again violent?' Wagner scored here a fine point in his genealogy of morals. Just as moments before Parsifal proved unable to distinguish between the cause of the death of the swan (his act) and the means applied (the bow), now he fails to distinguish between the cause of his mother's death and the cause of his grief (Kundry, the herald of bad news).

No moral education has effect on Parsifal, although he feels shame, although he sees the dead swan, and even understands the words and sentences addressed to him. As I have already indicated, he has no conscience, he does not know what responsibility is, he is ignorant in matters of cause and effect. Parsifal is a noble savage in a very Nietzschean way.[103] This self-made *Naturbursch* behaved – in the forest, fighting against robbers and beasts, yet also in killing the swan at Monsalvat – just as the noble warrior barbarians are supposed to behave in Nietzsche's genealogy. The 'fool' Parsifal was a blond beast without a pack; he was a lonely lion. Gurnemanz and the others tried to do something to Parsifal that Nietzsche described as follows in his *Genealogy*: 'to make the bird of prey *accountable* for being a bird of prey'.[104] And this approach remained without effect on Parsifal too.

The exterior features of the royal hall at Monsalvat do not fit into Nietzsche's vision of the the workshops where ideas are forged, for this 'landscape' reminds one more of the caves of the Niebelungen.[105] But the ideas he describes, the 'lies' that 'stink', are actually the moral ideas of this holy place.

Let us return again to *Parsifal*. Kundry, perceiving Parsifal's miserable condition, gives him water to drink. Listen to Gurnemanz: 'Well done, according to the Grail's mercy; they vanquish evil who requite it with good.' But listen to Nietzsche: 'His inability for revenge is called unwillingness to revenge, perhaps even forgiveness . . . They also speak of "loving their enemies" – and sweat as they do so.'[106] We shall return to the 'sweat' in the next lecture, but for the time being we still follow the moral education of Parsifal. After Gurnemanz has praised Kundry's goodness, she replies: 'I never do good; I long only for rest . . .' Is this so? Gurnemanz said that Kundry never lies. So it seems that one can repay evil with good, without doing good.

We know the rest. After attending the sacred ritual of transubstantiation in reverse (blood becomes wine, etc.) Parsifal says nothing and understands nothing, or rather, he is unaware of having understood something. His moral education was a failure. Yet during the service the divine voices repeat the promise: 'Enlightened through compassion, the innocent fool . . .' And we are familiar with the rest of the first essay in *On the Genealogy of Morals*. In the battle between Judea and Rome, Judea seemed to have won. Yet 'must the ancient fire not some day flare up much more terribly, after much longer preparation? More: must one not desire it with all one's might? even will it? even promote it?'[107] Both first acts end with defeat; sickness and decadence prevail. Yet both also intone the melody of the expectation of healing.

Act Two: 'Guilt', 'bad conscience' and the like

Several exciting topics are covered by the word *Verwandtes* ('and the like') in the orientational title of the second essay. Unfortunately, we cannot tackle all of them here. We will not speak about the kind of guilt that is not (yet) fused with conscience (which is not yet the sense of guilt); we will neglect the complexity of the discussion of punishment; we will avoid the question of justice (of barter, contract, exchange) as we have avoided already the preliminary approach to the virtue of justice in the first essay. True, all topics covered by the nonchalant word 'Verwandtes' play their part in Nietzsche's battle against *Parsifal*. But the themes of the second act of Nietzsche's opera are not always synchronized with the second act of Wagner's opera. We limit ourselves to the synopsis that encompasses both.

Nietzsche begins again at the beginning. The question is how to breed a human being from an animal. Man is an animal with the right to make promises ('das versprechen darf').[108] Forgetfulness, this active faculty of repression that makes room for new things, this doorkeeper, preserver of psychic order,[109] needs to be abrogated by the active memory of the will. 'Between the original "I will" . . . and the actual discharge of the will, its *act*, a world of strange new things, circumstances, even acts of will may be interposed without breaking this long chain of will.'[110] This is the long story of how responsibility originated.

Prehistoric labour made man predictable and rational. A man acquires the capacity to make promises after he learns how to distinguish between contingent and necessary events, between goals and means, as he also learns to think in terms of causality and to anticipate.[111] Obviously, the Parsifal of the first act of the music-drama has not yet gone through this 'prehistoric labour'. He has not yet acquired the capacity to make promises; in fact, he has not yet made any promises. In the second act, we still encounter the same Parsifal; he is still the blond beast, the noble savage, the man who has not acquired the right to make promises, the pre-rational, courageous, healthy, but uninteresting person.

Nietzsche continues: the ripest fruit of 'prehistoric labour' is the sovereign individual, the free man who is his own measure; the man for whom responsibility becomes an instinct and who calls this instinct his conscience. Nietzsche intones here the theme of an ethics of personality.[112] This theme interrupts the course of the narrative, and with good reason. This 'ripe and late fruit', [113] the ethics of Nietzsche's real heroes, of Goethe, of Napoleon and of Dionysus the philosopher (one of Nietzsche's masks) is, according to Nietzsche, not the ethics of *Parsifal*. The roots of the latter had to be sought in different quarters.

The main narrative tells the story of how blood, torture, sacrifice – that is pain – had been the most effective utensils of mnemotechnics. And it was pain that made Parsifal remember. One gets the impression that Parsifal's mythological story is translated here into the language of mythologized history. The kind of knowledge (*Erkenntnis*) that Parsifal gained (through pain) in the second act of the music-drama is the knowledge that makes men capable of making promises in such a way as to understand causality, to anticipate, to distinguish between contingency and necessity. Parsifal becomes man through pain, the pain of a 'wounded animal'.[114] Pain, and not Gurnemanz's or Kundry's moral education, transforms the innocent fool (the prehistoric man in an ontogenetic sense) into a moral person. It is now that Parsifal makes his promise, and he is going to keep it. Parsifal can keep this promise because he has gained the capacity to make promises. How much time elapses between Parsifal's victory against Klingsor and the Good Friday of his return, his 'bringing home' of the sacred spear? Who knows? Wagner indicates that much time elapsed. What kept Parsifal's promise alive in those worlds of 'strange new things'? Only the capacity that Nietzsche termed 'the memory of the will'.

Nietzsche recapitulates the drama of the transformation of Parsifal in his own story about the emergence of conscience. But at this stage we do not yet receive his whole story. In order to get the full picture, we first need to follow the story of another branch from Nietzsche's tree of genealogy.

I repeat with regret that we skip the story of debt and contract for the simple reason that there is no contract in *Parsifal*. Parsifal jumps over the debt-stage of guilt[115] as does Nietzsche's model of the ethics of personality. Parsifal has no inkling of the debt (guilt, *Schuld*) that he is supposed to 'repay' to his community (he has none) or to his ancestors (he does not know them) or to God (he has not the faintest idea about his existence). If he is punished at all, he is not punished by his ancestors, nor by his community, nor even by God, for his punishment (if it can be described in such terms) is immediate self-punishment. Moreover, this is not even the kind of self-punishment that ensues from reflection, but is rather self-punishment by instinct. May I say that it is sovereign self-punishment?

Again, Nietzsche comes very close to Wagner (or rather to Wagner's *Parsifal*); they are rubbing shoulders. Nietzsche is no more the enemy of suffering than Wagner. Both of them remain in debt to Schopenhauer on this count. In *The Birth of the Tragedy* Nietzsche is deeply committed to a Dionysian metphysics of suffering. Later the metaphysical foundation vanishes and suffering assumes an ethical significance in Nietzsche, but not a moral one. Suffering is of moral significance if it is suffering-with-the-other. Suffering is of an ethical significance, in the sense of an ethics of personality, if it enhances life. Nietzsche takes the side of Tannhäuser against Venus: suffering is, after all, life, and one cannot say 'yes' to life without saying 'yes' to suffering. 'What really arouses indignation against suffering', Nietzsche says, and repeats it on many other occasions, 'is not suffering as such but the senselessness of suffering: but neither for the Christian, who has interpreted a whole mysterious machinery of salvation into suffering, nor for the naïve man of more ancient times . . . was there any such thing as *senseless* suffering.'[116] But suffering and the suffering of 'bad conscience' are still not the same thing.

We can detect a similar brand of ambiguity in Nietzsche's genealogy of 'bad conscience' as it is found in his genealogy of responsibility-taking. Instincts turned against man himself, the discharge of instincts turned inward – this is how we could sum up Nietzsche's story of the genesis of bad conscience. The tamed animal, the fool (Nietzsche uses the term *Narr*, like Wagner in *Parsifal*) invented 'bad conscience'. And immediately afterwards you hear (yes, you hear) the Parsifal-cum-Zarathustra motif, of the redeemer sounding:

> From now on, man is *included* among the most unexpected and exciting lucky throws in the dice game of Heraclitus' 'great child', be he called Zeus or chance; he gives rise to an interest, a tension, a hope, almost a certainty, as if with him something were announcing and preparing himself, as if man were not a goal but only a way, an episode, a bridge, a promise . . .[117]

Then two branches of the same bough are again examined separately. One branch brings the wondrous fruit of an ethics of personality,[118] whereas the other carries the rotten yield of the Jewish-Christian-Kantian version of morality:

> Here is *sickness*, beyond any doubt, the most terrible sickness that has ever raged in man; and whoever can still bear to hear ... how in this night of torment and absurdity there has resounded the cry of *love*, the cry of the most nostalgic rapture, of redemption through *love*, will turn away, seized by invincible horror.[119]

Wagner's *Parsifal* is, in Nietzsche's mind, the fruit of this latter branch and not the sweet produce of the former. The second act of his Anti-Parsifal opera is about the parting of ways of the sweet hero of an ethics of personality and the repulsive hero of a morbid culture.[120] Both are also sick (man is, after all, a sick animal), but the first overcomes sickness whereas the second succumbs to it and infects others with it. In the second act of Nietzsche's opera there is both a Roman and a Jewish-Christian Parsifal. We shall see what will happen to them in the third act.

But in Wagner's opera there is only one Parsifal. The Parsifal of an ethics of personality and the Christian Parsifal are one and the same. What happens here?

We skip the flower maidens, and we return to the drama where it corresponds to Nietzsche's second act: at the dramatic encounter between Kundry and Parsifal.

Kundry: Parsifal, stay!

. . .

Parsifal: Did you call me, who is nameless?

. . .

Kundry: ... what drew you here if not the wish to know?
Parsifal: ... what now I see fills me with dread.

Parsifal hears his name. He is now named. This is the first determination of the contingent person. A name is nothing as yet. Kundry emphasizes the 'nothingness' of Parsifal's name in her etymology: Parsifal means just *fal parsi*, the 'innocent fool'. Yet the sound of his name arouses dreamlike memory traces in the youth, and together with them some recognition of his 'situation' emerges. His first feeling is dread.[121] At this point Wagner speaks Kierkegaard's language: the anxiety of the innocent is freedom's actuality as the possibility of possibility.[122] From anxiety one 'leaps' into freedom. This non-Nietzschean theme is episodic. The main motif remains knowledge (*Erkennen*) versus innocence-ignorance. Kundry, as we saw, challenges Parsifal at once: it is not by accident that he has arrived at Klingsor's castle, she says. He was obviously drawn by *der kunde Wunsch* (desire for the message). He was not 'driven', he was 'pulled' by it. Being pulled by *der kunde Wunsch* indicates the first stirring of destiny. Parsifal is still a fool, he has no memories, neither does he anticipate his future; still, something drives him towards something: he wants to know, without knowing either what he wants or that he wants and what he wants. Destiny begins stirring in Parsifal's soul as an instinct, as an affect – unconsciously. Both Nietzsche and Wagner think (and compose) in terms of a dramatic (of tragic) genre. This is why neither of them accepts the rude contrast between reason on the one hand and instinct on the other. The deepest-lying reason in a paradigmatic person's life is his love of (his) fate. The drive towards one's fate can be called reason and instinct alike. It is the reason (rationale) of the persons' life, but this reason is not always consciously pursued; it 'drives one towards' one's destiny, and it is rarely reflected upon. Parsifal is pulled by his destiny towards knowledge. Ignorance is innocence; is then knowledge guilt?

It is then that Kundry tells the story of Parsifal's mother, Heart's Sorrow, who bore the fatherless child and sheltered him both from his enemies and from knowledge. The Oedipal motif (kissing, embracing) appears for the first time. Kundry then continues: 'But you did not consider her woe . . . when you finally did not return . . . grief consumed her pain and she craved for death's release: her sorrow broke her heart.' Parsifal's reaction is 'terrible perturbation' and grief (*schmerzlich ueberwaeltigt*): 'Woe on me! Alas! What have I done? Where was I? Mother! Sweet mother! Your son, your son it was who killed you! Fool, blind blundering fool.' Thus suddenly, as knowledge dawns upon him in his pain, Parsifal assumes responsibility. What he could not understand after killing the swan, in spite of having seen the swan's wound and its glazed eyes, he now understands without sight, by gaining the capacity of memory and the power of imagination: Mother died – I was the one who killed her. Parsifal gains conscience through the sense of guilt. Actually, Kundry did not ask him, 'What have you done?' She did not accuse him directly of killing his mother for the simple reason that Parsifal had not killed his mother, at least not in the same sense as he had killed the swan. Parsifal is here Cain thousandfold in reverse. He does not just say, 'I left my mother, so I am co-responsible for her death.' He immediately exaggerates, he takes upon his newly-won conscience the burden of full responsibility as sin. This is precisely the gesture which is dictated by his destiny, the destiny of a redeemer.

This scene must have been a scandal for Nietzsche: So close to him, and yet so far! No one tells Parsifal that he killed his mother, no one even asks him the question, and yet he takes upon himself the guilt. So close to Nietzsche, since the feelings of guilt and bad conscience emerge directly in Parsifal's soul and heart as the answers to the pull of his own destiny. There is no authority to command Parsifal to regret his vicious deed. He does it on his own, he exaggerates, he spins the thread of bad conscience entirely from his own instinctual, emotional commitment. So close to Nietzsche and so far! For it is guilt, bad conscience, compassion, and all the 'sick' emotions from which Parsifal spins the threads of his own soul.

When Nietzsche hails the men of responsibility with their capacity to make promises, he praises prospective, never retrospective (retroactive) responsibility. As I mentioned in my first lecture, prospective responsibility has nothing to do with bad conscience or guilt. A strong and healthy person who takes upon himself responsibility for something will keep his promise so that he will not feel guilty. Parsifal's *amor fati*, to the same extent as his gesture of taking responsibility, was closely associated with guilt. Retrospective responsibility makes sense only if there is guilt, sin, misconduct, or some equivalent; something one has to acknowledge as one's own deed or as the result of one's deed; something one is ready to pay for at least by causing pain to himself. Parsifal will also assume prospective responsibility (to rescue the Holy Grail), but he can do so only after having already assumed retrospective responsibility (for having been guilty).

Still, there is nothing in the Wagnerian Parsifal that would disqualify him as the carrier of an ethics of personality. After all, he was following his destiny in assuming retrospective responsibility. This was his fate, so this was also the ethics of his personality.

Let us return to the story. From the recognition of guilt, remorse follows. Parsifal: 'How could I forget my mother – my mother! Ah, what else have I forgotten?' This is a dangerous moment for the seducer woman. According to her strategy, Parsifal was required to remember up to exactly this point. Without developing pangs of conscience for abandoning his doting mother, Parsifal would remain an ignorant innocent. Kundry could have made love to him, but she could not have seduced him, for there is no seduction without knowledge. The knowledge so far acquired by Parsifal was necessary, and also sufficient. But Parsifal pushes further ahead when he asks: 'What else have I forgotten?' Half-knowledge dooms Parsifal, full knowledge saves him.

Parsifal is drawn (by his own instinct) to remember Monsalvat, the Grail, and Amfortas. Kundry seizes the only occasion (of still half, not yet full, knowledge) and replies: 'Confession will end guilt in remorse, understanding changes folly into sense.' The content of the sentence is true, but in the context in which it is spoken, the truth becomes untrue. Nietzsche has said something very similar: the truth of sentences is context-dependent, or rather dependent on the perspective of the person who speaks and of the person who is spoken to. The real question is 'What are you doing with this sentence?' In this context Kundry's words mean: you have experienced remorse; enough now, you are no more a fool but a man of sense. Kundry must hurry up; she must seduce Parsifal before he remembers Amfortas. She therefore resorts to the most forceful weapon of seduction, the Oedipal motif. Parsifal should make love to her as if he were his own father and she, Kundry, his mother. She kisses him, and it is then that Parsifal is seized by the utmost terror (*höchsten Schreck*) and by agonizing pain. Parsifal: 'Amfortas – the wound! The wound! It burns within my heart!'

This is the very centre of the opera: in one shock Parsifal finds the path to his destiny and becomes himself. As Nietzsche says in *Ecce Homo*, he becomes what he is – through total transformation, transfiguration from an innocent fool into an ascetic priest. (In Szyberberg's film the reborn Parsifal is played by a new person, an actress.) Parsifal suddenly hears the Saviour's lament asking Parsifal to redeem him. Having assumed responsibility for his mother's death, Parsifal now resumes responsibility for the death of God: God, whom you have forgotten, is dead. 'Redeemer! Saviour! Lord of grace! How can I, a sinner, purge my guilt?'

A self-made man has grasped his destiny. Why is the story (so far) utterly fraudulent in Nietzsche's terms? We now speak only of the second act (of both *Parsifal* and *Anti-Parsifal*).

The identification of sexuality/guilt/knowledge is for Nietzsche an affront against nature, one of Christianity's sickest inventions, and – as it appears in the Parsifal-legend a simplistic idea into the bargain. Wagner harps on this motif while he invests his music with sensuality, with his power of sexual 'seduction' in support of the deadly enemy of the selfsame power. This is a very fine analysis.[123] After all, the wound of sexual love, the wound of sickness (decadence), and the wound of compassion are all the same wound. This is a multi-purpose motif. Parsifal could become a fully inner-determined man of the ethics of personality because his compassion was a feeling identical with the other person's feeling of pain. His destiny as that of an ascetic priest was prefigured in the exaggeration of his emotions. Just as he takes responsibility for having killed his mother (which he had not done), so does his compassion for Amfortas differ from 'normal' empathy. In the first act, Gurnemanz asked him to develop 'normal' compassion: to feel pain because another creature feels pain, accompanied by the readiness and the desire not to cause pain again. But no 'good man' wanted him to feel exactly the same pain as the person with whom he was supposed to empathize. This kind of sensibility is the Redeemer's mark of distinction, not the good man's character trait: Parsifal, who could not even feel sympathy with the suffering of others, now feels the very kind of suffering (on the same occasion) as the other. Absolute identification with the other calls for the absolute identity of the source of suffering. This source is Kundry's kiss. Although Parsifal is not wounded by the spear, he is wounded by the kiss, and this wound rescues him from the power of the spear. *He not only 'foreknows', but feels the consequences of his act before his act.* The act is prevented by the felt consequences of this very same act which is never going to be committed. This is how Parsifal rescues – through compassion – not just Amfortas and the Grail, but also himself, by realizing himself. Parsifal can become what he is only as the person who redeems the Redeemer. Empathy is his royal road to the throne of redemption.

I repeatedly referred to the Oedipal nature of Kundry's seduction. There are several similarities between Parsifal and Oedipus (that is, with the Oedipus who solves the riddle of the Sphinx), but he is also the opposite of Oedipus: the one who does not sleep with his mother, and who resurrects the father whom he helped to kill. Finally, we should remember the Troll motif. Not only the flower maidens, but Kundry too seduces her victims into regression. The Parsifal who returns in his mother's womb is not only guilty of moral transgression against a sacred law, he is also guilty of committing a crime against himself. To return to the beginning without, and instead of, fulfilling one's destiny is the opposite of the passionate acceptance of the eternal recurrence of the same. First fulfil your destiny, then wish to repeat it, or else you are a failure, a contingent person remaining contingent. Parsifal is not 'determined' by his world, knowledge or psyche. He is a projection, but not the kind a Nietzshe could love, approve of, or hope for.

Breathing in the mountain air of Sils-Maria (his Monsalvat) Nietzsche dreams of another kind of 'projection': of the man of the future 'who will redeem us', of 'this Anti-Christ and anti-nihilist; this victor over God and nothingness – he must come some day . . .'[124]

It was through compassion (*Mitleid*), a virtue that Nietzsche despised, that Parsifal became an ascetic priest. The third act of Nietzsche's music drama, of his *Anti-Parsifal*, speaks about this ascetic priest.

Act Three: What is the meaning of ascetic ideals?

'What is the meaning of ascetic ideals?' is the question which encapsulates the main theme of the third act of *Anti-Parsifal*, or rather the main theme of the whole *Anti-Parsifal*, and moreover, the main theme of the third act of *Parsifal* and of Wagner's whole opera; it appears immediately as the first sentence of the first paragraph of Nietzsche's third essay. All instruments in Nietzsche's orchestra sound the same theme, which later will be frequently repeated by one or another separate group of instruments. What I call a group of instruments is a so-called 'perspective'. Whatever your 'perspective', the ascetic ideal means something for you. It means something different to the artist, to the philosopher, to scholars, to women, to the majority of us mortals, to the priest, to the saint; but it invariably means something. Listen to the *crescendo fortissimo*: 'That the ascetic ideal has meant so many things to man, however, is an expression of the basic fact of human will, its *horror vacui; it needs a goal* and it will rather will *nothingness* than *not* will. Am I understood? . . . Have I been understood?'[125] This first paragraph is also an operatic trick, an 'orchestral prelude', as the concise anticipation of the whole act before curtain rise.

The curtain is raised and we see Richard Wagner, the 'failed swine', putting his antithesis, Parsifal, the country simpleton and ascetic priest, on the stage as a joke.[126] Thereafter Nietzsche 'eliminates the artists' from his 'orchestra' of the first paragraph and turns his attention towards the philosophers. What is the meaning of ascetic ideals to them? The first motif ('the first indication') is 'the gaining of release from a torture',[127] of sensuality or sexuality, not from virtue,

> 'but because their supreme lord demands this of them, prudently and inexorably: he is concerned with one thing alone, and assembles and saves up everything – time, energy, love, and interest – only for that one thing.'[128]

The supreme lord is philosophy, or rather the 'will to power' as the will to engage in philosophy – that is, in the philosopher's destiny. In full swing we now return to the initial motif of the 'overture' (see above). And it is only with the greatest regret that I jump over the following, perhaps (to me) the most beautiful, sections of the third essay, since we already have heard and seen as much as is necessary for the further elaboration of our limited topic. But the conclusion, if there is any, must be noted. Nietzsche writes, 'the most ancient and most recent experience of philosophers on earth: whoever has at some time built a "new heaven" has found the power to do so only in his *own hell*'.[129] I must insert a brief remark here: the same is true of Parsifal. Didn't he serve two lords at once: the lord of his destiny and the Lord of Heaven? And since these two coincide, what is, after all, the difference between Parsifal's and the philosopher's commitment to the ascetic ideal? And if Parsifal's compassion, the pain of the bleeding wound, and his pain of the sensual/sexual experience were but one, and if it was the immediate spiritual sublimation of desire that made him find his own life and destiny, hasn't he also found in the same act the power to build a heaven (not a work of philosophy, but a world) from his (newly gained) hell?

But we cannot ask questions of Nietzsche that he would not have already asked of himself. This is how he continues:

> the philosophic spirit always had to use as a mask and cocoon the *previously established* types of contemplative man – priest, sorcerer, soothsayer, and in any case a religious type – in order to be able to *exist at all: the ascetic ideal* for a long time served the philosopher as a form in which to appear . . . he had to *represent* it so . . . for the longest time philosophy would not have been *possible at all* on earth without ascetic wraps and cloak, without an ascetic self-misunderstanding . . . the *ascetic priest* provided until the most modern times the repulsive and gloomy caterpillar form in which alone the philosopher could live and creep about.[130]

What is common to Parsifal and the philosopher is also common to him and the caterpillar-philosopher, the philosopher's wrapping. And what is great in the philosopher is great in spite of this wrapping. To avoid misunderstanding, the wrapping is not an 'appearance' and the philosopher does not sit inside the wrapping in his very 'essence'.[131] Actually, from Nietzsche's perspective, the bipolarity of essence/appearance itself belongs to the metaphysical 'wrapping' of philosophy. The ascetic priest is the form of existence philosophers have assumed until now; it was the only (typical) form of their existence. But the 'genre' of philosophy has something else still in store: a new, and adequate, form: a beautiful appearance – whereas the ascetic priest remains self-identical. He has acquired his ultimate forms, he cannot assume new ones.[132]

Now we have to listen carefully: the theme of a Nietzschean redeemer appears here in an extremely interesting variation. Usually (and you may already recall two examples of this from the text you have read so far), Nietzsche lets the theme sound forcefully in the form of an exclamation, or as a prayer uttered with urgency, or as a strong appeal to the promised future. But here, the redeemer theme takes the form of a question which is not rhetorical, but real; a question to which the person who asks it does not know the answer. The question is also an appeal, for it is asked with the desire of ushering in the possibility of a redeeming 'yes'. The question sounds as follows: 'Is there sufficient pride, daring, courage, self-confidence available today, sufficient will of the spirit, will to responsibility, *freedom of will*, for "the philosopher" to be henceforth – *possible* on earth?'[133]

Yet the butterfly appears only in Nietzsche's lyric outpourings; we are in the second scene of Act Three, where the caterpillar (Parsifal) and its variants occupy the stage. Nietzsche approaches them from different perspectives. The ascetic priest enjoys his sufferings; he seduces through the image of torment and he wills to suspend all affects in order to castrate the intellect. But this (enigmatic) ascetic priest is the representative carrier of the ascetic ideals, of the protective instincts against a degenerating life, of the artifice of the preservation of life in a sick culture. The paradox is formulated in many variations and in different orchestrations but all of them boil down to a single one: the ascetic priest is sick and makes us sick; yet only this (sick) seducer, this enemy of life, can rescue life.[134] Is, after all, Parsifal still 'the redeemer' of Amfortas' decadent world?

And here Nietzsche goes one step further in the praise of (the sick) man. His praise of man is more modern, yet not less forceful, and it is perhaps more touching, than the well-known song of the chorus in Sophocles' *Antigone*:

Man. . . . is *the* sick animal . . . he has also dared more, done more new things, braved more and challenged fate more than all the other animals put together: he, the great experimenter with himself, discontented and insatiable, wrestling with animals, nature, and gods for ultimate dominion – he, the still unvanquished, eternally directed towards the future, whose own restless energies never leave him in peace, so that his future digs like a spur into the flesh of every present – how should such a courageous and richly endowed animal not also be the most imperilled, the most chronically and profoundly sick of all the sick animals? . . . even when he *wounds* himself, this master of destruction, of self-destruction – the very wound afterward compels him to *live*.[135]

The last sentence's reference to *Parsifal* is so obvious that it does not call for further elaboration.

But then Nietzsche changes his perspective. The more normal our sickliness becomes, the higher we should honour 'the rare cases of great power of soul and body: man's *lucky hits*'.[136] The referents of the term 'lucky hits' are here not men of an ethics of personality in general, but just the 'butterfly' men who have abandoned all ascetic ideals. It is from the perspective of the protection of the health of those 'lucky hits' that the 'ascetic priests' are now described and discussed. Unfortunately, we must skip many important points of this discussion, though they could bear further witness to the musical nature of this composition of Nietzsche's. For example, the main theme of the first act (*ressentiment*) returns here and is fused with the theme of the ascetic priest (*ressentiment* turning against ourselves); and the Christian themes of guilt, sin, depravity, damnation, and redemption (as separate mini-motifs) are absorbed by the main ones. The theme of the herd (and of the man-of-the-herd, also exemplified by Richard Wagner) becomes associated, not only with the herd, but also with the 'orgy of feelings' (see Wagner's music), which is also produced by the 'mighty sorcerers' (ascetic priests). The destruction of taste (by the New Testament, Luther and Wagner) is also a recurring theme.

Then Nietzsche switches his perspective again, not entirely 'back', but very close to 'back'. Now he will not discuss what the ascetic ideal has done but what it means.[137] At this point we begin to suspect what we have already guessed: Nietzsche's *Anti-Parsifal* is not a radical *Anti-Parsifal*. Despite Nietzsche's contempt for, and even hatred of, this late work of Wagner, it is not the struggle of two antagonists that we now witness. Or rather, something changes here while the drama of *Genealogy* develops. The first essay (first act) is a straightforward example of an indirect philosophical (and artistic) polemic. In the second essay (second act) many of Nietzsche's observations on ethics and morals may serve as interpretative devices in our reading of *Parsifal*, but Nietzsche himself never takes the standpoint of *Parsifal*. But something happens in the third part (or act) that turns the tables.

Nietzsche suggests that one read the third essay as a lengthy commentary on a sentence by Zarathustra: 'Unconcerned, mocking, violent – thus wisdom wants *us*: she is a woman and always loves only a warrior.'[138] This is one of Nietzsche's jokes, for the third essay is certainly not a 'commentary' of this sentence, although it is written (or composed) in the spirit of this sentence. But let us return to Nietzsche's question in paragraph 23, the question that also appears as the title of the third essay (What is the meaning of ascetic ideals?). The ascetic ideal is powerful, because it expresses a will, it presents a goal (one single goal) and it offers interpretation. 'Where is the match of this closed system of will, goal, and interpretation? Why has it not found its match? Where is the *other "one goal"*?'[139]

We learn that neither modern science, nor atheism, nor even radical enlightenment provides one. For whether one says that God exists or that he does not exist, one equally has faith in truth. The faith in truth, in the value of truth, is the ascetic ideal itself. Yet, 'from the moment faith in the God of the ascetic ideal is denied, a *new problem arises*: that of the *value* of truth.'[140] Here follows one of the most concise and brilliant discussions of the agony and death of God, of the emptying out of the old faith, where finally God is replaced by a question mark and everything is permitted; it is a discussion of passive and active nihilism, of the modern forgery of ideals. What happened to the belief in the Truth of the Christian God, Nietzsche asks, and answers his own question: 'All great things bring about their own destruction.'[141] Christianity as a dogma was destroyed by its own morality (the virtue of truthfulness), and Christianity as morality must perish too, for truth (the meaning of truth, the will to truth) is now being questioned. Morality will perish; this is 'the great spectacle in a hundred acts' reserved for the next two centuries; 'the most terrible, most questionable, and perhaps also the most hopeful of all spectacles.'[142] We may notice that Nietzsche says 'perhaps' only in the third case.

We need not return to *Parsifal*, for we discuss *Parsifal*, the 'Problem *Parsifal*', the problem of truth, the whole time. Parsifal's fate is to redeem the redeemer, to resurrect the dead God of a decadent world, to uncover the Grail: Truth. Parsifal develops the will to truth, and it is through this will-to-truth that he infuses meaning into a senseless world. Suffering has a meaning again, and so have life and death. There is, once again, a goal, an interpretation and a will where the only Truth has now been restored. On the surface, Nietzsche fights Wagner, who abandoned Feuerbach and succumbed to Schopenhauer. But deep down, there is something else and something more at stake. Whatever the 'content' of the Grail, Christian or pagan, it does not matter. For it symbolizes Truth, the only, the one, the saving Truth, the Truth of metaphysics.[143] This truth is not perspectivist, unlike the truth of Nietzsche. Parsifal cannot say 'this is my truth' or 'your truth', he just 'shows' truths. Parsifal thus performs the apotheosis of the Truth of metaphysics. Yet a morality which is embedded in the Truth of metaphysics 'does' all those things with the sick animal that traditional Jewish-Christian morality always did: it humbles them, it enslaves them, it de-sexes them. Moreover, since Parsifal is a modern, contingent man, and his world is a modern, decadent world, a mystery-play about rescuing the metaphysical Truth is an absolutely fraudulent gesture. Where the faith in God is already gone, no old 'redeemer' can restore it. Where the faith in absolute truth is gone, where everything becomes permitted, the gesture of 'unconcealing' (Aletheia) is false; the Grail is a forgery. The redeemer cannot be redeemed. The whole paraphernalia of its mystery is a lie, and in a work of art one should not lie. Parsifal, the repository of an ethics of personality, the contingent man who found himself, his own destiny, his own truth, should not have pointed at the Grail as Truth.

In the third act of Nietzsche's *Anti-Parsifal*, he speaks as much for Parsifal as against him. In fact, he composes a more modern opera on the theme of *Parsifal* than did Wagner; this is an opera that ends in a question mark. But how can an opera end in a question mark?

The finale of Nietzsche's opera (and it is a finale!)[144] begins with the sound of trumpets: 'Apart from the ascetic ideal, man . . . had no meaning so far.' Then an old theme re-emerges, played by the strings: 'The meaninglessness of suffering, *not* suffering itself, was the curse that lay over mankind so far – *and the ascetic ideal offered man meaning.*' 'This . . . brought fresh suffering with it, deeper, more inward, more poisonous, more life-destructive suffering: it placed all suffering under the perspective of *guilt* . . . But . . . man was *saved* thereby, he possessed a meaning . . . *the will itself was saved.*'[145] This will is, as resounding in the overture of Nietzsche's music-drama, a will to nothingness. And 'man would rather will *nothingness* than *not* will'. ('Lieber will noch der Mensch das Nichts wollen, als nicht wollen.'[146])

I indicated earlier that Nietzsche's music-drama ends in a question mark. I could have been mistaken. After all, the last sentence of the third essay is an emphatically firm statement. And this is, indeed, Nietzsche's last musical sentence. But is it also the last statement of the music-drama?

Let us return to the finale of the second act. We have quoted a few words from paragraph 24. Nietzsche yearns here for a redeemer, for the anti-Parsifal, for the victor 'over God and nothingness'. The finale (of Act Three) makes' no mention of such a redeemer. There is only one redeemer left: Parsifal himself, the ascetic priest with his nihilistic ascetic ideals, this forgery of the redeemer. But at the end of the second act (essay), another theme is resounding: 'But what am I saying? Enough! Enough! At this point it behoves me only to be silent; or I shall usurp that to which only . . . *Zarathustra* has a right.' This theme does not appear in the finale, or at least it does not 'resound'. The rest is silence. Silence 'behoves' (*geziemt*) Nietzsche alone. And Zarathustra? Zarathustra's dictum (you remember, it is about wisdom who, like a woman, loves only a warrior) is placed at the head of the third act (essay) as a motto.

Zarathustra is asked to intone the main motif that Nietzsche (his father) will interpret. We saw that this does not happen, we said it is one of Nietzsche's jokes. It is a deep joke. For, as Nietzsche says, only the ascetic ideals offer a truth, a goal and a meaning for interpretation. Zarathustra speaks truth, but Nietzsche shies away from stepping into Zarathustra's place to announce a new truth, a new hope for a new redemption, in the finale of his music-drama. On Good Friday, Nietzsche's (ambiguous, schizophrenic, *Doppelgänger*) Parsifal uncovers the Grail, but, just like Wagner's Parsifal in Act Two, he alone – as in a dreamlike frenzy, shattered by deep emotions – sees the blood, the gleaming hope, the uncovered Grail. The others, who surround him, whom he is elected to redeem, see nothing; Parsifal's truth is not theirs. There are no heavenly voices, no dove descends on Parsifal's head. He stands there alone, eyes fixed on his truth, and he sings. Yet the others remain silent. So does Nietzsche.

Lecture Five

As we know, the last paragraph of *Genealogy* begins with the sentence: 'Apart from the ascetic ideal, man, the human animal, had no meaning so far.'[147] One could say that 'der Mensch' stands here for the genus 'homo'; the yield of domestication and self-domestication; the 'sick animal'. At first glance, Nietzsche states something about humankind in general. At a second glance, however, we realize that Nietzsche does not refer here to humankind in general, but to those human groups, or (perhaps) also to whole peoples, who took upon themselves the travail of forging 'ideals'. He speaks about the pioneers who established the slabs of values for themselves and for others. Man has a meaning (*Sinn*), suffering has a meaning (*Sinn*), will is rescued if, and only if, there are groups of people who forge, maintain and also propagate ideals. The ascetic ideal, the will to nothingness, the result of the travail of two thousand odd years of old western culture, has no alternatives. If this is so, Wagner did the greatest service to the 'will to power' in creating Parsifal, the conservative hero, who brings back the world of decadence to its former, not-yet-decadent state; who dares to give back to an already weakened and discredited ideal its old lustre and truth; and who renders thereby meaning to life and to suffering. This conclusion would be unavoidable, if conclusions could be unavoidable for Nietzsche, to the man of radical enlightenment. But Nietzsche rebels against his own conclusion (because the conclusion results only from his own premises). Apart from the ascetic ideal man has no meaning *so far*. So far he has none, but tomorrow he may have one. Perhaps he will.[148] The 'perhaps' opens up possibilities. 'Perhaps' the butterfly of a new philosophy will fly out of the husk of the ascetic priest, 'perhaps' all values will be transvalued, 'perhaps' there will be another set of ideals, 'perhaps' man is only a bridge to something 'higher'. Parsifal is fraudulent because he deletes this 'perhaps'.

Radical philosophy indulges in shocking and provocative categorical statements. Nietzsche was a typical radical philosopher, and he too loved shocking and provocative categorical statements. Yet he also deconstructed 'necessity', historical necessity first and foremost, and this left him with a 'perhaps'. There is only one way to employ the 'perhaps' in the service of categorical statements, and this requires the idea of a wager in a very Pascalian sense. To speak with Nietzsche's voice but in terms of the Pascalian wager is not an absurd idea. In Nietzsche's philosophical mythology Pascal resembles a fallen angel: a great genius who discredited himself in a cowardly fashion by putting all his stakes on the wrong option, namely, on God's existence.[149] Both Pascal and Nietzsche used the 'throw of the dice' as their favourite metaphor in reference to contingency. Nietzsche does not 'bet' on the existence or non-existence of God, for the question concerning the 'existence of God' is, for Nietzsche, in itself a metaphysical speculation. The choice to live without God is an ethico-philosophical one:

> wir Anderen, die wir dem Werden seine Unschuld zurueckgewinnen wünschen, möchten die Missionäre eines reinlicheren Gedanken sein ... Es fehlt ein Wesen, das dafür verantwortlich gemacht werden könnte, dass Jemand überhaupt da ist, dass Jemand so und so ist, dass Jemand unter diesen Umständen, in dieser Umgebung geboren ist ... *es ist ein grosses Labsal, dass solch ein wesen Fehlt.* (We, the others, who are willing to restore its innocence, want to become missionaries of a purer thought ... There is no Being who can be made responsible for anyone's existing, for anyone's being such and such, that is born under these conditions in such and such a time ... It is a great consolation that there is no such Being.)

No one experiments with us to produce an 'ideal of perfection', 'an ideal of virtue', or 'an ideal of happiness'.

> Es fehlt jeder Ort, jeder Zweck, jeder Sinn, wohin wir unser Sein, unser So-und-so-sein abwaelzen koennen. Man KANN das Ganze nicht richten, messen, vergleichen oder gar verneinen ... zum Beispiel, *well es Nichts gibt ausser dem Ganzen.*[150] (There is no place whatsoever, no goal, no sense, to which we could relate our being such and such. One cannot judge, measure, compare or even negate the whole ... because, for example, there is nothing outside the whole.) (all emphases by Nietzsche)

It would have been unnecessary to insert this quotation to further underpin something that has already been said: namely that Nietzsche's relation to all ontological questions, including the question of Truth, was eminently practical. Instead of asking 'What is it?', he rather asked, 'What is its meaning for us?', or 'What does it do for us?' But the same concise quotation opens up (for us) a related field of interrogation. Nietzsche offers a very Leibnizian anti-Leibnizian interpretation of his own perspectivism. He agrees with Leibniz (without mentioning him) in so far as both hold that there is no privileged point, time, situation, nor is there a privileged group or a privileged personal standpoint in the universe or in the historical universe. All singular standpoints mirror (or express) the universe in their own unique way.[151] Every standpoint measures other standpoints against itself, by its own yardstick; there is no absolute yardstick. But still, in Leibniz an absolute standpoint had remained: the standpoint of God that unifies and totalizes all the particular perspectives. With one stroke of the pen, Nietzsche deleted this absolute standpoint. The gesture can mean (although it does not necessarily mean) that all standpoints are equally valuable or non-valuable, or rather, that all perspectives engender the most valuable (or the *only* valuable) ideals and commitments for those men and women who share them, but not for others. How could one pass a categorical and apodictic assertion against the backdrop of such a radical perspectivism?[152]

Here we return to the wager. Nietzsche's wager is not about the existence or non-existence of anything, particularly not of God. Nor is the wager about the question of meaning. Meaning resides, if our life is meaningful at all, exclusively within our perspective. Yet no perspective is privileged, as the container of totality or the repository of Truth, to serve as the yardstick for measuring others; our perspective can contain or carry 'our truth', a truth that enhances our life (and the lives of others too), although it does not necessarily do this. We engage in this truth. As Napoleon said, and as Nietzsche could have said (and perhaps he did say it somewhere): 'On s'engage, et puis on voit.' What is the significant aspect of the wager, then? Not the engagement, but the 'puis on voit'. The wager is on the future. First we commit ourselves to certain values, and then we will see what happens. But since we shall not live to see what is going to happen in centuries to come, we enter a wager concerning the future.[153] And perhaps . . . we put all our stakes on this 'perhaps'. You may recall paragraph 27 from the third essay of *Genealogy*. Nietzsche there says that 'morality will perish' in a series of spectacles: this is a categorical statement concerning the future. There is no 'perhaps' here. Yet at the end of the sentence Nietzsche also refers to this future as to 'perhaps the most hopeful of all spectacles'.[154] The sentence 'morality will perish' is, in Nietzsche's book, not a prophetic utterance but a mere extrapolation. It is a weak categorical statement, whereas radical philosophy requires strong statements. The 'perhaps' evokes something which is stronger, a kind of forceful hope. Nietzsche could not have said: 'perhaps yes, perhaps no', only 'perhaps yes'; although, logically speaking, 'perhaps yes' also means 'perhaps no'. 'Puis on voit' can be translated in the following way: perhaps we shall see success, perhaps failure. But if 'puis on voit' is preceded by 'On s'engage', then it means: although everything can happen, I bet on the good outcome. Good outcome can mean several things. Nietzsche also described what 'good outcome' meant for him in several terms. The more concrete his statements concerning the 'good outcome' are, the more disappointed the contemporary reader becomes. The emergence of a new society of castes, or that of overman (particularly if he is described in pseudo-biological terms), looks rather like a 'bad outcome' for some of us. But the less concrete Nietzsche is, the more sympathy we feel. If the emphasis is put on the engagement itself, and the bet on the future remains (or becomes) vague, as happens in the last period of the Nietzsche we now discuss, the more the present takes precedence over the future.

This is how the categorical sharpness of radical philosophy can be wedded with perspectivism and can cohabit with the wager (on the future) and with the 'perhaps' in the sense of 'perhaps yes'. Nietzsche's wager is eminently practical: it is wager through engagement. While engaging myself in something, I have already put my stake on a future that 'perhaps' will be. There is no absolute perspective in Nietzsche, but there is an absolute engagement; there is no totality, but there is total engagement, there is no Truth one should preach for all, but there is 'my truth' for which I wholly live. Friedrich Nietzsche engaged himself in transvaluing all values; and he meant '*all* values', not just a few of them. Friedrich Nietzsche engaged himself in 'taking back' the system of values of two thousand (plus) years of European culture single-handedly (or single-mindedly).

What is the problem here? What is wrong with shifting the concept of 'totality' away from the 'totality' of all perspectives (Leibniz's God or Lukács's proletariat) towards the 'totality' of personal engagement? On the one hand, this shift is a 'lucky hit'. A new concept of truth is dawning here, or rather a few new concepts of truth are simultaneously emerging; our century has not yet incorporated them all. Truth without a strong epistemological claim is 'truth for me'; it is just the thing I am totally engaged to do, due to my existential commitment. Friedrich Nietzsche chose himself as a philosopher; this is his total commitment, this is for him 'the whole'; and there is nothing left (for him) 'above', 'beside', and 'outside'. He was totally committed to becoming what he was. He listened to the voice of his 'affect', to his 'will to power', to his destiny, which gave his philosophy content and direction. It is thus that he became a radical philosopher engaged in turning the traditional system of values upside down; it is thus that Nietzsche constituted his truth. Until this point we are still told the story of an ethics of personality. Until this point the abandonment of epistemological totality for the sake of practical holism appeared rather as an asset. And what is an asset in Nietzsche's terms, as well as in my own – namely disconnecting total engagement from total knowledge – is a gesture or a sign of sincerity (authenticity). Kant wins a Pyrrhic victory here. For the division between knowledge and practical reason is here accomplished, yet universality is sacrificed. And, as happens with all Pyrrhic victories, this one too remains ambiguous, not only for universalists, but also for Nietzsche himself.

'Warum ich ein Schicksal bin' states the last subchapter of *Ecce Homo*. Within the framework of an ethics of personality the title is unpretentious. Every person who follows the ethics of personality is a destiny. He is his own destiny. As Lukács formulated the same idea roughly two decades later: 'From contingency to necessity – this is the way of every problematic individual.'[155] But when Nietzsche answers this self-posed question, he says something else and also something more:

> Hat man mich verstanden? . . . Die *ent-deckung* der christlichen Moral ist ein Ereignis, das nicht seines Gleichen hat, eine wirkliche Katastrophe. Wer über sie aufklärt, ist eine force majeure, ein Schicksal – er bricht die Geschichte der Menschheit in zwei Stuecke. Man lebt *vor* ihm, man lebt *nach* ihm . . . Der Blitz der Wahrheit traf gerade das, was bisher am höchsten stand . . . [156] (emphasis by Nietzsche) (Have you understood me? The discovery of Christian morality is an unparalleled event, a real catastrophe. The man who discloses it is a *force majeure*, a destiny – he breaks the history of mankind into two pieces. One lives before him, one lives after him – the lightning of truth struck the thing that until now stood the highest.)

Nietzsche is not only his own destiny, he is also a historical destiny. He does not merely represent himself, as all *vornehme* (noble) men are supposed to do; he also represents a historical juncture; moreover, the only decisive historical juncture for millenia. The question of truth returns here with a vengeance. Nietzsche now claims that it is 'the' truth that he is trumpeting, the total and absolute one, and not the truth 'for him', perceived from his perspective, but the good old whole truth for the whole world. Nietzsche speaks about the 'lightning' of Truth in the light of which every truth 'hitherto' is unmasked, annulled, and cancelled as a fraud. Certainly, Nietzsche does not return to the metaphysical concept of Truth; his project is different. He switches from one level of practice to another level. The truth of a person's personality (a person's philosophy) appears now as historical truth, Nietzsche's destiny equals history's destiny. The subjectivism of Nietzsche's concept of truth now backfires.[157] Had he acknowledged the existence of a yardstick to measure truth-untruth with, a yardstick to which the philosopher himself should or would commend his ideas for a check-up, Nietzsche would have preserved a few vestiges of a metaphysical concept of truth on the one hand and would have made a case for the historical relevance of his own truth on the other. This is actually what Lukács did with his overstretched Marx-interpretation. Historical truth was in this case attributed to a historical (not a personal) subject. Nietzsche rejected this type of approach as insincere (which it certainly was). But then he claimed historical truth, even absolute historical truth (as if there were such a thing) for the brainchildren of a personal subject: himself. And this is the logic of madness. Absolute commitment to personal perspectivism, to an ethics of personality does not mix with the concept of the world-historical subject.[158] The logic of madness leads to madness. *Amor fati?*

Nietzsche was well aware of one aspect of his problem. The ethics of personality has absolutely nothing to do with history. Once the 'travail' of prehistory was over, and once the men of the 'Sittlichkeit der Sitte' acquired the capacity to promise, there were always individuals who accomplished their destiny, who lived in the spirit of an ethics of personality: 'Dieser stärkere Typus ist oft genug schon dagewesen: aber als ein Glücksfall, als eine Ausnahme – niemals als gewollt.' ('This stronger type has been present often enough, but as a case of luck, as an exception – never as willed.') The other type (the 'Haustier', 'Herdentier', etc. the domestic and herd animal) 'war gewollt' (was willed).[159] Is, then, the historical task 'willing' the lucky throw of the dice? This sounds odd, for we know that even the person himself who is the very lucky throw of the dice cannot will himself consciously. A type, if willed by others (and a type is always willed by others) is by definition not the 'lucky throw of the dice' because he (or it?) is not autonomous. However, 'willing' a type does not mean to will one or another single exemplification of the type before he is actually 'there', before he presents himself. This 'will' rather concerns the elimination of the obstacles that prevent the great type's appearance. It is invested in paving the way for the recognition of the specimens of this higher type once they are 'here', once they dwell among us. A 'lucky throw of the dice' has no causes, this is why one cannot condition it. But one can still establish the most favourable conditions for a proper 'Rangordnung' 'innerhalb der Gattung Mensch'[160] (order of rank within the human species). This is a weak statement, and it has to be considered seriously. After all, our democratic age does not look favourably upon personal distinction, uniqueness, the quest for a personal destiny. The hideous growth of *ressentiment* cannot be stopped from flourishing, but its further increase can still be outweighed by a counterveiling passion vested in the recognition of the 'lucky throw of the dice'.

It seems easy to cope with the tension between the (timeless) character of the ethics of personality, on the one hand, and the actual task of creating optimal historical conditions for these 'lucky throws of the dice' to grow, on the other. But, as always in Nietzsche, the same theme appears in different variations and orchestrations. Sometimes a dissonance develops, without the possibility of resolution. Nietzsche then speaks of 'new philosophers', the men of the future, who transvalue eternal values welche in der Gegenwart den Zwang und Knoten anknüpfen, der den Willen von Jahrtusende auf *neue* Bahnen zwingt. Dem Menschen die Zukunft des Menschen als seinen *willen*, als abhängig von einem Menschen-Willen zu lehren und grosse Wagnisse und Gesammtversuche von Zucht und Züchtung vorzubereiten, und damit jener schauer – lichen Herrschaft des Unsinns und Zufalls, die bisher 'geschichte' hiess, ein Ende zu machen . . . [161] (which bind the present with coercion's knot, and compel them to go down new avenues. One should teach men the human future as something that depends on their own will, on human will-power, and propose great ventures and experiments in breeding and being bred, to put an end to the terrible domination of senselessness and contingency that had hitherto been called 'history' . . .)

Has it ever occurred to Nietzsche that the gravest accusation he ever mounted against Kant,[162] namely that the 'final purpose' of his world cancels his own morality, hits home, or rather that it hits home with him far more than it could ever hit his target, Kant? If contingency of history is cancelled, the lucky throw is also cancelled, and the ethics of personality is cancelled thereby. In an ethics of personality the person himself or herself is his or her own destiny: no one else can 'will' or 'breed' here. Every human being had already been 'bred' into a world of contingency and became contingent; if each is now going to be 'bred' into a world of necessity, we are all back in the world of 'Sittlichkeit der Sitte', before the sick animal began his sovereign journey on earth. Then is not Parsifal a greater promise? After all, he was not bred by anyone, he is not the product of the will of those suspect 'philosophers of the future', but he emerged just out of that 'schauerlichen Herrschaft des Unsinns und Zufalls' ('terrible domination of senselessness and contingency') which is history. Yet, Nietzsche would say, all this being granted, Parsifal's ideals, those ascetic ideals, nevertheless prevent the 'lucky throw of the dice' from emerging, for they promote a wrong *Rangordnung* (order of rank). But how and why? Is Parsifal himself not a lucky throw of the dice as well? Who creates the *Rangordnung*? What is it?

So far we have mentioned one tension (or occasional dissonance) in Nietzsche's ethics of personality. This is the tension (or dissonance) between the timeless character of such an ethics and the 'historical mission' such an ethics is supposed to fulfil for Nietzsche. This tension (or dissonance) leads directly to a second tension (and dissonance): namely to that between the form of an ethics of personality and its contents. We do not know anymore whether *every* man or woman who is a 'lucky throw of the dice' – who becomes what he or she is, that is, his or her own destiny – is regarded by Nietzsche as the repository of an ethics of personality, or if only a few of them are. If the former is the case, the ethics of personality is formal like the Kantian philosophy of morals, although its form is not universal, but individual, just like the form of an artwork. You become yourself, and yourself entirely, not 'humankind in' yourself.

As with formal ethics in general, a formal ethics of personality also allows for a great variety of substantive determinations. Quite different cases, entirely different personlities, can fit the bill. Owing to its liberalism, the formal concept could be embraced by an age like ours, which puts a bonus on pluralism. Soon we shall face serious problems, however. For example, Adolf Hitler would certainly qualify as an example of this ethics: he was a contingent person, he followed his destiny without hesitation, he became what he was. But it is an utterly revolting idea to describe Adolf Hitler in high ethical terms. But, I repeat, if we accept a merely formal concept of an ethics of personality, we cannot avoid including evil incarnate in it. Seemingly, Nietzsche could have hardly raised objection against including the epitome of evil within an ethics of personality. After all, he abused and ridiculed 'good men', and the only thing he praised about Hegel was the latter's appreciation of the positive historical role of evil. But, like Hegel, Nietzsche also had a very specific idea about evil, and not all the monsters fitted this idea. Some of them were the wrong kinds of evil. Nietzsche took first some commonplace features of the definition of evil, for example cynicism, sensuality, cruelty and egoism, and then, in reversing the signs, he declared those 'vices' to be so many 'virtues' in a Machiavellian sense: the kind of virtues that are becoming to the greatest, 'the really good' men. But some commonplace vices he just neglected, whereas others he too considered as 'bad' character traits (bad air!), such as vengefulness, vanity, envy, untruthfulness (lying).

All in all, Nietzsche was never entirely satisfied with describing an ethics of personality in merely formal terms. Frequently, although not always, he loaded his image of an ethics of personality with a series of substantive determinations. Sometimes, those substantive limitations did work. For example, in Nietzsche's terms, *ressentiment* disqualified a modern person from serving as an example of an ethics of personality. As a typical case of a man of *ressentiment*, Hitler could not have qualified for Nietzsche's ethics in Nietzsche's own terms. On the other hand, Nietzsche's substantive determinations can limit or narrow down the examples of the 'lucky throw of the dice' to the single type of Nietzsche's overman. And if Parsifal is not a 'lucky throw', who is? If the 'ascetic priests' (although not all repositiories of ascetic ideals) are excluded from the framework of an ethics of personality, who, then, is included? Or does Nietzsche distinguish between the ethics of personality in formal terms, on the one hand, and a substantively determined 'type' *within* this ethics (the one he most highly evaluated), on the other? And if so, is only this type appreciated? Let me take a random example. In his notebooks, among the entries of spring 1888, we find one entry entitled (by Nietzsche) 'Die *typischen Selbstgestaltungen. ODER: DIE ACHT*

Hauptfragen'[163] (*'The typical self-presentatives. Or: the eight main questions'*). Since Nietzsche discusses here typical cases of self-creation, there can be little doubt that all of them are cases of the ethics of personality. And yet there are typical differences between the modes of self-creation, and undoubtedly, one of those modes is more appreciated (more highly valued) by Nietzsche than the other. Sometimes there are more than two alternatives, but Nietzsche's perspective of evaluation remains clear. The eight questions concerning typical forms of self-creation are as follows: (1) whether one wills oneself *vielfacher* (manifold) or *einfacher* (simpler); (2) whether one wills greater happiness or greater indifference in facing both happiness and unhappiness; (3) whether one wills to be satisfied with oneself or be *anspruchsvoller* (more demanding) and *unerbittlicher* (more implacable); (4) whether one wills to be more human or more 'inhuman' (*'unmenschlich'*: inverted commas by Nietzsche); (5) whether one wills to be more clever or more reckless; (6) whether one wills to reach a goal or rather 'allen Zielen aus weichen' (to avoid all goals), 'wie es zum Beispiel der Philosoph tut, der im jeden Ziel eine Grenze, einen Winkel, ein Gefängnis, eine Dummheit riecht' (as, for example, the philosopher does, who smells in every goal a limit, a corner, a prism, a stupidity); (7) whether one wills to be respected or feared or despised (*verachteter*); and (8) 'ob man Tyrann, oder Verfuehrer, oder Hirt, oder Herdentier werden will' (whether one wills to become a tyrant, a seducer, or a shepherd or a herd animal).

It is obvious that Nietzsche's self-chosen type (undoubtedly himself) prefers one particular set of alternatives over all others. This in itself is already a kind of a *Rangordnung* (an order of ranking). We have assumed that this particular notebook entry is concerned with ranking the various types that are committed to self-creation. Among the self-created types, one stands higher on the ladder of ranking, while others presumably occupy lower places. Nietzsche wills his own compexity: willing complexity stands higher than willing 'simplicity'. Is not Gurnemanz rather 'simple'? And did not Parsifal, the simpleton, even after becoming enligthened, remain a simpleton in so far as he committed himself entirely to a very simple ideal? Nietzsche's self-chosen type (himself) rejects happiness; but is the felicity of redemption (Parsifal's felicity) not a version of Plato's experience of *eudaimonia*? Nietzsche's noble type is never satisfied. But how can the redeemer of the redeemer (or the good man) be more *anspruchsvoll* (demanding)? Gurnemanz and Parsifal are two anti-types to Nietzsche's most favoured type, although Parsifal does not stand entirely for such an anti-type. The very interesting last point (8) in the above quoted typology comes to our support. Following a Platonic tradition, Nietzsche distinguishes here four major character-types (or souls). The first and the fourth among them are the same as in Plato: the tyrant on one pole, and the *Herdentier* (the democratic soul in Plato) on the other. In between them there are the types of the seducer and the shepherd. (Actually both of them appear also in Plato, although not as alternatives to the tyrannical and the democratic soul.) Which of those two (middle) souls stand highest in the order of ranks? True to the spirit of Nietzsche, we must answer: certainly not the shepherd, this very Christian type. This leaves us with the seducer. But Wagner is a seducer, Socrates ditto, according to Nietzsche's own mythology. Does he rank them, in the spirit of point (8), at the highest place, alongside himself, Zarathustra and the overman? Parsifal assumes an ambiguous status in this order of ranking. One can say that he is, and becomes, a shepherd. Yet he is also a seducer. He was created by Wagner, the seducer (himself a Klingsor of a kind) in order to seduce.[164]

I cannot follow Nietzsche's manifold juxtapositions of different 'types of self-creation' any further; I merely wanted to make the following point. The fact that Nietzsche's hesitation between the formal and the substantive concept of the ethics of personality normally results in the predominance of the latter points again to the dissonance between his radical anti-historicism, on the one hand, and his radical historicism, on the other. Radical anti-historicism would have favoured a formal concept, whereas his radical historicism favoured a strongly substantively determined concept. Nietzsche's ideal types (this time we speak about the ideal types of the ethics of personality) mediate between a merely formal and an entirely substantive concept.[165]

It cannot be emphasized too frequently that Nietzsche's radical historicism is eminently practical. Radical historicism requires that the mere 'perhaps' of a promising future should be overdetermined, and practical historicism requires that this 'perhaps' should be overdetermined in practice. This can happen by and through the substantive determination of the exemplary carriers of this practice, that is, via 'that type of man' who could be 'the bridge' to this future. A man of this type is committed to an ethics of personality, he is a lucky throw of the dice, yet not merely that. It is determined in advance which particular number is the luckiest throw among many lucky throws of the dice. This particular number becomes what he is in accordance with the need of our historical times – when God is dead and there is no redemption.

The order of ranks (*Rangordnung*) is the very heart of the Nietzschean ethics of personality. Nietzsche deconstructs the Platonic metaphysics. Plato's many accounts of the soul's ascent from the lowest to the highest provoke Nietzsche's scorn rather than his sympathy.[166] None the less, he preserves the spatial vision of ranking which is so intimately linked precisely to metaphysics. The highest stands for the best, and the lowest for the worst. Moreover, Nietzsche also preserves another metaphysically underpinned terminological distinction, namely that between 'deep' and 'shallow', although he rejects the metaphysical distinction between 'essence' and 'appearance'. You may recall that Nietzsche speaks of our 'deepest self' (among our many selves) in the context of his ethics.[167]

There is a general order of ranks, yet within each order, there may be another order of ranking. The all-encompassing distinction is the one between 'high' and 'low'. In terms of Nietzsche's ahistorical, formal language, all those who embody an ethics of personality belong to the 'high types' whereas all others are ranked 'low'. But whenever substantive values and commitments participate in the procedure of ranking, the distinction becomes more complex, and it is sometimes blurred. For example, Jewish and Christian values stand low in Nietzsche's hierarchy of values; they are the values of slaves. Yet those who initiated the slave revolt (the first transvaluation of values) are ranked high on the ladder of evaluation, whereas egalitarian disbelievers and utilitarians are ranked low. The ethics of personality is associated with action, taking initiative, being creative. Thus everyone who is authentically creative and active, and who fulfils thereby his own destiny, stands high on the ladder of the hierarchy of ranking, even if his values are rejected by Nietzsche as slavish, dangerous or even perverted. The mode of distinction between good and bad, as Nietzsche describes it in the first essay of *Genealogy*, is typical of an ethics of personality in general. An autonomous person does not constitute his personality in accordance with the opinion of others, he defines the others. He looks down on others in general with slight contempt or indifference and also with pity (different from that of the compassionate Jewish-Christian type). He keeps his distance from others, not because he is haughty, but because this is his nature, – since he is noble (*vornehm*). In this way he is also 'inhuman'.

The noble man is also a good man, but in a sense entirely different from the way in which a Jewish-Christian is a good man. For the noble man there are no models of goodness to follow (for this is reactive); the needs of others do not appeal to him (this would also be reactive); he does not love in a Jewish-Christian sense, for he does not need this love (although he is capable of *amour passion*).[168] In his notebooks Nietzsche writes the following about conscience:

> Ehemals schloss man: das Gewissen verwirft diese Handlung: folglich ist diese Handlung verwerflich. Tatsächlich verwirft das Gewissen eine Handlung, weil dieselbe lange verworfen werden ist. Es spricht bloss nach: es schafft keine Werte.[169] (Once they had decided: conscience rejects this act; as a result the act was to be rejected. In fact conscience refuses an act because it has already been long rejected. It only repeats what has been said; it does not create values.)

This kind of reactive conscience is ranked low. But active conscience (of the autonomous man with the capacity to make promises) is ranked high, precisely because it is active and creative.[170] Nobility (as real goodness) is the greatness of the soul; its wealth (*Reichtum*) is the kind of wealth that pours out upon others spontaneously, without consideration. The wealthy, the noble person, offers presents (*schenkt, verschenkt*); his output is luxury and beauty.

Nietzsche keeps pondering the question of 'Was ist vornehm?' ('What is noble?') until the end of his conscious life. In *Beyond Good and Evil*, the book that we could describe as a kind of Nietzsche-Encyclopaedia, Chapter 9 (Neuntes Hauptstueck) is addressed solely to this task (although Nietzsche speaks about the distinction between 'high' and 'low' at some length at least in two other chapters as well). But I cannot discuss the narrative parts of Chapter 9 within this limited framework. In addition, these belong to the best known passages of Nietzsche's work (the distinction between *Herrenmoral* (master morality) and *Sklavenmoral* (slave morality), the noble barbarism of aristocratic cultures, and so on.) I do not particularly like these passages, and I prefer to speak about things which, even with a few or many provisos, I rather like.

Nietzsche continues: the morality of the noble ones is anti-utilitarian. A noble person does not even understand what vanity is, although he desires, and accepts, the recognition of his own value. He is a man of refinement. His ethics is subjected to the greatest trial when he is confronted with a person of the first rank without authority: it is then that he shows his *Instinkt der Ehrfurcht* (instinct of esteem).[171] Only the 'low' person (*gemein, Herdentier*) is envious and self-righteous. But the noble one is a true egoist, for he both takes and gives without concern. He suffers more deeply, he is also clean, or pure. The noble soul has self-esteem.[172] He is more afraid of being understood than of being misunderstood. He has the capacity of golden (olympic) laughter. There are normally three levels of evaluation, encapsulated in three questions: *who* is the person who says or does something; *how* does the person say or do this thing; *what* is the value of the thing said or done? Usually the answer to the first question takes precedence over the answer to the other two. But sometimes the 'how' co-determines the 'who' and sometimes, although less frequently, even the 'what' can co-determine it. We now turn to the short discussion of the intimate relation between 'who' and 'how'.

It happens later (in his notebooks of spring 1888) that Nietzsche will answer the question 'What is noble?' with the following sentences:

> Dass man sich bestaendig repraesentieren hat. Dass man Lagen sucht, wo man bestaendig Gebaerden noetig hat. Dass man das Gluck der Grossen Zahl ueberlaesst ... Dass man instinktiv fuer die schweren Verantwortungen sucht. Dass man sich ueberall Feinde zu schaffen weiss, schlimmsten Falls noch auch sich selbst. Dass man der *grossen Zahl* nicht nur durch Worte, sondern durch Handlungen bestaendig widerspricht.[173] (emphasis by Nietzsche) (That one has to represent oneself constantly. That one seeks situations where one needs gestures. That one leaves happiness to the great 'Number'. That one seeks instinctively for difficult responsibilities. That one knows how to make enemies, if the worst comes

to the worst, oneself included. But one constantly contradicts the great
number not just in words but also in deeds.)

The answer to the question 'What is noble?' serves here, as it does in
most places, as a kind of *Bestimmung* of the ethics of personality. There
can be no doubt that all enumerated features of 'nobility' of the soul are
ethical in kind, and that he who does not live up to these standards
disqualifies himself or herself in terms of an ethics of personality. This
time, the *Bestimmung* has no direct substantive features. Let us start with
the issue of representation. First, the noble person constantly 'represents'
himself. Nietzsche speaks here of a natural feature of traditional aristo-
cracies, but he attributes those features to non-traditional persons in a
non-traditional world. A modern contingent person is not born into the
role he represents. There is no role to represent in the modern world,
which operates with numbers, with quantity, while representation is
qualitative. Quality cannot appear in the form of role-playing as it does
in ancient barbarian warrior cultures, for utility has been substituted for
traditional representation. This is why representation must appear as
unique, as the exception. There are no ready-made contexts for the
representative gestures; a noble man of modern times is constantly on the
lookout for a situation that requires such gestures. Nature and ethics are
fused. The 'lucky throw of the dice' becomes what he is (otherwise he
would not be a lucky throw), but he also should harken to his internal
voice (will to power) in the search for situations which call for his
representative gestures.

Instinct and practical reason are here identical, but they are identical
solely in the representative noble person. The person's becoming
(his life's reason) is guided by his affect, his instinct-to-life. This is what
Nietzsche terms in one word 'representative': the fusion of reason and
instinct-to-life; the fusion of the matter and form of a man, of a unique,
exceptional person, of a 'thusness'. The fusion of instinct and reason
(matter and form, being and becoming) is beautiful. Everything
that grows from within is meaningful as the unity of instinct and reason,
and the meaningful manifests itself in meaningful and representative
gestures. Meaningful gestures provide the personality with form. The
ethical ideal is fused here with the aesthetic ideal. Not the artist, but the
artwork (more precisely, the modern artwork) will stand for the model of
Nietzsche's ethics of personality. The noble man must contradict 'the
greatest number' constantly, and not just in words but also in deeds, for
a perfect artwork must be entirely new, unsuspected, unexpected.
The aesthetization of the 'noble' type distinguishes Nietzsche sharply
from the Epicureans and the Stoics,[174] although his noble man has certain
Stoic or Epicurean features. For example, the noble man must seek
difficult responsibilities, he must know how to make enemies for himself,
he has to challenge the crowd, he must remain indifferent to good or bad

luck or to the opinion of the herd, and so on. Put briefly, moral (or ethical) aesthetics and moral (or ethical) psychology merge here in Nietzsche, but they do not merge in either the Stoic or in the Epicurean tradition.

It is time to sum up our preliminary conclusions. Nietzsche hesitates between a merely formal and a substantive definition of an ethics of personality. Owing to his practical commitment, he can never be entirely satisfied with the purely formal definition. But in his various attempts to determine the content of his ethics he will also explore two different avenues. In taking the first avenue, he overloads the concept of the 'lucky throw' with his own values, among them strongly historicist ones; so that finally only the 'bridge' to the 'overman' will satisfy its criterion. The individual disappears in a type that stands for a general promise. In taking the second avenue, he will overdetermine the merely formal concept of the ethics of personality with additional formal criteria, such as representation, gesture, uniqueness and sheer quality. In other words, he will overdetermine it aesthetically.

I have already expressed my objections to the merely formal concept of the ethics of personality, as well as to the Nietzschean attempts at a substantive determination of this concept. The merger of aesthetic and ethical forms looks more attractive, at least at first glance. The truth of the matter is, however, that in spite of its attractiveness, this is the theoretically least satisfying solution. All the problems of a merely formal concept reappear here, and none of its pitfalls have been avoided. We can recall the example of Hitler: one could say that Hitler made himself into a representative figure (a kind of artwork); that he was a man of gestures; that he took over weighty responsibilities and brought also something absolutely unique into the world (after all, Auschwitz was absolutely new and unique). But what kind of ethics is this?[175]

True, Hitler was the exact opposite of the 'refined' man in Nietzsche's model. True again, Hitler would have disgusted Nietzsche.

We must stop here for a moment. The affect of disgust plays an important role in Nietzsche's ethical-olfactory explorations. Nietzsche smells bad air; the impure stinks; the banausic man disgusts him. His disgust signals to him (as presumably to all noble persons) the fact that he has encountered an ignoble man or an ignoble deed. Disgust is, then, the manifestation of ethical taste. Just as the gourmet of French cuisine is disgusted by the sauce put before him in a bad restaurant, so is the noble man disgusted by bad manners and behaviour; by everything that is 'little', 'base', banausic and undignified. Undoubtedly, there is such a thing as ethical (moral) taste. But ethical taste is acquired – to an extent, although never entirely – in a way similar to how culinary taste is developed. We have to know how decent people behave and have to experience some decent actions first, before we develop an aesthetic taste for decency and begin to feel disgusted by indecency as a result. But if the ethical *Rangordnung* is constituted by aesthetic criteria alone, and if the 'high' and the 'low' rungs on the ethical ladder are eminently aesthetic positions, our disgust will manifest our aesthetic and not our ethical taste. Whenever ethics and aesthetics merge, something similar happens. And there are even further complications in Nietzsche's ethics. Since the noble man is not reactive, he cannot develop his aesthetic taste in a way similar to that in which he develops his culinary taste. Being the lucky throw of the dice, his instinct governs him only from within, and his taste is thus engendered by this instinct-reason alone. He is not disgusted because he finds the person disgusting (aesthetically or ethically), but the person is 'felt' to be disgusting owing to the experience of feeling disgust. Kant was, however, right. The 'genius' could perhaps develop all that which he is, solely from within, but the man of taste cannot. And this is true both of aesthetic and ethical taste.

Nietzsche must, then, introduce again a few substantive qualifications into his aesthetic model of ethics. Now he tells us *what* will disgust, what *must* disgust, and what actually *does* disgust the noble man, although all noble men develop their sense of disgust from within. This sophisticated version of the (aesthetic) ethics of personality now seems to click. But in fact it does not. Let us return to the starting-point: Nietzsche would have been disgusted by Hitler because Hitler was not refined, and refinement (as an aesthetic category) is attributed to all noble men by Nietzsche. But just as everyone who accepts that charity is a virtue will consider himself a charitable person, even if he is not, so everyone who subscribes to the value of 'refinement' will consider himself extremely refined, whether or not he is refined. The question is not whether Hitler lived up to Nietzsche's ethico-aesthetic standards (he did not), but whether these standards possess any ethical quality at all and whether they are reliable.

Without the introduction of at least one substantive and purely ethical (that is, not simultaneously also aesthetic) qualification, one remains entangled in mere formalism. I do not deny the importance of moral (ethical) aesthetics, but I would relegate it, to speak with Plato, to the second place after the moral concepts proper. *What* is valued and done, takes precedence over the 'who' (that has done it) and also over the 'how' (it has been done), although the beauty of an act, as well as the noble character of the actor, add a sublime dimension, a finishing touch, to the goodness of the act and to the decency of the person. In morals, the content is never entirely absorbed by the form.

The experiment with the aestheticization of the ethics of personality brings us back to the problems we have already encountered: I mean the problems emerging from the substantive overdetermination of the merely formal concept. Even in cases where the aesthetic qualification of the 'noble person' remains merely formal and the 'who' includes only the 'how' (representation, performance of gestures, uniqueness, originality), but not the 'what', the aesthetic forms themselves function as substantive qualifications from a purely ethical point of view. Such substantive qualifications are, for example, that the ugly person cannot be noble or that a person who shuns an act because her conscience rejects it, similarly cannot be noble (because she is not acting, but rather reacting). Whichever way I look at it, Nietzsche's ethics of personality falls short of being the kind of ethics that could possibly serve as an alternative to the moral pathos of a Parsifal.

But at first glance, this is exactly what Nietzsche suggests. There was 'so far' no alternative to the ascetic ideal. But from 'now on', from Zarathustra and Nietzsche onward, there is one. But is that so? Perhaps. At least Nietzsche said so.[176] But Nietzsche also said something else. He identified himself with the seducer as well as with the cynic: *cave canem*. Nietzsche warned us, and not only once, about his own ethics.

We are running out of time, I am afraid. And so we must now return briefly to the genesis of the ethics of personality according to Nietzsche, to the genealogy of morals, and also to Wagner's *Parsifal* and to Nietzsche's *Anti-Parsifal*. But let me first sum up some of our more weighty comments and objections. For simplicity's sake I will use the term 'ascetic ideals' in the broad Nietzschean sense. The concept then encompasses the values of the western culture of the last two thousand years, the tradition of Judaism, and also of Buddhism and other oriental religions. It encompasses metaphysics, that is, all philosophy 'hitherto', modern sciences, and the ideals of equality, universalism and democracy. It includes all references to the idea of truth, as well as to that of morality, and also to morals. It also includes all contents of traditional morals, their oppressive character, heteronomy, contempt for sensuality, and much else.

A purely formal concept of an ethics of personality cannot offer an alternative to the ascetic ideal, if for no other reason but for the most obvious one: namely that the representative figures of the ascetic ideal (Parsifal included) were also representative figures for the ethics of personality.

The substantively determined concept of an ethics of personality cannot serve, in any of its several versions, as an alternative to the ascetic ideal, for all these versions express the philosopher's own *Rangordnung*; they legitimate his own historical vision. From the standpoint of other perspectives they can be unattractive: in ethical terms rather horrifying, in aesthetic terms simply disgusting. And of course one assumes the existence of many other perspectives. Had Nietzsche been a new pagan Christ and had his *Zarathustra* become a new Bible, as he sometimes predicted it would, everything would be otherwise; but this was not the case.[177]

The aesthetic concept of an ethics of personality cannot be the alternative to the 'ascetic ideal', for it is valid only for 'the lucky throws of the dice' who create something new and unexpected and who render meaning for themselves (e.g. a Goethe, a Napoleon or a Picasso).

Finally, none of the 'virtues' that Nietzsche attributes to noble men have the capacity to give a content to the merely formal concept of the ethics of personality in a theoretically satisfying manner, because none of them are virtues which hit the moral centre. I would prefer to repeat what I have said in reverse: I call 'the virtues and values of the moral centre' those virtues and values which perform the task that Nietzsche hoped would be accomplished by his favourite virtues and values. Only virtues and values of the moral centre can determine the content of a formal ethics of personality to the minimal degree; that is, to the degree which is absolutely required for acquiring an intersubjective appeal (the lowest denominator for universality) without sacrificing its formal character.

Kant's substantive formula of non-instrumentalization (that is, that one should not use other persons as mere means) is well qualified for this role. But Kant's solution could not be appreciated by Nietzsche, if for no other reason than for its prohibitive character: the new ethics is supposed to liberate us from all 'should nots'.

Casting a glance at Nietzsche's list of virtues, we find among them such subtle ones as 'gift bestowing', good taste, capacity for great suffering, uprightness (*Redlichkeit*), the 'befehlerisches Etwas, das vom Volke der Geist genannt wird' ('that commanding something which is called spirit by the people'),[178] instinct for ranking, indifference, self-respect and many other virtues or values. But it is obvious that none of them fits into the moral centre, which means that none of them can perform the same task that the substantive formula of the categorical imperative so brilliantly performs.

But there is something on Nietzsche's mind that would be difficult to disagree with. Measured by ethicoaesthetic standards, there is indeed a *Rangordnung* (an order of ranking) unlike the 'order of ranking' performed solely by moral standards. And it is even questionable whether one can speak of an 'order of rank' in terms of moral criteria alone, without considering the aesthetic dimensions of characters or deeds in the slightest. I have already mentioned this matter briefly. It is an elementary experience that we appreciate the good deed more when it is done with grace than when it is done rudely, or formlessly. They are surely not the same deeds. And there is something in the personality (call it his or her essence, self, nucleus . . .) which instinctively plays a role in our moral evaluations. Alas, the lukewarm might be better than the cold (by moral standards), yet it is still spat out. But why? One willingly agrees with Nietzsche's intuition: the self-righteous person, even if he never does anything that he should not, is not particularily appealing.

While pondering this issue we shall soon realize that Nietzsche's *Rangordnung* is not alien from the old European tradition; instead it is deeply rooted in it. This comes as no great surprise. Nietzsche is, after all, a self-confessed old European. The distinction between following 'the letter' or 'the spirit' of the commandments, the equally important execution of ethical ranking according to the quality of the souls, and the eminently (although not exclusively) modern distinction between heteronomy and autonomy – all of them belongs to this tradition. They seem to be entirely and purely moral distinctions; the distinction between autonomy and heteronomy particularly seems to be of a Kantian provenance, but the sensitive recipients, for example Schiller, developed their aesthetic aspects very soon.[179] Moreover, even in the case of a purely moral ranking, the upper positions are normally occupied by the 'good' who is also 'great' in his or her goodness, for example a *megalopsychos*, a saint, or an (almost) fully autonomous being. Moreover, there had also been modern attempts at ethically ranking personalities on the basis on non-moral standards before Nietzsche. Hegel, for example, established his own *Rangordnung* by the standard of world historical importance. One could get the impression that Nietzsche wanted to rescue a very European thing in a modern egalitarian age. And also those who, like myself, are disgusted by Nietzsche's disgust of political equality, could possibly share Nietzsche's feeling that it is a valuable thing to preserve and to cherish the intuitive establishment of a *Rangordnung* among persons, in purely personal sense. For persons who are also personalities deserve higher appreciation than those who are not, and despite political equality, some of them still stand higher up, while others lower down, in an order of rank that we instinctively establish by the complex yardstick which allows for combining morals and taste.

Contrary to the pre-modern universe, where the rank-order of personalities was intimately connected to the social-political order, in our contingent world this is no more the case. As a consequence, it is difficult to describe, let alone to define, what exactly makes a high, or noble, or subtle, or sublime personality. One can hardly fathom it, one can hardly grasp it – how could one possibly breed it without losing it? But somehow, and here Nietzsche has a strong appeal, this ranking of persons as personalities, has to be cultivated on purpose; if you wish, it has to be willed . . . for if this yardstick is lost, and no one distinguishes between high and low, noble and base, one of the most precious traditions of the old European world, the old European culture will also be lost. Perhaps it is already lost. And what will then be the meaning of suffering?

The ascetic ideal – so Nietzsche writes –

> believes . . . in its absolute superiority of rank over every other power – it believes that no power exists on earth that does not first have to receive a meaning, a right to exist, a value, as a tool of the ascetic ideal, as a way and means to *its* goal, to *one* goal. Where is the match of this closed system of will, goal, and interpretation? Why has it not found its match? – Where is the *other* '*one*' goal?[180] (Nietzsche's emphasis)

We followed Nietzsche's search for this 'other' path, and we came to the conclusion that there is no such other path, at least not in Nietzsche's sense. The totalization of practice is no match to metaphysical totality. The 'other one goal', the closed system of will, goal and interpretation that does not raise claim to Truth, merely to 'truth for Nietzsche', will never meet the ascetic ideal on the battlefield as an equal. Nietzsche's ideals give meaning to his own sufferings; he will redeem himself, but not others. This sounds odd. After all, no philosopher of the last one hundred years exerted greater influence on European thinking than did Nietzsche. This is true, but it is also true that his influence had nothing to do with the single 'one goal', the 'match' to the ascetic ideal. As a metaphysician, which in any case he was not, Nietzsche could not offer an alternative. Who could? As a nihilist, he had a long list of followers. But if nihilism is the last word, victory remains with the ascetic ideal, at least if we think in Nietzsche's terms. However, we can think in other terms. One can leave behind not only metaphysics (or, least of all metaphysics) but also Nietzsche's ideal that praxis should replace metaphysics, that the absoluteness of the absolute, totality, truth should be vested in action, spurred by our 'will to power', performed from our own perspective. What if one abandoned the absoluteness of the absolute altogether? Would we thus surrender to the ascetic ideals? Perhaps; perhaps not. Perhaps this is a wrong alternative. Perhaps this is not at all what we need. What we need, and Nietzsche is right here, is to know the meaning of our suffering. But what does it mean to know the meaning of our suffering?

Let us return for the last time to the second essay of *Genealogy*, to the second act of Nietzsche's opera; his *Anti-Parsifal*. The story is about acquiring the capacity to make promises. Nietzsche discusses here 'the end' of this process, 'where the tree at last brings forth fruit':

> then we discover that the ripest fruit is the *sovereign individual*, like only to himself, liberated again from morality of custom, autonomous and supramoral (for 'autonomous' and 'moral' are mutually exclusive), in short, the man who has his own independent, protracted will and the *right to make promises* – and in him a proud consciousness, quivering in every muscle, of *what* has at length been achieved and become flesh in him, a consciousnes of his own power and freedom, a sensation of mankind come to completion [*ein Vollendungs-Gefühl des Menschen überhaupt*]. This emancipated individual . . . this master of a free will, this sovereign man . . . whose trust is a mark of distinction . . . will call the consciousness of his rare freedom his conscience.[181]

This passage contains the most concise and clearest description of Nietzsche's ethics of personality. It is clear, or rather pure, since all substantive determinants are still missing. The man of an ethics of personality appears in front of us as the individual who stands above

morals. Standing above morals implies two things: first, he is not subjected to morals; second, he does not subject anyone else to his morals
(since he has none). He looks down on others with contempt, but he does
not 'educate' them; he exercises his power without principles, goals and
ideals. He is thus neither a seducer nor a shepherd, nor is he the one who
would appear on the battlefield to present alternatives to the ascetic ideal.
He is simply himself. If we think in terms of *Rangordnung*, then this 'free'
or 'sovereign individual' will end up on the top by virtue of *what* he is.
Every man at the top of the ladder of the *Rangordnung* follows only his
own conscience. If we think in terms of a metaphysical concept of
'totality', we must admit that our free individual will not need it, because
he can do without it. If, alternatively, we think in terms of totality of
praxis, we will recognize that our sovereign individual does not need it
again, for he always possesses it. His suffering has meaning simply
because he is what he is and his suffering is his (he becomes what he is).
But this meaning is unique, it cannot be extended, not even to a single
other, a single second person. *For within the scope of this ethics there is
no other, there is no second person.* This sovereign individual is like an
artwork. It exists autonomously, but he exists also on his own. As the
existence or beauty of a sculpture has nothing to do with the existence (or
the beauty) of another sculpture, so the existence of a self-accomplished
sovereign individual stands for himself, whether or not there is a single
other like him. There are no connections between them, no influences, no
relations. Nietzsche is right: in this model morality is entirely missing.
This is so not because his sovereign person's conscience does not subject
itself to a universal maxim and rather listens to his solitary conscience
alone, but because there is nothing contained in this solitary conscience
apart from the programme (affect, will to power) of the individual's own
perfection or completion.

This sovereign man is a lonely man; he acts and sings solo; he does not
look in anyone's face. The others who lack the capacity to promise do
not matter anyway, because they are 'lowly' and they are treated accordingly. Those who have the capacity to promise do not matter either, for
reasons I briefly mentioned: the autonomous man does not need them
and they (being equally autonomous men) do not need him. Troll, be
yourself enough?!

In his last poem, 'Von der Armuth des Reichsten' ('From the poverty
of those who are the richest') Nietzsche writes,

> Still, meine Wahrheit redet!
>
> · · ·
>
> Wehe dir, Zarathustra!
> Du siehst aus, wie Einer,
> Der Gold verschluckt hat . . .
>
> · · ·

Zu reich bist du,
du Verderber Vieler!

. . .

Du möchtest schenken, wegschenken deinen
Überfluss,
aber du selber bist der Überflüssigste!
Sei klug, du Reicher!
VERSCHENKE DICH SELBER ERST, oh Zarathustra!

. . .

Du musst ÄRMER werden
weiser Unweiser!
willst du geliebt sein.
Man liebt nur die Leidenden,
man giebt Liebe nur dem Hungernden:
VERSCHENKE DICH SELBER ERST, oh Zarathustra!
– Ich bin deine Wahrheit . . .[182] (Nietzsche's emphasis)

This is not the voice of the Troll; this is the voice of Parsifal.

If we listen carefully, we still hear the solo voice of an ethics of personality. After all, Nietzsche says, 'it is my truth that speaks', and not 'it is the truth that speaks'. He says, 'I am your truth', and not 'I am the truth.' But this is an ethics of personality with a touch of humility, where self-abandon is given a higher rank than self-sufficiency ('im eigenen Safte süss geworden und gekocht'); where simplicity ranks higher than complexity; and where abandoning oneself (to the other) ranks higher than pouring out our superfluous wealth indifferently and without concern. Nietzsche remained to the last obsessed by Parsifal.

It was a 'failed swine', a role-player, an actor who set the opera stage for a musical mystery-play about the innocent fool, who became an ascetic priest, who found himself (and became himself) in-and-through the plot by abandoning himself entirely to the other. Knowledge, Truth, manifests itself in the uncovering of the Grail (*aletheia*), but it is not the Grail which is the Truth. Truth is practical, it is practical in moral terms. Truth is identity, but not the identity of subject and object; rather the identity of subject and subject. There is totality here, totality in praxis, total self-abandon, but the total self-abandon to one's own destiny is simultaneously also the total self-abandon to others' destiny. Wagner, the sorcerer, performed his magic. He (and not Nietzsche) resolved the tension, or rather the dissonance, between the formal concept of an ethics of personality on the one hand and its substantive qualifications on the other.

We know what the dissonance consists of. A merely formal concept of the ethics of personality is too broad (for example, even Hitler would qualify for it). The substantive determinations offered by Nietzsche will either narrow down ethics to the most preferred type (to Nietzsche himself, to his overman, his Dionysus) or remain unfit for intersubjective generalization. The simple story of *Parsifal* does a better job than

Nietzsche. Parsifal fits perfectly the formal concept of an ethics of personality. He is the free, the sovereign, the autonomous individual; he is the one who always acts, never reacts. He is the one who is not enlightened (about good and evil) through compassion, but only by the voice of his own conscience, from within. Wagner (and Parsifal) need only one single substantive value or virtue to determine Parsifal's personality so that his truth and 'truth as such' could merge. This sole substantive value or virtue is *Mitleid* (sympathy, empathy, not pity). Think it over. If *Mitleid* is the highest value or virtue for a man, he can freely follow his own star and become his own destiny; for this ethical destiny will be also the other's redemption. An ethics of personality that is substantively determined by *Mitleid* alone already contains morality. Yet it is not less an ethics of personality, not less the self-accomplishment of a sovereign individual. This is so, because *Mitleid* belongs to the virtues or values that constitute the moral centre. It performs the same task as the Kantian formula that prohibits instrumentalization, it gives the necessary qualitative determination to a formal concept. Since the formal concept in question is the formal concept of the ethics of personality, the qualitative determination is not a prohibition, not even an injunction. This is clear in *Parsifal*. No one tells Parsifal 'you should empathize'; he simply does.

Yet the morality of sympathy (*Mitleid*), so Nietzsche writes, is the most sinister symptom of decadence, nihilism, and pessimism.[183] It is a symptom of the victory of Jerusalem over Rome; it is a symptom of the fact that we are living at the expense of the future. The future is the future of the Antichrist, the anti-nihilist. *Mitleid* annihilates Will. But perhaps this is so only in Schopenhauer's setting. Perhaps we can imagine a *Mitleid* that does not annihilate will. After all, Parsifal's *Mitleid* did not annihilate his will. Parsifal's *Mitleid* fits very well into Nietzsche's own philosophy of will to power. And if we discuss will in a more traditional sense, Parsifal's will was rather enhanced by his *Mitleid*.

None of Nietzsche's major philosophical speculations, such as the eternal recurrence of the same or the will to power, are proper weapons against Parsifal. Nor did the ethics of personality qualify. The sabre that Nietzsche was able to carry into the battle consisted only of noes ('no' to *Mitleid*, 'no' to the redemption of the redeemer, 'no' to the traditional values of Jerusalem), whereas all the yeses were merely the reversals of a few substantive values. In this battle, Nietzsche, the radical nihilist, fought against the 'passive' nihilist; he radicalized evil. But he did this with a bad (not bad moral but bad philosophical) conscience. Man would rather will nothingness than not will, so far so good. But Parsifal wills (in Nietzsche's mind) a nothingness that others also will: the redemption of the redeemer through *Mitleid*. Whereas Nietzsche wills a nothingness that is nothing, a non-existing nothingness, the absent alternative to the ascetic ideals. The first can offer meaning, understanding, interpretation, the second cannot. But Parsifal kneels down before the Grail, he looks upwards, he humiliates himself before something that stands higher than himself, something that is transcendent. There is no morality, absolutely none, without the passionate acknowledgment that there is something (or someone) that is, or that stands above, all single men. One can call it 'the divine law', 'transcendental freedom', 'the suffering Other'[184] or something else, but such a value, moral law, or transcendent voice, must be presupposed. Nietzsche revolts: man is free; he must be fully autonomous. But is there such a thing as full autonomy? And if there were, could it be still called 'human'?

Heroic pessimism fights the mystery-play. This is a fight without the hope for victory; victory would also be defeat. This is why Nietzsche became obsessed with Parsifal. This is why he became obsessed by Wagner. The seducer became seduced.

It was a blessed obsession. For it was through this obsession that Nietzsche became what he was: the Sphinx who offers his riddles to wayfarers. Unlike his favourite, Oedipus, he was never the solver of riddles; and unlike the Sphinx, he indulged in setting up riddles that were not only unsolvable for us, as wayfarers, but also for himself. He went to the extreme; he could go no further. He said everything that there was – for him – to say. And we, children of the twentieth century, and also timeless wayfarers, address ourselves to his riddles; but we also set up our own. Some of us (like myself) will remain enchanted by the magic world of the sorcerer-composer, and will read *Parsifal*'s message in the light of Levinas's texts, whereas others will be deaf to his music or will turn away from the role-playing clown. But Nietzsche and *Parsifal* remain eternally tied together. (Excuse me, I was carried away.) Let me reformulate my last sentence: Nietzsche and *Parsifal* will remain associated, as long as the so-called 'ascetic ideals' still give meaning to human suffering.

Part II

Vera, or
Is an Ethics of Personality
Possible?

Three Dialogues

Dialogue One: Is There an Ethics of Personality?

(The dialogue takes place in New York, 1992. After attending a class on Nietzsche and Parsifal, *two philosophy students, Joachim and Lawrence, are heading towards home together. As usual, they are embroiled in a lively conversation.)*

Joachim: The course was interesting and enjoyable, I admit, but it did not seduce me. For I am not persuaded in the least that there is such a thing as an ethics of personality. Nietzsche is a fascinating thinker, a master of rhetorics, a poet – but an ethicist he is not. Neither are Wagner's music-dramas ethical parables. Ethics cannot be conjured up from within, from the depths of a single and unique human 'soul', it simply has nothing to do with an idiosyncratic personality. The essence of ethics is rather that it imposes the same standards on us all, or at least on all members of a group who share the same ethos. One does not need to be a dogmatic universalist to see this. The commandment says, 'Thou shalt not kill.' 'Thou' stands here simultaneously for a universal subject ('no one should murder') and for you, the single person, who should not.

Lawrence: You said that ethics imposes the same standards on all of us. But whatever is imposed on us, compels us. You identify ethics with compulsion. And this is precisely what Nietzsche accused morality of doing. He added: compulsion is unfreedom, it is crippling, ugly; it makes us ugly. But he also insisted that an ethics which breaks with the Judaeo-Christian tradition, an ethics which does not compel, is possible; this is the kind of ethics that we may call an ethics of personality.

Joachim: You want ethics without compulsion? My dear friend, nothing in human life, or at least nothing great or subtle can ever be achieved without compulsion. You disregard even your own darling Nietzsche. May I remind you, that Nietzsche's overmythologized genealogy of morals also tells the story of the series of other-imposed and self-imposed acts of violence which, in his mind, were simply necessary for moulding and shaping the human race? Since there is no ethics of personality without our capacity for making promises, and since this capacity has allegedly resulted from the most painful kind of 'prehistoric labour', the ethics of personality, if there is such an ethics, it is also the result of compulsion. You may retort that precisely this is why it has now become possible to exercise an ethics of personality without compulsion and force. But then, you see, your modern, even postmodern Nietzsche will resemble a very old-fashioned progressivist. How is it that now, and precisely now, a thing has become possible that had not been possible hitherto, namely exercising an ethics of personality; that is, developing an ethics fully from within, without force, other-imposed violence, compulsion. Something must have happened to 'human nature' that made force and compulsion superfluous or redundant. Your Nietzsche would say that our race has undergone degeneration but that the degenerated state of the race is also rich in previously non-existent possibilities. This way of thinking reminds me of Marx . . . Put bluntly, your ethics of personality is rooted in historicism. Either you believe that we occupy a privileged position in history, and owing to our privileged position we are not only entitled, but also able to exercise an ethics of personality, or you do not believe in any privileged position, and you have no reason to presuppose that we can live, or that we actually do live, a moral or even an immoral life without being exposed to compulsion, violence and force. In other words, we are in the same predicament as all human generations 'hitherto'. Let me repeat emphatically: there is no ethics without compulsion, because there is no human life without compulsion. We are no more 'civilized' than the first tribes of homo sapiens. Is it necessary to refer to Auschwitz and the Gulag to make my point? The question is not whether there is compulsion or whether there is none, but rather who or what compels us and to what?

Lawrence: You mix up everything! I never said that an ethics of personality is conceivable without any compulsion whatsoever . . .

Joachim: Yes you did . . .

Lawrence: But this was not what I meant. I meant that here the compulsion comes from within, out of the deepest layers of the personality itself. I meant that this compulsion – if you want to call it that – is not characterized by a command–obedience relationship. Or rather, my own instinct, that is, my own reason commands, and it is myself and myself alone that I obey when I do so. Obedience is, again, the wrong expression, for I am simply carried away by my destiny, towards my destiny.

Joachim: Identifying instinct and reason is typical of you.

Lawrence: Haven't you felt that they are fundamentally the same? Haven't you ever blindly accepted your instinct's guidance, only to discover later that what you have indeed followed was exactly the voice of your reason?

Joachim: No, never. Instincts and reason are opposites.

Lawrence: Always opposites in your own experience?

Joachim: No, I would not go that far. But generally, I cannot rely on my instincts. And not only in moral matters I am afraid – in many other matters as well. I normally make my decisions rationally, and in moral matters under the guidance of practical reason. And it is certainly not my destiny that I am following. Living is a problem one has to solve, a difficult task one has to perform honestly. But you are a seducer, aren't you? You have just seduced me into talking about myself. And if one begins to talk about oneself in matters of philosophy, one immediately enters the slippery grounds of an ethics of personality. This is what I try to avoid doing. While discussing ethics, morals, and the related field, we should resist to talk about Joachim or about Lawrence; we should talk about the general person instead, about 'X' who stands for every person, disregarding his or her concrete character traits, psychological endowments and talents.

Lawrence: Why should one resist? Why so many 'shoulds', again? Besides, it was easy to seduce you into talking about yourself.

Joachim: I do not like talking about myself.

Lawrence: Yes you do. For philosophizing is always about conducting a dialogue with ourselves about ourselves. Nietzsche said that philosophy is a kind of a memoir . . .

Joachim: Philosophizing may be about conducting a dialogue *with* ourselves, but we do not conduct the dialogue *about* ourselves. Philosophers rarely talk about themselves.

Lawrence: Perhaps they talk so rarely about themselves because they always speak about themselves, if not directly, then indirectly.

Joachim: Nonsense. Kierkegaard was the first to employ indirect communication philosophically.

Lawrence: Rather he was the first who employed indirect communication consciously, because, as a post-metaphysician, he could not proceed otherwise, at least not sincerely. In post-metaphysical thinking direct communication sounds fraudulent, for there is no absolute authority left to back the philosopher's truth claims. Nietzsche's perspectivism is also a kind of indirect communication.

Joachim: You have admitted then, that modern philosophers, post-metaphysicians alone, indulge in writing memoirs in the guise of a philosophy.

Lawrence: By no means did I admit this, only that metaphysicians did this instinctively (you see, their instincts and their reason were identical), whereas post-metaphysicians have lost this kind of *naïveté*. They have become reflective, they raise questions concerning the possibility of their genre without having an answer at hand, they defend themselves ironically. And irony is always also self-irony. Indirect communication is the alternative route for philosophers when the main avenue has already been barred. But even if I admitted that only modern philosophers indulge in writing their memoirs, which I do not, the theory would still fit your case, since you happen to be a modern philosopher, or at least a promising apprentice of philosophy in (post) modern times.

Joachim: This is all nonsense, and you must know it. We have inherited our categorial system, our language, from our philosophical ancestors. We all speak this language, we communicate through it. And language is not a means here, but the being of philosophy itself. Philosophy does not originate in the soul of the philosopher. When I speak this language I cannot use it as the vehicle of a private, individual experience. I cannot simply express myself *qua* myself through this medium.

Lawrence: But neither are memoirs nor autobiographies just means of self-expression. A philosopher cannot help but understand himself in the language of his philosophy, and he talks about himself without expressing himself, simply by speaking the inherited language, his language, his being . . .

Joachim: You have not convinced me in the least. The circumstance that the philosopher lives in his philosophy does not mean that he writes his own life as philosophy. You will not seduce me again, I will not let myself be seduced. If there is a subject/object-identity in philosophy, there is only one way to have it: the single exister must disappear in the object (the language), he must abandon himself to it entirely, he must get rid of the peculiarities of his own personality and character rather than overemphasizing them. One just lets philosopy speak for itself . . .

Lawrence: Letting philosophy speak for itself means that the philosopher lets philosophy speak, in following his own instincts as a philosopher . . .

Joachim: Even if I admitted this, although I would do it most reluctantly, your ethics of personality would score no points this time either. True, a person who is about to perform a task had better abandon himself entirely to the task, but this has nothing to do with the ethics of personality. In so far as I abandon myself to the universal, I am still abandoning myself to something other than my instinct or even to my personified reason. The Kantian reverence for the law is a kind of self-abandon, since I subsume myself, my singularity, my phenomenal self through *Achtung* entirely to the noumenon, the universal moral law. It is I who abandon myself to it, every single person does it for himself separately, no one can do it for me instead of me – this is why one can speak of the autonomy of the human personality. But autonomy (although never fully achieved) is posited as the identification of the individual with the universal. It is in pain that I perceive my smallness as against the moral law, but this pain also elevates me, for I discover – in myself – the absolute by myself.

Lawrence: Of course, one abandons oneself not to oneself but to some-one else or to something else; it depends on 'to whom' and 'how' and 'by the guidance of what' you abandon yourself, whether or not you aban-don yourself to your destiny. The problem with your Kantianism is certainly not self-abandon. Not even that you abandon yourself to the universal; but that you become, or make the effort to become, universal yourself. You are in duty bound to pay respect to humankind in the other, the moral law within the other, reason within the other. What you are thus duty bound to pay respect to in the other is exactly identical with the absolute that dwells both in you and in the other. Is this universalism not the most subtle form of egotism? Think it over: you are not in duty bound to pay respect to diversity, to the idiosyncrasies of the other, to the 'ipseity' of the other, to her single qualities, to her beauty. No, you just pay respect to humankind in her, you pay respect to a ghost, a nullity, a sheer empty concept.

Joachim: Egotism is a stupid word in this context, for where there is no ego, there can be no egotism. Only the idiosyncratic *homo phenomenon* can be egotistic, for he is the one who cherishes self-love over the universal law . . .

Lawrence: I used an improper word, but you know what I meant. Hegel, whom I don't particularily like, hit the nail on the head when it came to Kant's moral philosophy . . .

Joachim: Please, do not introduce Hegel into our discussion. In his system 'morality', as the moment of 'for itself' (negation, subjectivity), has to be overcome. Worse still, he discusses the so-called right to well-being as a manifestation of morality, and what is the worst, he gives preference to the *Sittlichkeit* of the state over individual morality. Actu-ally, Hegel annuls moral philosophy, to a lesser degree in the *Phenom-enology*, but almost completely in *The Philosophy of Right*. He falls back behind Kant . . .

Lawrence: In the main I would agree, and still there are elements in Hegel's critique of Kant that I rather like. Contrary to you, for example, I find it lovely that Hegel discusses the 'right to well-being' as one of the moments of morality, although 'right' is an improper term here . . .

Joachim: Improper for you, because you are thinking in terms of an ethics of personality. But 'right' is the proper term here, whereas 'moral-ity' is the improper one. I accept without hesitation that the 'pursuit of happines' should be a right in the modern world, that modern institu-tions should open up a wide territory for the development of individual abilities so that everyone can be happy in his or her own way, but I would not discuss the 'pursuit of happiness' (for this is what Hegel describes here) under the heading of morality.

Lawrence: Morality, no. But ethics, yes. Even your Kant, at least in his *Metaphysics of Morals*, condescended to speak about our duties towards ourselves – and the developing of the individual's talents and capacities occupies pride of place among those duties. I hate the word 'duty'. I do not see any nobility in duty. It reminds me of Eichmann, who also declared before his judges in Jerusalem that he had always performed his duties and nothing else . . .

Joachim: Dear me, my head is spinning . . . you jump from one topic to another and create the greatest mess. Let's make an elementary order. First as far as Kant is concerned: he surely discussed our duties to ourselves, and, among them, also the conditional, broad, and indirect types of duties; all those kinds of things that you would be happy to accommodate within your ethics of personality. But your attempt is bound to fail for many reasons. Let me enumerate just a few. First, among the duties towards ourselves, the unconditional ones have preference over all conditional ones – this is what 'unconditional' means. Although there are no conflicts of duties, there are conflicts among the grounds of duties: the famous *Verpflichtungsgründe*. If the ground of a conditional duty collides with the ground of an unconditional one, the latter must be given preference. Actually, all moral duties which cannot be at all (or at least not fully) external, such as the interdiction against suicide or against lying, are discussed – at least in *The Metaphysics of Morals* – among our duties to ourselves. Here Kant gets closer to Aristotle than is usually admitted. In Book Five of his *Nicomachean Ethics*, Aristotle defines justice, as (among other things) the sum total of virtues in relation to others. This means that moral virtues, such as courage or temperance, or even intellectual virtues like *phronesis* or wisdom, are virtues in relation to ourselves. In Kantian terms, they are duties towards ourselves . . .

Lawrence: The idea of duty is entirely alien to Aristotle as it is to all Greeeks . . .

Joachim: Let me continue . . . Second, even in the case of indirect duties towards ourselves, Kant rejects the claim to the pursuit of happiness. The happiness of others, and not of ourselves, is a matter of duty for us . . .

Lawrence: This is so because Kant has such a pathetically poor concept of happiness. Is there a greater happiness than the feeling that we have developed our powers fully?

Joachim: But we speak here about a universalistic ethics. While for Lawrence the highest happiness may consist in developing his capacities in full, his neighbours get the greatest kick out of torturing others . . .

Lawrence: Alas, alas, now you don't do justice to your own Kant. Although the promotion of other persons' happiness is a conditional duty, and one should promote the happiness of other persons in line with the conceptions of happiness of those whose happiness one is promoting, we certainly must not provide our neighbour with the means of mass murder or torture just because he draws his happiness from mass murder or torture. Your said yourself just a moment ago that unconditional, strict and direct duties always take preference over and above conditional, indirect or broad ones. Pay attention, Joachim, I shall be very logical this time: why can't I have a duty to promote my own happines, provided that I don't draw my happiness from torturing others or from similar unpermitted exercises?

Joachim: To promote your own happiness cannot be your duty, because you do it anyway, because you like doing it.

Lawrence: But if I like developing my own abilities, how can that still be a duty? A duty towards myself?

Joachim: I told you already: you must not think in terms of an alleged ethics of personality when discussing Kant. Kant does not speak about Lawrence or about Joachim. He speaks about everyone, and he also addresses everyone. That for a person called Lawrence, the performance of his duty is, by chance, also the source of his felicity is fine, but morally irrelevant. For happiness is not a matter of duty, but developing our capacities is. Many – most people, I suppose – would feel the happiest if they just could laze around and let their endowments remain barren.

Lawrence: I think that here you are wrong again, for most people enjoy the exercise of their endowments and powers . . .

Joachim: Whether I am right or wrong, it does not matter. For it still remains true that there are things that oblige everyone without being pursued happily by everyone. The first is necessary, the second is contingent.

Lawrence: Why is an empty necessity of the greatest moral value, why is a contingent constellation, the happy coincidence between character and fate, however valuable it is, so undeserving? Has this got anything to do with our own ethical concerns and judgements? Is it not philosophy, or rather metaphysics alone, that puts a premium on necessity, universality, inevitability, eternity, infinity, absoluteness and the like, instead of putting a premium on the contingent, the vanishing, the finite, the temporal, the single individual, the contemporary? You accuse me of seducing you; but you are yourself the dangerous seducer in your superimposing of philosophy's own madness, the pursuit of necessity, universality, eternity and the like – that is, the philosopher's madness, the philosopher's own destiny – upon all other earthly creatures! Listen to the Laughter of the Thracian woman! It is a good laughter, a liberating laughter . . .

Joachim: That philosophy, or rather philosophers, love all those great and high things that you just mentioned, I would be the last to deny. But, alas, when a Thracian woman bursts out in laughter, the last thing she laughs at is practical philosophy. Moral philosophy was not invented by philosophers. They just wrote long footnotes to the ever-current moral practices of the best of men, idealized them, made cases for them; they provided a consistent, well-shaped, subtle and sophisticated apology for the acts and lives of the best persons among them. Let me say with all due modesty: moral philosophy – if you compare it to other branches of philosophy, particularly to metaphysics proper – is an eminently low-key speculative exercise. Sometimes one gets the impression that all moral philosophers say basically almost the same thing, with a limited set of variations. If I disregard the greatest thinkers – Plato, Aristotle, Augustine, Spinoza, Kant – moral philosophers mostly are down-to-earth and sometimes even boring. Moral philosophers talk too much, they insist too much, they are repetitious, sometimes also sententious. Yet they speak the language of their contemporaries. True, they speak the language of eternity and necessity, but so too, normally, do their contemporaries. Ater all, an average Athenian citizen did not attribute a mere temporal value to courage or relative merit to men of wisdom. He was not yet a historicist . . .

Lawrence: But Kant already lived in a world of historicism. And yet, he – and to a degree Hegel, too – remained committed to necessity, universality and absoluteness in a world where the foundation, or the taken-for-grantedness, of these and similar ideals have already been undermined.

Joachim: This is true. But the things you dislike most in Kant are precisely the marks of his towering greatness. Heine, in his lovely book on modern German philosophy, once compared Kant with Robespierre. Of these two great men, Heine said, Kant was the greater terrorist; he had not been satisfied with killing people, he had cherished a higher ambition, he had killed God. Heine was less interested in Kant's lifelong concern to rescue morals and the absoluteness of morality, in a world where God is dead.

Lawrence: What you call 'lifelong' begins with his critical period. Kant created problems for himself, and then he came up with the solution . . .

Joachim: What you just said is entirely beside the point. I ask you, for the last time, stop inserting biographical elements into my interpretations.

Lawrence: But excuse me, there was no biographical pretension in my modest intervention. What I meant was that Kant had to clarify problems of moral philosophy which had been created as problems by his own system of philosophy. Till his mid-fifties, his mid-life crisis, he had no such problems.

Joachim: Is your mention of Kant's alleged mid-life crisis not a biographical reference?

Lawrence: Perhaps yes, perhaps no. You discuss a system detached from the author of this system. I also discuss the system but I do not detach it from its author. In the case of a Rembrandt imitation it is important, even significant, for you that you are able to tell the real from the forgery, even if you cannot distinguish them sensually, with naked eyes. What makes a real Rembrandt real, then? Is it not authorship or, if you wish, biography that authenticates it? Why is something self-evident for you in the case of Rembrandt but not in the case of Kant?

Joachim: Here I could score a point against you with your own weapons. As a kind of postmodern thinker, you are not expected to defend authorship – I am expected to do so. But for me, the system is actual, while the author is a mere name. When we discuss philosophy, dropping Kant's name serves as a kind of abbreviation; when I refer, for example, to Kant's moral philosophy, every student of philosophy understands what I mean, and so I spare myself the trouble of a lengthy explication. But the relationship between Kant and this philosophy is, in my mind, entirely contingent. You believe yourself to be very up-to-date, but you are an antediluvian philosophical animal if you try to establish a direct link between a philosopher's life and his work.

Lawrence: I thought that we had gotten over all this by now. Must I repeat everything that I have said about autobiography and memoir? I do not mean that a master philosopher has to live according to his philosophy, nor do I think that he will directly express his life experiences in his philosophy. What I mean is that philosophy is the philosopher's life, that he lives this life above all, and that he does not 'solve problems'. Or rather, it seems as if he also solves problems, but these so-called problems are, let me repeat, self-created ones, because these are the problems of his own world. In inventing his critical philosophy, a person called Immanuel Kant established a world for himself. It was in this world that he began to live from then onwards; in an enjoyable world, he lived an enjoyable life: his world, his life. But he presented his own world as 'the' world, as if it were a description, the only and sole true and right description of the world allegedly common to all of us. This was the game he was playing. He called us up in arms against our inclinations, promised us sweat and tears, while he was enjoying himself.

Joachim: I think we should stop discussing this issue if we ever want to get to the point. We wanted to find out whether an ethics of personality is possible. I said, or at least I tried to say, that a theory of personality is certainly possible but it will never resemble an ethics.

Lawrence: And I wanted to push you very far in one direction so that you would realize: no other ethics is possible in the modern age, at least no one which would be adequate to it. Either ethics of personality or no ethics. There are as many ethics of personality as representative ethical persons. Kant's moral philosophy is also an ethics of personality – the ethics of his personality, of course. But he was not sincere about it, or at least, his ethics itself barred the way to his sincerity. Kant had to present his ethics of personality in universal wrappings . . .

Joachim: Stop, for Heaven's sake, you mix up everything once again. I never denied that Immanuel Kant's personality is manifestly present in his system, I merely added that the system itself has nothing to do with this personality. Let me make it clear for the second time that I am the one who denies the relevance of authorship, not you. Unlike Rembrandt, Kant cannot be imitated. You are welcome to write a fourth Critique; the second is constantly copied – namely by the printer.

Lawrence: But you said, didn't you, that Kant was concerned about rescuing morality in a world where God had died. You dated him, you put him into his place, you historicized him. But history is an aspect of our biography. At the beginning of our dispute, you accused me of historicism; aren't *you* rather a historicist?

Joachim: I admit that up to a certain point I am. I put Immanuel Kant and his concerns in a historical context without discussing the system itself, the message of the *Critique of Practical Reason*, within this context. One can say, of course, that Kant formulated the absolute moral philosophy in and for modernity; and in emphasizing this connection, one introduces an element of historicism into the problem. But only an element of it, for one can still insist that there is only one adequate moral philosophy after the death of God for us, moderns, and this is the Kantian one. And if we reject the Kantian and begin instead to indulge in a kind of ethics of personality, we lose everything, we become unable to distinguish good from bad, good from evil. If I were to foresee Kant's demise, to suspect that the Moral Law will share the fate of the old God, I would be a thousand times grateful for not being bound to live in the next century. I am more afraid of the future than the past . . .

Lawrence: Here we go again. You employ forceful rhetorics against the ethics of personality, but on what grounds? Motivated by fears and gloomy premonitions that ensue from your own personality. If I read your Kant well, he was rather hopeful . . . but, alas, he had a different fate and also a different character . . .

Joachim: If I were you, I would say 'bingo!' It was an atypical *faux pas* on my part to speak about my personal feelings in an objective discussion . . .

Lawrence: But in the meantime you made me curious without satisfying my curiosity. You said that Kant came to the rescue of moral philosophy in a world where God was (almost) dead. And you also said that Kant's moral philosophy is the only moral philosophy of modernity; put bluntly: either Kant or nothing, either Kant or chaos . . .

Joachim: To continue: either Kant or the *Sittlichkeit der Sitte*. As your Nietzsche would have had it: life without conscience, without reflection, mere shame-regulation, legality without morality. And nothing and chaos, you are right, for mere legality, at least in the modern world, cannot survive for long without morality. Nietzsche speaks about willing nothing. But still worse is willing many things which amount to nothing as far as meaning is concerned.

Lawrence: We dislike the same things, it's just that we believe in different remedies. We know that philosophical remedies can also be poisonous. Plato's *pharmakon*, and not just in Derrida's sense, contains many a poisonous potion.

Joachim: Here again, we agree. But Kant concocted the sole remedy that is never poisonous.

Lawrence: This reminds me that you still owe me an answer about Eichmann's performing his Kantian duties . . . How would you meet this challenge?

Joachim: Easily. First, Kant was a sceptic and he knew much about the resourcefulness of human self-deception. He did not believe, for example, that even those who were acutely aware of the categorical imperative would actually live by proper, morally well-tested maxims, or even if they did, would always act accordingly. He found that if one applies only one single formula of the moral law one can still remain on slippery ground. He recommended that we test our maxims and intended actions by at least two, but preferably by three formulae, among them the substantive and limiting formula: the interdiction against instrumentalization. It is true, for example, that Kant said that disobeying the law of our state is morally impossible, but he also said that we should not use other persons as mere means. There are cases, I admit, where you cannot make a choice on Kantian grounds alone. Even Kant is not fail-safe when it comes to all those complex single decisions. He confronts such an example in his controversy with Benjamin Constant. To rescue another person's life is – in his mind – a conditional duty (an external broad duty) whereas the interdiction against lying is a direct and unconditional duty. As I already said, unconditional duties by definition always have priority. But it is not always possible even for an orthodox Kantian to establish the hierarchy of duties on the occasion of a collision between the grounding of duties. For example, how about obeying the laws of my state if those laws stipulate the use of other men as mere means? All these fine points are, however, of no relevance in the Eichmann case. Obeying the laws of the state is one thing, and voluntarily accepting the assignment that contributes to the murder of millions is another. Eichmann's reference to Kant was fraudulent and hypocritical; he did not know Kant . . .

Lawrence: And yet he could rationalize his actions with Kant . . .

Joachim: You can rationalize your action always and at any time and with anything. Whatever we write, whatever we do, can be used against us, against our intentions, meanings. Nothing protects us from misuse after our death. But as long as we live, we can still protest. And you cannot accuse Kant of neglecting this duty.

Lawrence: I don't accuse him of anything, that is, not of anything personal. I talk to you, not to him; it is you I want to convince that your defense of the Kantian moral philosophy is untimely and shaky. And although you have promised to tell me why Kant's moral philosophy is the only relevant ethics in – and – for modernity, you still own me the answer. Meanwhile it has gotten dark and cool and I am freezing, and I haven't yet heard the declaration of your truth which might have warmed me up.

Joachim: There is a nice pub on University Place, let's go and have a drink. That will warm us up. And I promise a great plea for the defence for Kant.

Lawrence: All right, but don't forget your promise.

(Change of scene. Pub on University Place. Lawrence and Joachim are seated around a table for four on the first floor. Joachim sips brandy, Lawrence drinks coffee.)

Lawrence: Wouldn't Kant mind your indulging in a brandy?

Joachim: How would a strong coffee and a Cuban cigar, these paraphernalia of a decadent culture, fit into the Dionysian ideal?

Lawrence: Indeed, it would befit me more to become intoxicated, and you to promote the wakefulness of mind with a nihilist touch.

Joachim: I was only kidding in your own style. There is no connection between our merely personal tastes and habits and our philosophy.

Lawrence: In this sacred moment, both Kant and Nietzsche would remind you of your promise. I am afraid you have to keep it. Why, then is Kant's moral philosophy the only possible one in-and-for the modern age?

Joachim: We agreed that morality had to be rescued after the death of God . . .

Lawrence: So you historicize Kant . . .

Joachim: I told you already that I do not historicize the categorical imperative; if I did, I would not be a Kantian. But I historicize its discovery. Kant himself admitted that he had merely offered a new formula; I historicize the formula . . .

Lawrence: Excuse me, but now you are the one hopelessly mixing things up. You cannot state three things in one. First, owing to the death of God, in order to rescue the old European conscience and morality one has to invent a moral law that dwells in all of us. Second, the moral law dwells in all of us eternally, but it had to be discovered (like America by the Europeans). Or third, the moral law had always been known (like Europe by the Europeans), but it could not be properly applied since the magic formula provided by Kant had not yet been available. Which is it?

Joachim: Certainly I did not mean the first.

Lawrence: Certainly? Not the first? Joachim, you are in trouble! Because if the moral law dwells in all of us anyway and we are aware of it, and if only the magic formula had been added by Kant, your claim that only Kant's moral philosophy can rescue us from chaos or absolute nihilism will be null and void – for the moral law could take care of this on its own. And if the second were the case, namely that Kant discovered the law just as the Europeans discovered America, a discovery of this kind, once made, could anyhow never be entirely forgotten. Alas, Kant said something very similar about the French Revolution. We would be in danger of being lost to chaos or nihilism without Kant if, and only if, the categorical imperative, the moral law, were Kant's own invention, the last life-raft thrown into the ocean of nihilism. Either we would grasp it or we would be drowning.

Joachim: I never thought about this in your way . . . But now I guess that the second interpretation would best fit my idea. For it is not true that if something has once been discovered, it will never be forgotten. You know this better than I do, for your Nietzsche wrote many interesting things about the economy of forgetting and remembering.

Lawrence: There is liberation in forgetting . . .

Joachim: True, depending on what we forget and from what we are liberated. Forgetting the moral law in us would be the a fatal kind of forgetting. What are Kantians – myself included – doing? We remind people of the moral law, so that it should be kept in memory, so that it should not be forgotten. As long as Kant's moral philosophy is kept alive, we can still have hope.

Lawrence: For the time being I accept your explanation without agreeing with your self-congratulatory conclusion. But we haven't yet arrived at the gist of the matter.

Joachim: Just because you do not let me speak.

Lawrence: I'll have a second coffee then, and get practice in listening.

Joachim: Kant's moral philosophy does not make men and women good; no moral philosophy can perform miracles.

Lawrence: Why not? Isn't that exactly the self-set task of moral philosophy?

Joachim: For Heaven's sake, you have promised to listen for a change!

Lawrence: Here comes my second coffee. Now I am really listening.

Joachim: Moral philosophy does not make men and women good. What it provides is a reliable crutch for enabling people to distinguish between good and evil. The point morality springs from is the ability to make this distinction, and to distinguish well and rightly. The crutch helps you out, it offers you the necessary support. If one relies upon this crutch, one will not mix up moral distinctions with other ones, such as the ones between successful and unsuccessful, useful and harmful, beautiful and ugly . . .

Lawrence: Excuse me for this one interruption: why do you want to avoid, as you say, mixing up good versus evil with beautiful versus ugly? Is the good not beautiful, is, for example, evil not ugly in your philosophy? And why haven't you juxtaposed the distinction between good and evil to that of true and false?

Joachim: I would have arrived at this problem anyway in due course. But let me see. Certainly, we can describe a good deed as beautiful, and an evil one as ugly, but only metaphorically. In a non-metaphorical, strictly aesthetic sense, the evil one can also be beautiful. The demonic powers are beautiful . . .

Lawrence: We cannot speak about beautiful and ugly, except in a metaphorical sense.

Joachim: Let us skip this mini-controversy and continue. I did not enumerate true and false (untrue) among the distinctions that one should not mix up with that between good and evil, because it is precisely at this point that Kant's moral philosophy proves particularly revolutionary. Greek, and especially Christian, thinking identified the good with the true (and usually also with the beautiful, as you suggested), because their moral philosophy was metaphysically grounded. God, the supreme goodness, was thought as supreme truth and beauty. Insight into the essence of the Supreme, the original and originating, the trinity Goodness–Truth –Beauty, opened up the avenue for also knowing with certainty the character and the content of the derived goodness, truth and beauty. Morals were strictly substantive, as well as heteronomous (at least in the Kantian sense), given that men were thought to have received the commandments from above. *Qua* creatures, they were the recipients of the catalogue of virtues and vices, and they were duty bound to obey the commandments and to practise the virtues as well as to avoid the vices enumerated in the catalogue.

Lawrence: Now you exaggerate. Nicholas of Cusa, for example . . .

Joachim: Yes, I do exaggerate. But in case of Nicholas of Cusa, despite his theory of learned ignorance, we were still guided towards knowing the precise character of goodness. For example, in his metaphor of the 'throw' the God-Man is at the centrepoint of the circle, as the single embodiment of Goodness and Truth; whereas men, creatures, try to approximate the centre of the circle, although they can never end up in the centre. Actually, Kant's categorical imperative has preserved the same model, yet without the metaphor. What does it mean for Kant to hit the centre? If one chooses all of one's maxims with the guidance of the categorical imperative, if one acts only out of duty and never simply dutifully, if, therefore, the law is, in the last instance, no longer an imperative because one cannot act otherwise, *then* man arrives at the centre. Yet man cannot hit the centre, he can only approximate to it. If one does not know what the centre is, then one has no yardstick, if the crutch is missing, then man is lost and cannot find his way towards the good. Yet this does not mean that anyone could be completely good . . .

Lawrence: This metaphor of the crutch troubles me. People who can walk on their own, freely, without help, with upright gait, need no crutch. Those who do need one are ugly and they are perhaps also crippled in spirit . . .

Joachim: Kant never mentioned the crutch; this is my metaphor. Still, Kant compared men to crooked wood who are difficult, if not outright impossible, to straighten. This crutch helps the *krummes Holz* to get closer to the straight one. In addition, the categorical imperative (the crutch) dwells in all of us, it is not superimposed, it does not infringe upon men's autonomy; rather, it warrants autonomy.

Lawrence: So, you mean that *homo phenomenon* uses his own *homo noumenon* (that is, the purely rational human person in himself) as his own crutch, and in this sense the *krummes Holz* relies upon himself to sraighten his spine and make his gait upright?

Joachim: Exactly. But let me return for a moment to Cusa's metaphor because it is a good one. When I said that moral philosophy provides us with a crutch, I could have formulated the same idea in the following way: 'moral philosophy points at our moral centre. If the moral centre is pointed out, we know precisely what to approximate.' See, Kant hardly believed that there can be a single person who always subjected his maxims to the scrutiny of the categorical imperative. At any rate, we cannot know whether there has ever been a single such person; we cannot know this about ourselves either. The main thing is not that we always do the right thing but that we always know what the right thing is, what we should do, and that we feel uneasy or sad or self-critical or guilty when we fail to live up to our commitment to the categorical imperative.

Lawrence: This is all very traditionally Christian. And what if we do not have such a commitment? Why do you presuppose that once our centre has been pointed out we will always try to approximate to it?

Joachim: 'Always try' – this is too much . . . Kant was too much of a sceptic to hold such beliefs. But yes, one always tells oneself: 'If conditions were different, that is, better, if I had the opportunity, if only I could do it without hurting my interests, my comfort – how wonderful it would be to approximate to the centre. But alas, times are difficult . . . etc.' You see that Kant, who employed the term 'radical evil', never ever believed in radical evil. What he called radical evil is actually neither radical nor evil, but rather the (in itself harmless) drive to follow the directions of self-love . . .

Lawrence: And this is what makes Kant sound so absurd. I would rather be left without a crutch than use his . . .

Joachim: Is that so? May I ask you why?

Lawrence: A good person distinguishes between good and evil because he is good, and he also does the right thing. He does not need the crutch. Only the *krummes Holz*, as you said, needs it, because his will remains always 'split', because he likes doing the wrong thing again and again although he does it with bad conscience and guilt, I admit. A good person can freely follow his self-love because he loves a good self. He does not need to approximate the centre of the circle, and he cannot even do so, because there are several circles and several centrepoints. Every decent person is his or her own centrepoint, a circle on his or her own, and very different from that of any other. This is why the good can also be beautiful. Your decent person is sweating, he is ugly . . .

Joachim: Let me first point out that you got very close to the concept of a single-centred person in what you said. Please, give it a second thought.

Lawrence: Let me correct myself. Every person is a circle with several, although limited, numbers of so-called centrepoints . . .

Joachim: Did you fail geometry? I would rather return to my simile of the *krummes Holz*. The problem is with your eyes and not with the picture. In Kant's mind the whole human race is like the *krummes Holz*, which simply means that we are no saints; we are, after all, humans. Under time pressure, plagued by dissatisfaction, spurned by ambition, man is simply a *krummes Holz*. If you do not accept this you are lying to yourself – which is a capital crime not only for my Kant but also for your Nietzsche. If you conjure up the mental picture of a hunchback, a kind of Rigoletto, or a pygmy, as the protagonist of the Kantian moral philosophy, then of course you will reject it in horror. So would I. But as you said yourself, the simile exhibits the relation between *homo noumenon* and *homo phenomenon*: the crutch inheres in all men. Haven't all philosophers suggested that man's desires, wishes, impulses should instead listen to the voice of reason, at least in practical matters? Besides, Kant's practical reason is fundamentally identical with free will . . .

Lawrence: We have just embarked into the safe harbour of philosophical platitudes. Kants's practical reason and pure will are gigantic platitudes.

Joachim: A platitude can be a truism and a truism can be true and right. In practical philosophy we deal with the good and the right, and they are sometimes uninteresting. But in moral philosophy the category of 'interesting' has no place. After having made this concession I still do not think that, in all fairness, you could call the manner in which Kant elaborated his idea of practical reason and pure will platitudinous. The identification of practical reason with pure will is so far from being a platitude that it is an innovation. You can read it in two ways. You may say that Kant eliminated an old independent philosophical character called 'Will', by identifying it with another old philosophical character called 'Reason', or you can say that Kant eliminated (at least from moral philosophy) the oldest philosophical character called 'Reason' by identifying it with 'Will'. For Kant's practical reason, given that it does not provide any kind of knowledge, can hardly be termed 'reason' in a strictly traditional way. Some people, you are among them, accuse Kant of having over-rationalized morals. If this accusation were correct, Kant would not have been innovative. Metaphysicians normally over-rationalize morals. This is what you called platitudinous. Yet one could come up with the diametrically opposite suggestion: Kant has eliminated rationality from morality by making his practical reason void of the capacity of providing knowledge of any kind.

Lawrence:　You are confusing matters and you 'postmodernize' your Kant without bounds. Would you then call Kant an irrationalist?

Joachim:　No, by all means, not! By the way, in Kant's days there was no 'irrationalism', although the first stirrings of the romantic movement irritated Kant as much as the fully-fledged romantics later angered Hegel. But was Kant, in his practical philosophy, a rationalist? Let me repeat another, and fairly old, truism: in his so-called epistemology, Kant supposedly combined the empiricist and the rationalist traditions. In his moral philosophy he certainly did not do this. The reversal of the sequence of the chapters of the *Critique of Pure Reason* in the *Critique of Practical Reason* and Kant's own explanation of his reasons for this reversal tell the whole story here, so I think that I do not need to discuss it. Thus, Kant's moral philosophy is obviously not a combination of the rationalist and the empiricist tradition. But does it follow from all that has been said so far that he followed the rationalist tradition? The categorical imperative, the moral law, transcendental freedom, pure practical reason, pure will – they are all encompassed in the 'fact of reason' . . .

Lawrence:　If I remember correctly, Kant made two attempts at the transcendental deduction of the moral law, both times in the *Groundwork*, only to come to the conclusion, which was to be guessed anyhow, that the question of *how* freedom is possible cannot be answered . . .

Joachim:　Yes, indeed. And this is why he gave up on such an attempt in the second *Critique*. Thus, the moral law is a fact of reason . . .

Lawrence:　The fact of reason, of course, and not the fact of human nature or the human condition or the like . . .

Joachim:　But where does this fact originate? From transcendental freedom? But you know about transcendental freedom only through the 'fact of reason.' However, should we ask this fact of reason the question, 'Who is your father?', it would, in a very Parsifal-like manner, answer, 'I don't know'; 'Who sent you this way?' 'I don't know'; 'Your name, then?' 'Kant described me through my acts and called me the categorical imperative, but my real name I do not know.' Why is the appellation of this unknown the 'fact of reason' and not the fact of human nature? Because the moral law, the crutch that we need to rely upon on the road of universality and necessity, is called reason. But the moral law, the crutch itself, cannot be explained. Here comes the *Parsifal* motif: its origins are unknown. It is just there. It is a fact.

Lawrence: A fact like the sun? Or a fact like the law of attraction? Or
a fact like in human (legal) law? I have lost track, I do not understand
what you are up to . . .

Joachim: I am now approximating the limits of reason, the limits of
rationality. I am about to show you that the limits of rationality are as
strict in Kant's moral philosophy as in his epistemology . . .

Lawrence: But this means, again, a very primitive thing. All those
Kantian faculties once had a common origin, and their origin could be
pointed at as long at there was a God and a human soul: the created and
the uncreated substances of Leibniz. Then you still had your pre-established harmony, all right. But take away the two kinds of substances and
all these faculties will be cut off from their place of origin, they will just
float in the air. After having them uprooted from their natural habitat,
you will be obliged to bind them together again, this time artificially. If
in addition you are unable yourself to perform even this trick, you will
just say: this is a fact, I am sorry, I cannot go further.

Joachim: But don't you see my point? Since the times that modern
natural sciences begun emerging, the whole world of knowledge has
become progressively – if I may use this word – decentred. If something
was held true yesterday, it will be held untrue today, be it a description
of facts, a so-called law of nature, or a paradigm. Perspectivism, historicism, relativism, have occupied the place of the absolutes, of the creed of
the eternal, unchanging, necessary, divine world order – of certainty.
This where we now are, this is the way we now know and forget, learn
and unlearn. If morals are tied to knowledge, full relativism and nihilism
directly follow. Moral philosphy, like practical philosophy in general,
has to be disentangled from the deadly embrace of philosophy of knowledge, the philosophy of the spectators. The Aristotelian distinction between practical and theoretical life is not radical enough for us; practical
and theoretical thinking must be juxtaposed to one another entirely. It is
a poor objection to Kant if you reproach him for having neglected the
consequences of actions as one of the foundations of good moral judgement. Kant was not silly enough to believe that consequences do not
matter, he just insisted that they cannot and should not serve as the
foundation for moral judgement and for the choice of moral maxims in
general. For if they did, knowledge could take preference over the moral
law, and the unavoidable relativism and perspectivism of the modern
vision of the world – *Weltanschauung* – would drag all morals along into
an early grave . . .

Lawrence: The post-Kuhnian conception of sciences can be described
as perspectivism, although not necessarily also as relativism. Modern
men and women are contingent, they are aware of their contingency, and
they are also aware of having been thrown into the prison-house of
temporality: historicity. The post-Kuhnian conception fits the natural
attitude of modern men and women perfectly well. Why is it that you

appreciate that Kant, despite his accepting the logic of the modern era in the case of theoretical reason, protests against it until his last breath when it comes to practical reason, instead of reproaching him for his inconsistency? Why do you remain conservative? Why do you preserve a dying species in ethics when you promote a new species in knowledge? For, I am sorry, I still do not see why the absoluteness of the categorical imperative and the phoney juxtaposition of *homo noumenon* and *homo phenomenon* would be the sole alternative to moral relativism. You have, as a matter of course, identified relativism with perspectivism. This is not at all a matter of course to me. There is no relativism except in the face of an absolute, and perspectivism has nothing to do with the juxtaposition of relative and absolute. Every perspective stands for itself. There are different worlds from each and every perspective, but these worlds, though different, are also shared; we understand each other to the extent that we can dwell in a common world. From a perspectivist standpoint truth can be either absolute or relative, but whether it is absolute or relative, does not depend on perspectivism in general, but on the concrete perspective of a person in particular. Nietzsche was a perspectivist, not a relativist; he saw in relativism the sickness of passive nihilism. Leibniz – as Heidegger pointed out, and our professor after him in our recent lectures – was also a kind of perspectivist. There are similarities between him and Nietzsche. You could say that in his own way Kierkegaard was also a perspectivist. Was his moral standard not high enough? I think that you cheat in the philosophical game when you try to sell the idea that the sole alternative to the categorical imperative, this oddest fact of reason, is no morals at all. Neither life nor post-Kantian philosophy bear out your claim. I stress this point passionately because my ethics of personality is also perspectivist. When you identified perspectivism with relativism, you have influenced people in a biased way against this ethics. Were relativism and perspectivism identical, an ethics of personality would be either impossible, or utterly banausic, and in the latter case it would have no interest for me. I see myself as a perspectivist who is committed to absolutes. And please do not interrupt me again by saying that for Kantianism a single person like Lawrence doesn't matter. For I insist that I should matter, and not just as a specimen of the species 'humankind', but also as a single individual, as myself, as 'the total concept of the substance Lawrence', to quote an old and defunct but clever metaphysician . . .

Joachim: Lawrence does matter, he matters very much for his friends and for himself. You matter for me, I love you, I care for you precisely as you are. But your 'ipseity' has no bearing on moral philosophy. Since all human beings live under the same moral law, in morals equality reigns supreme. Here there is no difference; there is neither *quod licet Iovi non licet bovi* nor *quod licet bovi, non licet Iovi*. But you see, this strictness, this rigidity, this formal equality does not enchain you; on the contrary, it sets you free. Once you have done your duty, as it is expected from everyone, you are just yourself, a butterfly who flies as no other butterfly does . . .

Lawrence: But is there anything more precious than caring for the other, loving the other? Why do you give preference to the moral law? Why should Lawrence and Joachim first be measured by a so-called universal standard in order to get the go-ahead signal to care for each other without measures?

Joachim: Because Lawrence and Joachim do not live together on a deserted island. On second thoughts, even if we did, we could hardly abandon the universal yardstick, because we do not know ourselves, or at least we are not entirely transparent to ourselves – and so many things could happen even between us that should not happen . . .

Lawrence: Dear me, you do mix up your metaphors! Is a beautiful butterfly also a *krummes Holz*?

Joachim: I am afraid so. Although you may not be, I certainly am a *krummes Holz*.

Lawrence: Do not say that! You are the most upright, honest person I've ever known!

Joachim: You say that because you are young, and, excuse me, a little naïve. But speaking on a non-personal level: a *krummes Holz* can be very upright and honest. It is perhaps easier to lead an honest life if you see yourself as a *krummes Holz*. To return to your objections more seriously, one can certainly live honestly without relying on the crutch of the categorical imperative if one has good luck and a good heart, and if one lives one's whole life in a familiar environment. But men of *amor fati*, the typical protagonists of your ethics of personality, are daring. They tread on new paths; they either have a good heart or they do not, they can have good luck as much as bad luck; moreover, they can have good luck without having good moral luck. Macbeth is a good example . . .

Lawrence: But Macbeth is also a good example for the impotence of a Kantian ethics. He could tell good from evil, he knew he was doing the most wicked things, but he went on doing them. Could a person who follows his instincts alone do a more bloody job than Macbeth?

Joachim: Perhaps not; but Macduff could have done a worse job and so could Lady Macduff. And without them and people like them, we would have no grounds to call Macbeth evil, for we (and not only he) would lack the yardstick to tell good from evil. But *Macbeth* was not a good example; it is a pagan play. Think rather of Iago and Iago's wife. In every Shakespeare tragedy there is at least one person who, without being personally interested in doing justice (sometimes even being interested in covering up for evil) still does justice and keeps the moral standards pure; Iago's wife, Kent and Horatio are such persons. If I were a better philosopher I would illuminate moral philosophy with Shakespeare rather than with Kant. For Shakespeare had such an unerring moral judgement. He also knew everything about the *krummes Holz*, think of Hamlet's monologue while he was waiting for Ophelia . . .

Lawrence: But he knew more about the ethics of personality . . .

Joachim: About both. But whenever I try to verbalize my Shakespeare experiences, I begin to behave as the proverbial bull in the china shop. And yet, I cannot help speaking about Shakespeare. So please excuse me for my clumsiness. There are two different ladders of value-hierarchy in Shakespeare, primarily in his tragedies but also in some of his comedies. One is the value-hierarchy of greatness, the second is the value hierarchy of morality. Those on the top of the first are never on the top of the second, and vice versa. For example, Hamlet is at the top of the value hierarchy of greatness, but on the value hierarchy of morality Horatio occupies the highest place; while King Lear is at the top of the hierarchy of greatness, it is not him, but Kent, who occupies the top position on the moral ladder. This is also an answer to your insistence that love should have ethical preference over the moral law. It is Cordelia who loves her father most, but Kent is the one who chooses to commit himself to doing justice, to standing for values for the values' sake . . .

Lawrence: I cannot follow you fully in your preference-game. I admit, there are two ladders, or, to speak with Nietzsche, orders of rank: one of greatness, another of morals. But why should I establish a hierarchy within the latter? Why should Kent stand higher than Cordelia? In addition, I also disagree with your description of the two value-hierarchies where one person stands at the top of the ladder of greatness whereas another at the top of the ladder of morals. In my ethics of personality, greatness, the significance or weight of the character, also results from, or is the manifestation of, ethics and ethical worth . . .

Joachim: You would not, I hope, see in Hamlet or Lear the exemplifications of your *amor fati*?

Lawrence: Not of 'my' *amor fati* perhaps, beacause their ethics of personality differ from mine. But they are both repositories of an ethics of personality in the tragic mood. Still, there are major figures in Shakespeare such as Antonys and Cleopatra, Julius Ceasar and Brutus, who fit my bill completely.

Joachim: But Brutus is also at the top of the moral hierarchy of values . . .

Lawrence: Now I begin to realize that there is a kind of 'lucky throw of the dice' in Shakespeare too – in the exceptional cases when the two 'tops', namely the moral one and one of greatness, overlap . . .

Joachim: There are very few such 'lucky hits' in Shakespeare's tragedies. You have mentioned only Brutus so far . . .

Lawrence: True, but there are many in his comedies; Beatrice and Benedict are perhaps the most lovely ones among them. And they are everyday persons, not heroes or authors or other kinds of historical luminaries. You see, I have Shakespeare on my side: an ethics of personality is possible, and not just as an exception . . .

Joachim: What a short memory you have! I rather like the expressions 'lucky hit' and 'lucky throw of the dice'; this is why I reminded you of them. But those 'lucky hits' do not fit the bill of your ethics of personality. Have you already forgotten that we set out to think of cases where the top of the moral hierarchy and that of the hierarchy of greatness overlap? This point of coincidence contains morality to the highest degree. I am sorry, but in the modern world the chances of such a 'lucky throw' have decreased. Not because there are fewer people of good heart, but owing to the rapid historical changes that every day confront people with new and newer situations, new kinds of choices. Yes, the chances are decreasing of 'lucky hits' and this hurts me, too.

Lawrence: You accused me of historicism, remember? Now you are intoning a historicist theme. If your categorical imperative is timeless, eternal and unchanging, and if man is, and remains, a *krummes Holz*, I do not see why our possibilities to be 'lucky hit' should decrease.

Joachim: We already settled the issue of historicism; please do not open it again! Neither the eternal character of the moral law nor the *krumme Holz* character of our nature has anything to do with the context in which we live and act. Nevertheless, Kant always contextualizes ethical problems. Whenever he gives examples for the choice of maxims in accordance to the moral law, he always chooses extremely contextualized cases. Can you imagine a more specific context than the problem of whether one is allowed to embezzle the deposit when the depositor is already dead and no one knows about it except the person who chooses between embezzling or not? I faithfully followed in Kant's footsteps when I introduced into our discussion the historical context in which we, modern persons at the end of the twentieth century, check our maxims and make moral decisions. In this concrete context (which differs dramatically from the context of a relatively closed society in the times of the Renaissance) a moral person, a person who consciously scrutinizes his maxims as to whether they qualify for the moral law, has decreased chances of being a lucky throw of the dice. He must be more conscious, he must make succinctly rational decisions, he can rely much less upon his instincts . . .

Lawrence: Wait a minute! Half an hour ago you tried to persuade me that Kant is falsely accused of rationalism, and you indulged in comparing the fact of reason to *Parsifal*. Now, however, you say exactly the thing I expected of you: we must think more, calculate with pluses and minuses more; we must be more conscious. This is rationalism proper, or logocentrism with a practical intent. But before you interrupt me . . .

Joachim: I never interrupt you, you keep interrupting me . . .

Lawrence: . . . let me make a solid remark. You have accepted that there is such a person whom we may call 'the lucky throw of the dice', although you still dismiss an ethics of personality. So far, so good. But if there are cases, or in certain historical contexts even several cases, of the 'lucky throw of the dice' (call them Benedict and Beatrice), don't you notice that you have accepted, even though only as an exception, the unity between your *homo noumenon* and *homo phenomenon*, that is, a unified single individual, an 'ipseity', who can follow his instincts and do the right, even the best thing, and can be happy and lovely and beautiful and witty and merry and refined in the bargain?

Joachim: Moral philosophy is as little custom-made for Beatrice and Benedict as it is for Lawrence. Haven't I told you that moral philosophy does not address itself to the exception?

Lawrence: But if you need a centre to aim at, cannot representative 'lucky throws of the dice' sit at this aimed-at centre?

Joachim: Here my darling postmodern friend suddenly becomes pre-modern. What robs us of our freedom? Not the categorical imperative, not the moral law, I can assure you. This is what we ought to approximate. But a sheer form can be filled with every kind of content; this is why Kant, who makes a strict case for the universal, makes also the best case for the uniqueness, for the unprecedentedness of the individual. No single and unique lucky throw of the dice can sit in the centre of our moral circle. All such lucky throws act in their own situations and contexts and not in ours, all of them are empirical beings like ourselves; but we are different, we are ourselves and not them. If you mean by the total unification of *homo phenomenon* and *homo noumenon* that someone never stops to reflect upon what he has done and what he is going to do, and he nevertheless always does the right thing, I don't think this is possible, nor do I think that Benedict or Beatrice would be examples of this kind of person; for they practised both prospective and retrospective moral reflection. Or if you mean thereby, in a philosophically sloppy manner, that after labouring for a sufficiently long time on our moral nature, our judgement becomes reliable and quick, I agree. Sometimes moral judgements appear as if they were instinctual, although they result from ascesis . . .

Lawrence: First, do not compare ethics to typing . . .

Joachim: Ascesis is not like a drill. Still, there is a superficial similarity between them, namely, both are acts that became quasi-instinctual without having always been instinctual. You can have an instinct of freedom . . .

Lawrence: Funny that a Kantian mentions an instinct of freedom . . .

Joachim: Kant mentions it himself. The instinct of freedom is not merely human; animals have it too; this instinct drives them out of the zoo (if they can, they escape). But there is another kind of 'instinct for freedom' – Kant would shrink back from the expression, I suppose – an instinct that results from ascesis, that is, from the ongoing labour on our empirical nature performed by the moral law. Or, if you prefer, from an ongoing labour performed by ourselves upon ourselves, a kind of autonomous labour. Freedom is the obedience to the moral law. In a more down-to-earth formulation: you are morally free if you do the right thing for the right reason, and if doing the wrong thing you will not – for you cannot – apologize later by pointing at something that has 'determined' you to do the wrong thing. You cannot say any more that you acted wrongly because of your unfortunate childhood, because you are a neurotic, because you wanted to defend your child or your country, because you had anticipated no serious harm, etc. You would rather say that you did it because you did it, it is fully your deed, you were not compelled or determined to do it. If someone attributes her deeds fully to herself while she is doing the right things fully spontaneously and unthinkingly, then we are entitled to speak about an instinct of freedom of the second order. In this case, you may have an ethics of personality, not because the personality is the embodiment of her fate, or at least not primarily because of this, but because morality itself has become her fate . . .

Lawrence: Do you know such people? I mean people for whom morality has become their fate?

Joachim: Not personally, but I can think of such people. Weber called them 'virtuosi'. Virtuosi of morality are possible. In their acts universality becomes individual . . .

Lawrence: I see that even moral instinct is possible according to your theory. I always guessed that you were not an orthodox Kantian. But despite your concession, you could not cover the traces of your hopeless rationalism. You could not even fathom that the secondary instinct of reason would have something to do with the primary instinct of reason . . .

Joachim: You understood me well . . .

Lawrence: Here Rousseau enters behind the back of Kant. The theory of the second denaturalization . . .

Joachim: If you ask me, in this respect Rousseau's shadow was always cast on Kant. But, hopefully, you will not find Rousseau guilty of unwarranted, extreme rationalism? Or logocentrism?

Lawrence: This is a complex matter. I prefer discussing issues to discussing authors. Kant stands for a typical modern moral philosophy, at least for me. For you, he stands for the only possible modern moral philosophy. 'Who said what' is of secondary importance. After all, we do not deal in copyright issues.

Joachim: I agree.

Lawrence: What I think is that one can tone down the Rousseau-like reminiscences in Kant and thus get an improved and more attractive Kant. By the way, I have made the observation that whereas Kant sees himself as the defense lawyer of transcendental freedom and the moral law, he says very little about his clients and prefers to discuss 'nature' instead . . .

Joachim: But this is easy to understand. The community of legislators, the kingdom of ends, embraces noumena alone, but if the hope of the possibility, not of the merger of noumenon and phenomenon, but of the progressive approximation to the noumenon by the phenomenon is being discussed, then by definition 'nature' must be the centre of interest. Little can be said of the eternal, but much of the changing, the temporal and the historical . . .

Lawrence: And the latter is also far more interesting. The technique of nature, the teleology of nature, the beatiful, the sublime, history, even the law and the republic, perpetual peace and the commonwealth of nations, the lovely idea of the ethical state – these combinations, links and approaches are rich, complex, and fascinating . . .

Joachim: Now it is my turn to warn you that we discuss moral philosophy and not the Kantian œuvre. Please exercise a topical asceticism.

Lawrence: What is a side-street for you is the main avenue for me. And I wouldn't want to exercise asceticism, topic-wise or any other wise . . .

Joachim: Your Nietzsche would have no objection to asceticism . . .

Lawrence: But he is a far more easy-going philosophical master than yours. He does not interfere with my own thoughts, and even less with my way of life. Yet now you are the one who acts like a Nietzschean thinker, constantly shifting, turning, reversing the topics, the signs and everything else. Let me ask again my old question, this time directly. Pay attention, you must answer it presently. You cannot twist and turn and change the topic, no more side-stepping, please. First question: is Kant, the moral philosopher, a rationalist or is he not? Second question: if there is a place in your thinking for something that Nietzsche calls the 'lucky throw of the dice', like Benedict and Beatrice, why can't your Kantianism-of-a-kind accommodate an ethics of personality? Why don't you acknowledge at least its possibility?

Joachim: First question first: whether I would call Kant a moral rationalist depends on my concept of rationalism. He is certainly not a moral rationalist in the traditional sense. In pre-Kantian rationalism – and later, in a certain way, in Hegel once again – good action hinges on true knowledge. In cutting the umbilical cord between knowledge and morality, Kant ceased to be a rationalist in this traditional sense. Moreover, let me repeat, the moral law as the only fact of reason cannot be explained. It is in this context that I referred earlier in our conversation to Parsifal. I should have perhaps added that whereas Parsifal's famous 'I do not know' underlies his contingency, the moral law's 'I do not know' emphasizes its own necessity. For it would be easy rationally to explain the very existence of an internal moral voice in men by utilitarian, historicist and other kinds of arguments. But the necessity and the universality of the moral law is beyond all rational explanation. Transcendental deduction is, you would agree, a strong version of rational explanation. The trouble spot has not just recently been discovered. One could rather say that this is the starting-point of moral philosophy from the beginning. When Socrates argues, for example in *Gorgias* and the *Republic*, that it is better to suffer injustice than to commit injustice, he deploys all the paraphernalia of rational argument in order to prove the truth of this crucial statement – but he fails. It becomes obvious that the founding statement of moral philosophy, its *real arché*, that 'it is better to suffer than to commit injustice' cannot be proven. But if this sentence is untrue, then there is no morality. If there is morality, the sentence is true. What can you actually prove? That for a good person it is indeed better to suffer injustice than to commit injustice, and that for a bad person it is better to commit than to suffer injustice. We are left with ultimates: there are good persons and there are bad persons. But these ultimates are tautological, commonsensical, pre-philosophical; as a result, they cannot be accepted as ultimates. We must go ahead and prove that which avoids proof. So Plato went forward and began to speak about the ideas, only to arrive at the supreme idea, the idea of the Good. He invented the philosophical myth of recollection to prove his point, and in the same act he invented the language game which we have since been calling metaphysics. Through this detour he finally succeeded in connecting knowledge and morals. If you know the idea of the Good – you are good. The idea becomes the source of knowledge and of goodness. It *is*, it is the Supreme Being – and so on and so forth. Kant undermines metaphysics when he cuts the umbilical cord between morality and knowledge. He had to perform this operation because knowledge, as I said, had become de-centred and, as a result, the former pride of the moral centre – to be safely encapsulated in the metaphysical centre of Absolute Certainty – was humiliated. Kant was a modern thinker. He saw that if we continue to rely on knowledge, we shall be thrown back on the foundational statement of moral philosophy (that it is better to suffer than to commit injustice), on the *arché* which by definition cannot be proven. Kant's moral law occupies the vacated place of the idea of the Supreme Good. 'It is better to suffer injustice than to commit injustice' is true, and absolutely true, for to act in conformity with this sentence is obedience to the moral law; it is paying reverence to the law. The sentence of Socrates manifests, although in a clumsy way, precisely the universal-necessary-absolute something. If you ask the question, 'Why is that so?', 'Why is it better to commit justice than injustice?', your very question will place you outside the moral sphere. A question like this is not a moral question at all. The moral questions are, 'What should I do?', 'What is the right thing for me to do?' If you ask these questions of yourself you turn to the Moral Law by yourself in yourself, for this Law is the crutch you can and should rely upon to find the right answers to your moral questions. When

Kant says that the moral law dwells in all of us, he means that everyone carries in himself the supreme authority which he should consult. But he does not mean that we normally do consult this authority, even less that we normally – let alone always – follow this authority's advice. Let me now come back to the question of rationality. To consult the moral law in ourselves is rational since *what* we consult is rational (it is reason) and *that* we consult an authority which we should consult, is also rational. But if knowledge and morals are disconnected, why should we call the authority 'Reason'? This is a crucial point, and not only in Kant, I believe. His reason thinks, it does not know. What I mean is that Kant distinguished strongly, more strongly than anyone else, between thinking and knowing. I admit in brackets that Kant's reinterpretation of the Leibnizian distinction between truths of fact and truths of reason is somewhat shaky, and I also admit that his identification of the rationality of practical reason with the 'truth of reason', which excludes self-contradiction, makes concessions to a then still respected tradition. Moreover, I also admit that thinking is too narrowly conceived in the Kantian moral philosophy. Thinking is just an act of subsumption; to subsume a maxim under the law is determining judgement. I could, if you were patient enough to listen, make a case for a more broadly conceived Kantianism and include reflective judgement into moral thinking (*The Metaphysics of Morals*, or already *The Critique of Judgement*, offer many clues for the broadening of this concept); but since we do not discuss Kant, rather his philosophy as the only moral philosophy of modernity, I will stick to the basics. The statement that the moral law dwells in all of us is the explanation of the inexplicable, namely that we are free, that we can initiate something absolutely in the world of nature. We can do many things in and through nature, our nature and the external nature, but then we remain within the chain of causal determination. In this sense we do not introduce anything entirely new into the world. But in a moral act we do just this. And you see, Kant says that everything that is not inserted into the chain of natural causality comes from somewhere else. This 'somewhere' is not to be thought spatially – Kant is no Plato – but there must be a 'somewhere else'. To cut a long story short: goodness cannot be explained, moral freedom cannot be explained, but it can be thought. And it is thought as the universal law, the only possible competitor to the laws of nature. This is rationalism of a kind, no doubt, for it does not acknowledge a single empirical, sensual, unique, idiosyncratic, personal moral motivation as the foundation, or even as a partial source, of morality. All this boils down to a simple statement: nature cannot determine freedom. Kant would be outraged by the identification of instinct and reason, and so am I. Yet one does not need to be Kantian to see that for us moderns it is thinking, first and foremost thinking, and not impulse, that serves best as the moral guide. Although I do not particularly like Arendt's analysis of Eichmann, and I previously criticized one of her points in another context, in one respect I fully subscribe to her point: Eichmann was a man who was never thinking. A modern man must always think about that which he is doing. Before you do something, before you join an institution, a party, a movement, before you engage in a new relation, think it over first, think over what you are doing, what it means morally. One cannot stop pondering the moral meaning of one's actions. I sail here on non-Kantian waters, but I am certain that we are in need of a kind of moral hermeneutics. Thinking about what we are doing is not just an act of subsumption; it is also an act of interpretation. I notice that I have gone too far . . . I am sorry. Just let me make one thing clear: the interpretive work should not trespass over a limit. This limit is still demarcated by the rightness of our maxims, particularly by heeding the Kantian formula of non-instrumentalization. It is from the standpoint of the moral law that we engage in the labour of ethical hermeneutics . . .

Lawrence: My dear Joachim, would you be so kind as to turn finally to the second question . . .

Joachim: There is still so much to be said about the first. But I see it is late and you might be getting hungry. We should be home by now.

Lawrence: Never mind, we can order a meal here. I am too fascinated by your speech to interrupt our conversation. Go on, please.

Joachim: Now I have forgotten what else I wanted to say. So let us go straight away to the second question. Yes, I am inclined to believe that there is such a thing as the lucky throw of the dice. You are one of them, Lawrence. Or rather, you are like a plant: everything that you do somehow grows organically from within you; you keep growing, you keep stretching out your branches beautifully, your tree will bear fruits. And you are also a decent, honest person, an upright man. You do whatever you do rightly and still without effort, at least without the overt signs of effort. You have no bad instincts; this is why you believe in the unity of instinct and reason. You perhaps have no need to consult the moral law. Yes, there are a few lucky ones who obey the moral law without ever have passed a conscious moral judgement, who never use others as mere means, because they are just this kind of person. But one cannot shape an ethics after the model of the lucky throw of the dice, for they are few. I have told you this so many times already that you must be getting bored. Besides there is another point. There are so many different kinds of the so-called lucky throws of the dice, and not all of them are also morally 'lucky throws'. There exists the lucky throw of evil. A lucky throw of the dice becomes what it already is – and only few of them become good, only those who are already good. Even if I accepted that being a lucky throw of the dice is ethically relevant (provided that the lucky throw is also a moral person) because his morality does not smell of sweat, I could still not subscribe to an ethics of personality in general. It is too broad a concept, which also embraces people from whom heaven should save us.

Lawrence: You are like your own philosophy – I love you but I do not love your philosophy. I wonder . . .

Joachim: This is also how I feel and how I think. I love you as you are, but I am convinced that your philosophy is false. But this is, so to speak, natural in my case. I have properly distinguished between reason (thinking) and instinct (feelings). But you have not. How can you dislike something, the very personal embodiment of which you love? Can't you distinguish between reason and instinct in your *judgements* at least?

Lawrence: Since I believe in indirect communication, I shy away from the direct kind. I do not like speaking about myself in an expressive manner, but rather from behind a mask. Why do you think that I am identical with my mask? Why not just let me take up this mask?

Joachim: Don't frighten me, please . . .

Lawrence: Why not? Alas, in the life of a repository of an ethics of personality, his judgements likewise reveal his fate – when he loves someone, he loves his fate, when he dislikes a philosophy, he loves his fate also. I do not think about loving you – there is no thinking about such things. But I certainly think about my dislike of Kant's moral philosophy; I am a philosopher (perhaps), and philosophy is the language game of our thinking. My dislike itself, however, does not originate in my thinking but in my instincts, and I am aware that all my arguments against your Kantianism are nothing but rationalizations of my aversions.

Joachim: Do you have an aversion against a steak?

Lawrence: Not the slightest. A good steak is welcomed by my fate . . .

(Change of scene. Lawrence and Joachim are consuming their dinner. As they eating, a young girl dressed entirely in black approaches their table.)

Vera: Joachim? Lawrence?

Joachim: Do we know each other?

Lawrence: How do you know us? How do you know our names? I don't recall ever having met you.

Vera: We did meet but you won't be able to remember.

Lawrence: Since you addressed us by our first names, you could be an acquaintance from our common dreams. Sit down and join us, let our dreams continue . . .

Joachim: Is one of your near relatives recently deceased? For whose memory are you dressed in mourning?

Vera: For yours.

Joachim: Pardon me?

Vera: Until I noticed you here about an hour ago, I believed both of you to be dead.

Joachim: When were we supposed to have died, if I may ask?

Vera: You, Joachim, a little over twenty years ago, at a very great age; you, Lawrence, you died young, in 1911.

Joachim: Are you mad or just playing theatre?

Lawrence: O no, just listen! She knew our names, didn't she? Tell me, how old was I when I died?

Vera: Twenty-three.

Lawrence: This is my age, I mean my age now. What a fate, what an *amor fati*! The eternal recurrence of the same . . .

Joachim: I'm afraid that you have read too many Mishima novels about the three reincarnations of Kiyoaki . . .

Lawrence: You don't understand. A young lady who mourns for the still living is called wisdom and we are supposed to love her. What is your name?

Vera: I am called Vera.

Joachim: At least she knows her name. She is not a fool like your Parsifal . . .

Lawrence: Or your moral law . . .

Vera: It is now you who play the fools. I apologize, but I listened in on your conversation. I was not eavesdropping, there was no need for it. You were so much engaged in your dialogue that you did not noticed how loudly you spoke. Do you see all the empty tables around you?

Joachim: Your eavesdropping explains how you got to know our names. We addressed one another by name . . .

Vera: When I met you for the first time, you were already – or still – young, noble and enthusiastic. And of course you discussed matters of the highest interest. At that time, in 1908, you were deeply engaged in a discussion about Goethe and Sterne: Johann – or Joachim – Goethe and Lawrence Sterne. The dialogue was committed to paper by the then still young Gyorgy Lukács, and it was dedicated to his friend, Leo Popper. What a complex series of reincarnations: Joachim Goethe, Gyorgy Lukács, Joachim by Gyorgy Lukács, Joachim of New York – Lawrence Sterne, Leo Popper, Lawrence and Leo by Gyorgy Lukács, Lawrence of New York.

Lawrence: Please, tell me something about the centennarian Joachim and Lawrence: What did they say? Were they interesting, attractive and deep? Did they love you? Did you love them?

Vera: Read the dialogue and you will know what they said. Whether they were interesting or attractive – you decide. They wanted to please me but they did not love me. They were interested in one another and not in me. I just listened. I do not love people to whom I do not speak.

Lawrence: Why then are you in mourning?

Vera: Because I could have loved them. They were my possibilities.

Lawrence: Are we your possibilities?

Vera: I doubt it.

Lawrence: Why?

Vera: Because you are not patient enough.
Lawrence: Why have you, then, accosted us at our table?
Vera: I wanted to listen.
Lawrence: What did you want to hear?
Vera: I wanted to hear something about the occasion.
Lawrence: The occasion of what?
Vera: Of your discussion.
Lawrence: This is a very humble request. Joachim and I, we have been attending a course on Nietzsche and *Parsifal*. We were fascinated by the topic and we enjoyed the elaboration. Still, something was missing. More precisely the 'point' was missing. Many questions were left open, presumably quite deliberately. Today, after the last class, we felt the urge to go after those open issues; they were like open wounds, we had to close them . . .
Vera: Did you close them?
Lawrence: No, not at all. Or rather, we have come to the conclusion that since Lawrence is Lawrence and Joachim is Joachim, our wounds are different, and so is the *pharmakon* or the magic sword that might close them . . .
Joachim: Excuse me, this was perhaps your conclusion, but it was certainly not mine. Besides, you explain our controversy in leaps and bounds – no one would understand a word of it. Let me do the explanation. First, forget about *Parsifal*. That was a side-track. The main issue was the following: Nietzsche, so our professor contended, elaborated an ethics of personality. This ethics can be described by the following constituents: we follow the guidance of our own reason-instinct, we love our fate, we let ourselves be carried away towards our own fulfilment and without letting ourselves be determined by our past. If we were to choose, we would live the same life over and over again – because for us there is no alternative. The main virtues of an ethics of personality are authenticity, sincerity, truthfulness, nobility, pride, all the paraphernalia of an intellectual and emotional aristocracy. We acquire the capacity to make promises, we take responsibility. But no norm, no commandment that comes from the 'outside' or from 'above', can or should be obeyed. An authentic person is never reactive, but always active. Our professor further distinguished between different conceptions of an ethics of personality. One of them is an aesthetic conception, the other is a merely formal conception, and there are still some others. She said that if we find one substantive value or virtue – like the virtue of compassion, or the Kantian non-instrumentalization formula of the categorical imperative – as the substantive determination of the mere formal conception, an ethics of personality might be viable as a kind of moral philosophy. But this last issue remained obscure. This is why we got entangled in our discussion. Is an ethics of personality possible or not? I said no, Lawrence said yes. This is all. Instead of a formal introduction

I might have added that, in rough outlines, I am a Kantian and Lawrence is rather a Nietzschean . . .

Lawrence: There are Kantians, but no Nietzscheans. I am just myself and I am also a person who likes Nietzsche.

Vera: Tell me, Lawrence, is Joachim a decent, upright person?

Lawrence: He is absolutely righteous.

Vera: And you, Joachim, tell me, is Lawrence morally reliable?

Joachim: You must have overheard what I just told him: he is the most honest, decent person I have ever met.

Vera: You Joachim, are fully committed to the Kantian moral philosophy, whereas Lawrence sympathizes with Nietzsche's ethics of personality. Yet both of you are good.

Joachim: I protest, I am not good, I have so many bad instincts . . .

Lawrence: I protest, I am not good, I merely follow my destiny . . .

Vera: Good is the person who is good in the judgement of the others. In the judgement of the friend, the lover, the debtor, and the creditor, and also in the eye of the beholder. No one is the judge of her own goodness.

Joachim: But I know myself better than the others do . . .

Vera: First, no one is entirely transparent to himself . . .

Joachim: True enough . . . but even less is he transparent to the other.

Lawrence: Whether less or more, this is an open question, but I agree.

Vera: But does it matter? I mean, does it matter ethically?

Lawrence: Excuse me?

Joachim: Excuse me?

Vera: If you do the right thing, if you are an honest man, is it important for the other to find out why this is so, why you aren't rather wicked?

Joachim: Excuse me, this is a naïve question. We are philosophers; it is our passion as well as our interest to ascend to the ultimate reason of things. You can say that Lawrence is decent and Joachim is decent, we care only for their decency and not for their ideas. But we live in those ideas and also for them . . .

Vera: I understand that you live in your ideas. But, excuse me, your decency has little to do with those ideas. I know a few decent persons, among them Voltaireans, devout Catholics, Hassidic Jews, whereas many other Voltaireans, devout Catholics and Hassidic Jews are quite indecent. As also many Kantians and Nietzscheans are indecent or even wicked . . .

Joachim: This was also my point against Lawrence. There is no direct connection between a philosopher's personality and his work.

Lawrence: Yes, there is.

Vera: Let me then formulate naïvely: in certain cases there is, in certain other cases there is none. At any rate, to employ Joachim's lingo: there is no necessity in the connection.

Joachim: This is beside the point. Moral philosophy does not make people honest, but rather tells us why and how they are wicked or honest.

Vera: Sorry, I am not a philosopher. But I listened to your conversation attentively. You, Joachim, said that the question 'How is transcendental freedom possible?' cannot be answered, that the moral law is the fact of reason. It was you and not I who have quoted Parsifal's famous words about his unknown origins. The moral law is simply there. The question of why we act accordingly or why we do not is not answered by your Kant, for to insist that it is self-love that carries us away is a poor answer. It is because we could ask, we do ask further: Why does self-love carry us away? And your Kant is too sincere a thinker not to have understood that he had arrived at point zero. Although I am not a philosopher, I am a reader of books on philosophy. One brief footnote in *The Metaphysics of Morals* particularily caught my attention. Here Kant asks the same question that I have right now naïvely asked: Why do we follow our self-interest against the call of obligation? And he says outright that he has no answer to the question. Nature is mysterious; why we do not do what we should do is, after all, not explicable. This can never be explained, do you understand? Neither the fact that we follow nor the fact that we do not follow the command of the categorical imperative can ever be explained; moreover, the categorical imperative itself cannot be explained . . .

Joachim: That I concede. But let me repeat: moral philosophy does not make you good. It describes why and how pople can become good . . .

Vera: It describes? You mean that moral philosophy knows why and how people become good rather than wicked? Yes, I know that philosophy is in your mind a system of rational knowledge, Kant's *Vernunfterkenntnis* in concepts. It is *Vernunfterkenntnis*, all right. It is a kind of knowledge that knows that morality itself is not based on knowledge, but on thinking and on obedience to the law. There is a tension in 'practical philosophy', for philosophy is eminently impractical . . . .

Joachim: It is my turn to wonder what are you up to . . .

Vera: I am the one who wonders. I am in wonderment about a philosophy that, *qua Vernunfterkenntnis* proper, declares the only truth about morality, but says in the same breath that it cannot explain why Joachim or Lawrence become good rather than bad. Moreover, it cannot explain the sources of morality, nor can it explain why anyone listens to self-love rather than the voice of conscience. It is a poor truth.

Joachim: You overstretch yourself. You began to listen in on our conversation on Kant. But you have missed an elementary point: Kant invented only a formula, he drew his ethics from the practice of everyday life . . .

Vera: So he drew his idea of good persons from the good persons themselves. This is straightforward. But we have just agreed that one of such good persons is a Hassidic Jew, the other a Nietzschean, the third a Voltairean, the fourth a devout Catholic – each of them draws strength for their respective goodness from another well, and each believes that their respective well is the only source of goodness. What makes you so sure that only the Kantian formula makes sense of the goodness of all these good people? For if a philosophy resigns from explaining the sources of morality and fails to give an answer to the question of 'why', why is someone good rather than bad, when it admits that the Socratic claim cannot be proven true or false, why doesn't it draw the conclusion than the goodness of the good ones can be described in-and-through different formulae, or that perhaps one does not need any formula to account for it. One can simply point at the decent persons: here you are . . .

Lawrence: This is what I have always said . . .

Vera: Allow for an attentive listener to express her doubts. You said, just as Joachim did, that you have no knowledge of the source of ethics. The 'lucky throw of the dice' means 'I don't know'. And just as Joachim – who did not answer the question concerning the source of morals – was confident about knowing the grounding, the determination of the morality of each and all, so you too were confident that you knew the telos of the ethical life in general: *amor fati*. I am not a very logical person and I have no strong objections to logical circularity, nor do I stick to identity logics beyond reason. But let me modestly point out your poor logic.

Joachim: There are people of good will – it is from the very existence of good will that we become aware of the moral law – but it is the moral law that determines the goodness of the man of good will.

Lawrence: There are people who love their fate, who become what they are – their own destiny; they are the lucky throws of the dice; the lucky throws of the dice are people who love their fate and fulfill their destiny.

Vera: Joachim has his strong point: universality. Lawrence also has his strong point: singularity. Joachim has a strong point: necessity. Lawrence also has a strong point: contingency.

Joachim: I do not mean to be rude, but it is obvious that you are not a philosopher. How can you consider both necessity and contingency, both universality and singularity assets in the description of the goodness of the good person. Or are you a secret disciple of Hegel?

Vera: I am not, although I have no objections to a kind of dialectics. But let me, the layperson, beware of philosophy: *cave canem*. When speaking about ethics, one can claim knowledge concerning the preference of the universal over the singular, or vice versa, only if one has knowledge about the source of morality. But both of you are modern philosophers; neither of you claims knowledge of the source; neither of you insists that he can answer the question of why it is better to suffer injustice than to commit injustice; both of you admit, although not in so many words, that the source of morals is above your, or above our heads, that it is transcendent, metaphysical. It depends on your philosophy or religious creed what expressions you would prefer to use to describe your shared conviction about your shared impotence. But if this is so, we all fall back on the only experience we can: there are good persons – period. A Kantian would refuse to speak about experience in this case, but I allow myself, a non-philosopher, to be eclectic with this issue too. I prefer Hegel's concept of experience, and if one takes his concept seriously, then we do have experience about the existence of good people. And who a good person is, we have already described. Good is a person who is perceived to be good by her friends, lovers, debtors, and creditors (of course in a metaphorical sense) and who is also decent in the eye of the beholder: the impartial judge, the voyeur, the reader of novels, etc. So we do not need to define or to determine the single constituents of good people. If we know many of them, we also know how different they are. One is like Lawrence, the other like Joachim; one has great talents, the other has none. Everyone is good in *his or her own way*, idiosyncratically – this will please Lawrence; and *everyone* can be *good* in his or her own way – this will please Joachim. Now you can see why I love Joachim's universalism and Lawrence's individualism, and both alike. As once Sören remarked, there is no such thing as 'the duty'; you do your duty, I do mine.

Lawrence: I see, I see. You are very shrewd. You knock out our heroes only to put your own hero in their place.

Vera: Sören was not a philosopher, but an existing thinker. So are we all. Sören invites us to become the existing thinkers that we already are. I do not put him in the place of anyone; his place is among us.

Lawrence: God, you are a little hypocrite! I have rarely come across as sophisticated and complicated a philosopher as Kierkegaard! It gives me far more pain to understand him than to understand Kant. If I understand one Kantian sentence I will surely understand the next one. Not so with Kierkegaard.

Joachim: And with Nietzsche?

Lawrence: Well . . . let's let sleeping dogs lie. But at least I always know what Nietzsche is up to.

Vera: I do not need to know what Sören is up to. He sets me free. He wants me to do my own thinking, to arrive at my own conclusions, to live my own life . . .

Lawrence: Absolutely   wrong . . . He   always   addresses   someone, preaches and teaches . . .

Vera: Not he, it is the pseudonyms that preach. And they address quite different persons and, in so far as they preach, they preach different things. Sören speaks only in his edifying discourses: they are religious discourses, they do not address the ethical sphere or stage. But you must be familiar with all this, I heard you making mention earlier of indirect communication.

Lawrence: Excuse me, why do you speak about Kierkegaard as 'Sören', whereas you never mention Kant as 'Immanuel' or Nietzsche as 'Friedrich?' Did you know Kierkegaard personally?

Vera: I knew all of them personally. But Sören is my friend. I call my friends by their first names.
Lawrence: That's flattering for us.
Vera: Please, don't misunderstand me. I call you by your first name because I do not know your last names.
Lawrence: Neither do we.
Vera: Sören does not make me say anything, but he lets me say what I am about to say: Lawrence and Joachim, you are both decent persons. The source of your decency is entirely the same, albeit entirely different. Both universal and idiosyncratic.
Lawrence: You remind me of the Sphinx; you speak in riddles.
Vera: It is easy for a lonely wayfarer to solve them. Lonely wayfarers are particularly good at solving the easiest riddles . . .
Lawrence: I still humbly ask our dear Sphinx to unveil her secret herself.
Vera: Irony suits you well. Lawrence and Joachim are both decent persons; I assume that they have both chosen themselves existentially as decent persons. They become what they already are: decent persons. The choice of goodness represents the element of universality; but Lawrence chose Lawrence and Joachim chose Joachim; this represents the element of uniqueness or singularity. Once you choose yourself as a good (decent) person existentially, you choose under the category of universality, for you choose something everyone else can also choose – but you choose no one but yourself. Since you choose yourself and no one but yourself, you do not choose goodness but you choose yourself as a good person and thus become what you are; this is an ethics of personality. It is an ethics of personlity which includes universality. For, let me quote Sören again: in the sphere of morals the individual is the universal. Lawrence, Joachim: assume that both of you have chosen yourselves as decent persons and you have begun to become what you are. In the process of becoming what you are you sometimes seek a crutch; a crutch you can rely upon to help you to become decent – and not help you to be decent, for you are already decent. Without having been decent first, without the resolve to become what you are, you would not seek a crutch, for you would not need it. Precisely as you begin to become what you are, you will ask yourself the question: what is the right thing for me to do, here, now, in this conflict, in this context, in this situation? Many a moral philosophy, religious and secular, can serve you as a crutch.
Joachim: It is here that Kant enters the picture . . .
Vera: Further, to choose yourself as a decent person does not require much thinking, sometimes it does not require thinking at all; whether this choice is rational or instinctive cannot be answered. One might say either that it is both, or that it does not matter, or that the question is irrelevant. But you do engage (for you need to engage) in a process of serious and conscientious thinking whenever you seek advice: how to become, here,

in this context, good (that which I already am)? Kant's formulae of the categorical imperative, as Joachim so beatifully put it, are crutches which may be of help in such times. One person may need them, the other person may not. But whether or not you need them, the crutches do not make you good if you are not already good; and no *amor fati* will be of the ethical kind unless becoming good is the fate of the men and women in question, the fate they love. Everything depends on the existential choice. You spoke rightly when you said that the sentence 'it is better to suffer injustice than to commit injustice' is true for the just and untrue for the unjust. It is a creed. No creed will turn the unjust into the just. But the just person, who knows that this sentence is true, who is committed to the truth of this claim, whose creed it is, will certainly ask questions such as: why is this or that called just, how can one act justly or more justly, how can one avoid causing another person avoidable sufferings, and so on. Kant's opening gambit in the *Groundwork* is beautiful: good will is like a jewel, it shines. This good will is the ultimate, there is no other ultimate beside or beyond it. Choose yourself as a good person choose yourself as a person for whom the Socratic claim is true.

Lawrence: I understand what an existential choice is, and how it differs from all other types of choices. I heard much about it in our university lectures. In choosing yourself you choose your destiny and you follow your destiny. But how do you know that people have ever actually made such a choice?

Vera: I could answer that many men and women are aware of having made such a choice. I could refer to recollections of childhood experiences, I could also refer to spiritual events that Christian religions associate with rebirth. But I forgo such clinging to examples; Kant would have done better too, had he resisted the temptation to show with unconvincing examples that we are all aware of the moral law in us. I would rather say that we know about the existential choice of goodness from its manifestations. *There are* good people: this is the proof that they have chosen themselves existentially as good persons. We do not need other proofs. You see, I say the same thing that you two were saying, but I say it differently.

Joachim: I don't get your point.

Vera: It is easy. How do you know about the categorical imperative, Joachim? From its manifestations. How do you know about the lucky throw of the dice, Lawrence? Though its manifestations. How do we know about the existential choice? Through its manifestations. When you, Joachim, see a good person in action, you say to yourself: she acts dutifully, and continuously so, without hope of profit; so I guess that, at least sometimes, she also acts out of duty. If you, Lawrence, see a good person you say: this is her fate, she loves it. If I see a good person at work, I say: she has chosen herself existentially as a good person.

Joachim: This is just another way of saying: she is a good person. Philosophically, this business of the existential choice is meaningless.

Vera: You said yourself: moral philosophy is the explication, the exhibition, or the interpretation of goodness. Goodness must be there for philosophy to interpret it. Soren, my friend, has interpreted it otherwise than either of you. The business of the existential choice is a philosophical business.

Lawrence: Wait a minute! You said just five minutes ago that Kierkegaard was not a philosopher. Still, I find your suggestion interesting; there is wisdom in it . . . Instead of saying: decency manifests the work of the moral law in us, you say: decency is the manifestation of the existential choice. We all agree that the source of morality is transcendent, metaphysical, or something similar. That means that the source of goodness is beyond knowledge, beyond explanation, that we cannot derive it or transcendentally deduce it. We just accept it as a fact. Since the origin of goodness is unknown, we point at it; this is a gesture. At the beginning, there is a gesture. But what are we pointing at with this gesture? You can point at a law of freedom (the moral law), you can point at the contingent result of the whim of nature (the lucky throw of the dice), and you can also point at just another gesture – for the existential choice is but a gesture. You think of a gesture as a 'pointing at'. You identify 'pointing at' itself with what has been pointed at. This is philosophically interesting.

Vera: I like watching how you compose variations on a simple theme . . .

Joachim: Lawrence is an enthusiast, he becomes easily enflamed. But let me ask you to describe the existential choice. For even hypothetical starting-points must be described . . .

Lawrence: It was described by Kierkegaard succinctly. Choosing yourself as a good person is tantamount to choosing yourself as a person who makes choices, who – above all – chooses between good and evil. To choose yourself as a good person is to choose yourself as a person who gives priority to the moral distinction between good and evil over all other distinctions. Let me remind you, Joachim, that when you defended Kant as the person who maintained and protected the moral centre, you also argued that without relating ourselves to a moral centre we cannot make the moral distinction. Finally, the Kierkegaardian description of the existential choice is also a way of preserving the moral centre while cutting the umbilical cord between knowing and goodness; the new-born is autonomous morality, isn't that so?

Joachim: But Kierkegaard's centre is a lousy centre. If the categorical imperative is the centre, I know exactly what I should approximate, for I am presented with a fixed and eternal centre: the moral law. But if I say that I choose myself as a good person, I do not really have a centre, let along a fixed or an eternal one. Since I do not know what goodness is all about, how can I become what I am?

Lawrence: But don't you see, this is exactly the point; this is how the umbilical cord is really cut. This is how you avoid the moral law in you, reason, this universal ghost, being autonomous 'in' you, over you and against you. Instead, you as a whole human person will become the repository of moral autonomy. You choose yourself as you are, *you* become good as you are. You choose your own crutches, the crutches that fit you better custom-made crutches that enable you to become what you are. The existential choice is a leap, and the term 'leap' stands for the same unknown as transcendental freedom, for no determination 'by nature' can be found to explain it. But the leap is the leap of the person, of a person who is not split into noumenon and phenomenon, who is a single exister and who becomes good as a single exister, as an ipseity.

Joachim: And what about our dangerous instincts, our self-love? We cannot become good without suppressing them . . .

Lawrence: But don't you understand, the existential choice means that we choose ourselves fully, and we choose ourselves fully as good. When I choose myself, I choose my instincts, the good and the dangerous ones alike, my self-love, my infirmities, and also my environment, my parents, my country, my age, to sum up: all my determinations, and I say: 'Here I am, this is what I am as I am; and I am a good person and I become what I am.' Previously, you too envisaged something similar, don't you remember? You spoke about the 'virtuosi' of morality.

Joachim: There are superficial similarities, but my virtuosi do not choose their infirmities, they do not choose themselves at all. What does it mean to choose our infirmities, anyway? Do you mean that the sadist chooses himself as a sadist?

Lawrence: Yes, also as a sadist. He will say: I have sadistic inclinations, I choose them too when I choose myself as a good person – and I become good as I am.

Joachim: But a sadist cannot become good without compelling himself, without putting pressure on himself.

Lawrence: Indeed, but since he is good, he will seek advice on how to become good, even though he is a sadist . . . He will not practice sadism of course . . .

Joachim: I am sorry, but if there is hyperrationalism, then this is it. How could Kierkegaard believe in this nonsense?

Lawrence: Just as you believe in it. You say: what we ought to do we can do. He says: what we ought to choose we can choose. Kierkegaard never says that he who chooses herself as a decent person existentially will always act rightly and choose the good . . . Only the ones who make the distinction between good and evil can also do evil.

Joachim: How can a good person do evil things?

Lawrence: Ask your Kant first!

Joachim: Oh, my God, how Lutheran all these philosophers are!

Lawrence: But we speak here about common wisdom. And also about approximation, your favourite topic, Joachim. No one ever hits the centre fully – but this is not the point. The point is approximation. It is secondary to find out what we approximate, the primary thing is the resolve to approximate.

Joachim: Listen, Vera! You've got a disciple . . .

Vera: I am not a philosopher, I don't need disciples.

Lawrence: What you must understand is that the existential choice of ourselves as decent persons is philosophically equivalent to transcendental freedom. If a person who has chosen herself existentially does something that is considered by others (or herself) as unrighteous or wrong, she cannot say: I did this because of my bad temper, because of my misfortune, because I was born with this and this nature, because I was educated in this and this environment. By choosing herself she has chosen all of those things, so they do not determine her – nothing that you have chosen by choosing yourself determines you, for freedom (your choice) alone determines you. It is thus that you take responsibility for everything that you do. And Kierkegaard does not ponder whether you have to take into account foreseeable consequences of your action, nor how far you need to mobilize your knowledge, nor whether you act out of empathy, love, instinct or on the grounds of purely rational reflection – for all these are of secondary relevance. The issue is: you take responsibility, your acts are your acts, and since you have chosen yourself as good, they should be good acts, because it is through good acts that you fulfil your destiny, that you become what you are – and fully so. This is why the ethics of existence is an ethics of personality, an ethics of the love of fate, of self-fulfilment. I love it. I love Kierkegaard.

Vera: It was not Kierkegaard but Judge William who made a case for the existential choice as just described by you, with some modifications by you. Judge William is one of Kierkegaard's masks. He is not a philosopher, he is a decent person who advises a young man to despair. For, in Judge William's mind despair can be the occasion (never the cause, of course) for lifting ourselves from the aesthetic to the ethical sphere, to the sphere of the authentic either/or.

Joachim: Are you in despair, Lawrence?

Vera: That was the wrong question. Lawrence is a decent person. In Judge William's mind he, in all probability, has already made his existential choice of goodness. He will not despair. But he could still end up in the state of resignation; other personae of Kierkegaard, such as the Pastor from Jutland, Silentio, Climacus and Taciturnus detect the condition for the leap into the religious stage in resignation. That is how you become a disciple . . .

Joachim: Quite an exercise in spiritual acrobatics. One leap just finished, and you leap once more . . .

Lawrence: Stop! This I don't understand. If I choose myself existentially as a decent person, I become what I am. How can I leap once more? Are many subsequent leaps or existential choices possible?

Vera: Sören could not answer you. You see, this is why he is no philosopher; it is not he who is speaking. He does not attribute to himself such authority. One of his characters advises one kind of a leap (into the ethical), another of his personae makes a case for another leap (the ethico-religious), a third pseudonym again speaks of the leap into the religious with the suspension of the ethical. All those characters are thinking, reflecting; we, as single existing thinkers, are also thinking, reflecting – alongside them, against them, in dialogue with them. One pseudonym appeals to one existing thinker more than another, and vice versa. You choose your sphere just as you choose your crutch.

Lawrence: The religous stage is quite an odd conception in a world where God is dead.

Vera: Why do you become captive to a slogan? 'The death of God' is a slogan.

Lawrence: But excuse me, our whole discussion would become meaningless without taking this slogan seriously. It is because of the death of God that the umbilical cord, as Joachim said and you repeated, between knowledge and morals must be cut . . .

Vera: You know that I am a good listener. There was no need for God in Aristotle's *Nicomachean Ethics* either; there is little metaphysics left in his ethics.

Joachim: Good point for a non-philosopher. But Aristotle philosophized in a closed world of *Sittlichkeit* – the ethical world.

Vera: Good point for a philosopher. The slogan 'The death of God' does not stand for the death of God, but for the death of the closed world of *Sittlichkeit*.

Lawrence: But in a Christian tradition the two amount to the same. God was the source of the Christian – and also of the Jewish – *Sittlichkeit*. When the closed, homogenous world of *Sittlichkeit* dies, God also dies.

Vera: But then does God die only as the source of the homogeneous, unique, single *Sittlichkeit*?

Joachim: One may say so. He may live in some sense but He becomes morally irrelevant. This is why the moral law has to replace God. But, of course, the decomposition of *Sittlichkeit* is just one reason to speak of the death of God; the second is the dominating role of the modern kind of knowledge; scientific knowledge, the third is the end of metaphysics . . .

Lawrence: Please, stick to the topic. It is enough to say that morally, God has become irrelevant.

Joachim: All right, I will say just this.

Lawrence: But then you may be wrong. For if we choose ourselves as decent persons and become what we are, and we can also choose which crutch to rely or not to rely upon, is it not allowed, is it not still possible to choose the old God as a crutch?

Joachim: Logically, it is possible. But then God is a crutch for one person, yet not for the other. But a God who lives for some and not for the others is a dead God, isn't He?

Lawrence: I don't think so. For if you tell me that the categorical imperative is an absolute, why can't you accept God as an absolute? Although I am well off without your categorical imperative, you still refer to it as to your absolute, and I accept your philosophy as your personal creed.

Joachim: You relativize truth.

Lawrence: By no means. I just told you what Kierkegaard used to say: truth is subjective.

Joachim: Whatever is subjective is also relative. Only the objective can be universal. The subject–object identity . . .

Lawrence: I believed that we already settled this controversial issue at the beginning of our conversation. But now it seems as if this settled issue has returned with a vengeance. Perspectivism is not subjectivism. The sentence 'truth is subjective' does not even presuppose an entity called 'subject'. Actually, Kierkegaard does not speak about subjects at all; he is anti-Cartesian. It is not the subject but the exister who experiences, chooses, believes and thinks. Truth *is* subjective, for my truth is my truth and your truth is yours.

Joachim: If this is not subjectivism, I don't know what it is.

Lawrence: Again, we have settled this issue already. 'Subjective' dooes not mean that 'anything goes', but that by reflection I approximate the answer to a question about right or truth, and then I leap: I passionately embrace it by faith: It is mine – my truth. The embrace is total. But the embrace is preceded by the labour of approximation. Without the labour of approximation, an exister cannot embrace anything as his truth, for it will always remain something received, a token 'truth' coined by others, that he could never call 'mine'.

Joachim: You now speak the language of love: 'I embrace it', 'it is mine'. I never understood you to be in love with truth. This is quite unlike Nietzsche, don't you see?

Lawrence: Please, don't watch over my orthodoxy. Kierkegaard says: when I say 'mine', I do not mean something that belongs to me, but something to which I belong. When I say 'I embrace it', truth does not belong to me – I rather belong to her.

Joachim: You said 'to her'. I never thought of truth as a woman . . .

Lawrence: This is just a gender issue, it is a matter of language, it is inessential. But let me return to the issue. If you do not do your best to approximate, you will never be embraced by your truth; and if you never leap, if you do not embrace her and do not make her yours, then and only then will you become a relativist. For what can only be approximated always remains questionable. Scepticism leads to relativism . . .

Joachim: Your sudden disappointment with scepticism astonishes me. Just yesterday you were a great friend of Voltaire, weren't you?

Lawrence: Voltaire wouldn't have strongly opposed what I am going to say: God can also be a person's truth, just as the categorical imperative or the love of fate can. In this sense, God is not dead . . .

Joachim: We are getting sidetracked again. Vera does not interfere, she is just listening, and this is a bad sign . . .

Vera: It is just a sign of fatigue.

Lawrence: But we have got somewhere, haven't we?

Joachim: Where, if I may ask?

Lawrence: To the end station. We decided to discuss the matter of whether an ethics of personality is possible. We have weighed all the pros and cons, and this has taken a long time. Then Vera interfered, uninvited, and we began to rush fast towards the terminus. She suggested that all decent people of modernity choose themselves existentially as decent people: they become what they are. The practical ethics of modern men and women is nothing else but an ethics of personality. Modern decent persons are all practising ethicists of personality. What kind of theoretical framework we choose in order to make sense of this ethics speculatively is philosophy's business. Philosophy does offer speculative interpretations for an ethics of personality, but these interpretations do not need to be moral philosophies of personality. Isn't that so?

Vera: Approximately.

Lawrence: And now I embrace this approximation and I hold to it fast with maximum passion: it is my truth.

Joachim: I am afraid that you are guilty of spiritual promiscuity. For the kind of ethics of personality that you now embrace is not the same kind of ethics of personality you embraced at the beginning of our discussion. And if your truth is not the truth that belongs to you but the truth to whom you belong, you must figure out first to whom you verily belong. For the exister who has chosen himself existentially as a decent person is not the lucky throw of the dice. Or at least he can be this as well as not. Isn't this so, Vera?

Vera: Yes, it is.

Joachim: My dear friend, have you already forgotten the lucky throw of the dice and his love of fate – where fate can be everything and not just the humble destiny to become an ethical person? What about your passionate defence of the gift of nature or grace? What about sincerity and authenticity as the main, or rather sole, virtues of a man? Become yourself, be true to yourself – yes. But what has all of this to do with the choice between good and evil? Or, to follow my old Kantian habits, is there a necessary connection between choosing myself and making the distinction between good and evil? Or is this connection just contingent? And if it is, then your triumphal tone was premature. Because then I will return to my conviction and hold fast to it: it is contingent that you are a person who has – presumably – chosen yourself ethically. Others choose themselves in very different ways and they will not make the moral distinction because they will not be decent persons. Perhaps there is such a thing as the morally lucky throw of the dice – these are the ones who choose themselves as good persons. They are the exception, not the rule. For even if I agree with you that we all know a few good persons in our would (even now), I would exaggerate if I said that I know many.

Lawrence: Excuse me, I cannot follow you. It is getting very late and I am exhausted.

Joachim: But we cannot finish our discussion in complete disagreement . . .

Vera: Why not? This is the best way to finish a discussion. But you will never finish. As long as you live you will go on.

Lawrence: What Joachim really meant was that we have got used to you, that we will miss you, that we could not possibly continue the discussion in your absence . . .

Vera: If you will really miss me, I shall be with you.

Lawrence: Wonderful! Tomorrow, in our apartment. Here is the address.

Vera: At noon?

Lawrence: Gosh, no! At five in the afternoon.

Vera: I will be there.

Is There an Ethics of Personality?

Dialogue Two: If There Is, How Can We Describe It?

(The living room belonging to Lawrence and Joachim. Shortly before five in the afternoon.)

Lawrence: Should I make coffee or tea?
Joachim: Wait till she arrives. Ask her, not me.
Lawrence: What about some cake?
Joachim: She does not look like someone who would be on a diet.
Lawrence: You are awful. Don't you like her?
Joachim: There is nothing to like about her. I don't know her. How can I know whether she is likeable or not?
Lawrence: But it was you, and not I, who wanted her to come . . .
Joachim: Memory cheats you. It was you who invited her.
Lawrence: But I fulfilled your silent wish.
Joachim: Do you know what I now wish?
Lawrence: Yes. Inspiration.
Joachim: I wish I knew why I wanted to continue our discussion. Yesterday I felt that there was something important that we must think about, but now my mind is blank. I have no idea of what I am going to ask, or even if I need to ask anything.
Lawrence: We do not need to be clever. Let's just make small talk.
Joachim: With Vera? Out of the question. We must have a fresh idea. Or rather, you must have a fresh idea. The ethics of personality is, after all, your pet. As far as I am concerned, I have exhausted the topic.

(The bell rings. Lawrence opens the door. Vera enters.)

Vera: Here I am, as I promised.
Lawrence: Would you like to drink tea or would you rather have coffee?
Vera: Tea and some madeleines, please.

Lawrence: To recollect the ideas?

Vera: To replay how to become ourselves.

Lawrence: To paint grey in grey, then?

Vera: Des Lebens Goldenbaum ist grün.

Lawrence: This is one of Goethe's most beautiful lines. The metaphor seems awful, but it is still beautiful in its awfulness. Goethe speaks about a golden tree. But a golden tree is dead. It cannot bear fruit. You cannot eat a golden fruit. What does it mean that the golden tree is green? How can a golden tree be green?

Vera: Perhaps like the stick of Tannhäuser.

Lawrence: The stick of Tannhäuser is dead wood. The divine miracle of grace alone can make it bloom. But the golden tree is the tree of life. The golden tree of life is supposed to be green. It does not need divine grace to flourish.

Joachim: The metaphor is polemical, and Vera threw it into the discussion polemically. The golden tree of life is contrasted to 'theory': Grau sind alle Theorien, all theories are grey. However, by contrast, life's goldentree (written in one word!) is green. I wonder why all theories are grey? I also wonder why Hegel chose to pick up this disquieting metaphor from Goethe and, in addition, why he applied it to philosophy? To interpret philosophy as recollection is a trick as old as philosophy itself. To substitute the recollection of history for the recollection of ideas also makes sense. But why the hell did Hegel say that it is now that darkness has set in? His description of the modern world is otherwise rather flattering. True, when he said 'darkness', he could have meant the darkness of redemption, the darkness of shining light, of the last judgement, salvation, end of history – that is, if he had intended to follow the footsteps of certain great mystic thinkers whom he otherwise admired. But if 'darkness' stands for the light of redemption, then Hegel would not have picked up Goethe's metaphor about the 'grey' theory which has nothing to do with the mystic's shining darkness. I agree with you, Lawrence, that Goethe's metaphor, unlike the metaphor of the blossoming dead stick, does not evoke the vision of divine grace; perhaps there is no place left for divine grace. Let me reiterate: philosophy paints grey in grey: philosophy has no colour. Neither golden nor green. Only life's goldentree is green. But what is life if history is grey and painted in grey? The problem with the metaphor is deeper than I suspected.

Lawrence: 'Life's tree is green' would be unsuitable for a poetic line. Platitudes are unpoetical. Goethe's poem became beautiful, moreover, it became a poem at all, through the word 'golden'. 'The golden tree of life' – this is paradoxical.

Joachim: The goldentree of life is an old mystical – sometimes magical – symbol. The paradox lies in its being green. But whether paradoxical or not, the whole poem is a mess. Why is life green? Why is theory grey? What is life after all? Why is theory juxtaposed to life? And, to return to

Hegel, if philosophy is recollection, and recollection means painting grey in grey, where and how can we pick from the goldentree anything that is green?

Vera: For example, in loving.

Joachim: We love truth, this is our *métier*. But, according to Messieurs Goethe and Hegel, our *métier* is grey.

Vera: A metaphor is polysemous.

Joachim: But in no interpretation would I consider philosophy, or even theory in general, grey. And I still do not know for what the goldentree of life, in juxtaposition to theory, stands.

Vera: Philosophy may not be grey, but it is certanly black and white – and neither gold nor green.

Lawrence: You speak in riddles . . .

Vera: Not at all. Reason and being are the main protagonists of philosophy. Have you ever thought of reason or being in colour? Thought in general has no colour. Spirit has no colour, nor does the soul. When you – philosophers – speak of truth or falsity, you employ metaphors of light and darkness. You envisage the Sun and the Cave. Philosophers see – but what do they see? Did they ever see colour? The straight line, the circle, the triangle – did you ever imagine them red or green? And the numbers? The one and the many? And necessity? And certainty? Is determination, perhaps, pink? Feelings, emotions, sentiments – they are colourful; hope is green, love is red, sadness is blue . . . But you exiled them from philosophy, you stuck to your black and white. Colour is subjective, the experience of colour is not the same for me and for you, but philosophy has traditionally cared only for what is, or seems to be, the same for all of us, for the subject. But the subject writ large is both colourless and colourblind. Only life's goldentree is green.

Lawrence: Nietzsche is not colourless . . .

Joachim: I admit that the first and the second Critiques are written in black and white, but you cannot miss the experience of colour in the third . . .

Vera: There are colours in Nietzsche, I admit. Musical compositions are not black and white. One can tell when thinking replaces metaphysics and traditional philosophy, for it is then that colouring appears. There is colour in Wittgenstein, for example. And some, although not much, in Heidegger. Yes, Joachim, it appears also in the Third Critique, although Kant wages a rearguard battle against colour. You will remember how important it is that the sheer form of purposefulness elicits the judgement of taste. There is some colouring in Hegel's *Phenomenology*, too . . .

Lawrence: You give him more credit than he gave himself . . .

Vera: In that book he let the configurations, the *Gestalten*, of consciousness speak for themselves. And they did not let all of their experiences be reduced to the experience of the spirit, although all of those experiences had been recapitulated by the spirit.

Lawrence: What about painting grey in grey then?

Vera: Hegel was sincere. Think it over: what do you do if you want to understand Cicero? You cannot re-experience what Cicero experienced. You can, however, try to re-think what he thought. Pure thinking alone can be recapitulated, or if you wish, remembered. True, even pure thinking cannot be fully recapitulated, for it is always a person, an exister who acts as well as thinks. You will never be able to think exactly what someone else has thought, because you cannot feel and experience all the historical and autobiographical connotations of their thought. It never ever comes to the fusion of horizons. Hermeneutics makes a case for the impossible. Speculative philosophy at least makes a try. It is a modest, a very modest, venture- a thoroughly self-restrictive one. Thought alone, and nothing else but thought, will be recapitulated. But thought is colourless, and this is why we paint hopelessly grey in grey . . .

Lawrence: Excuse me, I do experience when I am thinking . . .

Vera: Yes, you do, but then you do not recollect thought. You are an exister, you are an existing thinker. You experience as all the existing thinkers do. Life's goldentree is, after all, green. As long as you live, you think as a living being. Your thought cannot be disconnected from your existence and experience. It is the false pretension of the old philosophy allegedly to disconnect 'thought' from the person who thinks, as though thought could think thinking. God as a pure Spirit is created by men to be thought, and not to be loved or to be cherished . . .

Joachim: If you cannot think thinking that thinks, you have no philosophy . . .

Vera: You can think thinking that thinks, and you can pretend that pure thinking is 'thinking as such' while *you* are thinking, but this is precisely painting grey in grey . . .

Lawrence: Listen Vera! Painting grey in grey can also be experienced as the goldentree of life. I am thinking thought (or at least, as far as I can do so, I am thinking thinking), and I enjoy doing it, and I actually, although indirectly, manifest my full personality through those allegedly pure thoughts. Don't I, then, paint grey in grey while sitting on the top of the goldentree of life?

Vera: I see you climbing the goldentree . . . Yes, you do that. You might express yourself more arrogantly: all creative existers sit on one or another branch of the goldentree of life. In other words, all creative existers make the goldentree of life blooming. You think thinking, but it is not thinking that thinks thinking, it is *you* who do that. Because you think thinking, or at least you try hard to think thinking alone, your philosophy will be black and white, but you – the man-who-thinks, who thinks originally – you are full or colour and so are blessed!

Lawrence: Vera, you flatter me!

Vera: Kundry never lies, you know.

Lawrence: But you are not Kundry and I am not Parsifal ... Tell me, what does it mean to think originally? Your (or my) Goethe said that no one is entirely original.

Vera: Entirely not; actually yes.

Lawrence: Nietzsche said that philosophers are ascetic priests who enjoy their asceticism for they enjoy that which they are doing. You said something similar. You said that philosophers are existers who think thinking. To think thinking is an exercise in black and white (perhaps similar to painting grey in grey), for it never captures experience, the goldentree of live. But philosophers, as existers, as men and women who are doing thinking, live this way: they experience their thinking, their triumphs, their sadness, their loves, their hopes. So they are 'in colour'. This is what the original meaning of philosophy, the love of wisdom, expresses. Wisdom (in philosophy) may be black and white, but the love of wisdom is red, it is scarlet, like all kinds of love.

Vera: I spoke with Climacus (one of the pseudonyms of Soren) and he said something similar. *Amor fati* ...

Lawrence: I never heard your 'Sören' mention *amor fati*.

Vera: Not in so many words.

Lawrence: So this is why you threw the Goethe quotation in our discussion as if it were a colourful ball.

Vera: It is a colourful ball, but I only threw it back to you. You came up with the puzzle of painting grey in grey. I could not resist the temptation ...

Lawrence: Do you ever resist temptation?

Vera: Never, but I am very rarely tempted.

Lawrence: The happy throw of the dice is then a branch on the goldentree of life ... But somehow the two metaphors do not match. The branches of trees, they grow quite naturally ...

Vera: You spoke about the instinct for life and creativity that works from within, that keeps one growing like a plant ...

Lawrence: When our professor explained to us Nietzsche's concept of *amor fati* she said that the men of destiny are pulled, not pushed; their past does not push them, because their future pulls them. They follow their fate almost blindly, toward fulfilment ...

Vera: So they do; I knew a few of them.

Lawrence: Is death fulfilment?

Vera: Not death as such. The future that pulls those men of destiny can be their death, if death is their fulfilment. I did not miss one of your professor's points: all tragic heros are repositories of an ethics of personality. But they are not the only ones. That which pulls those men and women of destiny is their own fulfilment; the fulfilment of their chosen destiny, whatever it is. And each chose a destiny for himself or herself.

Lawrence: What about living toward death, then?

Vera: Heidegger relapsed into generalities. His *Dasein* is fundamentally the human condition. He still (or already) considers it aphilosophical to speak about the single exister. Sören, my friend, spoke about the single exister. What is fulfilment for one exister, is not fulfilment for the other. Wise are the existers who choose the hour of their death at the *limes*: the moment of their fulfilment.

Lawrence: How do you know about the moment of fulfilment?

Vera: Again, there is no general answer. Again, I have to remind you of your lectures. Your professor said that Kierkegaard died at the very moment when he, as a philosopher and as a religious thinker, could not go further, and that Nietzsche sank into madness exactly at the same ontic juncture. They chose the proper moment of their real or mental death; in all probability, instinctively. But one can also choose it consciously. Oriental cultures know more about this than our occidental-Jewish-Christian one. You mentioned Mishima when I discovered in you and Joachim the reincarnations of my two old/young friends. The same Mishima decided that at the very moment that he finished the main work of his life, his great cycle of novels, he would depart from life. And he did so. In the morning, he committed to paper the last sentence, in the afternoon he committed ritual suicide – *seppuku* – and died. *Amor fati*. But it was not in death that he saw his fulfilment, but in the cycle of novels which he had just finished. He believed that having accomplished the main work of his life, he would begin to decline as an author, and he did not want to decline. There is no life after fulfilment, just survival . . .

Lawrence: Excuse me. While listening to you, one thing caught my attention. You said that people of destiny have chosen their destiny. Moreover, you stressed the verb 'to choose'. But the blessed ones – whether blessed by God or by nature or by chance – should be called 'the chosen', not 'the ones who choose'. How can one choose to be or not to be a lucky throw of the dice? How can one choose to grow or not to grow on a branch of the goldentree of life, to bear green leaves?

Vera: Why the contrast? Why the juxtaposition? Why do you abruptly start to think in the bipolar model that you otherwise distrust?

Lawrence: Choosing or having been chosen is not one of the binary opposites of ancient metaphysics . . .

Vera: But contingency/necessity are; and so are external/internal . . .

Lawrence: Don't continue, I understand. When we think in terms of the 'lucky throw of the dice', we think the 'throw' in terms of initial contingency. When we think in terms of having being chosen by divine ordinance, we think of ourselves in terms of determination, that is, necessity. The description 'having been chosen' fits only the latter, not the former. It is hard to describe the lucky throw of the dice as 'having been chosen'. But all this does not yet suggest that we can choose the throw as a 'lucky' one – for it *is* either lucky or unlucky. You mentioned another binary opposition: it was external/internal. Both the lucky throw of the dice and divine election are, so to speak, 'external' . . .

Vera: If fate is external, why do you love it?

Lawrence: Perhaps because it is so. But I understand what you are aiming at. In the case of a lucky throw of the dice, fate cannot be external. It is external in so far as it has come about by chance. But the external is here verily internal, I suppose. For *I am* the lucky throw of the dice, and this throw is *my* fate. Nietzsche has already overcome the metaphysical binary opposition of external/internal, and also that of chance and determination. Chance itself is taken up by the lucky throw of the dice as its own determination . . .

Joachim: This is also a trick of good old metaphysics: the intellectual love of God, the recognition of necessity, and so on. I do not mind. You must not think that metaphysicians were always wrong. In these matters one can hardly speak in terms of right and wrong. But why do you associate your Nietzsche with old metaphysics?

Lawrence: I do not associate him with old metaphysics, but Nietzsche . . .

Vera: It is now my turn to repeat what you, Joachim, said yesterday. Please listen: I am not facing Nietzsche but Lawrence. I talk to Lawrence, not to Nietzsche. I am interested in Lawrence, not in Nietzsche. Please, do not hide behind Nietzsche's broad back.

Joachim: Excuse me, I thought that you were talking to both of us . . .

Vera: By talking to Lawrence, I talk to both of you. You just listen.

Joachim: Women are whimsical.

Lawrence: True, but so is fate. I love surprises . . .

Vera: Fate is full of surprises. But a few minutes ago, while hiding behind Nietzsche's broad back, you announced that chance is taken up by the lucky throw of the dice as its own determination. But if there is self-determination, there remains little room for surprises. Nothing will be whimsical in this fate, it will not resemble women – to quote Joachim. I would be sorry if he took offence at what I said.

Joachim: I am listening . . .

Lawrence: You mean, Vera, that although we can safely account for a 'lucky throw of the dice' as the child of chance, it would be odd to add that she was chosen, and also odd to add that she is going to determine herself through insight and thus create her destiny . . . This is why you came up with the as yet unspoken idea of the lucky throw of the dice 'choosing herself'? What are the theoretical and practical advantages in saying that you 'choose yourself' instead of saying 'you {yourself} determine yourself'?

Joachim: Yesterday Lawrence asked me not to hide behind Kant's back, today you asked Lawrence not to hide behind Nietzsche's back. Yet you hide behind Kierkegaard's back. Is this fair?

Vera: My old friend Sören inspired me. But he would not take responsibility for all that I am going to say. I am taking the position of one of
his pseudonyms. Call this pseudonym Vera for change's sake. It is I, not
Kierkegaard, who speaks . . . But let me return to Lawrence's question.
For you, my dear, this formulation offers great theoretical advantages.
Lawrence: Go on, please.
Vera: First, you need not answer any metaphysical questions. You do
not need to say that men are contingent, nor do you need to confirm the
idea of the lucky throw of the dice in an ontic-ontological orchestration.
You can answer the question Gurnemanz asked, 'Where are you coming
from?' with Parsifal's reply, 'I do not know.' You may recall that this was
also Joachim's answer when you made inquiries about the parentage of
the categorical imperative. Thus you can enjoy the benefits of the Kantian
doubt. When I propose to think that a 'lucky throw of the dice' chooses
himself or herself, I leave all ontological questions open. After all, it is of
no relevance in the case of self-choice whether the dice was thrown by
God on purpose or whether it was lost by the child Heracles who was just
playing with unrelated dice cups without a purpose . . . Choosing yourself does not require such knowledge. Moreover, if you knew what you
do not know, choosing yourself would become meaningless.
Lawrence: I see that there is some theoretical benefit in accepting your
language game. But I don't understand why you protest against the term
self-determination. Only because it has a metaphysical past? I would
agree with Joachim on that point at least: one can still fall back on old
metaphysical thinking for illumination . . .
Vera: The metaphysical parentage of self-determination is not the
reason for my reluctance to accept it. Try to think self-determination for
a moment! Do it sincerely and without presuppositions, as far as it is
possible. Philosophers are just like average everyday actors: they talk in
categories without thinking over what they are speaking about. Self-
determination of a 'lucky throw' can mean, then, the following. Once I
accept that there is a chain of determination – whether I do it in a
traditional metaphysical, in a Kantian, or in a Humean sense, makes no
difference – what I accept is that all features that constitute 'me' result
from previously existing facts or factors, and that those features come
about by sufficient reasons (causes), or at least that this is the best way of
understanding (describing) them. If this is so, self-determination means
the following: I know all my determinations (in the previous sense) and
it is through this knowledge that I can predict what I am going to do,
how I am going to act, and so on. This is, of course, sheer absurdity. You
yourself said – and so did my Sören – that we can never become completely transparent to ourselves, we do not even know about our 'features', much less about the factors that sufficed to bring about these
features. The 'self-determination' story, then, obliges you to take the
position of a theoretical attitude. Allegedly, the clearer the ideas that you

get about the world or yourself, the freer you become. The creative person, the creative genius, the 'lucky throw of the dice' whom we now try to understand, is certainly not this kind of a person. She acts, creates, and it is through her acting and creating that she fulfils her destiny. For one person, contemplation can be the fulfilment of her destiny, but for others, it cannot. Metaphysicians start with a great advantage (or disadvantage). They pick one possibility among a thousand and baptize it the only actuality. Self-determination is not just an empty word but it gives you a false idea about men and women who have *amor fati*.

Lawrence: I still do not see how choice can replace self-determination . . .

Vera: But you do, if you remember our discussion of yesterday. We spoke about the existential choice of ourselves.

Lawrence: But this is an entirely different thing. Moreover, I have always found your conception shaky. For example, I cannot grasp why you maintain that to choose ourselves as good persons is a so-called 'existential' choice.

Vera: Funny, your mentioning that you have 'always' found my conception shaky. So you admit, unknowingly, that we have already met one another long before yesterday . . . But enough of reminiscences. Back to the present. Choosing ourselves and beginning to become what we are is an existential choice. The existential choice is a leap. If you think of the world in terms of spheres, you may say that you leap into a sphere: into the religious or the ethical sphere, or into the sphere of politics, erotics (Max Weber distinguishes an erotic sphere as well), into the sphere of creative art or aesthetics, and so on. But you never choose a sphere, and this is decisive. You do not choose philosophy, but you choose yourself as a philosopher; you do not choose politics, but you choose yourself as a politician; you do not choose your beloved, you choose yourself as a lover. You can talk about the leap in other terms too. But in terms of our present discussion I would say that to leap means to destine yourself – and not to determine yourself.

Lawrence: I still do not see the difference between choosing, that is, destining myself on the one hand, and determining myself, on the other.

Vera: These alternative concepts – destining or determining – describe entirely different ways of thinking the existential turn. You must remember how someone chooses herself existentially as a decent person. She says: I choose all my determinations, all my character traits, my context, etc., thus as I am I become what I am: a decent person. This is how someone destines herself. Choosing one's own determinations does not presuppose that one knows them. It does not even presuppose that one thinks in terms of determinations. It is indifferent from this point of view whether one cherishes a Kantian, Humean, Spinozian, or Nietzschean concept of causality, determination, motivational forces or necessity. It is indifferent whether I presuppose that my origin, my childhood, my historical context, my knowledge, my unconscious, etc. are or are not decisive for what I choose, for I choose it (myself) fully. I become a decent person (I am one), regardless of where I was coming from.

Lawrence: You said that we are pulled by our future. But this is just to replace *causa efficiens* with *causa finalis* . . .

Vera: Yes, if one jumps, one switches from being pushed to being pulled. I admit, the expression 'being pulled' is somehow related (in the sense that Wittgenstein speaks about relatives) to *causa finalis*, but it is not *causa finalis*. If one chooses oneself existentially under the category of the universal, that is, as a decent person, the force of the 'pull' cannot be localized, not even metaphorically. Every moment is fulfilment as long as the person becomes what he is . . .

Lawrence: What does 'as long as' mean? Can you eventually revoke the leap?

Vera: An existential choice is existential because it cannot be revoked. But it does not necessarily come off, for there is no necessity in destining ourselves. If your existential choice does not come off, you will lose yourself, you will be void of the possibility of 'becoming': a failed exister. He or she who never dared to leap is not a failed exister – he or she is not an exister at all. He or she is determined by others – but not in an onto-metaphysical sense of determination. To be determined by others means that others tell you what you are, that others make you what you are, that you become an object, an artefact manufactured by others. The person who loses himself, the 'failed exister', resembles those who have never existed – with a difference. Those who have never chosen them-selves have neither won nor lost. The failed existers have lost, they have lost themselves as existers, and they are aware of it. Despair becomes them, this becomes their fate.

Lawrence: If one chooses oneself, then one takes a great risk.

Vera: There is no authenticity without risk.

Lawrence: Nor is there inauthenticity without risks.

Vera: But they are incommensurable.

Lawrence: Now I understand better than yesterday why the choice of oneself as a good person is an existential one. But I am afraid, we are still far off the mark. We didn't get one step closer to the understanding of the self-choice of the 'lucky throw of the dice'.

Joachim: Although I acquiesced in remaining silent, I must now inter-rupt. Vera, seductress, you go too far. You describe the existential choice of decency in such terms that no decent or good person would recog-nize himself in it. This apple of yours hit the ground far from the Kierkegaardian tree. What was your description of a failed exister? Do I remember accurately? You said: others tell him who he is. Others will determine him. But is ethics not about the others, about our relation to the others? How can you speak about centring without pointing at the others? You said that we choose ourselves as decent persons under the category of the universal. But how does the universal manifest itself? How does its universality show? It must show itself, and first and foremost, in our relation to others. I realize how anti-democratic you are: you take on aristocratic airs, you teach Lawrence to indulge in his genius instead of humbling himself before the moral law . . .

Vera: Let me address Lawrence first, then I will turn to you.

Joachim: I am patient but I expect to get my due.

Vera: I am sorry, thinking is not always the friend of justice. Although you will not get your due, you will get, at least for a while, the leading role in the theatre of discourse. this much I promise. For the time being, let us return to the so-called 'lucky throws of the dice'. they choose themselves not under the category of the universal, but rather under the category of difference . . .

Lawrence: Why not under the category of the singular, of uniqueness? All of them are unique, aren't they?

Vera: Yes, but all who choose themselves existentially, choose themselves entirely, and all of them are, in this sense, unique and inimitable. This is true about men and woman who choose themselves under the category of the universal as much as about those who choose themselves under the category of difference or the particular . . .

Lawrence: Why the particular?

Vera: We have already discussed this matter. They choose themselves as philosophers, politicians, tragic authors and the like . . .

Lawrence: But this is what Nietzsche also said. You remember, when he asks the question about the meaning of the ascetic ideal, he too mentions artists, philosophers, scientists, women; that is, different categories . . .

Vera: Silence, please . . . We agreed to speak only about one another.

Lawrence: I now understand the expression 'difference' or the 'particular'. But I still do not see what *choice* has to do with all this. Have I chosen myself as a philosopher? Let me see, this is the wrong question, because I know that I did. I remember also when I did it. As a young boy, I wanted to become a physician. Then, by chance, or rather by Joachim's insistence, and very reluctantly, I accompanied him to a philosophy lecture by his favourite professor. I didn't understand a single word of what he said. But one thing I did understand: I have to stake my whole life on understanding this matter, precisely this and nothing else. Oh, yes. Up until that point I was pushed, from that moment onward I was pulled to become what I already was.

Joachim: You make things too simple. It is easy to evoke the decisive turn in our lives retrospectively. And why did you become my friend and not a friend of someone else before your so-called existential choice that you have just discovered? I had already studied philosophy then. Was not my studying philosophy the source of my so-called attraction?

Lawrence: This is a 'why' that will never be followed by a 'because'. There are no answers. Or do you want me to pull your objection apart? Was your studying philosophy an addendum to you, a piece of garment which you could put on and take off by wish and at whim? Or may I ask whether you were attracted to me because you had a premonition about my future turn towards philosophy, something that I had absolutely no presentiment of at the time of our first encounter?

Joachim: But I want to understand all this. I know that it can never fully be understood, or rather that it can be understood in a hundred different ways. Still, I want to know it. I always want to know. I want to know, for example, why you are attracted to Vera, whom you do not know.

Lawrence: You think I am attracted to her? I have known her all the time, perhaps in another shape.

Joachim: I had really better remain silent amidst so much madness.

Vera: Lawrence's personal experience has touched me. Still, here I join forces with Joachim; it is irrelevant whether you preserve a strong recollection of an existential choice or not. And in the case of an existential choice, memory is highly selective. But, and this is the gist of the matter, a modern man or woman cannot be a man or woman of destiny without having chosen this destiny for himself or herself. Whether you remember the choice or not is not the issue. As it was not the issue when we discussed the existential choice under the category of the universal . . .

Lawrence: Let me remind you that we began to speak about the theoretical advantages of replacing self-determination with self-destining via an existential choice. You mentioned some, but you promised to come up with more. And you have not yet said one single word about the practical advantages of your conception. I know I ask questions in a pragmatic vein. But N– – I do not dare to mention his name before you, Vera – also had some affinity with pragmatism.

Vera: Both Nietzsche and Wagner made existential choices. Nietzsche chose himself a philosopher, Wagner chose himself as a composer of music-dramas. An existential choice is a commitment for life. It is not just a conscious commitment: the person-as-a-whole chooses himself as this or that as-a-whole. This is why your Nietzsche could not tell his reason from his instinct. The maximum actualization of the philosopher Nietzsche pulled the philosopher Nietzsche, the maximum fulfilment of the composer-dramatist Wagner pulled the composer Wagner. The maximum realization of Nietzsche as philosopher is not the maximum realization of 'philosophy'. Philosophy is not an exister, it cannot fulfil itself. To continue to speak about existers: fulfilment is different in each case. The person who has made an existential choice has a 'feel' for his fulfilment, he 'feels' that something is still there 'in him' that waits for actualization, or that he has fully actualized his destiny and can die or just rest. Let me recall Mishima again, this time not his story, but the story of his young hero, Isao, who felt that the whole of his destiny had been fulfilled at the age of twenty-three. Fulfilment does not depend on age . . .

Lawrence: But it obviously does depend on talent. What is fulfilment for Feuerbach is not yet fulfilment for Kant, the man of far greater talents . . .

Vera: Talent is a mysterious thing. Sometimes I have the impression – particularly if I observe smaller children – that there is something one could call a 'talented person' in general. One can see there a talent that has not yet taken shape, as if existence were still resting in the state of waiting or hesitation. It has not yet chosen itself as this or that. It could choose itself as this and also as that, and it could become what it chose itself to be: this or that; and once 'this' or 'that', then entirely, fully. At other times you have the impression that a person is endowed with a talent for a particular thing. If this is so, the talent itself works as an instinct, it gives signs, it pushes. It pushes, but it does not yet pull. Only after the leap, once the person has chosen his destiny, will the endowments begin to pull. However, the expression 'after the leap' does not account properly for something that one cannot pin down in time.

Lawrence: What makes a person leap?

Vera: You know quite well that, again, you have asked an unanswerable question. If there are original endowments-towards-something, you may say that the push itself is a condition of the pull, although this is not so if we speak about a 'generally talented' person. Since a philosopher – unlike a pianist or a painter – does not need a specific skill (e.g. a talent), no 'push' is here the condition of the 'pull'. But an endowment is an abstraction. Your 'lucky throw of the dice' is not a man of the best abstract endowments. He has endowments too, and brilliant ones, but they are, in all probability, deep-seated in the 'general' character and can hardly be separated from it. Given that we live in a historicist age, we know better than thinkers before us, how important historical conditions may be for the appearance of a lucky throw of the dice. One should not forget that moderns are 'thrown' from different, unrelated dice cups. From one dice cup, the character is thrown, from the other, the historical time, from the third, a specific skill; and out of all those combinations, one can make a lucky hit, the other a less lucky one. In everyday parlance we speak of 'greater talent' or 'smaller talent', and we know roughly what we mean: not just 'natural' endowments, but endowments that have already been practised, that have become manifest. The existential choice – whether conscious or unconscious – is a decision, and *a final one*. You throw your own existence wholly into one single task, or at least, into one overwhelming, all-decisive task. This is what you are; you become what you are in following your star. Yes, you follow your own star, but you choose your star first . . .

Lawrence: Sorry, Vera, all this is beautiful, particularly what you said about our star, but I still do not see the pragmatic benefits . . .

Vera: The existential choice cannot be revoked, it cannot be taken back. This is so if you choose yourself under the category of difference to the same extent as it is in the case in which you've made an ethical self-choice . . .

Lawrence: I understand this in the second, but not in the first case. Suppose that I have chosen myself as a decent person – this must be final, for I cannot choose myself as an indecent person. I can, of course, be an indecent person, provided that I haven't chosen myself or that I have lost myself. But I do not see the same connection in the case of our lucky throw. Assume that Nietzche had chosen himself as a philosopher, but his choice did not come off, and so, realizing this he then chose himself as a composer, or something else. What is absurd in this? If one choice does not come off, there are still plenty of things to choose for yourself to be. It would be nonsensical to say in this case that you lose yourself if your first-and-only choice does not come off.

Vera: An existential choice is unlike choosing a profession. You can begin to study philosophy, then switch to law, then again, switch to psychology. It may happen that you do not choose yourself as a philosopher, lawyer or psychologist at all – none of them. Once you have chosen yourself under the category of the universal – becoming a good person – it is of secondary importance whether you are a splendid lawyer or a psychologist or a philosopher, for you still become what you are. Perhaps you have not chosen yourself at all, but rather let others choose for you. If this is so, you are not an exister, but you can still be an expert in one thing or in more than one thing. Yet an exister is a person who had made an existential choice under either the category of the universal or that of difference. Metaphorically speaking, an existential choice is envious, or rather jealous: one cannot choose twice. An existential choice is the state of monogamy. A bigamist by definition has not chosen existentially, for he has not chosen himself as a person committed absolutely to one thing for life.

Lawrence: You mean that if I choose myself a philosopher, I cannot paint, or write poems . . .

Vera: No, that would be absurd. But if you have chosen yourself as a philosopher, you become a philosopher; this will be your fulfilment, and your reason-instinct will pull you towards fulfilment. You can also do many other things – with interest, with gusto, as a profession – but they will not be your fulfilment. You can take them up or drop them without losing yourself. You can write poetry for a while and then stop writing it, you can practise law and be involved in it, you can make photos or begin to paint instead – you will still remain yourself. But if you stopped doing philosophy . . . but this, of course, is nonsense because you could not stop. For if you had chosen yourself as a philosopher, you could not live without philosophy, you could not take a breath, just as the person who has chosen himself as a painter cannot take a breath without painting; as a lawyer without practising law, as a politician without continuous and active political involvement. And so on ...

Lawrence: But this could also be true about dilettanti, I am afraid. I am not so sure that since I have chosen myself as a philosopher, I also am, and have become, a philosopher. I agree that the choice of ourselves does not depend on our endowments, at least we do not know if it does; but whether the choice comes off does depend partly on those endowments, and not simply on the choice. I can put all my stakes on something, and still, if my talents for this thing are meagre, my so-called existential choice will be null and void. I would also reiterate Joachim's objection. Joachim said that in your defence for the existential choice under the category of the universal you have forgotten the Other as if the other men and women were not existers of a kind. Now, in your defence for the choice under the category of difference, you have repeated the same blunder. Assume that I have chosen myself as a philosopher and that I have become what I have chosen myself to be. Can I, then, have really become a philosopher, without it being the case that certain others at least recognize me as one? Or am I a philosopher even if my thinking appears to others platitudinous or, alternatively, as sheer madness? Yes, dear Vera, what about Descartes's old problem? What about madness? Does a madman also choose his own madness? And can it happen that by choosing myself as a philosopher I choose nothing but my madness? Is the path that leads to fulfilment not too narrow? More narrow still than Kant's path towards virtue? Is not the path between failing as an exister on the one hand, and choosing ourselves without receiving recognition, that is madness, on the other – the narrow path of a self-chosen talent that is also recognized, that shines in public, and that is also fulfilled, in brief – the road to triumph – is not this the narrowest path of them all and the most difficult one to follow?

Vera: Difficult is the wrong word; for those whose path it is, to walk on it is easy.

Lawrence: You avoid giving a straight answer.

Vera: What kind of straight answer do you expect me to give?

Lawrence: The choice of ourselves as good people is shown by its manifestations; we become what we are: good persons. Is the choice of ourselves, for example as philosophers, shown by its manifestations? Will philosophy be our destiny? Everyone can be a decent person. Can everyone, who so chooses, be or become a philosopher?

Vera: This question cannot be answered. How could I know? If you *are* a philosopher, then you have chosen yourself. This is the only thing I know.

Lawrence: And how could I know that I *am* a philosopher?

Vera: You know it. If you are destined, you cannot do or be otherwise.
Lawrence: And the triumph? The uncovering of the Grail?
Vera: If you choose triumph, you do not choose yourself. If you choose yourself, there might be triumph, but there might also be none. Triumph does not depend upon you; it does not depend upon your choice. It is grace. We agreed that choosing yourself under the category of difference is risky. And grace cannot be willed or chosen or deserved. It is a gift from above.
Lawrence: This sounds too solemn for my taste . . .
Vera: You give thanks for it, if it occurs; you do not blame it if it does not.
Lawrence: Although you took great pains to distinguish, and distinguish radically, between the existential choice under the category of the universal and the one under the category of difference, finally the yields of the two kinds of choices seem very much alike. If you choose yourself as a good person, then you are decent and activity itself is your triumph. If you choose yourself as a philosopher, a healer, a composer or the like, then again the activity itself is your triumph. That kind of triumph that is outside and above activity itself will not result from your self-choice in either case.
Vera: And neither being good nor being good-at-something warrants grace.
Lawrence: That's very unfair to the decent ones.
Vera: This was a problem for the prophets, the wise men, the philosophers for many a thousand year. It would be just, if happiness were granted to the just, but alas, if this were so, there would be no decent or just or good people at all. For one is good if one does the right thing irrespective of the consequences for one's own life that might ensue from the act. And of course, this is also true of all those who choose themselves under the category of difference: they act following their own chosen destiny, irrespective of the consequences for their own lives and the lives of others . . .
Joachim: Here is the gist of the matter! Here lies the decisive difference between the two kinds of existential choices. I waited for it so long. Irrespective of what you choose under the category of the universal? Irrespective of the consequences that ensue from your act for your own destiny? And irrespective of what you choose under the category of difference? Irrespective of the consequences that ensue from your act for your own *and* for the other's destiny? But no act of moral content is ever performed 'irrespective of the consequences that ensue from it for another person's life'. Caring for the other, respecting the other, paying attention to other person's autonomy, suffering, sensibility – all these 'respects' belong to the activity and to the attitude of a righteous man. And this is not so, not at all, whenever you choose yourself existentially under any category of difference.

Vera: This is so. Although decency does not warrant triumph or happiness, it warrants at least one thing: decent persons do not make others unhappy by pursuing their own destiny. But this is indeed not so in the case of the existential choice under the category of difference. I choose myself as a composer, I become what I am. I then pay no regard to myself, to my everyday kind of happiness, but I also do not pay any regard to any other people either – they do not exist for me if they bar my narrow path to becoming what I am. I may torture or instrumentalize them as Wagner did; the only thing that matters to me is then the actualizing of my destiny. In moral terms, he who chooses himself under the category of difference can be evil, demonic, wicked – or just entirely unconcerned.

Joachim: We have arrived at a conclusion that is far off the mark. You promised to introduce us to the mysteries of an ethics of personality. Just now we have come to the conclusion that he who chooses himself under the category of difference can be an entirely immoral, or non-moral, or amoral being. That this so-called lucky throw of the dice may, in addition, be unhappy, that he may live and die in solitude and remain unrecognized, does not make his figure more attractive or more ethical in my eyes . . .

Lawrence: But it does in mine. And, excuse me, but your Kant was more sensitive to this type than you are. At least he admitted that men who sacrifice their lives for freedom, or for any other idea, elicit our enthusiasm. To sacrifce ourselves to an idea is at least a kind of *analogue* to obedience to the moral law, for it requires many things that pure morality also does; among others, humiliating our normal, everyday egoism and self-love for the sake of something that stands higher.

Joachim: Pardon me, but as I see it, we were not speaking of self-abandonment to an idea. I admit, if someone dies for his conviction, this may elicit our enthusiasm. But why would we vest our enthusiasm in a philosopher who philosophizes and in a tragedy writer who writes tragedies, just because they are unrecognized by the crowd or are badly paid? There is nothing resembling the self-abandonment to an 'ideal' in just doing what one likes doing best. Since they would not abandon what they were doing for the sake of anything anyway, they cannot expect us to regard their activity as a manifestation of self-sacrifice.

Lawrence: And this is one of Kant's weakest points. And, like all his weak points, this too results from his splitting a human person into two unrelated persons. Yes, a person can suffer even if he is doing the only thing he likes doing best. If he is crucified because he has chosen himself as the man who is to be crucified, is the experience of being crucified less painful? Or less deserving?

Joachim: Less painful perhaps not, but certainly less deserving. For it is not the fulfilment of your own life that is deserving, but the fulfilment of the other's life – unless, of course, the fulfilment of the other's life is also the fulfilment of your own. But this can be so only if you choose yourself under the category of the universal, imitating, perhaps, the Man on the cross. And it is not this kind of existential choice that we are now discussing.

Lawrence: And what about the gifts that we receive? Are the poems of Baudelaire, the 'flowers of evil', not gifts put on our birthday table? Or the paintings of Van Gogh, or the music of Beethoven? Are not presents under our Christmas tree? Could we live meaningfully without them? Are their authors undeserving, because they could not live otherwise but by doing what they have done, because they have not created that which they have created for the purpose of presenting Joachim and Lawrence and Vera with their gifts? Just a few minutes ago Vera said that grace, blessing, comes from above. No effort warrants it. But it does not come without effort. Joachim, you have an extremely reduced perception of human existence if you believe that to love and to suffer are two different things.

Joachim: Thank you. I have better style than to call them 'things'.

Lawrence: Don't be offended. I did not mean you, I meant your mentor, Kant.

Joachim: Forgiven, forgotten. But you meant me and not Kant. You could not have meant Kant. In addition, you shifted ground; or was it just a slip of your tongue? Instead of saying 'to triumph and to suffer' you have said 'to love and to suffer'.

Lawrence: No, no, I meant love. I spoke about *amor fati*. This is the kind of love for which the lucky throw of the dice is crucified . . .

Joachim: Whether 'triumph' or 'love' of 'fate', we are back to Nietzsche again. The man who lets himself be pulled by the fate that he loves is the giver of presents. If I understand you well, it is to this spot that you now fix the centrepoint of your ethics of personality. Let me reiterate: the man who has chosen himself as a composer, a politician, a poet or the like becomes what he is; he leaps; he follows the command of the pull. He sacrifices many of the pleasant and gratifying preoccupations of everyday life, for he is obsessed with this one task, this one goal which is not a goal at all. He runs blindly on his narrow path toward the fulfilment that may occur or just as well may not. There is suffering, work, effort, and also great love – the love of fate. But the person who creates in joy and suffering prepares gifts, not for himself, but for others. Am I far from your point if I hold your ethics of personality to be consequentionalist? It is only when labour is crowned by success, when its works are received as great birthday presents by contemporaries and successors, that the creator of the works will be ethically credited for doing something for others which no one else could have done in lieu of him; something incommensurable, essential, eternal. But if the work is not crowned by success, if triumph fails to materialize, if there is no blessing from above, then the creator of the work cannot be ethically credited, irrespective of the suffering he may have endured. He is still the man who had chosen himself, who has crucified himself to the cross of his vocation, but there is no resurrection, no eternal life – just a cadaver.

Lawrence: Do you remember Vera saying that there is no justice in the ethics of personality?

Joachim: And I cannot stop asking: is there ethics without justice? Is there ethics where credit does not depend on the creditor, because the creditor is not the actor, rather some unknown grey eminence that we call 'grace'? Why are we, who – I grant you this – enjoy all the gifts, debtors to a mere vehicle of blessing? Why don't we rather recognize our debt to the grey eminence itself, the very source of blessing? The quality of the wine that pours from the vessel is not to be credited to the vessel.

Lawrence: You like to tear things apart. True, there is no gift without triumph. Yes, there is an element of consequentialism in the ethics of personality . . .

Joachim: Not if you choose yourself existentially under the category of the universal.

Lawrence: Now you begin to think in our terms . . .

Joachim: In 'our' terms? Why this *pluralis majestatis*?

Lawrence: I refer to Vera and myself. And you are right, as you always are when it comes to discovering weak spots in an argument.

Vera: And you, Lawrence, expose those weak spots. Because we came to the conclusion yesterday that there is no other ethics in modernity than the ethics of personality, yet that there are different types of this sort of ethics, we decided to discuss the two main types separately. An ethics of personality is consequentialist if one chooses oneself under the category of particularity (difference). If one chooses oneself under the category of universality, it can hardly be consequentialist, for a decent person wears the green crown of the goldentree of life on work-days. This is her triumph; she is both the wine and the vessel; she is in no need of grace. She can still be blessed, but the gifts granted to a decent person are like luxury goods: she manages to become what she is without them.

Joachim: Please do not bang on open doors. I have already accepted an ethics of personality; you *can* describe the morality of modern persons well with the help of Kierkegaard's philosophical metaphor of an 'existential choice'. There are, in my mind, other relevant descriptions, but this is among the best. But as far as your second type is concerned, that is, the one who chooses himself under the category of difference, you have convinced me of nothing. Let me sum briefly up my objections: it is a consequentialist theory, in which the consequences themselves cannot be credited to the actor, but must rather be credited to grace. To your claim that a blessed person presents us (the others) with the gifts of his hand and mind, I would retort that this is of no ethical relevance because it is not he who presents us with the great gifts, but his blessing; this blessing he cannot choose, cannot extort, cannot even help receiving. On second thoughts, then, it becomes irrelevant to speak about him the way you did, in terms of his choosing himself as a philosopher, his becoming what he was, etc. Because if triumph, gifts, blessing and the like cannot be expedited, or achieved at will, no person could possibly choose himself as a philospher, etc. I return to an earlier stage of our conversation: the man of choice is in fact never the chooser, he can be chosen as well as not, by the whim of alien powers. If he suffers (and he might), he suffers heteronomously, for he is an utterly heteronomous creature. Further, let me speak briefly about the gifts we receive: drama, poetry, constitutions, etc. We neither encounter nor communicate with the dramatist, the poet, the creator – only with their work. The creator, the initiator, is nothing, the work is everything. Artists are particularly uninteresting and unattractive – they are like an empty husk, not even a vessel. Why should I be interested in this empty husk? Finally, and here I return to my starting-point, in morality, and ethics is morality, the other is not just the recipient of a gift; the other also communicates with the giver of the gift. Morality pertains to a relation between persons, not between a person and a work. You try to interrupt me to say that the work is also in individuality, that the person is objectified in this work – but this is all nonsense. When I conduct a conversation with a work, I do not conduct a conversation with the author of the work. The author is absent . . .

Lawrence: My dear Joachim, we are back at the beginning of our conversation of yesterday about the connection between biography and work . . .

Joachim: I am aware of this, and I insist, that my position be taken seriously for a change. I communicate with the first critique and not with Kant. I have no relation to Kant. The gift I have received is his work. Kant does not answer to me, he does not correct me, he does not scorn me, he does not laugh at me, he does not smile, he does not hold my hand, he does not help me in dark times, he does not lend me a cent, he gives me no advice when I am in trouble . . .

Lawrence: But I thought that he did all those things for you . . .

Joachim: Worse still, I cannot do these things for him. I do not hold his hand, I do not rebuke him, I do not sit beside him at his table, and I do not assist him in his hypochondria. This is why I think that ethics has nothing to do with a so-called 'work' at all. There is no objectivation in ethics. Everything in ethics happens between people, nothing remains for the third party to see, to feel, or to think. Ethics is fluid – yes, it is life, it is the green crown on the goldentree of life . . .

Vera: Beautifully said.

Lawrence: Vera, don't betray me! All joking aside, I don't think that even our second type of ethics of personality is entirely consequentialist. That there is no necessary connection between work and grace does not yet mean that there is none at all. No blessing comes without effort, sacrifice, passion, despair . . .

Vera: True, Lawrence, true. But I am surprised that neither of you has yet recalled your professor's interpretation of Nietzsche . . .

Lawrence: Had you not censured me for my mentioning Nietzsche, I would have returned to those lectures long ago. But what exactly do you have in mind?

Vera: The one thing that binds together all kind of ethics, how different they may be.

Lawrence: I have already mentioned sacrifice and effort. I even added passion and despair, though not all kinds of ethics cherish them.

Vera: You have quoted the sentence of Socrates and you have added that it is true for the righteous and untrue for the wicked.

Lawrence: 'It is better to suffer injustice than to commit injustice.' But this is irrelevant in our case.

Vera: Why is that so?

Lawrence: Because you yourself said that the second kind of ethics of personality is not about justice.

Vera: The meaning of the sentence is rather: it is better to suffer wrong than to wrong another person.

Lawrence: It is still irrelevant to the case under discussion. The person who chooses himself under the category of difference (for example the person who chooses himself as a statesman) wrongs many people, sometimes on purpose. What carries him through the narrow path is his destiny, his *amor fati* – but we have gone over this a hundred times already.

Vera: Can you do wrong to your work?

Lawrence: Certainly. And perhaps a work, be it a painting, or a novel, or a philosophical treatise, or perhaps even an economic programme, is like another person; if you do wrong to it, it beseeches you to stop. A work can cry out, it can weep, and it can also take revenge.

Joachim: But if your work is your own life, how can you distinguish between harming the other and harming yourself?

Lawrence: Perhaps you can't.

Joachim: But no one harms himself on purpose. Why would a person harm himself knowingly?

Lawrence: Why do persons harm other persons knowingly?

Joachim: Because the impulse or the drive of self-love carries them away and they do not listen to the voice of their conscience. But in your ethics of personality, self-love is a moral factor, and not an immoral one . . .

Lawrence: Why don't you get rid of your transcendental anthropology? Why do you presuppose two selves, one intelligible, one sensible? Why don't you assume that there are many selves, none of them merely rational, none of them merely impulsive, and that an existential choice means only a simple gesture, namely the placing of one among those selves into the centre while letting the others circle around without being annihilated or even oppressed.

Joachim: This is how *you* interpret Joseph's dream! Jacob's son was also a man of destiny and a lucky one . . . But do you think it possible that one of those several selves may successfully take over the central place from its previous occupant? If this is possible, who do you term the choice of our centre existential?

Lawrence: We agreed that the existential choice is irrevocable. Although the existentially chosen centre cannot be replaced by another 'self', you can lose the centrepoint of your life. Your life can become entirely de-centred. That is when we can speak of an existential failure. But an existential failure is not a social 'failure'. He can become a very wealthy man, a producer of renown, a publisher, a general, a prime minister, etc.; he can be very successful in many respects, but he remains an existential failure. An existential failure can also be representative in his failing. He is representative when the temptation that he has succumbed to is demonic and representative.

Vera: You see for yourself: even the second kind of ethics of personality is not merely consequentionalist. If so many selves try to remove the self chosen in the existential choice from the centre place, continuous effort is required to keep it there . . .

Joachim: We always return to the same deadlock. If some one loves to do something and does it with full passion, why on earth would he (or one of his selves) allow the centrepoint of his life to be removed and annihilated?

Lawrence: And you still continue to think in the systematic framework of a Kantian transcendental anthropology. Kant wants to answer the question 'What is man?' I want to answer the question 'What is this or that man?'

Joachim: There are no philosophical answers to those questions, because they are aphilosophical ones.

Lawrence: Perhaps. But raising precisely such questions is certainly not an offence against the resolve to think what we are doing.

Vera: Please, do not yet abandon the man who has chosen himself under the category of difference. You have agreed that in choosing himself existentially, he chooses a centrepoint of his existence. He is a philosopher, a dramatic poet, a politician, a military man, a teacher, a lawyer, a prophet, a lover and so on . . . because he has chosen himself as such. His centrepoint is his passion; he loves his fate. But he is also tempted by many of his heterogeneous selves who attack this centrepoint rather than circle around it peacefully. If the attack is successful, the person becomes an existential failure, just as he also becomes de-centred. In terms of the Socratic master-sentence this could be expressed as follows: one pursues an ethics of personality unfailingly if one prefers to suffer wrong or injustice rather than lose the centre of one's life. For a person who has chosen herself under the category of difference and whose choice has come off, the statement 'it is better to suffer injustice than to wrong the centrepoint of my life' is true.

Lawrence: How can we wrong the centrepoint of our life?

Joachim: What are the virtues and what are the vices of a repository of this kind of ethics of personality?

Vera: The main virtue is authenticity. A person is authentic if she is true to herself.

Joachim: This is also the case with the good person. She too is authentic. She too is true to herself.

Vera: Yes, authenticity is the main virtue, or one of the main virtues, in all ethics of personality. If you fail to be true to yourself, you lose yourself. Needless to say, for a person who has not chosen herself existentially, who is not an exister and lets others choose for her, authenticity is not a virtue. From this it does not follow that she is inauthentic. Inauthenticity is the vice of those who have lost themselves. She who has never gained herself is neither authentic nor inauthentic – these ethical categories have no relevance for her. She wants to 'look' like something, or to 'seem' like something, but she neither *is* nor *becomes*. Many people do not exist ethically, and from this perspective they *are* not. For the most part they are far from being wicked, but they lack moral autonomy.

Joachim: I see that even you cannot get rid of my transcendental anthropology. Heteronomous are the people who pursue their self-love.

Vera: They are rather like the people mentioned in the Passover ritual: the ones who cannot even ask the question. But let's return for a moment to the question concerning the virtue of authenticity. I would not say that authenticity is 'the main' virtue of a decent person. Authenticity is the foundation. But if I choose myself as a good person, my main virtues develop in the process of becoming what I am. Every person is good in her own way. Yes, the good, the decent persons are the green crowns of the goldentree of life. They are not grey, neither are they alike; each of them is entirely unique. It is not difficult, however, to enumerate the main virtues of those who have chosen themselves under the category of difference: they are decisive, but they are few. For the distinctive mark of these people rests in the creative process, in the work they create, and not in the catalogue of their virtues. Whereas in the case of the decent person, where decency, action and works coincide, no representative catalogue of virtues can be designed. Only writers can do justice to decent persons, yet even they can hardly grasp their own inimitable 'ipseity'.

Lawrence: Now it is my turn to ask you to please return to the topic. You said that authenticity is not the main virtue of decent people, but rather of the repositories of the second kind of ethics of personality. But what is authenticity in this case? What does it mean to remain true to

ourselves? Does it mean to remain true to our work? To remain true to
that which we have chosen?

Vera: Yes, to remain true to the centrepoint of our life, true to our own
existence. Authenticity blends two virtues: that of truthfulness and that
of fidelity. The same virtues that need to be blended in our intimate and
close relationship with a few chosen others, or perhaps to a single other.

Lawrence: Authenticity means, then, being my own best friend?

Vera: An authentic person is at least one of her own best friends. But if
you choose yourself morally, it is not you who are your best friend but
another. If you choose yourself under the category of difference, you are
your best friend as long as you are your friend at all. When you cease
to be your best friend, you will become your worst enemy. This is
certainly not the case when you choose yourself under the category of the
universal.

Lawrence: This means that the man of an ethics of personality of
the second kind must be very lonely. If you are your best friend, and at
the moment you cease to be your best friend, you become your greatest
enemy, you must be very lonely.

Vera: Yes, in this ultimate sense, men and women who chose themselves under the category of difference are lonely. Their highest loyalty is
to the centre of their life. All representative others in their life are
expected to cherish and to respect this centre. Otherwise they could not
become representative others for them. And here comes the first temptation, the temptation to vacate the centrepoint of life for an other. This
other is not necessarily a person, it can also be an idea or a cause which
is alien to, or in conflict with, the centrepoint of life. If the centrepoint
of life is vacated and comes to be filled by an exterior other (a man,
a woman, an idea, a cause), the person loses himself – his life is in
shambles . . .

Lawrence: I understand now why authenticity is loyalty. You never
betray the centre of your life for anything or anyone. Not even once. For
once betrayed means betrayed absolutely; there is no second time . . . But
I do not understand why truthfulness is blended with loyalty. Truthfulness means first of all telling the truth about yourself. But painters or
novelists, for example, do not disclose themselves; and although – if you
ask me – philosophers do, although indirectly, Joachim thinks that I am
wrong. Truthfulness can also mean to telling the truth, and nothing but
the truth. But what is truth in painting or in politics or in fiction? Or even
in philosophy? I am a perspectivist; I think that I have my truth and you
have yours. Does truthfulness enjoin me to remain loyal to my own
truth? This is just loyalty, and nothing else. Why do we speak about a
'blending' if there is nothing to be blended?

Joachim: It may come as no surprise to you that I understand what
truthfulness does for the virtue of authenticity, but I have problems with
loyalty. You should never lie; this is a univeral moral maxim. As a

universal moral maxim it must be valid and it is, in all kinds of ethics. No ethics can allow falsity. But loyalty to myself is not loyalty – this is the wrong expression. I cannot be disloyal to myself in so far as I follow my interests. I can only be loyal to something or someone other than myself – to a person, an idea, a cause – even if it hurts my interests. To speak about the pursuit of a cause, of an idea, or of the absolute loyalty to a friend as temptations that could result in the loss of oneself is a scandal of reason and a scandal of the heart . . .

Lawrence: You are straying away from Kant this time. Kant would not always appreciate your self-abandonment to a cause, or a friend, let alone your mention of the scandal of the heart.

Joachim: I know that I was unorthodox but I do not mind. Loyalty to a friend is the best, it is the highest virtue, or rather the supreme good in life. You do not lose yourself in friendship, but rather gain yourself. Friendship is the green crown of the goldentree of life.

Lawrence: Provided that friendship is the centrepoint of your life. Otherwise, it is temptation, perhaps the strongest of all temptations.

Joachim: Don't resist temptation!

Lawrence: I am stupefied. You, the Kantian, tell me, the Nietzschean, that I should not resist temptation? And I, the Nietzschean should answer you, the Kantian, that yes, one must resist temptation?

Joachim: But why?

Lawrence: Wrong question, again. Still, I have the answer: in order to remain what you are.

Vera: Yes, a repository of an ethics of personality resists temptation. He throws the inkstand in the face of the tempter: 'Here I stand and cannot do otherwise.'

Joachim: Is the friend then the devil?

Lawrence: Everything and everyone who tempts us to be untrue to ourselves is the devil. The sweeter, the more devilish.

Joachim: For Heaven's sake – you speak like Immanuel Kant!

Lawrence: And like Friedrich Nietzsche. The ethics of personality is, after all, an ethics. But I still wait for Vera's answer to my question.

Vera: Hasn't Joachim answered it?

Lawrence: Not quite. Joachim said that, of course, truthfulness means that we do not lie. If one thinks in his terms, one can keep the virtue of loyalty and the virtue of truthfulness apart. But why does authenticity require that we should not lie? In addition, what does it mean that we should not lie to ourselves? We need to know first what truth is before we can tell the truth to ourselves or lie to ourselves. What is even worse, we should know ourselves. But if we neither know the truth nor know ourselves, the demand that we should not lie to ourselves becomes meaningless, or at least very vague . . .

Joachim: Distinguishing between lying and telling the truth belongs to our capacity to tell good from evil. And although I agree that we can never fully know ourselves, the ancient moral injunction 'know thyself' remains valid. It is an imperative because we are not entirely transparent to ourselves. Not lying to ourselves cannot possibly mean telling the whole truth about ourselves to ourselves – if there is such a 'truth' at all – but rather, being candid with ourselves as much as possible, not flattering our dear ego, trying, really trying, to illuminate our motives, and to beware of taking our ego-ideal at its face value. Like every kind of knowledge, self-knowledge is also approximate . . .

Lawrence: You are again in trouble, Joachim, and since you are honest with yourself, you realize it. As a good Kantian, you have severed knowledge from morality once and for all. From your perspective, the whole issue of knowing yourself in terms of being candid with yourself and finding out your motives must be either irrelevant or of tertiary importance. It is only in the ethics of personality for which I am standing that 'being true to ourselves' matters and where it matters above all. To know my destiny is to know myself. And this is all I need to know, I do not need to be fully candid . . .

Joachim: You are as inconsistent as I am, even more so. If *amor fati* is an instinct, or at least a blend of reason and instinct, if you are pulled and never pushed by the will to power, the whole issue of knowing yourself is idle – and far more so for you than for me.

Vera: You do not notice that you say the same thing, although you express it otherwise. You agreed in your disagreement that being true to ourselves is something other than knowing ourselves. If the centrepoint of your life pulls, obedience to this pull is being true to yourself. Your shadow-boxing fixed us to the same point; we have still not distinguished truthfulness from loyalty.

Lawrence: I now begin to recall something that our professor said about Nietzsche's concept of truthfulness: never lie in your work. One remains true to oneself if one never lies in one's work. Joachim is right: 'You should not lie' is a general moral maxim.

Joachim: But in your ethics of personality that we are now discussing, the general moral maxim is not employed as a general moral maxim. The injunction 'you should not lie' is entirely different from the one 'you should never lie in your work'. The second injunction is specified. You can lie as well as not on any other occasion or context, but in your work, and in that alone, you should not lie!

Lawrence: But if it is true that the centre of your life and of yourself is your work, and you never lie in your work then the centre of your life remains pure, unspoiled. But again, how do you know? How do you know whether you are lying or being true in your work, whatever this work may be?

Vera: At the beginning of the century when I used to listen to the conversations of the other Lawrence and the other Joachim, it was my task to grind coffee for all of us. As long as the mill was full of coffee beans, grinding was difficult, the moment that there were no more beans left in the mill, it became very easy. If grinding is very easy and you still pretend to grind those coffee beans, you are lying. You are lying if you continue grinding nothing.

Joachim: This sounds Kantian, or rather Stoic: if you have a choice between doing something that is difficult and doing something that is easy, choose the difficult. But this hardly fits into your scenario. Whatever is supposed to make up the centre of your self, you pursue with passion, and self-abandon – absolutely. This is far easier than succumbing to temptation. I do not see here any temptation.

Vera: The trouble with you is once again your transcendental anthropology. Your scheme is too simple; the whole traditional 'picture' of the self is too simple. You keep forgetting things we have already discussed: suffering and felicity are not contraries, and to be true to our absolute commitment is to be crucified to the task. I love my fate and I am also crucified to my fate. It is not the love that I am tempted to abandon, but the bitter cup. If grinding coffee is your self-allotted task, you always concentrate on grinding coffee. People may come and go – you grind coffee; interesting things happen around you – you just grind your coffee. Others are happy in an ordinary sense – you just grind coffee. You are lonely, isolated . . .

Lawrence: My dear Vera, wake up! We are no more at the beginning of our century, but at the end of it. Today is May 1992. We are not your old friends Joachim and Lawrence, we are a new Joachim and a new Lawrence. Talk to us!

Vera: I know, I became a little old-fashioned. But if I am antiquated, it is not my fault.

Lawrence: Whose fault is it then?

Vera: Perhaps there are no longer men and women who have chosen themselves under the category of difference. Perhaps no one is any more pulled by her fate. Perhaps no one any more loves her fate. In the times of my old friends Joachim and Lawrence, they still did.

Lawrence: My dear Vera, you sound like a cultural pessimist à la Nietzsche. But Nietzsche had said all this before your old Lawrence and Joachim were even born. The predictions concerning the demise of old-European high culture were proven wrong. And as long as this culture exists, there will always be men and women who choose themselves under the category of difference . . .

Vera: I said perhaps' I have not predicted anything . . .

Lawrence: Yet you have interrupted yourself with your recollections. We still want to figure out something about truthfulness in our ethics of personality. I liked your simile of coffee-grinding, thought. But this is still very vague.

Vera: Here you enter again the territory where you soon encounter the limits of reason and of knowledge. We do not know how another person is able to distinguish between telling the truth and lying. We just know that he can. For example, someone writes a novel and at a certain point she commits a sentence to paper and immediately gets the feeling 'this is not right, this is not me, this is a lie, I should not leave this sentence as it stands', and she is about to delete it. If she does not delete this sentence, she begins to err in her distinction between 'true' and 'false', becomes untrue to herself, and probably loses herself. I read a funny thing somewhere that it is the 'absolute spirit' that whispers into our ears 'Don't write this, this is a lie, one should not lie', I found it a nice, although a too Hegelian, metaphor.

Lawrence: But why would anyone decide not to listen to the whisper of the absolute spirit if she hears it distinctly?

Vera: Because not everyone resists temptation. I mentioned the subtle temptations to you: causes, ideas, love – but there are less subtle ones, like position, money, fame . . .

Joachim: Kant all the time!

Vera: Yes and no. Yes, because wealth, fame and power are the great tempters. No, because following my instinct-reason is the best protection against temptation. Of course, that's only if I have chosen myself under the category of difference . . .

Joachim: And yes, because it is absolutely decisive that you never make an exception for yourself. You cannot say: this time I lie, next time I will not. To make an exception is morally wrong.

Lawrence: And not because your expression 'to make an exception for yourself' makes no sense here. You are yourself, you are an exception . . .

Joachim: The gist of the matter is, however, that you do not lie even once.

Lawrence: The gist of the matter is, however, that lying and telling the truth means something different in a universalistic context from what it means in the context of my ethics of personality.

Vera: In telling the truth, in resisting temptations, be they subtle or profane, you keep your promise . . .

Joachim: Kant says that you should never make a promise without having the resolve to keep it. This is true for your ethicist of personality too.

Lawrence: Yes, but here you have made the promise to yourself, not to others.

Joachim: Kant would raise no objections to this interpretation. I remind you for the second time that he classified lying among the vices we commit against ourselves. And now, about the infamous whisper of the 'absolute spirit': isn't it just another way of describing the voice of conscience?

Lawrence: Yes and no. Yes, because the whisper advises you about right and wrong in an ethical sense. If the voice tells you 'go ahead' this is an ethical approval, but if it whispers, 'stop, do not lie' it is a warning. No, because it is a warning and not an absolute interdiction. And no again, because if you defy the voice you harm first and foremost yourself and not others. You do not harm the moral law within yourself, you rather destroy your destiny.

Joachim: Wrong, for it was you and Vera who insisted that the repository of your ethics of personality creates something for others; that she bestows a gift; a gift for which you have not laboured, a gift you will not reciprocate; a free gift which elevates you above your daily cares and brings you felicity . . . If she becomes untrue to herself, if she fails to keep the promise she made to herself, if she is weak and cowardly or ambitious and vainglorious, and fails to resist temptation – she betrays you, not just herself. She makes you poorer while withholding her riches.

Lawrence: At first you denied the possibility of our ethics of personality, and now – lo and behold – you not only accept it, but even over-ethicize it . . .

Joachim: One cannot 'over-ethicize and ethics'. And mind your style . . .

Lawrence: Yes one can, and never mind my style as long as you can understand me. You seem to forget again that we still speak about an ethics that you have denounced as consequentialist. And it *is* consequentialist. For how do I know that you have remained true to yourself? From the work of yours in which you have never lied. But how can I possibly read from the text of an average work that, had the author been authentic, he would have written or painted or composed a greater, a better, a superior one.

Joachim: Be honest, in many cases you can see it quite well. You know of poets, philosophers, or painters who authored important and promising works which were not followed by others of their kind because their makers betrayed their destiny.

Lawrence: I see your point and I agree. Yet still, the lucky throw of the dice is such a complex coincidence of factors. Two persons can equally choose themselves as poets, but the first has more brilliant endowments than the second. Assume that the one with more brilliant endowments betrays his chosen destiny to a degree, but not entirely. As a result, there will be false notes in his work, but there will remain also true ones. The man of weaker original endowment, however, remains through and through true to himself. For us, the others, the recipients of the gift, the ethical difference does not really matter. Both of them endow us with gift of a kind. We are interested in the gift itself, not in the author's ethic. Hannah Arendt once discussed Bertolt Brecht from this perspective. Had Brecht not lied in his poetry, Arendt claimed, he would have become a far greater poet, he would have endowed us with greater gifts. Still, he endowed us with some gifts, maybe ones as good as those of Auden, who had good morals and whom Arendt approvingly quotes.

Joachim: I might have over-ethicized your ethics, but I still do not take your point. As far as moral relevance is concerned, I do not see the sharp contrast between the two kinds of ethics of personality. If someone helps you in your sickness, you are not interested – to speak with my Kant – in whether she did it out of duty or simply because she likes you, or just has a good heart. As far as you are concerned, you have received the same help. And you cannot even tell the difference. But from the moral respect the difference is still enormous, because one acts rightly on principle and the other by impulse. Something similar, although not the same, can be said in your cases. For the recipient of the gift, a beautiful poem is a beautiful poem. It is pointless to ruminate about whether the author, had he been more sincere, could have written an even more beautiful poem or not. But for the poet himself this is not a matter of indifference. Because, as you have admitted, we cannot ignore the voice of conscience, or if you wish, the whisper of the absolute spirit. The author himself – he knows about his possibilities, he is aware of the betrayal: he cannot keep it entirely hidden from himself that he could have done better and more, that he could have bestowed more precious gifts on his neighbours had he remained true to his internal guide. People who are existential failures are aware of it, if only faintly. They are aware that there is no fulfilment in their lives. Your poet of minor endowment is fulfilled for she becomes what she is. Your poet who has betrayed himself never is. This is the ethical difference.

Lawrence: In your mind, consequentialism is a serious accusation, and you did your best to defend our ethics of personality against it. Thank you for your noble efforts. But I think you went too far, because you have universalized something that you cannot. I would not deny that some authors who have betrayed their chosen talents feel the burden of their betrayal – others, however, do not. Many remain convinced that they made a turn to the better in becoming successful at any price. The eye of the other is not always an ethical judge; it can measure by the yardstick of semblances.

Joachim: You now just made a very Kantian statement: good men are worthy of happiness, but they are not happy.

Lawrence: Yes, roughly this may also be said about the heroes and heroines of our ethics of personality.

Vera: At least we have arrived somewhere. For even Joachim agreed that there is a non-univeralistic ethics which still remains an ethics in so far as it shares decisive categories with the traditional ethics of old religious and lay moral philosophies.

Joachim: Let me formulate it more succinctly. Yes, I agree that there is an ethics of personality. But the bearer of an ethics of personality is not necessarily also a moral or ethical person. She is a moral or ethical person only under the condition that she has chosen herself under the category of universality. You see I am not doctrinaire. For the time being I will not push the issue of universality further. Still, you must admit that a person who is neither good (decent), nor ready to subject herself to valid norms or rules of decency, goodness, or justice cannot be termed a moral person, even if she has an ethics of her own. She is not the green crown of the goldentree of life; she endows this crown to others in the form of a gift.

Lawrence: We agreed that regardless of whether someone has chosen himself under the category of the universal or under the category of the difference, we speak in either case about an ethics of personality. In modernity no other ethics is possible . . .

Joachim: 'Why not?' is still an open question. Yet I will accept this too. Still I insist that only those who choose themselves under the category of the universal are to be termed moral subjects. And to avoid any misunderstanding, I do not speak here about the subject in a Kantian but rather in a Kierkegaardian sense. We can ignore the epistemological subject, the transcendental subject, and speak about the exister alone.

Vera: Sören used to distinguish between aesthetic and ethical existence. The third is the religious . . .

Joachim: We discuss only the aesthetic and the ethical exister now. But contrary to Kierkegaard, and in the spirit of Nietzsche, we also attributed a kind of ethics of personality to the aesthetic exister. Now, very much in the spirit of Kierkegaard, we might also attribute a kind of 'aesthetics of personality' to the ethical exister.

Vera: You do not know Sören well if you identify him with Judge William . . .

Lawrence: Excuse me for interrupting. It is seven o'clock already. One cannot discuss marriage, which is also a matter of household, on the meagre diet of cake and tea. I propose that we dine first and continue to live on spiritual food afterwards. Let me call the Chinese restaurant and order some food. They will deliver it in no time.

(After sharing a Chinese meal with wine, Vera and the two friends remain seated around the table.)

Vera: Joachim, it is your turn. You have promised to speak about the aesthetic dimension in the life of the moral exister in Judge William's terms.

Joachim: Sorry, I haven't promised anything of the kind. I just made an innocent reference to one of Kierkegaard's pseudonyms in order to underline my conviction that the signs must now be reversed. We now must speak about the aesthetic dimension of the ethical. But I prefer to do this in my orthodox Kantian manner. I would speak about beauty as the symbol of morality, about the intellectual interest in the beautiful; that is, about the good man who adores the beauty of nature, and about refinement and grace as the decoration of good deeds . . .

Lawrence: That would be grossly unfair on your part. We should honour symmetry. Till now, that we have been speaking of men and women of *amor fati*, we have not treated ethics just as a decoration or addendum to the aesthetic dimension. Rather, we discussed the ethics of personality, remember? Ethics, so we said and you agreed, inheres in the way of life of all those who are pulled by their destiny. Please do not repay us in small change. If you take the challenge seriously, you must tell us how the aesthetic dimension *inheres* in your ethics . . .

Joachim: It does not.

Lawrence: A poor answer.

Joachim: Here I stand and cannot do otherwise.

Vera: I shall be the mouthpiece of Judge William, then. To choose ourselves as good, decent people is to choose ourselves back into the human race. Goodness is goodness in relation to the other. Among all these relationships there is an absolute relationship. Let me abbreviate Judge William's long explanation with a metaphor. The centrepoint of ethics is not the conscience of the single person, neither is it humankind in us (or in others), but the relationship between two persons. Neither One nor All: *Two is the moral number*. Judge William – so he says – is nothing without his wife, and his wife – so he says – is nothing without him. I choose myself as a decent person absolutely in-and-with the absolute relationship; we two together become what we are – decent persons. There is only one history: that of becoming what we are, and this is the lived history of the absolute relationship . . .

Joachim: There are things that you have said with which I sympathize. First, the moral actor relates to the others directly, while for the lover of fate she is just the unintended receiver of a possible gift. I sympathize too with the term 'absolute relationship', for absolute is also unconditional. There is no morality without an unconditional foundation. Finally, and this follows from the above, I have never liked the idea of an ethics of loneliness. I agree with Hannah Arendt that loneliness – in contrast to solitude – is something essentially anti-ethical and unpolitical. What I do not like, you will easily guess: two is the wrong number in morals, the relation of two cannot be absolute, for it cannot be unconditional. Every concrete human relation is fragile, for it includes many contingencies. And since Judge William speaks about his marriage, I must now turn Lawrence's accusation against me back on to you, Vera: you are conservative and pathetically so. There is no more 'till death do us part' in modern life. I do not mean that it is counterfactual, but that it is not even desired or idealized. Humankind in us, reason, does not succumb to change, it is not fragile, it resists contingency . . .

Lawrence: Dear me, and you call Vera conservative! True, 'till death do us part' is not a social norm any more, and the marriage vow is normally taken lightly. But this is a point that speaks for Vera – or Judge Wiliam

– not against them! Because it is only now that a marriage vow can become a fully autonomous gesture, that it can inhere in an existential choice. Please, do not forget that one chooses all contingencies as one's own destiny. 'Till death do us part' as a marriage vow has become contingent, and that is precisely why can you transform it into your common destiny.

Joachim: It is difficult for me to think in terms of marriage vows.

Lawrence: But don't you see that there is not just one kind of absolute relationship. A friendship can also be an absolute relationship – in this respect there are no social conventions. You must see the weakness of your objection clearly . . .

Joachim: I see now that the demise of social conventions was a bad counter-argument. But I am still afraid that absolute relationships are fictitious. There are no absolute relationships.

Lawrence: So you just approximate. Don't you remember? You always just approximate the centre of the circle – you never end up in the centre. The absolute relationship of two persons is the moral centre – we approximate this centre. That we never 'have' an absolute relationship absolutely, is not an argument against the absolute relationship, the 'unconditional' of our Judge William.

Joachim: But what makes the absolute relationship absolute? What makes it unconditional?

Vera: The existential choice. In the orchestration of Judge William, choosing ourselves existentially as decent persons is tantamount to choosing the absolute relationship. It is unconditional precisely because it has been chosen absolutely, unconditionally. You become what you are – one of two persons in an absolute relationship.

Joachim: And what if a third person enters and the relationship breaks apart?

Vera: If you choose existentially, this will not happen. Third persons can enter the scene, but the relation will not be torn apart for it is unconditional, absolute.

Joachim: Yet I still ask, if I may, what happens to these friends if the relation nevertheless breaks apart?

Vera: The same as in all other cases in which an existential choice does not come off: they lose themselves, they become failed existences.

Joachim: Is it that simple? I choose myself together with another absolutely – and then I am suddenly in an absolute relationship?

Vera: Yes and no. Yes, because the relationship will be unconditional. No, because you will from then on become what you are; it is then that you both will *begin*.

Joachim: Begin what?

Vera: History, lived history. Lived history in general is becoming what you are. If two people together become what they are, that is lived history in an ethico-aesthetic sense.

Joachim: Excuse me, I have an additional objection. On second thoughts I do not think that an absolute relationship can be called ethical. Two devils can also enter into an absolute relationship. But even if they two were angels, a person is decent if she is decent towards all persons whom she encounters, not just towards one.

Vera: Whether two devils can enter an absolute relationship does not concern us here. Judge William discusses two persons who have chosen themselve existentially as decent persons in this absolute relationship. But in the mind of Judge William and a few other pseudonyms of Sören, two devils cannot enter into an absolute relationship in principle. For the moral attitude is the attitude of disclosure, whereas the morally evil person stays in an 'enclosed reserve'.

Joachim: We can mutually disclose ourselves in our wickedness, too.

Vera: Sören does not think so. And alas, this is not so far away from your Kant. Given that you are at least obscurely aware of the moral law in you, you would not disclose your resolve to infringe upon to anyone on purpose. Evil persons could not then have an absolute relationship, according to Kant. Or so it seems if we try to examine this possibility in his terms.

Joachim: We agreed yesterday that Kant did not really conceive of radical evil. What about Macbeth and Lady Macbeth, then? Was this not an absolute relationship of two evils?

Vera: In Shakespeare's play the absolute relationship of two evils is madness: this shows that it is beyond the capacity of our soul to bear such a relationship. But the existential choice of decency is a choice under the category of the universal; it is open to all, not just to the exceptional person who goes to the limits and beyond. Only if the absolute relationship is ethical can a man and a woman, or two men, or two women mutually disclose themselves to one another.

Joachim: But why is mutual disclosure ethical? I admit that confession brings relief and mutual confession brings mutual relief. But relief, if too easily achieved, might be morally problematic . . .

Vera: Mutual confession is not a proper description of Judge William's idea of disclosure. An absolute relation is absolute because the two persons in the relationship make themeselves transparent to each other.

Joachim: We already know that we are not even transparent to ourselves . . .

Vera: We speak about approximation, once again. Two people make themselves as transparent to each other as they can; perhaps they will be more transparent to themselves while they disclose themselves to the other. Transparency stands for absolute confidence, trust . . .

Joachim: How can you trust a human being absolutely?

Vera: This was Sören's question too. But there is no answer to this question within the ethical sphere. In the ethical sphere you have expectations of the other. One can have absolute trust (not just approximation), only if one does not expect anything from the other. It is questionable whether we can still speak about an absolute relationship here. I suggest, however, that we return to ethics. In ethics the absolute relationship is entirely symmetrical; this is why disclosure is also mutual.

Lawrence: This absolute mutual disclosure bothers me too. How can another person remain interesting if I know him inside out? What can I expect in this relationship that I do not already have?

Vera: Joachim once said: ethics is not about the interesting. And he also said that it is not about knowledge. Ethics is about doing things, relating, acting, communicating, but first and foremost about becoming.

Lawrence: But I am not Joachim. I love the interesting, the surprise. I would be rather attracted to a demonic, even evil, character than to some meek lady who keeps disclosing herself to me and expects me to disclose myself to her.

Vera: You borrow your image of mutual disclosure from an analytical session. Analytical disclosure is a disclosure of suspicion. Existential disclosure is the manifestation of absolute trust.

Joachim: I still do not understand why disclosure is ethical. I am not made good by disclosing myself, even if I disclose that I am good.

Vera: This remark reminds me that I still owe you an explanation. Earlier you said that a person who has chosen himself ethically should be decent to every person he encounters, and not just to one single person with whom he stands in an absolute relationship. You remember that when someone chooses himself existentially, he chooses himself back into the human race, into his family, country, age and so on. He then chooses himself back into a world of duties, virtues and obligations. You become what you are – a decent person – if you do your duties, honour your obligations, practise those virtues, keep your promises and so on. This is what it means to be a decent person. Judge William speaks about those duties – his duties as a judge, as the subject of his state, as the father of a family and so on – but he does not speak about his duties towards his wife, nor about his wife's duties towards him. For as you see, in an absolute relationship there are no duties. The absolute relationship is the lived history of a decent man, it is the unconditional foundation of a decent woman's decency, it is the *arché* of an ethical life; but taken in itself it is not 'ethical'. Sören would not subscribe to Hannah Arendt's suggestion that a decent person converses within himself with his own other self just as Socrates did. Socrates was an exceptional man, the Judge would tell us, but we are not exceptional people, we are just common men and women. We do not conduct ethical discussions within our soul with our other self, we need another flesh and blood person, another exister. Two separate persons, two existers in mutual disclosure and trust replace the dialogical relations of 'two in one'. Not 'two in one', but 'one in two'. With 'two in one' there can be suspicion, but with 'one in two' there cannot, for these two love one another. They love one another unconditionally. The unconditional love of existential equals (and if both existers have chosen themselves under the category of universality, they are ethically equals) is tantamount to the absolute relationship.

Joachim: Briefly, ethics is based on love. This is an old story. Why sell it in new wrapping?

Vera: Worse still, at least for you, is that not just the wrapping is new. Ethics is based on love; but not on *agape*, not on *caritas*, not at all. Ethics is based on Eros, on erotic love. Yet erotic love is by definition aesthetic.

Joachim: Then ethics is based on very slippery ground . . .

Vera: Sorry, I got carried away. Actually the Judge's ethics is not *based* on erotic love; how could he perform his duties as a judge if it were? His ethics is based on the existential choice of himself as a decent person; so is his wife's ethics. Erotic love is not the basis, not the foundation, but the vessel of ethics. It is the lifeline of ethics. Do your duty – this is far off from the image of the green crown of the goldentree of life! But the goldentree of life of decent persons who love one another erotically is – verily – green. The eternal spring is green.

Joachim: Vera dear, this is bad poetry . . .

Vera: Bad poetry perhaps, but good life. And the expression 'eternal spring' means something very specific here. Through an absolute, unconditional relationship, two persons become together what they are. This is lived history. But throughout this history – long or short – they never grow old. They discover each other every day. This is the first love which is also the last.

Lawrence: Now that you say it, and say it with such gusto, I see the attraction of this ethico-aesthetic life. I was wrong. History of the eternal spring is interesting, colourful and warm. But alas, it is entirely impossible. I said earlier that neither do we desire an absolute relationship, nor is it possible for socio-historical reasons. I have changed my mind: I desire it, and the issue of socio-historical possibility is entirely irrelevant. But it is still impossible. Psychologically impossible. We are not always good. We cannot constantly disclose ourselves, and even if we could, we do not want to. There is always a third person intruding into a relationship between the two. And if you object that the choice of an unconditional relationship is the unconditional choice, and we either do what is difficult to do or else we lose ourselves, or that we should approximate the choice we once made, I tell you that none of these well-known tricks of your friend Sören work this time. Because if becoming what we are turns out to be a thorny road, what is the difference then between the rigorous judgement of the moral law and the erotic love of one's friend or wife? Moreover, what has aesthetics to do with the latter if it has nothing to do with the former?

Vera: Dearest Lawrence, you have made my task too easy. The only thing I need to do now is to throw back at you your own arguments in defence of a Nietzschean ethics of personality. Suffering and enjoyment, felicity and being crucified, so you said, should not be juxtaposed to one another for they are intimately interwoven. So be it. And if you know the difference between the autonomous man of Kant and that of Nietzsche, you must also understand the difference between Judge William's absolute relationship and Kant's unconditional moral law. The dividing line is not between the easy and the difficult. Everything good – and not just in a moral sense – is difficult. What we sought we have found.

Joachim: Yes, we have.

Lawrence: I think that, rather, we found something that we have not sought. We were seeking the aesthetic aspect of the ethical and we found erotic love's absolute relationship as the alleged vessel of the ethical. But why is erotic love of aesthetic *valeur*? Clichés like 'eternal spring' are – I'm sorry, Vera – less than helpful. 'Aesthetic' can simply mean sensual or sensible, particularly in the presence of a Kantian friend. But when I say 'aesthetic' I mean beautiful, well formed, tasteful, creative and so on. Erotic love's absolute relationship is, I admit, 'aesthetic' in a strictly Kantian sense, but not in my sense. At least I do not yet know whether it is aesthetic in my sense.

Joachim: It is my turn now to be flabbergasted. How can you have doubts that erotic love is aesthetic both in a Kantian and non-Kantian sense? Have you forgotten your Plato? The attractiveness of the beautiful body of a boy? Or of the beautiful soul of the mentor?

Lawrence: No, I remember it well. But Vera has left us in darkness concerning the beauty of the body of Judge William or his wife. Their souls seem all right, but their bodies could be ugly. And, of course, if they grow old together, their bodies would be ugly.

Vera: The Judge says that for him his wife is the most beautiful of all women, and he also says that her beauty increases with age.

Lawrence: There are now two alternatives. Either there is a canon or some criteria by which to tell beautiful from ugly or for everyone the beloved will be the most beautiful and the one disliked will be ugly. In the second case we can forget about distinguishing between beautiful and ugly, for 'loving' or 'disliking' can be substituted for the distinction. What will be beautiful for me, will be ugly for you. I think that this is childish nonsense. There are criteria to tell the beautiful from the ugly, even if – I agree – only approximately.

Joachim: You never cease to surprise me, dear friend of mine. Yesterday you denied that there are criteria to tell true from false. Today, however, you make a case for a common, intersubjective criterion of the beautiful, you even suggest that perhaps there might be a canon that performs a so-called 'objective' distinction. If you can say 'my truth', why cannot poor Judge William address his wife 'my beauty' with at least the same justification. I may have problems here, but you should not. You ought to admit that when Judge William sees in his wife the most beautiful of women, a woman he loves with the eternity of first love, he does love beauty, just as the lovers did in Plato's dialogues . . .

Lawrence: I am not convinced.

Joachim: Then you should rethink all of that which you have said about truth.

Lawrence: And even if I were convinced, I would still not admit that we have so far dealt with any of the central issues of the aesthetic aspect of the ethical.

Vera: What are those 'central aspects' then?

Lawrence: At last, you have asked a question. This is perhaps your first. But let me see. You wanted to convince us that an aesthetic aspect inheres in the ethical when we choose ourselves under the category of the universal. Inherence means here that the aesthetic aspect is not an embellishment, a mere decoration of the ethical, but the ethical itself is impossible without it. If erotic love and its absolute relationship is indeed the vessel of the ethical, you have made your point. What bothers me is that we still remain under the umbrella of the category of the universal. True, in Kierkegaard's sense the individual is the universal, but you have also said in another context that every person is decent in her own way, that every decent person is different, and so on. I still do not see how beauty can mark the difference among decent persons. Not all decent persons are beautiful – or are they? And even if they were, they could not be equally beautiful. In cases of beauty, 'equality' makes no sense for there is no comparison between one beauty and another, and yet there is still less and more, and 'yes' and 'no'. And I can tell a beautiful personality from a less beautiful one even if both are decent and good. What are your criteria, where do you make your distinctions? Or why don't you make distinctions?

Vera: I would happily make all these distinctions, but they do not belong to the ethical. And we are discussing the aesthetic aspect of the ethical.

Lawrence: Wrong! Please don't let yourself be influenced by Joachim's boring universalism. I admit, your universalism is more bearable. You have annulled the annoying distinction between humankind in us and us as whole humans, but you still stick somehow to the category of the universal with statements such as 'everyone can do it', 'eveyerone can choose oneself', and so on. But dear Vera, not everyone can be elegant and beautiful and noble and tactful and deep and great – yet all of these are aesthetic categories, although ethical ones as well.

Vera: I thought that we had discussed, or at least had alluded to, all of them before dinner. I remind you of our lengthy controversy about the existential choice of ourselves under the category of difference . . .

Lawrence: But I do not speak of them. More precisely, from my point of view it does not really matter whether someone has chosen himself under the category of the universal or under the category of difference. There are people of the one kind as well as of the other kind who stand out; they are the more noble, the more subtle ones. Your differentiation may be important, but it overlooks an essential category which is neither that of the universal nor that of difference. Correction: the term 'category' is unsuitable, for there is a tremendous difference here – and not the difference between the poet's creativity and the creativity of the philosopher. It is rather a difference similar to that of the greater and lesser artist, yet at the same time, quite unlike it. For it is not the ability for something that makes the difference here, but the way 'to be'. Moreover, this is a 'to be' that has nothing to do with 'to become'; it is a fact. Not a fact of reason, but a fact of personality. Not an eternal fact, but a temporal fact: the fact of finitude. Is there anything more important in a man than this fact of finitude?

Vera: You become what you are till the end of your days. Only the eternal *is*, without becoming what it is. Joachim's 'fact of reason' is eternal. Since you refer to the fact, or rather to *a* fact, of finitude, your fact cannot *be* without *becoming* that which it is. One does not need to be a philosopher to understand this practical commonplace. A child is born, it comes into being, it exists. Living is nothing other than becoming what you are in the broadest sense. In a narrower sense – and you know this from experience and observation, and not from philosophy – you are born as a bundle of practically infinite possibilities. You can – *in abstracto* – become each of them, but you *will* become only a few of them. Every becoming annuls another becoming. If you fail to choose yourself, a few of the initial possibilities will randomly be selected, others ignored, but none of them will be chosen. What you are and what you become is determined by exterior and interior (psychological) conditions, by other contingencies. You are, then, heteronomous. But we have already covered all of this. This is why I really do not understand what you mean by 'a kind of being that does not become' and why you point at a phantom with such an unmistakable pathos.

Joachim: Our dear Lawrence may have taken a sharp turn towards traditional metaphysics. He may have in mind individual substances – although even a Leibnizian individual substance becomes what it is with God's foreknowledge. But Lawrence's individual substance is the eternal that changes only its accidents, its contingent manifestations. But why then is the eternal termed 'a fact of finitude'? Oh my dear, you have created such a mess!

Lawrence: There is a mess here, but I wonder whether I was the one who created it. How can you philosophically describe the fact that someone is a significant personality? Is this so 'by nature'? No one can be a personality 'by nature'. On the other hand, do you *become* a significant personality without having been one? No, wrong, again!

Joachim: But it is still right!

Lawrence: No, it is wrong. By relying on her untutored wisdom, Vera has nicely summed up one of the conclusions of our conversations. You either choose yourself existentially, one way or another, and then become what you are autonomously – where autonomy stands for being pulled by your destiny and not pushed by contingent determinations; or you fail to choose yourself and still become someone, but not through your choice – rather through a determined, conditional process of random selections. This kind of person *is*, but he does not *exist*, for he is not an exister. Of course there is the third eventuality. This we encounter whenever an existential choice does not come off. Then the exister falls apart and remains a failed exister. However, we have not yet considered the 'something' which is not chosen, but also not determined by others. This 'something' is not a phantom: I call it 'personality'.

Vera: Why do you think that a personality is not chosen?

Lawrence: Because, you see, we cannot lose it. Even if we go to pieces, even if we are failed existences, our personality remains. This is what I mean when I refer to it as an unchanging fact of finitude, a being that does not become. But the philosophical language has left me in the lurch. I cannot express what I mean philosophically. The personality is not a substance in an Aristotelian or in a Leibnizian sense. It 'has' no accidents, it does not manifest itself in phenomena, it is not an essence that appears, it is nothing 'metaphysical'. Nor can it be described in the language of the ontology of *Dasein*. It is not the 'human condition', it does not belong to historicity, and – this was my starting-point – I cannot describe it in the language of the philosophy of existence. Neither can I decribe it in the Kantian language. Philosophy has obviously never taken notice of this fact of being, for it is neither a 'subject' nor an 'object', even less a subject-object – and it has no epistemological or ethical relevance. This finite fact of being is a giver of gifts without giving gifts, it is a gift itself without a giver. But – how can I express myself? – it is the salt of the earth. Or, if you prefer your Goethan metaphor, it is the green crown of the goldentree of life . . .

Vera: Lawrence, now you are a poet, but a dilettantish one, I am sorry to say. You still speak about 'personality' as if it were a phantom or a mystical something . . .

Joachim: Excuse me, you said that your phantom-like 'personality' has no ethical relevance. Why then do you introduce this character into a discussion that we conduct about the possibility of an ethics of personality?

Lawrence: Let me first answer Joachim, for that is easy. I said that a great personality is like the salt of the earth. We become what we are – decent persons, poets, politicians, philosophers and so on – through the existential choice of ourselves. But the choice does not provide the salt. We become what we are, with or without salt, for we have chosen ourselves. But still the presence or absence of the salt makes a tremendous difference. If your being is heavy with significance, your actions will also be heavy. If your being is beautiful, your actions will also be beautiful. If a personality is significant and beautiful, her presence changes everything around her. Judge William, as we learned from Vera, described the erotic love of the absolute relationship as the vessel of ethics. The salt is as important as the vessel . . .

Joachim: No, it is not as important. We came to the conclusion previously that the aesthetic element inheres in the existential choice of ourselves as decent persons, but, at least as far as I have understood you, one can be a decent person or a good poet or a lawyer without being a great personality in your view.

Lawrence: Perhaps personality also inheres in our choices, at least in our choices under the category of the difference.

Joachim: But you said a minute ago that we do not choose it at all. If it were the necessary condition of the choice, we would be pushed rather than pulled. If we actually leap, then what you call a 'personality' may be one – although only one – of the internal conditions that we actually choose. We become what we are: among other things, this and this personality. I am sorry, you cannot escape logic.

Lawrence: I don't care. If you probe somewhat deeper into the beautiful sentences and arguments of Plato, you will see that he too often settled arguments with metaphors.

Joachim: He invented better metaphors.

Lawrence: He benefited from being first-born. Clothes are worn out when the last-born finally inherits them. Sorry, I have not answered Vera yet. Yes, what we call personality is something mystical, not just because one cannot explain what a personality is, but also because personalities are surrounded by an aura. They are like works of art. They are hermeneutically inexhaustible, and although they may be fully reliable, they still remain unpredictable. I cannot describe them without pompous words. I am not a poet, my poetry is bad. But my bad poetry, my pompous words and my ill-expressed pathos are nothing but hints.

Vera: What are you hinting at?

Lawrence: At nothing. Perhaps this is what you describe as indirect communication.

Joachim: Bad poetry is indeed a hint; it indicates that the ideas are meagre. Your ideas, Lawrence, are meagre. Think of it, just think a little about what you are saying.

Lawrence: I am thinking of it . . .

Joachim: In your youthful way, yes. But not in a mature way.

Lawrence: Please do not act old with your mere thirty years . . .

Joachim: Thirty is still more than twenty-three. But this is neither here nor there. Do you remember how you introduced the theme of 'personality' into our discussion?

Lawrence: I have not introduced the theme of 'personality' into our discussion. Have you forgotten that we address ourselves fully to the question of an ethics of personality? We do not speak of anything else but personality.

Joachim: Don't defend yourself before having been criticized. While we discussed the ethics of personality, we concentrated on ethics and ignored personality itself. I would not say that we took 'personality' as such for granted, but we made our interpretation of personality dependent on our main concern. You are right that it never occurred to us to discuss phenomena like 'the greatness' of personality separately. We presupposed, and to my mind rightly so, that if someone chooses oneself as a decent person and becomes what she is, she will be a personality through and through – a quite unique being. That some good persons can be more significant than others may be true – in fact, it is true – but it does not matter in so far as both the more and the less significant ones are good. You say that it does matter, and you may add that it even matters ethically. Let me express myself in a Kantian manner – it *should not* matter ethically. Ethics is not about difference, it is about universality. At least in one sense everyone can choose himself, namely as a decent person. Let me repeat, ethics is democratic, it is egalitarian, even if only a few men and women make the effort to approximate the centre. If you begin to speak about personalities not in terms of the things they do *or refrain from doing* but in terms of their *being alone* – to quote your Nietzsche, this time with sympathy – we shall be in greater trouble than you now think. I am sure that you will manœuvre yourself into a host of theoretical difficulties even though certain empirical observations might support you. I may add that if you want to theorize about the representative cases of creative personalities, you will also run into difficulties. But the latter is not my major concern.

Lawrence: What does it mean to say that 'ethics is egalitarian' if everyone is decent in his or her own way; if they cannot be measured or compared; if they, together with their acts and works, stand beyond, or rather above, justice?

Joachim: I've told you already. Everyone can choose himself as a decent person. I would not say that all have equal access to the existential choice, for this would sound stupid, but all of them can leap, and none of them more or less than any other. Everything depends on the resolve.

Vera: Excuse me for interrupting you, but I reccomend you to read the works of another pseudonym of my Sören, Johannes Climacus; particularly the chapter on Lessing in *Concluding Unscientific Postscript*. He speaks specifically about the leap of faith – yet finally, every leap is the leap of faith. What you call 'the weight', the 'beauty', the 'greatness' of personality may ease the leap, but they may also make the feet of the ones who leap heavy. The leap does not depend on them.

Joachim: Let me continue. What you call 'personality' is sometimes identical with 'character'. But the word 'character' is also polysemous. For example, a 'man of character' is a man of good character, a decent person. A man of bad character is an indecent person. To analyse 'character' in those terms would add nothing to our discussion. One can also speak about a 'noble character'. Here we get closer to your problems. But still not close enough. A decent person is a noble character, in spite of the fact that 'nobility' is neither an accident nor a character-trait of a substance called 'decent character'. Every decent person has a character of her own, and so do many indecent persons, although not the majority. Most of them are simply characterless; like aeolian harps, they sound when the wind blows. When one has a character there is an intimate relationship between the 'ipseity' of that character and the person's fate.

Lawrence: All of what you said sounds interesting but irrelevant.

Joachim: This is exactly my point. It is irrelevant. Because you do not speak about personality as such, nor about character, but about the so-called 'facts of personality'. You enumerate a few, such as nobility, subtlety, greatness, beauty, weight (or heavy weight?) and so on, and you add that all those facts are mysterious. Furthermore, they just 'are' and do not become, which is why a personality-of-a-kind simply *is* without becoming what it is.

Lawrence: This is what I take to be relevant.

Joachim: Please think it over. If you speak of nobility and of baseness in this sense, you return to the Nietzschean distinction between noble and base. And this is a class distinction. I am not afraid of the term 'class', but I am afraid that it unmasks your mystery. Persons become noble because they are bred to be noble, whereas people remain banausic or base because of a lack of breeding or of good breeding. Your noble personality is like a beautiful racehorse. You see, I said a 'beautiful' racehorse, for I do not deny its beauty. But your noble-beautiful man, just like the beautiful racehorse, comes from a good family, looks back at distinguished ancestors, is reared and educated to follow in the ancestors' footsteps, and in addition he also practises continuously. Every day he disciplines himself, he works on himself – just as diligently as the others work on him. This is how he becomes the perfect noble personality of yours.

Lawrence: Already Nietzsche went beyond all that. You do not need class to be of a noble and subtle character. What you need is culture . . .

Joachim: Now you have fallen into your own trap. Whether or not it is rooted in class or in culture, there is nothing 'mysterious' about the 'fact of personality'. First of all it does not exist without becoming. You are 'born' noble if your parents, owing to their good breeding by their class or by their culture, are noble. If you choose yourself existentially, you choose everything that you are – obviously your class or culture too. You centre yourself and you begin to become. I do not see your 'fact' making any difference here. Needless to say, I could refute you also in Kantian terms, but I wanted to show that I can defeat you on your own grounds too.

Lawrence: That is Vera's ground.

Joachim: Before dinner you still spoke the language of *pluralis majestatis*: and I am entitled to assume, unless you prove me wrong, that you still fall back on to the hermeneutics of existence.

Lawrence: I fall back on to it in the state of emergency, but otherwise my paths are my own.

Joachim: Have I missed your point?

Lawrence: You did not, and yet you did. You did not, for there are no 'great', 'beautiful', 'noble', or 'subtle' personalities without upper class, high culture, or both. The Greeks had both, the feudal age had the upper class, while we are not in the position to have either the upper class alone or both, but we may still have high culture, And yet you did miss my point, because I would not admit that 'great', 'beautiful', 'noble', 'subtle' personalities are determined by the very existence of those classes and cultures. Neither would I admit that you can become noble and subtle and great as a personality through breeding, practice, exercise or drill. Noble personalities are unlike racehorses, although even racehorses require a very specific personal quality to make them good racehorses; pedigree and training alone will not do the job. The beautiful, noble, subtle personality 'feeds' on class or culture, but it is not made by them . . .

Joachim: This feeding worries me. The salt of the earth feeds on culture. Dear me, this is a double salto.

Lawrence: Please do not let yourself be misled by your own quip; your laughter is not like that of the Thracian woman. Whatever is dear to me is also dear to you.

Joachim: Yet your thesis can still be ridiculous. A Nietzschean should have a better sense of humour and a deeper sense of irony than a Kantian. But you are deadly serious, I am afraid.

Lawrence: Yes, I am serious, for what I say now is serious matter for me. But I will try to find a better metaphor. Let me start from the beginning. The 'greatness', the 'beauty', the 'nobility', the 'subtlety' of a personality are the facts of the personality precisely because they are neither chosen nor bred. But this 'fact' of personality is formed by class or culture . . .

Joachim: Here we go again: matter and form . . .

Lawrence: I cannot express myself otherwise. You can destroy or deconstruct metaphysics, but one thing you cannot deny: the philosophical concepts and characters of metaphysics are the sublimated versions of everyday concepts and characters. We cannot speak without them. They just come to our lips.

Joachim: That was Heidegger's point, particularly in his criticism of the Aristotelian and the Hegelian concepts of time . . .

Lawrence: But he thought that that speaks against metaphysics, and I rather think that it gives metaphysics credit. The language of the child is warm and cosy and the childish questions are always to the point. Metaphysics indulges in speaking the language of children. Please do not censure me if I borrow some of these childish questions, notions and characters. They are good characters, even if no longer trendy . . .

Joachim: Heidegger also asked the childish questions . . . But once again we are getting side-tracked; this time it is my fault. I would grant you, then, that high culture forms something that you call the 'fact of character'. This something is not created by culture, but it needs culture, otherwise the character remains raw and clumsy. But how can the so-called facts of personality, like 'subtlety', 'nobility' and 'beauty' remain raw and clumsy? And if perhaps it does make sense to think in terms of 'personality', what is the ethical relevance?

Lawrence: Everything whose opposite has an ethical relevance also has an ethical relevance.

Joachim: I agree.

Lawrence: Egalitarianism is the institutionalization of *ressentiment*. When I say 'egalitarianism' I do not, of course, mean political equality, equal rights or equality before the law. I am as much in favour of liberal-democratic political institutions as you are. Equality is a value, but it is not an end-value, rather it is a means-value. For example, I claim equality in rights, in freedoms – that is, my end-values are rights and freedom, not equality. What I claim is that the high values mentioned above should be allotted to all persons of a civil body without discrimination and without conditions. For an egalitarian, however, equality becomes the end-value, and other values – freedom included – are degraded to the level of means-values. That is what I term – after Nietzsche, and with some additional clarifications – institutionalized *ressentiment*.

Joachim: You embarrass me. First, there is no such thing as institution-alized equality, with the exception of the kind of equalities for which you yourself stand. And in spite of your reassurance, I smell the fragrance of anti-democratism in your vehemence, even if not in your words.

Lawrence: It is interesting how an otherwise impeccably noble person begins to talk like an unthinking member of the crowd when it comes to the issue of equality. 'I am embarrassed', you said; but only banausic people are embarrassed when suddenly confronted with a theory that does not suit their prejudices. You 'smell' certain 'fragrances' in my words; that is, you do not trust them, you harbour suspicions – these are all manifestations of something that is base. You prove my point indi-rectly. *Ressentiment* is not a personal feeling, it is not envy. I have not met a person who would be more resistant to envy than you. But one cannot defend equality without expressing *ressentiment* . . .

Joachim: Excuse me, but you are the one who proves my point. You make mention of the 'crowd' with the kind of contempt that, I am sorry, does smell of anti-democratism.

Lawrence: I do not mind the smell. I am ashamed that I have to tell you twice that in my mind there is no alternative to the liberal-democratic political arrangment in modernity, for all alternatives to it are lethal. But if you transform equality from a means-value into an end-value, equality rises to the position of the supreme value in everything. That all men are equally endowed with reason and conscience, that they were born equally free, these are meaningful and necessary modern fictions. But if you say that all men are equal, and if you mean thereby that every single person is of equal, quality and worth, you do manifest *ressentiment*. And since democracy allows for the extension of the value of equality above and beyond its optimal limits, and this extension is built into democratic imagination, I dare say that egalitarianism *is* institutionalized in modern democracies and *ressentiment* has become rampant.

Joachim: I do not see how all this is relevant for an ethics of personality.

Lawrence: I am surprised. If equality is a substantive value, and the highest one, then the distinction between high and low character, between the noble and the banausic, the beautiful and the ugly, the subtle and the rude, no longer makes sense. Yet since all those things are 'facts of personality' they still exist – but they remain unacknowledged. The one who acknowledges them, the one who recognizes this difference, is excommunicated or sent to the psychoanalyst. Public opinion, the democratic dragon with a million heads, then abuses the unequals as 'mad', 'deviant', or as 'eccentric' at best. Everything that is allowed becomes obligatory. The exception, the person who stands apart, becomes suspect. The dragon with a million heads has a good sense of smell: it will detect even the slightest scent of difference . . .

Joachim: I am amazed at what you have just said. Isn't difference rather highly respected nowadays?

Lawrence: You mean the difference between two infirmities? I guess so. Every person has to belong to a pack of wolves and to remain true to his own pack. But you're right, there are more packs than one. Each pack is a so-called 'difference': but each wolf is nothing whenever it differs from the rest of the pack.

Joachim: You now repeat the oldest objections to democracy.

Lawrence: They are as old as Socrates and Plato. And still true.

Joachim: But Plato was not a great liberal either . . .

Lawrence: True, but I am. You now classify me as a liberal anarchist, I suppose. But I am not an 'ist' of any kind. I disdain all 'isms'.

Joachim: I do not want to pigeonhole you as a person, but I can still place your views somewhere . . .

Lawrence: Why do you need to treat my view separately from my person?

Joachim: Because a personal acquaintance is private, whereas his views may be public. People who do not know you may still know your views.

Lawrence: They may not know me as a single person, but they could still believe in the relevance of singularity.

Joachim: You said that you see no alternative to democratic institutions, because the alternatives are lethal. How then, can you be so bitter, so pessimistic, when it comes to the description of the selfsame institutions?

Vera: Yesterday, without hiding your irritation you asked me why I addressed you as if you were Lawrence from the beginning of our century? But today you speak exactly as this other Lawrence did. A hundred years do not matter after all.

Lawrence: They do and they do not. Years matter, for at the turn of century your old friend Lawrence did not defend the institutions of liberal democracy against all alternatives. But they also do not matter, for the problems with substantive or communitarian democracy remain the same.

Joachim: But if you dismiss all alternatives to political democracy, and you still think that democracy has the tendency to become substantive and embrace *ressentiment*, what is the practical intent of your practical philosophy? Is it just a kind of cultural criticism, or also an ethics?

Lawrence: Every ethics of personality is also a kind of cultural criticism. This is as true of Kierkegaard as of Nietzsche or the young Lukács. I add my modest token to the work of my distinguished forbears. But this is a variety of cultural criticism with a timely practical intent. One can cherish great hopes, one can cherish few or none, but in both cases one still tries to find ways to stop the glorious forward march of *ressentiment*.

Joachim: What remedies are there in your old-fashioned but supposedly timely pharmacy?

Lawrence: Culture! If one abolishes the distinction between high and low culture then there is no remedy left in this pharmacy. It is the distinction between high and low culture that can replace the division of high and low classes. The class division will not return, as far as I can see, and it is a good thing that it will not. But something needs to fill its place. Hegel called it the 'absolute spirit'. If there is no difference between high and low culture, and no difference between a subtle and a banausic person (or if the difference remains unacknowledged), and if thus the earthly foundation of everything that is 'high' is lost – there will no longer be heaven, God or gods, ideas and ideals. There would be simply nothing that would stand higher than man, or rather, higher than the dragon with a million heads. If this happens the Leviathan, or as your Kant formulated it, Nature, will suck us back.

Joachim: What can the distinction between high and low culture achieve?

Lawrence: High culture can form the mysterious things which I termed 'the facts of personality', it can preserve distinction, greatness, subtlety and beauty. And it can also preserve the acknowledgement of all these facts of finitude. That the same respect is due to every person – this is just the most appalling idea of modern American political philosophy. Why should I respect a banausic person to the same extent as a noble one? This injunction is just the expression of the deepest *ressentiment*: that equal recognition is due to all persons is right and fair. At this point, however, I prefer your Kant. For equal recognition is still due to the moral law in each of us, that is, to the maximum ethical possibility that dwells in us all. But since some have made much use of this possibility, whereas others left it barren, why on earth should equal respect be due to all of them?

Joachim: This is a sweeping generalization about American political philosophy. Rawls, for example, would join you in giving preference to freedom as against all the other values . . .

Lawrence: True enough, and I appreciate that. But Rawls is also guilty of *ressentiment*. He says that nothing specific is 'due' to talents because talents have been won on the 'natural lottery'! I won't go into the character of the empty generalization represented by the term 'natural lottery' since you know my view on this. So let us assume that we have won our talents on the 'natural lottery' – why then should nothing specific be 'due' to those talents? Is the beauty of a man less worthy of adoration because at least certain conditions of it were won on the natural lottery? What is 'due' to a cat or to a tree that is not 'due' to a man? The puritanic steamroller of *ressentiment* does its equalizing work so well, that it occurs no one to object . . .

Joachim: Many have objected to it . . .

Lawrence: Yes, they have, for they believed that there is no talent without merit. But it occurred to no one that respect, adoration, love can be vested in undeserved endowments – perhaps just because they are undeserved. Listen to Hamlet. What has a child 'deserved'? Can't we adore a lovely child and overwhelm him with presents just because he is what he is?

Joachim: Personally, yes – but not socially.

Lawrence: So, would you cut the heads off the tall poppies? Or rather let them grow?

Joachim: Rather let them grow. But I still don't see the ethical relevance of the question.

Lawrence: That's funny, you just spelled it out. I asked whether one should cut the heads of the tall poppies, and you answered: let them grow! This 'let them grow' is an eminently ethical commitment. The readiness to acknowledge the greatness of the great, to be pleased to meet someone superior to yourself, the capacity to enjoy the personality of another for her personality's sake alone and not for one's own sake, the taking of disinterested pleasure in the works of fine and subtle human creatures, the love of useless things for their uselessness if they are only beautiful or lovely – this is what I call nobility. The *megalopsychos* of our age is a tall or not so tall poppy in his disinterested respect and adoration for the few tall poppies. I mean adoration without humiliation; dignified adoration, and not hero-worship. For hero-worship is just the other side of the coin of *ressentiment* ...

Joachim: But these are ideas from the *Critique of Judgement* ...

Lawrence: Yes, your Kant was an old-fashioned European after all. He stood for liberal democracy (he termed it 'republic'), for a universalist-democratic ethics, but also for a cultural elite. The dragon with a million heads would be a very inappropriate subject for the disinterested liking of things of beautiful nature. But we have agreed that we are not going to hide behind the broad back of Kant or Nietzsche.

Joachim: I didn't refer to the *Critique of Judgement* in order to take refuge behind Kant's back. His back was far from being broad enough anyway. I humbly referred to the circumstance that democracy does not necessarily breed *ressentiment*.

Lawrence: Kant knew nothing of really existing democracy. What he knew was from books, particularly from Plato, and this is less than impartial testimony. But I repeat, the trend toward the deluge of *ressentiment* can be counterbalanced by high culture. This counterveiling force still exists in Europe. It does not exist here.

Joachim: But Europeans invented cultural criticism. They must have detected the dangers in their own house *ante portas*.

Lawrence: They were able to detect them because they had the standard for detection at hand; although in my father's time the standard for detection was not yet entirely absent in our quarters either ...

Joachim: I think that this topic has by now been exhausted. Vera, can I ask a favour of you?

Vera: It is granted.

Joachim: I want to talk to you alone.

Vera: Why?

Joachim: Never ask this question.

Vera: Tomorrow at five, then. In our pub on University Place. I realize that it is time for me to leave too.

Lawrence: No, no. Joachim may have exhausted the topic, but I have not. Please stay.

Joachim: Meanwhile, I'll go for a walk. It is my habit to take a long walk before midnight every day. So long!

(Joachim leaves. Lawrence and Vera remain seated.)

Lawrence: Vera, Vera, tell me, what am I?

Vera: Do you really ask me to tell you what you are?

Lawrence: I have chosen myself as a philosopher. I even remember when and how. But you and Joachim have called me a decent person. So

I must have chosen myself as a decent person. Which one have I chosen? Which one am I going to become? Can one leap twice? Can one make two leaps at once?

Vera: One leaps only once.

Lawrence: Who am I? What am I? Which was my existenial choice? And which is merely the contingent or secondary choice?

Vera: You do not know, I do not know, Joachim does not know. And if you are lucky – you will never know.

Lawrence: Is luck something other than destiny? Is it something external?

Vera: Your existential choice is internal. To go on towards your fulfilment – this is your destiny. But you do not know whether becoming a philosopher or becoming a good man is your destiny. And I said that if you are lucky, you will never find out. For if you are lucky you will become one of them, but you might also become the other. If you have chosen yourself as a philosopher, you will become one – and if you are lucky you may also become a decent person. In reverse, if you have chosen yourself as a decent person, you will become one, and if you are lucky you may also become a philosopher. Luck is not entirely external to the choice, but it does not inhere in the choice. Luck depends on the juncture.

Lawrence: What kind of juncture?

Vera: A very common juncture: the crossroads of fate. One can arrive in one's life at a juncture at which it becomes apparent which of one's choices was the existential one. This may happen to you as well as not. You will arrive at the crossroads if you find that you can become a philosopher only through moral offence, or if you find that you can become a decent person only by doing harm to your philosophy. If you arrive at such a crossroads you are unlucky. Then you must find out which one was your existential choice. If you do not arrive at the juncture, you will never find out. Then you are called lucky. There is an either/or, but not always and not for everyone. But you must know, Lawrence, that there is the either/or. You cannot prepare yourself for the juncture, but you must know that your happiness depends on it.

Lawrence: Does my luck depend on me? Please answer!

Vera: Yes and no. Yes, because there is a silent conspiracy between fate and character. One is not just catapulted to a crossroads by demonic or angelic powers, one also walks into the trap. No, because one of your demonic playmates is history; it is whimsical. Whether or not it will play its tricks on you I cannot foretell.

Lawrence: What do you know then?

Vera: The most important thing.

Lawrence: What is the most important thing?

Vera: The secret of felicity.

Lawrence: What is felicity?

Vera: Never to find out whether you have chosen yourself under the category of the universal or under the category of difference.

Lawrence: Then is no one happy before death?

Vera: Well said.

Lawrence: And if one dies at twenty-three, like that Lawrence of yours almost a century ago? Your secret is not worth knowing . . .

Vera: What secret is worth knowing?

Lawrence: I know of one. Vera, do you love me?

Vera: I don't know.

Lawrence: I know of another: Vera, will I ever hear the twelfth stroke of the bell?

Vera: I don't know.

Lawrence: I know of a third: Vera, what is my name?

Vera: Your name is reveRENCE for the LAW.

Lawrence: Vera, Veronica, Verity, please tell me: can I hope?

(The rest of the evening is left to the reader's imagination.)

Dialogue Three: If There Is, How Can We Practise It?

(The same pub as in the first dialogue. Joachim is sitting beside the same table; he is sipping his brandy. Having climbed the stairs, Vera approaches the table.)

Vera: Have you waited long?

Joachim: I arrived early. Sit down please. Do you want some tea? And perhaps your favourite madeleines?

Vera: No thank you. I remember things past without props. I would like to have a drink with you. Your favourite brandy.

Joachim: Since we have come to talk, let us talk. You asked me yesterday why I wanted to talk to you tête-à-tête. I refused to answer. Now I will answer. First, because you are not a philosopher. You do not catch me at my contradictions, you do not confront me with my own inconsistencies. And also because you do not love me, you do not want me to match your idea of me. You may understand me better if you look at me indifferently. Perhaps you could also accept me better then.

Vera: You have chosen me as a confidante? Because I am not clever?

Joachim: I have chosen you as a confidante but I will not take you into my confidence. I have chosen you because you are wise.

Vera: What can you tell me in confidence if you do not take me into your confidence?

Joachim: You will see. It is about my relation to the Kantian philosophy.

Vera: This is not a confidential topic. But if you speak about it in confidence, it becomes one.

Joachim: Excuse me, it is so difficult for me to commence . . . But please let me do so. The day before yesterday, at the beginning of our fateful conversation, Lawrence played on one of his favourite Nietzschean themes. Philosophy is like a memoir, he said, a kind of autobiography, philosophy is the philosopher's life, and so on. As was to be expected, I rejected his subjectivism. Afterwards you arrived, we indulged in a few thought-experiments concerning the philosophy of existence; we rehabilitated one or two brands of ethics of personality and defended them against the accusations of relativism, nihilism, etc. You two dragged me deeper and deeper into the discussion till I began to speak the language of your *amor fati*, till I agreed that we are pulled by, rather than pushed toward, our destiny. You let me forget the abyss that divides transcendental freedom from nature.

Vera: You now feel that yesterday we dragged you into our discourse. Did you make any statement then that you would not repeat today, something you are ashamed of or embarrassed about?

Joachim: No, no, by no means. Although I get more intoxicated by the spirit of discussions than by my brandy, I never become intoxicated enough to say something that I could be ashamed of the next day. I normally think matters over before I open my mouth. Or else I correct myself in the next round of discussion, if I am convinced by counter-arguments. No, something far more complicated happened to me yesterday. Although you two dragged me into the discussion, whatever I actually said about *amor fati*, about being pulled and not pushed, about being destined, about becoming what one is – about the ethics of personality in general – I believed to be true. And I still do.

Vera: What is wrong, then?

Joachim: Everything, Vera, everything. For when I spoke about all those things, I simply described Lawrence. Whatever I said, I said it about Lawrence. It was so easy and so enjoyable to speak of Lawrence. All the things I said about Lawrence are true. He is the man of *amor fati*, he is pulled by his destiny and not pushed by his past. He has chosen himself, he practises the ethics of personality, he is even the paragon of this ethics. Don't you see? I spoke the truth, but it was Lawrence's truth. Not mine. It was the truth about Lawrence, not about me. For I could not have possibly described myself in the same terms. I am a *krummes Holz*, I am not pulled by my destiny, I am haunted by my past, and – all right, I need not continue – do you see how deep my problem lies? I happily went along with you in describing Lawrence, telling the truth about Lawrence, the truth of Lawrence. But if this is the truth about Lawrence – and alas it is – and if my truth is of another kind, what follows from this? Briefly, that my own conception of truth has gone to pieces. Worse still, my own Kantian moral philosophy has gone to pieces. Do you hear?

Vera: I am listening . . .

Joachim: Good. If I am still capable of conducting a logical argument, let me try to see what follows from all this. I describe Lawrence and I describe him truly in terms of the philosophy of existence tinged with some Nietzsche. Yet I cannot describe myself in the same terms. I can describe myself only in terms of the Kantian moral philosophy. Whatever Kant said about morality is true of me. Yes, I can understand myself as two persons in one: a rational being, the beholder of the moral law, and a natural being, constantly resistant to it, but whose resistance can be mitigated, or rather broken – through sweat, great effort, and constant practice. I will not continue. Kant's moral philosophy is my truth, it is truth for me, it is a moral philosophy shaped to my personality. But I cannot say this. Why not, you may ask? Simply because the Kantian philosophy disallows the acceptance of the idea that there is a truth for Lawrence and another truth for me; that a Nietzschean kind of moral philosophy is true for Lawrence, whereas the Kantian is true for me. In terms of the Kantian philosophy you cannot say that Joachim carries the categorical imperative in himself, he listens to the moral law, he considers what kind of maxims he chooses, he checks them, and so on and so forth, because all of us are supposed, rather we are obliged to do exactly the same. If I am a Kantian as a person, and I am aware of being a Kantian, I cannot be a Kantian in my philosophy, because Kant's philosophy cannot be understood as a memoir or an abbreviated or stylized autobiography. It is supposed to be necessarily and universally true.

Vera: 'Only the truth that edifies is truth for you.'

Joachim: Of course the Kantian moral philosophy edifies me, it describes me, it elevates me. I said it is a crutch – it is my crutch for it is I who need it. I am a Kantian, for this is the crutch that I need. But as a Kantian, I cannot possibly repeat with you that only the truth that edifies is truth for me . . .

Vera: Why not?

Joachim: Don't be naïve.

Vera: This is not the first time that you censure naïvety; yet philosophy is supposed to raise childish questions. My question was, I admit, childish. Still, you should answer it: why can't you repeat with Sören that only the truth that edifies you is truth for you?

Joachim: Because my edification is not the proof of truth or untruth.

Vera: But this is not what Sören meant. He did not say, 'Whatever edifies you is truth for you'. He said, 'Only the truth that edifies or uplifts you is truth for you.' Edification is not the criterion of truth or falsity, but of something that the sentence spells out clearly: it is the criterion of whether a truth is truth for you.

Joachim: You mean that there are several true moral philosophies, and the one which edifies me is truth for me?

Vera: Yes, this is what I mean. And then you can add without embarrassment: this moral philosophy is true for me, that moral philosophy is true for Lawrence.

Joachim: But what does it mean to say that a moral philosophy edifies? Does it uplift you like the sight of a beautiful painting? And what is the truth of a moral philosophy?

Vera: Simple questions, simple answers. Moral philosophy, as you said yourself the day before yesterday, is our crutch. Most people need a crutch. The kind of moral philosophy which is the most reliable crutch for helping to be (become) a person who rather suffers than commits injustice or wrong 'edifies' you – is the truth for you. If you become a good person in using the heavy crutch of the categorical imperative, this is the truth for you; and when Lawrence becomes good by using the light and almost invisible crutch of following the pull of his destiny – this is his crutch and thus his truth. Don't you see? The question is not, *From where do we get the strength to be decent*? The important thing is *that* we be decent.

Joachim: I see what you mean by the term 'edifying'. But if there are many truths in morality, what are the criteria of 'truth', and how can you tell truth from falsity?

Vera: Excuse me. I haven't said that there are many truths in morality. I did say that there are many true moral philosophies. That's because in morality there is only one truth and that one is unconditional and absolute. The old truth, the eternal truth, the transcendent-transcendental truth that you embrace with a gesture: it is better to suffer wrong than to wrong others. But you can make a case for this single eternal true gesture in many different ways. Every moral philosophy which you can rely upon, in so far as it offers you a crutch which enables you to suffer injustice rather than commit injustice against others, is a true one. One of them will be true for you, others will be not.

Joachim: I am afraid that we are shifting ground. You said, if I recollect your simple arguments well, that all true moral philosophies offer crutches to people who are ready to be good, who prefer to suffer wrong to wronging others. So far so good. But I said something else, or at least I formulated another problem as well. I spoke about description. One moral philosophy describes me, the other Lawrence. What tortures me is the idea that you choose a moral philosophy not for moral, but for psychological reasons . . .

Vera: This may be the case. But why does this thought 'torture' you? Isn't this an exaggeration?

Joachim: Excuse me, I should have said 'it bothers me'. And it bothers me on many counts. First because psychology is an empirical science, it operates with natural causality . . .

Vera: I am not a philosopher, but I have some inkling of psychology. There are as many kinds of psychologies as there are moral philosophies, perhaps more . . .

Joachim: It is now my turn to warn you about over-complicating things. My thesis is simple. All psychologies refer to something that we can call 'psyche' – whatever they may mean by that. This 'psyche' is supposed to be 'there' (in our mind, body, soul, heart) prior to morality. It is normally described as the context, the foundation, the obstacle, the precondition, the determination of morality and of other so-called 'spiritual' things. This is not just a modern invention, it has accompanied us since Plato and Aristotle . . .

Vera: Excuse me, Joachim, you raised an objection to the introduction of psychology. And in order to prove how wrong this is, you refer to the example of philosophers, moreover to the founding fathers of metaphysics. Don't you think that your description of 'psyche' is a metaphysical description? Don't you think that it is the objectivation, or rather the fossilization of heterogeneous happenings, occurrences, movements and the like?

Joachim: Occurrences of what?

Vera: This is a metaphysical question. You except me to answer: 'Psychological occurrences "of that"', you expect me to speak the language of substance/accidents . . .

Joachim: This may be so. But let me throw the ball back: people have recognized themselves in those metaphysical constructs. They have been satisfied to know that the structure of their soul is accurately drawn by the designs inherited from the venerable Plato, or Aristotle, along with all of their followers . . .

Vera: I can catch this ball easily. Metaphysics describes our experiences as long as we can understand our experiences through the guidance of the old map of our soul drawn by metaphysicians. Wittgenstein used to say: let us try, perhaps we can look at the issue in another way for a change. And we can. Yes, people can look at an issue in many ways. The question is simply whether there is an 'issue' here – in this case a 'psyche' – which must be mapped, catalogued, classified, divided (for example in two or three parts), or instead, not. We can still look at our experiences through the looking-glass of metaphysical constructs; it's just that we do not need to, because there are at present many other looking-glasses at our disposal; as your friend Lawrence would say, there are many perspectives to take. Nowadays your psyche is unlike the psyche of your neighbour, your friend, your spouse, for each can pick a different kind of 'psychology', each can pick the one that is best fitted to describe the self-understanding of his or her respective experiences.

Joachim: But none of them describes our moral experiences. I told you, the psyche, whatever it is – and you may be right that at least within metaphysical psychologies, it is but a fossilized entity constructed from occurrences, fluid states of mind, and so on – is not supposed to be a moral actor or entity, but rather the determining ground of such an entity. To repeat: it is presupposed that first you have a psyche, then you have morals. Unfortunately, on a primitive empirical level this is roughly true, because the new-born does not yet relate – so she has no 'morals'. From this temporal sequence determination follows: since psyche comes first and morals second, it must be the psyche that determines, over-determines, limits and obstructs moral experiences. This is why I do believe that whichever psychology you choose – it will be irrelevant to moral philosophy. And not just in transcendental philosophy where this is a matter of course. Transcendental psychology has only an epistemological, but no moral relevance. The whole of Kant's criticism against Stoicism and Epicureanism is based on the total rejection of all kinds of psychological determinations in matters of morality. And even if I were no Kantian, I would still hold that this is one of the most sensible and relevant points in Kant's whole philosophy.

Vera: But didn't Kant simply take over the entire paraphernalia of traditional metaphysics in his description of the empirical psyche? It is still the old psyche that resists reason, it is still the wild horse that must be controlled by reason, which holds the reins with firm hands.

Joachim: There are many things is common, but not the essentials. Given that psyche *qua* nature is not prior to morality and it does not determine it in the slightest, that only freedom can determine nature, Kant's philosophy forecloses the psychologization of morality. And I still suspect that I became committed to Kant's moral philosophy for psychological reasons . . .

Vera: I, however, think something else: you are wrong if you continue to doubt the possibility of a moral psychology. You might say that I am partial, but Sören's existential psychology is a kind of moral psychology. Think of his *The Concept of Anxiety*. Anxiety from freedom, guilt, good – these are all syndromes. There is no determination here, even less is the psyche treated as a thing, or made an object and petrified . . .

Joachim: Yes, you are partial. Existential psychology is no psychology at all . . .

Vera: One cannot receive a good mark from you. You suspect psychology because it translates the temporal priority of no-moral-interior-occurrences and experiences as against moral experiences into a chain of determination. But if someone does something entirely different, you accuse him of having fallen short of conceiving a psychology altogether. In addition, you repeatedly complained that your moral–philosophical choice seems to be determined, or at least forcefully conditioned, by your psyche, or even worse, by your psychology. Your complaint gave the impression that you originally accepted what you immediately after-wards began to refute: namely the affinity between what you call your own 'psychology' and what you call your own 'morality'. What is the truth that you really want to convey to me about yourself?

Joachim: Now you speak as a philosopher. Dear me . . .

Vera: You mean that I don't want to understand your point. But I do. Don't speak about your psyche as a kind of a separate entity. If I assume that you have chosen yourself existentially as a decent person, I also assume that you have chosen everything that you are, your emotions, drives, inclinations – all interior occurrences and mental states that our metaphysicians used to construct, describe, and call 'psyche' – and that you have begun to become decent as you are. You see yourself as a *krummes Holz* because you are a moral person; were you not, you would not describe yourself a *krummes Holz*.

Joachim: This is a truism. Nietzsche said something like: we cannot reproach the wolf for killing and eating the lamb, and he draws some parallels here with human wolves. He says that we are wrong when we reproach human wolves for killing and eating human lambs. We make the reproach because we know – or at least we are supposed to know – that eating and killing human lambs is wrong, because we are so taught by our parents and teachers, and because we are punished for expressing our desire to eat lambs. It is thus that we develop shame and the sense of guilt for about secret desires. The end-product is the guilty animal, the sick animal in Nietzsche's interpretation, and the well-behaved man and woman of *Sittlichkeit* under the traditional moral-philosophical interpretation.

Vera: Mind you, this is extremely un-Kantian.

Joachim: I spoke about the truism, not about Kant.

Vera: I have as little to do with this truism as Kant does. Only my story is different. I think – together with my friend Lawrence – that the division of man into 'noumenon' and 'phenomenon' is a clumsy and inelegant way of rescuing the moral centre . . .

Joachim: This is a bad judgement of taste . . .

Vera: Perhaps, perhaps not. But still, I should not have said what I said. It is tactless to tell you that the moral philosophy that you have chosen as the best description of yourself is lacking in elegance.

Joachim: From bad to worse. You are not a flatterer, are you?

Vera: I hope not. But it amuses me that you suddenly seem to attribute some value to such a vanity as elegance. This would suit Lawrence better, don't you think?

Joachim: Vera, you witch, you caught me this time. Allow me then to translate your demonstration in the manner of Diogenes into philosophical language.

Vera: Hear, hear!

Joachim: No moral philosophy or psychology describes a person fully. When I said that the Kantian moral philosophy is my truth, this was not entirely accurate. It was rather an approximation. I understand myself best in the framework of Kant, but I am not Kant, I am Joachim. My emphases may be – wittingly-unwittingly – different from those of Kant. I can think like Kant, but I do not feel like Kant – at least, certainly not on many issues; and as far as other issues are concerned, I don't know. Here we return to one of our former disputes: hermeneutics of experience is a hopeless business – there will never be a fusion of the horizons.

Vera: But if you can think like Kant but not feel like him, if your experiences are supposed to be different from those of Kant – why have you told me – confidentially, yet with reluctance – that it was for personal psychological reasons that you chose Kant as your moral-philosophical mentor?

Joachim: This time you will not confuse me. When I think of the Kantian description of the human condition, I find there the speculative framework and interpretation that best matches the description of my self-experiences.

Vera: But the description of your self-experiences, isn't this also approximate?

Joachim: Certainly. There are two aproximations here. They are the crutches that help me walk.

Vera: So you are walking on two crutches, not one?

Joachim: Terrible comparison, I admit. But no, I do not walk on two crutches. The approximation of my own experiences, the principle 'know thyself!' conditions me to find the proper crutch for myself.

Vera: We are back to the vicious circle, Joachim. Because it was with the help of that crutch that you become able to begin to approximate yourself . . .

Joachim: No, no, this is wrong, I had embarked on the approximation before I became a Kantian. Now I see – you push me into making a confession. True, it was not Kant who made me aware that I am a *krummes Holz*. I had known about it before. I became aware of it on a Sunday, twenty-six years ago. I was running around like crazy with a stick in my hand in Central Park. I perhaps fancied myself a soldier, and – by accident – I bumped into another boy and hit him in the eye. He was bleeding, shouting, screaming; I can still hear it; I hear it now. He was rescued, but he almost lost his eyesight. I felt terrible, worse than terrible, it has tormented me. But I never said, 'I did it.' I tried to persuade myself that it was the stick that did it, without success. It was then that I became a Kantian.

Vera: Excuse me. You said that your psychology made you a Kantian. But the experience you just described – have you soaked a madeleine-cake in your brandy by any chance? – was also a moral experience. I would say, it was primarily a moral experience. Why do you tell me then that it was your 'psyche' and not your morality that made you a Kantian?

Joachim: Don't you understand? There was nothing in me that you could describe as 'natural commiseration'. I did not run to the boy, I did not ask my nanny to accompany him to the hospital, I never visited him, I never cried for him. No, I went home and I was sitting there in a dark corner swallowing my own guilt in torment. I could not persuade myself that the stick did it. So I said to myself, 'You will never ever run around with a stick again. Beware of hurting others' – and so on. You may say that it was my morality that made me Kantian. But this morality grew from the obscure awareness of my moral infirmity, of the absence of a good moral instinct, of the absence of compassion, of the feeling that is so abundantly and obviously present in Lawrence. What you call a moral experience was in this sense a psychological experience. I understood myself – should I repeat it again? – as *krummes Holz* that will never be straightened out, that always needs a crutch . . .

Vera: A crutch to help you become a decent person . . .

Joachim: Yes, perhaps, although I did not know it then; I knew only one thing – the torment I felt was worse than anything. The thought of the categorical imperative that dwells in all of us made me understand this experience better than anything else. It was in torment that the four-year-old child payed reverence to the law. This was my primal scene.

Vera: Anxiety before evil . . .

Joachim: Yes, you could also describe my experience in Kierkegaard's terms. But Kant provides a stronger crutch.

Vera: I still don't understand why you said that it was your psychology that made you a Kantian.

Joachim: You and Lawrence agreed that each and every person becomes decent in his or her own way. To become decent – this is the moral issue; but 'in our own way' – this is the psychological one. I became what you call a decent person, and Lawrence became upright and good; but it was and is difficult for me, as it was and as it is easy for him. He can rely on his natural sense of commiseration, compassion, openness, friendliness. He can disclose himself, whereas I must remain in a closed reserve, a burden to myself.

Vera: Why don't you describe yourself in terms of Freud, then?

Joachim: I have been expecting this question since I told you the story of my 'primal scene'.

Vera: A good Freudian will enlighten you to the fact that this is just the tip of the iceberg. Your 'real' primal scene has still remained unconscious.

Joachim: Of course, he would enlighten me. But we should come out from under our self-incurred tutelage on our own. Only through self-enlightenment can one become autonomous.

Vera: A Freudian would deny it. He would, perhaps, promise you autonomy through analysis. He would offer you a dialogical situation in which one person (the analyst) helps you to engage in a hermeneutical inquiry into your own unconscious. You said, and not for the first time, that what one *can* understand is another persons's thought, but *not* his experiences. A so-called 'fusion of horizons' can only be approximated to, if one rethinks another person's thoughts; one cannot think or rethink another persons' preconceptual or non-conceptualized experiences, one cannot tell the interpretation of the experiences from the experiences themselves.

Joachim: This was not exactly what I said. I am not enough of a fool to believe in entirely uninterpreted experiences.

Vera: But you still believe in the existence of unconsciously interpreted experiences. Since unconsciously interpreted experiences are not grasped in thought – they do not become experiences of consciousness – the interpreter has no access to them.

Joachim: Indeed. We have a privileged access to our non-conceptualized experiences.

Vera: How can you have such access if you do not conceptualize them?

Joachim: Although the experience itself cannot be grasped by the medium of conceptual thinking, it is, nevertheless, in this medium that we communicate it at first to ourselves. This is what I call conscious interpretation of experiences (of unconscious interpretations). Without the medium of conceptual language no conscious interpretation would be possible. But what the language offers is but a report of the experience. I can give you an idea about my new apartment in a letter in which I describe it. But you will not have an experience of my new apartment, you will have an experience of the description of this apartment. Just a few minutes ago I made a conceptual report about the torments of the four-year-old child that I once was. What you received was the evocation of the torment by a thirty-year-old, not the actual torment of the four-year-old. I too have the thought of the torment, but by recalling this painful experience a feeling arises in me: a sad and painful feeling, a kind of recapitulation of the experience, a repetition, a recollection, a sensual, or rather, sensitive remembrance. Not a conceptual remembrance that we can evoke together, but an experience-like remembrance that we cannot share. My thoughts and feelings can remember together, because they are interlocked. But if you tell me about your torments I will think them, I will understand them, I may feel many things in conjunction with them, but my feelings will not inhere in my thinking of an experience. This is what I termed 'privileged access'. Let me return to psychoanalysis. The analyst robs me, or at least takes pains to rob me, of the privilege of my access. This is how he robs me of my autonomy. He pretends to have better access to my experiences than I do, that he can perform a trick which I cannot, the magic trick of deciphering the unconscious interpretations of my experiences hidden behind the veils, or rather behind the barricades, of my self-defenses, and so on. The analyst violates my experience . . .

Vera: Joachim, one way or another you remain an unreconstructed Kantian. You think only in terms of a single person who has remained alone with himself and his soul. But we are not isolated thinkers, we live with people. Why do you think that another person cannot help you to understand yourself better than you could without her help? Yesterday you defended democracy against Lawrence's elitist predilections, but now it is you who protect a privilege absolutely, because the privileged access to yourself is an absolute privilege.

Joachim: I will certainly not resign my privilege to an analyst. And please do not mention hermeneutics in this context. For at least I have some respect for my own personal experiences. I do not know in advance what my unconscious is hiding. I do not know my secrets, not even their character – what kind of secrets are those anyway whose type or character we know? – for I am aware of my 'ipseity'. I don't remember which of us mentioned the bull in the china-shop. I guess I did. This is a good simile. The analyst is the bull in the china-shop: he destroys everything there, all traces of the entirely unique experiences which are mine and mine alone. He typifies me, classifies me, so that he can conjure up from my soul – may I ask you what? Precisely the same things that he conjures up from the so-called depths of all other persons' souls. While pretending to perform an interpretive work, psychoanalysis is the most primitive brand of universalism. It makes the souls of all of us alike; it attributes the same complexes to all of us, it knows at what age everyone goes through the same experiences. No, Vera, this is not my cup of tea.

Vera: Excuse me, dear Joachim, is not every construction of the psyche or the soul doing exactly the same thing? Did not your Kant tell you beforehand what you were going to find 'within' yourself? Did not Plato and Aristotle draw maps of your soul quite meticulously? Isn't it true that all speculations about the secret called a 'man' are universalized speculations, for they all address the 'human condition' or if you wish to modernize the concept, they all address *Dasein*, and none of them the single exister? Why is Freud worse in this respect than the common tradition of Judaeo-Christianity? Why does it hurt you if your 'soul' is divided into id, ego and super-ego, instead of body–soul, or body–soul–spirit or vegetative–attentive–rational soul, or the like?

Joachim: I'll tell you why. First of all, because all of the old classifications of the soul were dividing and subdividing the psyche with a moral intent. Further, they never pretended to speak to you or to me or to any single exister – they did not pretend to turn to you and to you alone. This is the incredible and unbearable *tartufferie* of analysis . . .

Vera: You employ Nietzsche's word . . .

Joachim: Yes, I am aware of it. The horrible *tartufferie* of analysis is that analysts *expect you* lie down on the couch and believe that the story is about you and no one else, that it is your problems, your sufferings to which they attend, and that your self-revelation may bring about your salvation. But alas, they explain you – yes, they do not even bother to interpret you – they explain you with the high-and-mighty self-complacency of the so-called positive sciences. They explain you as if you were nature, the passive result of determinations . . .

Vera: You said sometime ago that all kinds of psychologies employ causal explanation . . .

Joachim: Yes, but the others are unpretentious and they don't create the make-believe idea that you are the protagonist of a fully-fledged mythology, a new Oedipus, a new Electra. Instead of helping you to get an insight into your idiosyncrasies, analysts teach you to discover in your tired, old and mediocre parents the threatening mythological figures of a defunct past; every papa becomes a Laius . . .

Vera: But what if a person says, 'Freud described me, he did it well. Psychoanalysis is my truth.' You cannot deny that hosts of men and women have felt and said so in the last hundred years. If someone understands himself through Freud's description, why is that worse than your understanding yourself through Kant's description? Let me provoke you a little: are the 'psyches' described by Kant and by Freud not very similar? Couldn't you describe yourself in Freud's categories? Couldn't you say that I have a strong super-ego and I need it, because I have a rebellious id; and that I suffer because my ego is squeezed dry between the two enemies, but I still bravely follow the super-ego? And couldn't you describe Lawrence in the same terms? Couldn't you say that Lawrence is a person who has strong and good instincts, whose unconscious impulses are obviously all right; that he does not need a strong super-ego at all, and this is why his ego is not squeezed between super-ego and id, but develops freely? You began your self-description by contrasting the person who is pulled by his destiny, the man of *amor fati*, with another kind, who is pushed and determined. You said you resemble the second type, and this is why an ethics of personality is unsuitable for you. Couldn't you make your case more convincing in Freud's terms than you actually did in Kant's and in Nietzsche's terms respectively? It would be easier and simpler, I assure you. Because until now you have confronted one description (that of Kant) with another description (call him Nietzsche), and you have said that the first is your truth, whereas the second is Lawrence's truth. Had you taken Freud only somewhat seriously and checked your tantrum, you might have arrived at an interesting conclusion. Joachim, relax: I can tell you that I have never seen you so enraged, so out of your normal self during this long conversation as at this time. I could ask you: why are you so angry? But I will not ask this question because I can guess why. I am sorry, but this time it is left to me to draw the interesting conclusion: Kant describes you, Nietzsche describes Lawrence; Freud can describe you both.

Joachim: You are right, wise lady, I am angry. Freud has stepped on my toes, I admit. I think that he has stepped on my toes because he cannot describe me, you think that he stepped on my toes because he can. But whether my or your interpretation gets closer to my unconscious interpretive experience is of little relevance here. Let us assume that Freud can describe the structure of the internal landscape of my soul and he can also describe the internal landscape of Lawrence's soul – using in both cases the same building blocks, but arranging them in different ways. However, he can only describe – if at all – the structure and not the dynamics. More precisely, he can perhaps describe the dynamics of my 'soul'. I have admitted, that I am after all determined by my past in one way or another. But he certainly cannot describe the dynamics of Lawrence's soul – there is no place in Freud's *œuvre* for the fate of the pull, even less for the love of this fate. The Freudian and the existential psychology describe two entirely different dynamics. Here there is an either/or. Moreover, if I return to my case and admit that Freud can describe, not only the landscape, but also the dynamics of my so-called 'soul', he is still unable to describe me. He cannot tell me anything about the experience of the four-year-old me. No fear of the father or of punishment, no Oedipal feeling or the like were present in my four-year-old self (I never knew my father). In addition the so-called causality of my soul, which boils down to an urge to repeat my past, to copy with it repeatedly, can hardly be termed a 'complex'; the whole theory of 'complexes' is, at any rate, the worst kind of the objectifying, fossilizing understanding of our emotional and instinctual happenings and occurrences through their traces.

Vera: Sorry, you begin to manœuvre yourself back into the state of anger. And in the meantime you have forgotten something important.

Joachim: What have I forgotten?

Vera: The most important thing.

Joachim: What would that be?

Vera: Your very privileged access to your own inner life. The exclusion of another human person from participating in the interpretation of your experiences.

Joachim: I told you that I chose you as confidante without taking you into my confidence. But you push too hard. The insistence of your fragile being weighs heavier on my life-economy than all the school-books on psychoanalysis do. So be it.

Vera: So be what?

Joachim: Mother-confessor as old as the world, hear my confession. I know, I know for sure, that no one, no single being, human or divine, has access to my internal experiences. But there is nothing that I desire more than what I know to be impossible. I desire for the miracle to happen, I am longing for someone, for one single person, to do the impossible, to ease my resistances, to make me transparent to himself, and through himself, to myself. I see what felicity could be: Judge William and his wife, 'one in two' instead of 'two in one', the lived history of shared experience. But Lawrence, our dear Lawrence, seeks another brand of felicity . . .

Vera: I know . . .

Joachim: So you know it too. You must also know how high he stands above me. The great child in search of his truth. The son of Zeus who has received the world as a plaything.

Vera: Does he play with us?

Joachim: Yes, but he is not aware of it. He is just unconcerned.

Vera: But you spoke about his natural capacity for commiseration, of his goodness, of his compassion . . .

Joachim: They are all there; all the royal virtues, none of the simply human ones. I hope I serve him well. But he is in love with *you*.

Vera: He said so.

Joachim: Will you love him?

Vera: I don't know.

Joachim: Do love him – please.

Vera: I don't love on request. Do you believe that I could not love you?

Joachim: I am sure you could not – because Lawrence is ten times more important to me than you are.

Vera: You think that I am predictable, don't you? That I cultivate reciprocity instead of endowing my sympathies by whim? So I would rather tell you a tale. It won't be a tale from the *Symposium* – a glass of brandy does little for divine inspiration – it will just be a poor little grey modern tale about the human condition. Since we are supposed to paint grey in grey, I hope it will do the job.

Joachim: 'The goldentree of life is green.'

Vera: I haven't forgotten the golden tree, don't worry. Once upon a time – and every day is once upon a time, for once upon a time is every day – very special beings are born into the species *Homo sapiens* . . .

Joachim: Do you mean that some beings who are born into the species *Homo sapiens* are special, or that all new-borns of this species are special?

Vera: You have a sharp mind, Joachim. You want to catch me before I really begin my narrative. 'Now I will make Vera take sides,' you think, 'for if she says that the species is what's special then she loves me, but if she says that there are special beings born into the species *'Homo sapiens*,' then she loves Lawrence.' But you cannot make me take sides. For I meant both. Indeed, every member of the species *'Homo sapiens'* is special, because each of us is a 'throw'; every single person is entirely unique . . .

Joachim: There are no two leaves of a tree which are alike. Uniqueness is not the unique attribute of the human singularity. Every living being can be said to be a throw. As a humanist myself, I do not have any objections to humanism of sorts, but I warn you that your conception of universal uniqueness will not be welcomed by our dear friend Lawrence . . .

Vera: My narrative is a narrative about the genealogy of the problem, not the solution. Whether you see man as the lord of beings or as the shepherd of Being – you are assigning, in either case, a special task to 'men', and to each and every human being. Not our special destination, but the character or the 'essence' of this destination is nowadays frequently called into question. Let me speak about the 'throw'. Neither plants nor animals originate in the throw. Having been thrown is the human speciality. Perhaps this is why human thinking never stops asking (and answering) the question, 'Who (or what) is the one that throws?' Mythologies asked it, philosophies asked it, religions asked it. They all gave their answers. There will be no final answer. However, when no one asks anymore, 'Who or what is the one that throws?' human singularities will cease to be 'throws' and thereby they will also cease to be humans.

For they will lose their specialness. They could still have brains like multifunctional computers, they would remain bipedal and omnivorous, but not humans as we know them.

Joachim: Vera, are you also a cultural pessimist? Or do you echo Heidegger's dictum that only a new god could rescue us?

Vera: You told me – you are not a flatterer either, you know that – that I am as old as the world. I have not learned history from books, I have my personal experiences. I have seen too much to be a cultural pessimist, and particularly to believe that human beings will eventually stop asking their eternal questions. Although the currently fashionable outbursts against metaphysics annoy me still, my anxiety is soothed by the discovery that most of the scholars who abuse metaphysics do not know what they are talking about. The future always remains open. But let me return to my narrative. Once upon a time – and every day is once upon a time, for once upon a time is every day – very special beings are (were) born into the race of *Homo sapiens*: they are (were) thrown into the world . . .

Joachim: Stop for a moment. You (or perhaps Lawrence?) presented yesterday – or was it the day before yesterday? – a perspectivist conception of the world. You said, if I remember well – in reference to Leibniz and Nietzsche – that everyone has his or her 'own' world, although we also share a common world. How can someone just be thrown into 'a world' pure and simple?

Vera: Did you ever have a child? I have had many. One was born in a tent in the desert, another one in the jungle, another in the cottage of a fisherman, another in a thriving old city, the last in your metropolis. They were boys and girls; they were born into the families of lords and of servants, of the highly and of the lowly placed, of princes, beggars, and burghers, of knowledgeable and of ignorant people, in times of war and of peace, in the years of plenty and of starvation, into mild and harsh climates – and I could go on. None of this can happen with plants or animals. A human being is a throw, for at the moment of her birth she 'has' two a priori, not one: a genetic a priori and a socio-cultural a priori. Both are a prioris because they are prior to the single person's experiencing. All my children – just like all leaves on the tree – were unique; but so were the worlds into which they were thrown. More precisely, this is why there is a throw. A wolf is born as a wolf. A human person is not born entirely as a human person, merely as the potential for becoming what she is. It is in and through relating herself to the world that she is thrown into, that she becomes what she is. Yes, I said that she was thrown into a world, for she was not thrown into 'the' world – there is no such a thing. Yet she did not (not yet) have 'her' world, for she only began to acquire 'her' own world at the moment of her birth. My old friend, Hannah Arendt, termed the throw 'natality'. Natality is the throw.

Joachim: You speak about configurations we have already discussed. You become what you are in and through an existential choice. But what is special in an existential choice, when you – as a throw – become what you are anyway, namely a human being, through relating to a world which is thereby transformed into 'your' world.

Vera: Indeed. For the existential choice is the *repetition*: the repetition of the original human condition. In this sense it is the repetition of the same. I will come back to this question. Let me first go on with my narrative. I spoke about natality; we are thrown into a world where we receive our human destiny, to begin to become what we are – human beings. But we are all different. We are born with an entirely unique assortment of endowments. Let me call it, in a modern language – although we could also describe the same thing in an antiquated metaphysical language – genetic a priori. Thus the moment of the throw is the moment of absolute contingency – because it is a throw from two entirely unrelated dice cups. The dice cup 'genetic a priori' is unrelated to the dice cup 'socio-cultural a priori'. When I am pregnant, I move from one place to another, from one century to another – so all my children, and they are all mine, are thrown into an entirely different socio-cultural a priori. Where they are born does not depend on them. What depends on them, and increasingly so, is to become what they are. But they must become what they are (human beings) exactly in that socio-cutural habitat where, by accident, they have been thrown. One of the accidents, I repeat, is genetic – they are all the unlikely products of one sperm and one egg whose 'meeting' could not have been predicted by anyone – and this unique creature of genetic accidents has now to cope with a situation that was thrown (for her) from an entirely unrelated dice cup. This I call a throw! This I call a task! This I call destiny. Men and women are destined by the throw ... But I run ahead too fast. Let me return to the two a prioris, the genetic and the socio-cultural. In order to become what we are – there is an built-in teleology here – we must, we should dovetail the two a prioris. I said we must, I said we should – yes, there is a constraint here and an obligation. Dovetail or perish.

Joachim: We are born to suffer ...

Vera: And to experience joy. The dovetailing of the two a prioris is suffering, but it is also joy. Have you seen a child's face when she has first suceeded in grabbing something? When she has just made her first steps? When she has smiled back at her mother?

Joachim: I have had no opportunity to make those observations. But I trust you. As far as I can remember, I always longed to be a grown-up. It was so terrible being a child.

Vera: I know a few men and women who were happy during childhood but fell into despair as adults. What is hell for one, is paradise for the other. But I come soon to the end of my tale of dovetailing. Dovetailing is never completed, or at least we do not know whether it is ever completed. There remains a tension between the a prioris. This tension can be severe or mild. It is this tension itself that we interpret, understand or explain in psychology.

Joachim: You mean that the genetic a priori is nature, the socio-cultural a priori is spirit, and the synthesis is the soul?

Vera: Not at all. The genetic a priori is not 'nature' for humans who are born in order to lead a human life; the throw is not just nature. And a world (the socio-cultural) is not spirit. Of course, much depends on your philosophical language. Kant calls this socio-cultural a priori 'nature', whereas Hegel terms it 'spirit' (objective and absolute spirit). In Hegel's scenario, dovetailing could be described as the self-concretization of the subjective spirit. He elaborates something like this in his *Phenomenology of Spirit*. But if you do not construct a system, but rather, simply tell a tale, you are not obliged to dovetail your system with your tale. But when I said that owing to the incompleteness of dovetailing, a tension remains between the two a prioris, I did not point at an object, at a thing; tension in our dovetailing is not an object, not a thing; I did not mean a thing like the 'soul', let alone a soul as 'synthesis'.

Joachim: But you said that it is the tension that 'psychology' is busy trying to understand.

Vera: More precisely: the tension is the *problem* for psychology. The vegetative soul (in Aristotle) does not play a part in the 'psychological problem', yet in Freud, for example, in his theory of anal erotics, it does. This is because the vegetative soul is not party to the tension for Aristotle, but it is for Freud. Cognitive psychology does not – normally – treat 'psychological problems', unless it is engaged in the study of mental deficit or creative surplus . . . But it is almost dinner time; I do not wish to drag my narrative further. Let me sum up that for a 'throw' becoming what we are means living in tension – because there is always a tension between becoming what we are to be by the norms and rules of the socio-cultural a priori, and becoming what we are in and through our specific endowments . . .

Joachim: Long as your story was, does it not boil down to the old and boring problem of nature versus nurture? We are determined both by nature and culture . . .

Vera: On the contrary – we are conditioned by both, but we are not determined by either. We are thrown, let me repeat, from (at least) two different dice cups and none of them can 'determine' us, for the other a priori puts up resistance. What you call culture resists the excesses of our so-called 'nature', yet our so-called nature also resists the pressures of so-called 'culture'.

Joachim: So here we are, poor creatures, suffering under dual resistance and constraints.

Vera: Or enjoying ourselves in exercising our powers. Of course, resistance is just one aspect of the game. The tension is creative, it *transcends the world in which we had been thrown*. This is how we develop our own world, our own perspective, as Lawrence would have it. And also our own dreams. The tension is the energy of transcendence, the source of imagination . . .

Joachim: Now you begin to introduce a vitalistic language that I despise. Your energies smell of defunct natural sciences.

Vera: Or of Nietzsche's will-to-power. I agree, the term is misleading for it has been misused. Should we rather speak of creative imagination? This was, after all, one of the favourites of your Kant?

Joachim: I accept 'creative imagination'. But would you identify 'creative imagination' with the tension that ensues from incomplete dovetailing?

Vera: Incomplete dovetailing is not the cause of tension, it is the tension. The tension itself is not the cause of creative imagination; but it is the condition of creative imagination.

Joachim: The greater the tension, the greater the chances of creative imagination? Of transcending, both in conscious and unconscious dreams, the common world of facticity?

Vera: It is now you who begin to think in terms of quantitative energies. The question is not whether the tension is 'great' or 'less great', although tradition holds – without speaking about dovetailing and the like – that there is a relation here. This is why madness and creative imagination are often identified. But then it is rather the certain quality of the tension, the character of the tension, that may offer the best conditions for creative imagination. And of course, if we speak about the quality of the tension, we must have in mind not just one a priori (namely the genetic one) but both a prioris. People wonder why certain ages are so beneficial for the outpourings of creativity, whereas others are not. The 'world' does not determine the creativity of the so-called geniuses who always go beyond *the* (common) world in so far as they bring something entirely new into it – something that is '*their* world', something that becomes *a* world only after it had been brought into the world, nevertheless, *this* world is still the kind of a priori which gives rise to the kind of tension that bears the fruits of creativity. It is the goldentree of life that becomes green.

Joachim: Vera, you are shrewd as always. You began to tell a story of the human condition in order to illuminate the speciality common to the human race, and then – without letting me notice it – you transformed the topic of your tale so that you arrive finally at the specificity of certain human persons. You began with universality and you ended up with difference.

Vera: There is no shrewdness in it. The tale has told itself.

Joachim: Let me reiterate how I have understood your point. We are all thrown into the world from two unrelated dice cups. This is our contingency . . .

Vera: Not quite. This is the throw, the accident of the throw. But contingency is something else: it is the consciousness or rather the self-consciousness of thrownness. We become contingent if we understand ourselves as accidental – after the breakdown of mythologies, of metaphysical systems. We are contingent if we do not have the answer to the question, 'Who (what) is the one that throws?' What you called 'the death of God' in our first conversation (though I did not particularly like your expression) is the historical condition of cosmic contingency. In addition, modern men and women are thrown into a kind of world entirely different from that of their pre-modern ancestors. This world does not superimpose upon you your way of life. In this repect you are free, free to choose among your infinite possibilities, and you are also empty. The throw is a throw into freedom, that is, into nothing.

Joachim: Is this what you are saying: in a pre-modern world we are thrown into a world by accident, whereas in the modern world we are thrown into nothing? Is it the latter throw that you call contingency?

Vera: Roughly. But we moderns are also thrown into a world. It's just that the character of the socio-cultural a priori is now different. In a pre-modern world you received your destiny as a birthday present, whereas now you do not receive a birthday present. Or rather, you receive another one, an undetermined one: the possibility for self-destining. This can be termed empty freedom; this empty freedom, however, is the condition of all the modern freedoms. This is why you should destine yourself.

Joachim: Now I begin to see what you meant by 'repetition'. In the pre-modern world, as well as today, you are thrown into a world from two uninterrelated dice cups. As far as the genetic a priori is concerned, nothing has changed, as far as the accident of natality is concerned, nothing has changed either. It is the human condition. The human condition is, briefly, that you must and you should become what you are. But in the socio-cultural a priori of the ancients our destiny awaited us at birth. As far as the genetic a priori was concerned, you were just a unique person; as far as the world into which you had been thrown was concerned, you were born a potential hunter, a potential shepherd, or master, or slave, a potential king, and so on – and you had to become what you were, otherwise you perished. But now that the socio-cultural a priori no longer prescribes your destiny, you are simply born a 'human being'. You are born free. What does it mean, then, that you should, you must become what you are? You are not destined to being anything specific, you are just thrown into freedom *qua* nothing. Thus to become what you are means to become free – or to become nothing; to gain yourself or lose yourself. This is the stake. *The existential choice of ourselves is the repetition of the human condition under the condition of freedom or nothingness* that is, of modernity. And since the socio-cultural universe does not determine you, you will 'be', provided that you choose yourself, and you will become what you have chosen yourself to be. Is that so? Is this what you meant by repetition? Is the choice of ourselves our autonomy? For if it is, and you suggest that it is, we do not repeat the original scenario entirely. I cannot say, 'you should, you must, become what you are – otherwise you perish', but rather 'You do become what you are, what you have chosen yourself to be' yet the alternative is the same: 'Otherwise you perish.' Still, 'perishing' means something other than it did in the first case. It is tantamount to losing yourself. The loss of ourself is not a visible thing – rather, it is something invisible. The person who perishes, perishes before one's eyes; he cannot maintain himself in his destiny-given community. But the modern man who loses himself can be successful, adored and respected. Isn't this true?

Vera: That is why my Sören used to say that the internal is not the external . . .

Joachim: Yet this is so only in the case of authentic persons. The persons ready for repetition . . .

Vera: About the existential repetition . . . What Nietzsche termed the eternal repetition of the same is not the existential repetition. True, the possibility of a Nietzschean repetition is opened up by the existential repetition.

Joachim: My dear Vera, I have listened to your lengthy tale about dovetailing, the two a priories, the throw and the repetition. I understand why human beings are special among all living creatures while some human being are special cases within the special condition of humans. The latter are, of course, the lucky throws of the dice. We all live in tension, thus tension does not explain the lucky throw of the dice. What explains it?

Vera: Who, or what, is the one that throws?

Joachim: I don't know.

Vera: Then you cannot explain the throw, neither the lucky nor the unlucky one.

Joachim: I am satisfied. You have done better than you promised. Your tale was colourful and not grey. But you still owe me some wisdom about the goldentree of life.

Vera: I mentioned it briefly. The goldentree of life grows tall and beautiful on the soil of tension.

Joachim: From suffering?

Vera: And from joy. And now you see for yourself why you said that it was your psychology that made you choose Kant. Your psychology is the specific, unique tension. It is the tension between your two a priories and your openness for something which is not-yet. One releases the tension, yet also lives with it. But ethics, and particularly morality, is not a cap thrown on the top of the tension. You congratulated me for my tale, but you were too polite; my dovetailing tale is a modest story, it has only one advantage: you can describe with it yourself, Lawrence, and also me. It is not my truth about morals, nor is it Lawrence's truth, or yours. It is the tale about the condition, or if you wish, the possibility, of good and evil, right and wrong, that accounts for the plurality of truths.

Joachim: But if it gives a true account of the plurality of truths and about the common source of my truth in ethics, of Lawrence's truth, and of yours, why are you warning me from accepting your tale as the account of truth about morality?

Vera: Because the tale does not answer the question concerning truth in morality. What the tale points at is men's and women's openness to this truth. It is the openness to this truth that is common to Lawrence, you and me. But the truth about morality is the gesture that points at the source of morality, the centre of the centre. Nothing remains for me at this point than to repeat what you have said more than once: the truth of morality – it is better to suffer wrong than to wrong others – cannot be proven. Those who embrace it, embrace it with a gesture. They point at the source of morality, at the centre of the centre. True, the need for knowing the centre of the centre remains. Your Kant called it the need for metaphysics. But the God of Israel said: those who look into my face, will die.

(Lawrence appears, and remains for a second standing behind them.)

Lawrence: And all those who do not look into God's face will also die. For example, my namesake, Vera's old acquaintance, died at my age. And there are no reports of his having looked into God's face, although he was one of God's elected people. Sorry to have intruded, anyway. It is getting late, and I believe that you have already finished your tête-à-tête . . .

Vera: At this very minute or at a time many centuries from now . . . we could finish it any time, but we shall never finish it. Welcome.

Lawrence: Have you already ordered some dinner?

Joachim: We had no plans to dine here.

Lawrence: But now we can start planning. Mussels for starters. They have excellent venison too. Their beef dishes are lousy, I would not recommend any of them. But their lambsteak is quite enjoyable. Except for the French, the Indian and the Chinese, there are no cuisines of excellence; all other traditions and combinations require concessions and compromises. Culinary culture is on the decline. So get the best from the worst. Let me see the menu.

Joachim: You order for me. Salad and very little meat . . .

Lawrence: Salad? With this awful dressing? I am afraid that you have lost your sense for telling high culture from low . . .

Joachim: You know that this is not so. Yesterday, you may recall, you associated 'high culture' with the Hegelian absolute spirit and with Kant's aesthetic judgement. But cuisine, good or bad, cannot be related to either Kant's or to Hegel's ideas. I prefer to eat simple things – I am this kind of a person.

Lawrence: You mean that eating tasteless things belongs to your personality? I hope not to the ethics of your personality? But before you answer this difficult question, let's hear Vera's order.

Vera: You can order for me too. Choose what you consider best; I rely on your taste.

Lawrence: Vera dear, why don't you come with me to Paris! I would order you a royal meal there. But as things are, I am ready for the compromise.

(The discussion starts anew during dinner.)

Lawrence: Joachim, my friend, you still owe me an answer. Does your preference for tasteless and boring food belong to your personality, particularly to your ethics of personality? Your mentor, Immanuel Kant, used to invite several friends for luncheon. Those were splendid luncheons, also foodwise.

Joachim: Kant was a great host, a very urbane person. His table was loaded with spendid food and good wine so that all of his guests could eat and drink what they liked best. But these luncheons served a goal other than eating; they provided a framework for the cultivated discussions of select guests. Otherwise Kant kept himself on a strict diet; he ate little . . .

Lawrence: Yes, and he got up at dawn and washed himself in cold water, we know. He was an ascetic priest in Nietzsche's sense. But I asked about you, not about Kant . . .

Joachim: Excuse me, you were the one who introduced the theme of the Kantian luncheons into our discussion. Let me take up the challenge then: true, everything a man does belongs to his personality, either closer to the centre or closer to the periphery . . .

Lawence: Is the personality, then, one-centred?

Joachim: Please, do not introduce one of the most boring and most irrelevant questions of some recent debates into our conversation. If you take your ethics of personality seriously you cannot even raise it. In our long discussion of *peri psyche*, Vera and I came to the conclusion, among others, that what we call our 'psyche' is the tension between the two a prioris – the genetic and the socio-cultural – and that the two a prioris are always incompletely dovetailed. To cut a long story short, the psyche is not an object. So we cannot say that it has one centre, or two, or a hundred. We can only say that one person can describe his psyche better with a one-centred model, the other with a two-centred model, the third with a hundred centred model.

Lawrence: Excuse me, you forget that I have not participated in your conversation and cannot have any recollection of it. I would rather discuss problems that you two have not yet touched. Let's go back to the good luncheon's relation to an ethics of personality.

Joachim: External behaviour like being civil, urbane or rude, yet also matters of taste, regardless of whether they concern preference for a lean diet or sophisticated culinary art, opera or rock music and the like – do belong to our personality. But they are not indications of our autonomy. This is very Kantian, I know, but I don't think that we have become any wiser. For the only thing that all those heterogeneous manifestations of personality have in common is just the negativity I mentioned. Their ethical relevance is very different. Wicked men can have excellent taste in music or may behave with the greatest *politesse*, and they can certainly have unerring judgement in assessing wine. But if a person is decent, it is ethically far more relevant that she be urbane than that she have outstanding culinary taste. This brings us back to Lawrence's point concerning the weight of personality – noble or base, beautiful and ugly, and so on. He made a case for some aristocratic, or at least elitist, virtues. Now let me add to the list a few, similar but democratic virtues. Civility and urbanity are such democratic virtues. No exceptionally weighty personality is called for, for the practice of civility. Civility and urbanity are forms of human commerce which ease difficulties in our communication, which help the other save his face and so on. They are also forms of self-protection. The internal is not the external. We can protect our 'interior' by behaving with the utmost *politesse* externally. All in all, these forms have an ethical, although no moral, relevance. Nothing like this can be said about things like culinary taste. Excuse me, Lawrence, this belongs to your 'elitist' culture, not just because few can afford to pursue a life-style that allows for the refinement of taste. The same may also be true about taste in furnishing your house or room . . .

Vera: Here I protest. Two pots of flowers can change the atmosphere of a room entirely. And the apartments of the wealthy that are furnished by professionals in the image of the most current models of high-brow magazines look – more often than not – like the deserts of taste. They are entirely bereft of personality and more depressing than the smallest holes.

Lawrence: Hear, hear! But let's go back to your point about urbanity and civility. You, Joachim, have compared urbanity and civility – these democratic virtues – to the virtues of my (or Nietzsche's) noble and beautiful character. But the comparison is wrong and you yourself spelled out why. You said that virtues like urbanity and civility ease communication, smooth the hard edges of human commerce, protect the other person's, as well as our own, autonomy. But neither civility nor urbanity manifest one's own autonomy. On the contrary, my (Nietzschean) virtues of personality do manifest a person's autonomy;

they come from within. They do not protect the other, they rather superimpose themselves on the other; neither do they protect the so-called 'interior' of the great personality – for it is the 'internal' that is fully exposed by them.

Joachim: I would not object to this. But please, do not forget that the latest round of this marathon-discussion was occasioned by your taste for refined culinary art and my indifference to food. Is your culinary taste the manifestation of your personality? Of your ethical personality? And finally, of your autonomy?

Lawrence: Good questions.

Joachim: They were your questions.

Lawrence: All the better. The first two questions are quickly settled. My culinary taste is certainly one of the manifestations of my personality. And also of my ethics. As a sworn enemy of the ascetic priests – at least in theory, though in life I am rather attracted to them – I cultivate a kind of Epicurean ethics. About the third question, though, I have some doubts. For it would be ridiculous to say that my autonomy manifests itself in my culinary taste.

Joachim: Why would this be ridiculous?

Lawrence: I could make a decision now at this very minute: 'from today onward I will eat only bread and drink nothing but tapwater'. And from today onward till the end of my days I could then indeed drink nothing but tap water and eat nothing but bread. This is why culinary taste does not belong to my autonomy.

Vera: What about, for example, stopping smoking cigars?

Lawrence: This is my last cigar. I will never smoke a cigar again.

Vera: What about your predilection for strong coffee?

Lawrence: I will never ever drink another cup of coffee.

Vera: You are dangerous. You resemble too much an ascetic priest. Please stop exercising your autonomy for a while.

Lawrence: I'll stop when it pleases me. This means I would never stop. I have always exercised my autonomy.

Vera: What is this, your 'autonomy'?

Lawrence: The capacity to make promises. Whatever promise I make, I keep.

Vera: What can you promise? What should you promise?

Lawrence: I can promise everything that I will keep without losing myself; and I should promise everything that carries me towards my destiny. Everything that I *can* is permitted by my autonomy, everything that I *should* is guided by it.

Joachim: I don't trust my ears! Saulus/Paulus – Friedrich/Immanuel?

Vera: Let me continue to interrogate you. You said, Lawrence, that you are an Epicurean, that you taste the flavours of life fully and with gusto. But when I began to tease you, you resigned without hesitation two of your favourite pleasures: drinking coffee and smoking cigars. And I know that you will never ever smoke or drink coffee again. I also understand that you will not lose yourself for dropping those habits: you made promises that you were permitted to make in the spirit of your ethics. Still I do not understand why you have made these promises at all? Not, I am sure, in order to boast about your will-power; this would be so much unlike you.

Lawrence: No, no, it was not about will-power. While you were teasing me, something struck me like a flash: to be dependent on a habit does not suit me. To be dependent on anything 'external' does not agree with me. Cuban cigars are, for example, 'external' goods of this kind. Although I took pleasure in smoking them, I was not dependent on them. I knew that if anything happened – a trade blockade for example – and I became unable to procure them any more, I would not have 'withdrawal symptoms', I would simply discontinue smoking them.

Vera: Excuse me, now I understand you even less. If you were not dependent on the habit, why do you drop the habit? What came to you in a 'flash'?

Lawrence: Although I was not dependent on the habit, I was dependent on a contingent event – the possibility or impossibility of the procurment of cigars, and on a contingent time – somewhere, perhaps in the future. But why be dependent on contingencies? Why 'some time from now'? Why not 'exactly now'? And why not abslutely?

Joachim: Kant's rigour is child's play compared with your absolutism. I would not resign the pleasure of brandy, this innocent pleasure that does not hurt the moral law.

lawrence: And why should you?

Joachim: There are moments when I am tempted to follow you. To follow you absolutely and blindly. But then I reconsider. Perhaps your friendship with me is also a habit of yours that can be dropped at will, absolutely.

Lawrence: No, no, Our friendship cannot be described as a 'habit' because you are different and new every single minute . . .

Joachim: And dependence? Is friendship not a kind of dependence?

Lawrence: As long as it is mutual, it is not. If your friendship cooled down – yes, then it would become dependence.

Joachim: If your friendship cooled down, I would still cherish mine.

Lawrence: Are you, then the practical perspectivist, or even the practical relativist? And am I the practical absolutist? At least in matters of the psyche or the soul?

Joachim: You could say so.

Lawrence: But let me return to your most ambiguous sentence. You said that sometimes you were tempted to follow me, absolutely and blindly. But if you did, this would really be the end of our friendship. Thank God that you have always resisted this temptation.

Vera: I don't understand your vehemence. After all, you are a philosopher, and philosophers, just like religious leaders, need disciples who disseminate their ideas and bring the news about the good tidings . . .

Lawrence: They used to need disciples, but they no longer need them. If you discover the absolute Truth, the universal and necessary only one, then you need disciples. For a perspectivist like myself, a disciple is just an echo or the echo of an echo. The time of 'isms' is out.

Vera: And what about perspectivism, then?

Lawrence: Perspectivism is out too, although not the various perspectives.

Joachim: You have referred to yourself as an Epicurean. Your ethics, however, does not seem to resemble the teachings of Epicurus or Lucretius. And now you dismiss the 'garden' too.

Lawrence: No, not at all. My soul embraces the garden of Epicurus. In my garden there are no teachers or disciples. There are just friends. Each of them thinks in his or her own way, a unique way. Each of them is decent in his or her unique way. Yes, I embrace absolutely the idea of the beautiful community of equals.

Joachim: Are *you* saying this? You who abused equality just yesterday?

Lawrence: Yesterday I abused the substantive concept of equality. Today I speak of the equality of the chosen few. The equality of the wise men and women in Epicurus' garden, and of the knights on Monsalvat.

Joachim: This is beside the point. If the concept of substantive equality is wrong, and if no two persons – *qua* persons – can be compared, how can you speak about equality in a world where there is ethics beyond justice?

Lawrence: By 'equality' I meant something negative, not positive. The absence of hierarchy, the absence of the master–disciple relation, the absence of dependence, the absence of *ressentiment* . . .

Joachim: You forget what you must have learned about *das krumme Holz*, as always. If someone loves another who does not love him, there is already dependence. And if someone is more brilliant than another, there is, again, dependence. You still think that you can get along without the crutch. One day you will despair.

Lawrence: Faith is beyond despair.

Joachim: Or perhaps, faith *is* despair. Now, let us get back on the main track. I agree with you that what we once called 'philosophical schools' are no more, or they have become – to use your Nietzschean terms – banausic. In the present every original philosopher speaks his or her own language. Yet thousands of others earn a living by teaching philosophy, so they must learn how to speak another personality's language. A follower is nowadays just like a worker in a chemical laboratory who carries out the other's orders, with the difference that in philosophy the idea does not need technical application. Precisely this is why – apart from your Utopia of the 'garden' or Monsalvat – I still do not understand what you want from Epicureanism.

Lawrence: Funny that you associate Monsalvat with Epicureanism – or was it I who did so first? But I like this association. *Procul negotiis* – far from the business of the world, far from all the things that people normally care for, far from anxieties and from the fear of death, enjoying the life of spiritual concerns with a few chosen friends. What I call Epicureanism has nothing to do with the doctrines of this venerable philosophical school. They were thin metaphysical doctrines; I do not think that anyone so far has cared for them. When I say 'Epicureanism', I mean an attitude, a very practical attitude that one takes towards the common practices of the social world. Epicureans – of my kind – share this attitude.

Joachim: How can you reconcile your ethics of personality with your concept of a shared attitude?

Lawrence: There is no need for reconciliation for they are intrinsically connected. For simplicity's sake let me formulate in Vera's, or rather in her Sören's, terms. A person who chooses himself or herself existentially, chooses himself or herself either under the category of difference or under the category of universality. Then he or she begins to become what he or she is. The decent person asks 'What is the right thing for me to do?', while the man of destiny follows a different 'pull'. But both the decent person and the man of destiny assume thereby the attitude that I called 'Epicurean'. If they do not assume this attitude, then they fail existentially. You become what you are when you assume an attitude of indifference or of neutrality to everything that you are not. Or – and this is what I call the 'garden' or 'Monsalvat' – you also place yourself into a situation, a context, where you are no longer tempted. This is why I said that the Epicurean attitude belongs to all kinds of ethics of personality.

Joachim: Why Epicureanism and not Stoicism? But let me ask first another question: why *procul negotiis*? I can hardly imagine how a decent person could become decent *procul negotiis*?

Lawrence: *Procul negotiis* is not a place that one occupies above the social world, for one can stay far from the cares of the social world everywhere and in all occupations. For example, the person who rather suffers injustice than commit injustice does the right thing irrespective of the consequences to his own life that may ensue from the good deed. *Procul negotiis* means here a kind of indifference towards those possible consequences. There is commitment, even passionate commitment to the other's welfare, yet we make this commitment without also letting ourselves be exposed to the whims of fate. In another traditional way one could also formulate this as 'one does the right thing without fear and without hope'. But *procul negotiis* can also mean the withdrawal from all earthly cares, if this is what our destiny wants us to do – or rather – to be.

Joachim: This is not a moral attitude . . .

Lawrence: I thought that we had already settled the issue. It is not necessarily a moral attitude, but it is an ethical attitude. This is why it is shared among all men and women who are committed to an ethics of personality; among all men and women who have chosen themselves existentially; among all authentic and – relatively – autonomous modern men and women. Only some of them are moral in your Kantian sense; all of them are ethical in my sense.

Joachim: Again, why Epicureanism and not Stoicism?

Lawrence: Stoico-Epicureanism, perhaps.

Joachim: Isn't it frivolous to arrange a hyphenated marriage between two inimical philosophical schools? Stoicism as an attitude without doctrines appeals to me; if so understood, I could describe myself as a kind of Stoic. But I could never describe myself as a kind of Epicurean.

Lawrence: Still, you are the special friend of a confessed Epicurean – no enmity whatsoever; rather alliance. And this is my point.

Joachim: Your point is that we love our opposites?

Lawrence: My point is that we are not opposites. We are just different. As attitudes, Stoicism and Epicureanism are no longer worlds apart; pure Epicureanism or pure Stoicism – if they still exist at all – are the two extremes of a continuum – of the hyphenated Stoico-Epicureanism. What they share is a fundamental attitude; what they do not share may be everything else.

Joachim: What is this fundamental attitude that they share?

Lawrence: The practice of fencing off heteronomy. The practice that alone makes the good life possible.

Joachim: What is the good life?

Lawrence: Becoming what we are.

Joachim: What is happiness?

Lawrence: Ask Vera, not me.

Joachim: What is happiness, Vera?

Vera: Never to find out whether you have chosen yourself under the category of the universal or under the category of difference. Lawrence must know that, for I told him yesterday . . .

Lawrence: It's just that I did not believe you. The good life makes sense to me, happiness does not; particularly not the kind of happiness Vera just suggested. If you are taken seriously, it follows that no one can be happy before death. How archaic and insensitive . . .

Joachim: It appeals to me.

Lawrence: This is a sign of your Stoicism. But if there is felicity in the world for me, it will not wait for me on my deathbed. My felicity, if there is felicity in store for me, will grasp me as the timeless moment of eternity that arrives unprepared for and unwaited. As an indescribable joy ...

Joachim: This sounds mystical rather than Epicurean.

Lawrence: Both mystics and Epicureans experience joy, felicity and pleasure – or anticipate them.

Joachim: You said that your indescribable joy arrives – if it arrives – unprepared for and unawaited.

Lawrence: The joy of fulfilment comes unprepared for – but it privileges men and women who keep themselves in the state of readiness for felicity, pleasure, song, dance, gaiety and joy. The table for the Messiah must be set with heavy dishes and shining candles ...

Joachim: But your Messiah comes – if he comes – because the world is hollow, sad, guilty, hopeless and dark. And it is immoral to rejoice in a world that is hopeless and dark.

Lawrence: In what kind of world can we rejoice then?

Vera: Lawrence and Joachim, stop for a moment. you – the two extremes of the continuum of the so-called hyphenated Stoico-Epicureanism – you really go to the extremes. Your vision of happiness or felicity tears you apart, but your idea of the good life can bring you together again.

Joachim: 'Live according to nature' means for me: live according to your noumenal nature.

Lawrence: It means for me: live according to your self-chosen nature, your nature to be.

Vera: It means for me: as every exister, you too live according to your 'ipseity'.

Lawrence: Foul play, Vera. You spoke only about existers ...

Vera: Didn't you also? Only in the cases of existers can you refer to the self-chosen nature. Joachim alone, as a true universalist, appealed to everyone.

Joachim: 'To live in necessity is misery; but it is not necessary to live in necessity' means for me: your acts can (and should) be determined by transcendental freedom.

Lawrence: It means to me: *amor fati* lifts you beyond necessity.

Vera: It means to me: don't hesitate to leap.

Joachim: 'As long as we are, there is no death; where there is death, we are not' means for me that we are responsible for our actions and that we act as long as we live; to live honestly should be our main concern; death can take us when it pleases.

Lawrence: It means to me: the goldentree of life is green.

Vera: It means to me: live authentically; face your mortality sincerely; yet the telos of your life is not death but another person's life.

Joachim: 'Live in hiding' means to me to live modestly; one compares oneself with the moral law, not with one's fellow creatures.

Lawrence: It means to me: do not disclose your most interior self directly.

Vera: It means to me: fear nothing but envy; beware of making your fellow creatures envious.

Joachim: Be indifferent to the whims of the tyrant. Keep your dignity.

Lawrence: Be indifferent to the whims of the crowd. Keep your dignity.

Vera: Don't be indifferent to betrayal – but endure it. Keep your dignity.

Joachim: We could go on till morning without getting to the end of the Stoic or Epicurean commonplaces. But this suffices to establish Lawrence's claim. There is a general attitude that all three of us share. And why not term it Stoico-Epicurean? On this note we had better terminate our discussion. It is late, time to go home.

Lawrence: Terminate our discussion? And go home? Go home empty-handed?

Vera: What do you mean by 'empty-handed'? Haven't we scrutinized your 'ethics of personality' from many, or at least from three, perspectives? We have thought over what we are, what we are doing, and what we are living for. Could we have done more?

Lawrence: But Vera, don't you see? This is nothing, nothing at all. you payed us a visit, you lured us into a conversation as you have once lured the other Joachim and the other Lawrence into a conversation at the turn of the century, and as you have, perhaps lured many others before. You were our promise, you were my promise. Old witch, you betrayed us, you betrayed me. You brought me nothing, you told me nothing, you have not even promised me anything. You don't know whether you love me . . . you don't know even whether I can hope. If you don't know anything, why did you join me, why have you raised my expectations? Listen Vera, it is the Truth I want to know, I want to know the Truth!

Vera: The Truth about what?

Lawrence: About Truth. Lift the veil, uncover the secret!

Vera: Lawrence, keep silent . . .

Joachim: Lawrence, dear, your insistence is uncivil.

Lawrence: Civil or uncivil, who cares – I don't. Vera, I don't care for you either; with you or without you I will pursue, I will overcome, for I must.

Vera (putting her hand on Lawrence's): I love you.

Joachim: I see it now. 'Unconcerned, mocking, violent – thus wisdom wants *us*: she is a woman and always loves a warrior.'

Lawrence (freeing his hand, he quietly embraces Joachim): My dear Joachim, the words of Zarathustra do not suit you. Trust me. I would be most surprised if wisdom were unpardonably one-sided. I guess that the lady has many tastes.

Vera: Keep guessing and live well. Adieu.

Part III

Letters Concerning Moral Aesthetics: On the Beautiful and the Sublime Character, on Happiness and Love

Samples of the Correspondence between Mrs Sophie Meller and her Granddaughter, Fifi

Fifi to her Grandmother

Dearest Granny,

Can I ask you a favour? Of course, I know your answer, I heard it so many times as a child: 'You can ask me anything unless it is indecent.' Since I knew what was decent and what was not, I also knew what I might ask and what I might not. Don't worry, the favour I now ask is not indecent – this is why I know that I can ask you to do it. I'm asking you to read a manuscript for me. Not instead of me, for I have already read it three times. It is a manuscript written by a philosophy student, a fellow student of mine, a young man of my age. I have formed not just one opinion of this writing but many different ones; to tell the truth, the manuscript has confused me. I have been unable to sleep quietly ever since I have read it. Until now I trusted my ability to tell right from wrong; I have learned from you how to do it. You never scolded me for having soiled my dress or for having received a bad grade in school, you never preached, you were never pointing at model children I should emulate. Still, in your own way, you were very strict. You demanded that I respect others – adults and children alike, that I pay attention to their needs, that I care for their suffering. You demanded that I should not lie, but you also respected my need for secrecy. This was finally all that you meant by 'decency'. You could express your disapproval straightforwardly when I failed to keep up with this standard. For example, I remember that once I combed the hair of a friend of yours who complained about a bad headache. She asked me to stop, yet I did not. You just looked at me and said quietly, 'Stop doing it'. And then I stopped immediately, for in a flash I understood that I was doing something indecent. I never heard you raise your voice. You did not need to raise your voice. When you said 'stop it' it sounded like advice. But in my ears it was an imperative. Lawrence, this young man whom I have mentioned to you, the author of the manuscript I'm sending to you by separate mail, would, perhaps, say that it was a categorical imperative. Although you did not teach me many moral norms, and I felt myself more free to do what I liked best than all the other girls I knew, my upbringing cannot be described as 'permissive'. I grew up as a girl who knew that she had responsibilities, that she had a conscience to answer, that not everything is morally allowed. You never spoke about God, neither did you refer to divine ordinance or punishment. Or of any kind of punishment. On second thoughts, I do not think that you have punished me even once; your quiet disapproval was punishment enough for me. True, you never promised presents in exchange for my good behaviour either. I never heard you saying, 'If you are good, you will get this or that'. You never even used the terms 'bad' or 'good' in this context. You never said 'you are a good girl' or 'you are a bad girl'. Your praised and blamed only my acts, my deeds. I remember: sometimes you treated me with humour, particularly because of my inclination to be over-enthusiastic about just everything and everyone, without selection. Sometimes you forewarned me that if I followed my enthusiasm blindly, I would hurt myself. But you did not forbid me to do it; you did not even advise me against it; you gave only hints. The risk was mine. Do you remember how I used to lavish my little presents on a classmate who never reciprocated them? You just asked me whether this unreciprocated relationship did not humiliate me, and whether it was possible that the other person perceived my constant gift-giving as rather a nuisance. You asked this very tactfully, and still, it did hurt. How grateful I now am that you hurt me then. I guess what you are thinking: you have not educated me at all, you spoke to me the same way you normally spoke to your friends. I was – I am – your friend. And this is the 'natural' way to speak. Or the sincere way.

I can hear you telling me: 'Please, Fifi, stop, enough for now', because you do not like to talk about yourself, neither do you like to listen to people who are praising you highly. Not because you are embarrassed (I never saw you in the state of embarrassment) but because it hurts your sense of tact. But please, understand: I praise you not just in order to praise you – I praise you because I begin to see that all that you said to be 'natural' is not natural at all. Rather, it is something exceptional, unique. It is you and you alone. I begin to realize that you are a moral authority for me. Moreover: you are the only moral authority for me. And not just for me, I guess. I have learned to know many of your former students. In my eyes, of course, they were old ladies. I saw how reverently these old ladies spoke to you, how they sought your advice. How they listened to you. You were the moral authority for those former students of yours too, and not just for me. How did you perform this trick? You were right to say that there was no trick – it was just 'natural'. It was natural – for you. It emanated from your character. I try to express myself clearly. I do not think that your natural moral authority is rooted only in your upright-ness, decency. You also have an ability to create the atmosphere of decency around you – not many women can do it, sometimes even the best of them cannot. For example, they treat others permissively, or they preach too much, yet perhaps they do behave exactly like you. It's just that the others to whom they turn, be they children, adult friends, students, or almost strangers, would not listen to them the way they listen to you. Whatever you say is always received approvingly. I cannot help repeating myself: you never needed to raise your voice in order to be obeyed. But you were obeyed. Not in the way a command is obeyed, but in the way that an absolute insight is instinctively obeyed. How can I express myself? Everything emanates from your character. You have a good character; but also an imperious character. This is why your pieces of advice remind me of the categorical imperative.

But it is not to tell you all this that I began to write you this letter. I want to ask your advice. Since you are my moral authority, I must turn to you to seek advice about a book, or rather about the content of a book, which I received from a colleague for my perusal, a book that I have already read through three times, a book because of which I cannot sleep. I received it from a boy of my age (or have I told you this already?). He has very deep dark eyes. There is something in him that reminds me of you. Of course, nothing external. You have blue eyes and you are an old woman, although with upright gait and a quite angular physique, a woman with white hair (once blond and never dyed), Nothing in Lawrence reminds me of you, either, that I could define as something intellectual. You are the most refined and cultivated woman I ever knew; music and poetry are parts of your life. You understand how to surround yourself with beautiful things, without spending much money to purchase them, which you could not possibly afford from the small pension you receive as a schoolteacher. Only your love of beauty is comparable to your sense of humour. There is nothing of any of these feautures in Lawrence. Although he talks constantly about beauty, he never cares for it. Beauty is a kind of idea for him that has nothing to do with his life. His room looks miserable, no taste (not even bad taste) is traceable there, his books are thrown randomly one upon the other, and I had better remain silent about the cockroaches. Still, as I said, Lawrence talks constantly about beauty, he elaborates theories of beauty, particularily in ethics. He also lacks a sense of humour although he likes to discuss humour; he treats others with irony but he is too sensitive to tolerate being treated with irony. He has – as you will see for yourself – a great intellect. He cares for nothing but philosophy, all his passions are vested in thinking. It is this that makes him attractive, in spite of his neglected exterior and his obvious indifference for everything unphilosophical. Shortly: you are many-sided, he is one-sided. Why does he remind me of you all the same? I think I know: he is, like you, an imperious character, a commanding personality. He does not need to command anyone with words, he commands them through his being. But his is still a different kind of command from yours. For, when you command, no one really obeys although they do whatever you have commanded; you never restrict our freedom – for you convince us that we would do on our own the same thing as your personality has commanded us to do. But when Lawrence's personality commands, the others in fact obey. Being attached to Lawrence's commanding personality may result in the loss of one's freedom. I do not mean that we all fall in love with him. Not quite, although I confess, that if I consulted my feelings sincerely, I could detect there some stirrings that may resemble love. But this is not what I mean, for even if

I love him I know that he will never be interested in me in the way that lovers are interested in their beloved. My love – if I love him – will remain unrequited, and unrequited love is unlike requited love. It will never come to a relationship. True, the anticipation of my limited chances does not hurt. This is a love that resembles Spinoza's *amor dei intellectualis*. Don't misunderstand the expression 'amor dei' for there is nothing godlike in Lawrence. There is no touch of a Greek god in him, despite his great love for all things Greek. He is what I just called a commanding character, an imperious character, who commands through his intellect and his passion; this passion is, however, not vested in the people whom he commands, but in something else. He is also a man of gestures.

Why do I tell you all this? Perhaps because I love talking to you, and perhaps because I want you to see the context of my request fully. And, perhaps, also because I know your predilection for details. And there are still more details to tell. Surely, you must be curious to find out how did I get hold of this manuscript. I assure you, Lawrence is not the kind of person who would give you his manuscript to read just because he has met you by chance. Still, we did meet by chance. As I began to write my paper on Shaw I knew that I would not do it properly before acquiring a deeper insight into Nietzsche. This is how it occurred to me to take a course on Nietzsche, the same course Lawrence also attended. After class, a group of students would go together to a pub on University Place. I was one of this group. Lawrence talked much, so did his special friend Joachim. I rarely intervened, not because I am shy – you know that I am not – but because my philosophical culture is not up to standard; I learned more about philosophy, and particularily about ethics, from Shakespeare than from all the philosophers taken together. Besides, I was brought up by a person who never spoke just in order to show off or to emphasize her presence, who intervened only when she had to say something of importance. I had a brief conversation with Lawrence about Shakspeare; we discussed Beatrice and Benedict and whether their ethics could be described in Nietzsche's terms. He said yes, I said no. I added that Beatrice reminded me of my grandmother. He asked me to tell him something about my grandmother. So I did, very inadequately. Lawrence listened attentively, which rarely happens to him, and then he said that my story corroborated his judgement about Beatrice and not mine. For, he continued, 'your granny is a typical Nietzschean character'. I answered that he was entirely wrong, and that he misunderstood me and you. Then someone joined us and the conversation ended. Half a year later – a week ago – we met again. I was sitting in the same pub with my friends from a Shakespeare class. He came in and joined us. Better to say, he joined me, and asked me about you. But I wanted to avoid discussing you. Instead, I began to talk about a moral issue that had bothered me for a long time. I spoke about Shakespeare first, about Richard III in particular. Maybe Richard III is the only (literary) person who can be descibed as 'radically evil', because he chooses to do evil just for the sake of it. He does not do evil as people normally do, in order to achieve 'good' things – so-called material goods – such as power, wealth, sensual gratification, success. That is, Richard's relation to evil is the mirror image of Aristotle's definition of virtuous activity: vice is – for him – an activity one practises solely for its own sake. Yet in the last moment the selfsame Richard confesses to himself that he hates himself and hates his crimes. But, I added, if one follows the newspaper reports about mass-murderers today, at least here, in America, the first thing that will amaze one is that almost none of them confess to their crimes. They deny having committed their deeds before the verdict. And even after the verdict, five minutes before entering the gas chamber, or being chained to the electric chair, they still keep denying. Lawrence said that he has not made this observation because he never reads the crime pages in the papers. But, he added, when he came to think about it, he saw my point. For example, he continued, when Hegel wrote about capital punishment in his *Philosophy of Right*, he first said, that only murder should carry capital punishment, but murder always and absolutely. Hegel adds that capital punishment will best put the moral order right if the murderer confesses to the murder, and he adds some hints that the murderers usually do confess. Indeed, in Hegel's times, murderers normally confessed to their crimes, and not just while waiting for execution, but even during their trial. This brought us back to Nietzsche, to the death of God. In Hegel's time murderers still stood before the face of God. They were not afraid just of death, they were also afraid of divine retribution. When they had five minutes left for repentance, they repented. Lawrence interrupted just to remark that people cannot tell good from evil as things stand now. I objected, for I think that they could if they believed that they should. Lawrence, however, scolded me for my *naïveté*. Why should people do unpleasant things unless they need to do them? And then he begun blaming you for my *naïveté*. It is because of you that I, supposedly, believe in the impossible. Everyone who thinks of the exception as if it were the universal, believes in miracles. But he hoped, he added, that my granny – this Nietzschean exception – did not believe in miracles. *You* do, he said, because you are still young. This surprised me, because – as I've told you already – we are exactly the same age. And then, he turned to me and asked, 'Would you mind reading a manuscript that discusses similar matters?' 'Whose manuscript?', I asked; this was stupid of me – or tactful? – because I knew the answer. Lawrence continued, 'It is a dialogue I wrote; a report on conversation – partly real, partly imaginary – that took place between me, Joachim and a mysterious woman. I offer this dialogue for your perusal.' The following day he waited for me after my Shakespeare class to give me his manuscript. The manuscript was in an awful shape, as is everything around Lawrence. Sentences were left unfinished, the typing was a mess. But the content was a different matter. I would say, disturbing, or else fascinating. And sometimes puzzling too, but this, perhaps, only because I am not a philosophy student.

What is it that disturbes me? you will ask. Many things. But I stop here and won't tell you anything. For I really want to hear what you have to tell first. Just one word more. After reading the dialogue, I had to realize that Lawrence was right: I am naïve. Whatever I have learned from you without being taught, is the exception. It resembles a secrete alliance, an intimate tie; it is like a private language. It has no relevance to anyone else. But now I really stop. Please, answer soon.

I kiss you – Fifi

Mrs Sophie Meller to her Granddaughter, Fifi

My dearest,

To receive a letter from you is always a holiday. I did with your letter the same thing that you did with Lawrence's manuscript: I read it three times. You see how deeply I am already involved in your experience! I speak of Lawrence as of an old common acquaintance. I sympathize with him, because a strong passion vested in something spiritual shows a noble character. Judging from your story, he belongs to those young men who believe that everyone loves them; he is not yet fully grown up. He does not seem to be narcissistic – he does not speak about himself at all – but there can be other reasons for a kind of judgemental absent mindedness. In your portrayal I see a young man who does not observe other people, for he spontaneously assumes that they are like him. Since he is not envious, he does not notice the signs of envy in another; since he is not vain he acts as if no one were. I learned from you that he attended a class on Nietzsche; as a very knowledgeable youth he would be able to give a lengthy lecture about *ressentiment* on the spot. But one can know everything about something without recognizing the same thing as it actually appears before one's nose. Great theorists can be very poor judges of character. So can be beautiful souls. You mother was like this. She was always telling me funny stories about vain and envious musicians, their competitiveness and meanness. Still, she was absolutely confident that everyone liked her. When she finished at the top of her class in the conservatory, and I vaguely hinted at the possibility that not all of her friends felt happy about it, which was so obvious that even our little dog felt it, she was taken aback and shocked as if she had never heard about jealousy in her life. My dear, I am getting chatty, and what is worse, I'm indulging in reminiscences. Let me return to your Lawrence. I sympathize with him, in spite of his obvious lack of judgemental powers, for he is lovable, at least in your portrayal. But – I am sorry to come to this 'but' – I cannot read his manuscript; I cannot even glance at it. This young man Lawrence offered his manuscript for your perusal, not for mine. it is a private manuscript. You have sent it to me because you wish to have my opinion – but, perhaps, the author does not wish me to form an opinion. I am always reluctant to say 'no' if you ask anything, yet this time I must, unfortunately, say 'no'. I return the manuscript. But if you described the things that puzzle you, if you spoke about the thoughts that make you uneasy and take away your sleep, I could talk them over with you. So far, you have kept both your problems and your thoughts secret, and only expressed your feelings vaguely.

I must confess that I am more curious than worried. There is a certain kind of uneasiness that is more wholesome than a good night's sleep. Yours seem to be of this kind.

Love, Granny

Fifi to her Grandmother

Granny dear,

After receiving your letter I called Lawrence and asked him whether he would mind if you were to read his dialogue. He answered that on the contrary, he had expected me to send you the manuscript. He knew that I was going to do this. And you said that he was a bad judge of character! By the way, I got the impression that he gave me the manuscript specially in order to have your opinion, not mine. The manuscript has just arrived – and it goes right back to the sender. I am glad that things happened this way, perhaps also because I do not need to write a whole essay in letter form to explain to you the things that worry me.

One word more: you never ever before told me the story about mamma. You are shrewd to tell it now. For the story corroborates Lawrence's judgement concerning my *naïveté*, and my judgement of Lawrence's neglect of other people's opinions. Are you suggesting then that Lawrence and I, in one sense, resemble each other?

I expect your letter very, very soon (and a very, very long letter). Do not refer to your age – you have no excuses!

Kisses (many, many), Fifi

Mrs Sophie Meller to her Granddaughter, Fifi

My dear Fifi,

The dialogue you sent me made enjoyable reading. I spent four wonderful days together with it. After so many cold and rainy days the weather has suddenly turned warm. So I was sitting in the garden in my fancy rocking-chair, tasting the rays of the sun and listening to the song of the birds in the background while reading Lawrence's dialogue on the ethics of personality. When, in the future, I recall this dialogue, this glorious day will come back to me in a flash: the smell of late spring, of June, of the youth of nature, the youth of Lawrence and yours.

Yes, your Lawrence is a remarkable young man, although not the model of modesty. He made that obvious in his tête-à-tête with Vera, and particularly in the closing sections of the dialogue, where he tries to find out passionately whether he is a great philosopher or not, and he makes unmistakable hints to the reader that he is one. The Nietzsche-reminiscences are here too obvious. Lawrence is badly in need of the spice of self-irony. So is Joachim, who – as you mentioned – is modelled on a real-life figure. The sole person with a sense of humour is Vera, but she is a composite figure, glued together from a young girl (who lived at the turn of the century), as well as from Kundry, Ariadne, Veronica, and the goddess of wisdom – or perhaps, even the goddess of truth. This is too much. However, there is true wisdom in Vera's answer to the impatient insistence of your young friend to know all about felicity or happiness (she said, you remember, that you are happy if you never find out what exactly your primary existential choice had been), but she is too solemn, at least too solemn for my taste. The fault lies with the portrayal. Your Lawrence always puts one more piece of coal on the fire in addition to the amount sufficient to keep us cosy. (I almost added that he also overwhelms us with too many metaphors, but I realized in the meantime that I am guilty of the same misdemeanour and so I must keep silent.)

You were right in your observation that your friend has no sense of humour, and he is certainly not a man of understatements. He has no sense of proportion either. He likes to speak about 'the goldentree of life', yet there is more of the grey theory in his work than of this famous green 'goldentree'. I do not blame him for this. Some people say that lightheartedness befits youth best; life experience and work will teach us to take things seriously. I think that this so-called wisdom is modelled on morally worthless people, for whom 'making a living' and a good life coincide. It is 'making a living', such as acquiring a high position or earning a lot of money that they take seriously, not the resolve to become what they really are, not the existential choice – as Lawrence (or Vera) puts it. The youth of a person of worth is the most serious season of his or her life. It is then that it is decided whether a person will be pushed by her past, by her environment, or rather pulled by her character, whether she will become a personality or not. I like the metaphor of the existential choice, because it is simple and enlightening: it concentrates all of what must be said about becoming ourselves into one forceful central image. In the eye of the beholders of philosophy – and I am one of them – the metaphor of the existential choice has some adherent beauties. With the help of this image one can lift an everyday experience on to the level of philosophical speculation, on to a higher level, traditionally speaking. An everyday experience, separated from the everyday context, will then be an independent actor, eager to play a significant role on the stage of the philosophical world-theatre. As a good actor, it will play the role well, it will fit perfectly into the play, will skilfully interplay with the other actors, with the older, the more traditional philosophical characters, such as 'spontaneity', 'choice', 'the universal', 'the particular' and the like. But I hope, my dear, that you will never be tempted to judge all single characters and personalities by this standard. You will, I guess, not say, 'Here is my friend Fanny, so let me quickly find out whether she has chosen herself, and if yes, whether she did it under the category of the universal or under the category of difference. And when? And does she remember?' For, my dear Fifi, when you say – together with your friend Lawrence – that every person is unique, your cannot take this idea lightly, for it is not just a figure of speech. You must willingly admit that no two persons acquire uniqueness through performing the same kind of leap. Whether you will be an essential person or a superfluous one, three dimensional or one dimensional, whether you will resemble the stone or the husk of the fruit, is not decided in one way alone. I understand, the theory of the existential choice does not call for empty generalizations, for it has not escaped my attention that everyone supposedly chooses himself, himself entirely and himself alone. But, you see, here I feel the need to object. Sometimes one chooses oneself, but doesn't do so entirely. I even guess that this is what generally happens, this is the way that one can best describe what generally happens. Lawrence suggests that if I fail to choose myself entirely, I haven't chosen myself at all. My judgement of human character suggests otherwise. There is more and there is less. If one is not entirely oneself one is still not a mere husk. I know that you suspect expressions like essence or husk, they taste unsavoury on your generation's cognitive palate. I remain old-fashioned. One metaphor is as good as another if it helps to make plausible what one has in mind. So I stick to my vocabulary of 'essential or husklike', and it is my conviction that it is plausible to think of them as a continuum.

My dear, the word 'continuum' reminds me that I have forgotten to tell you what I began to say. I spoke about the seriousness of youth and then my thoughts began to wander. Whatever philosophical language I speak, whether I employ the metaphor of existential choice or choose another one, I will still continue to believe that it is in one's youth that it is decided whether one will turn out to be an essential personality or just an empty husk of a man, or closer to the first than to the latter. You will say: it is now you who is over-generalizing. I try to avoid it.

I am not talking about everyone. In the life of some people everything of importance is decided early in childhood, in the life of others perhaps later in life, but generally, and for the most, the question of being substantial or of lacking substance (or being closer to one or other of the extremes) is decided in youth. Youth is a difficult period in life; it is a painful age, the age of suffering, at least for the deep characters. Once Kierkegaard said (in reference to practising Christianity) that one takes the good position if one suffers. If one feels easy one must know that one has taken the wrong position. When you have a bad tooth, seriousness requires you to touch it with your tongue; the tooth will become healthy (or pulled out) if no pain follows whatever position you take. You see now what I mean when I refer to the seriousness of youth. Your Lawrence, for example, constantly touches the aching tooth. This is why he writes in utter seriousness. This is why he has no humour (yet). Perhaps later, after the bad tooth has healed or has been pulled out, he will learn how to speak will humour, how to employ understatements and the like. People who are inclined to become rather husklike avoid the period of seriousness. They will not touch the aching tooth; in their perception they have no bad tooth. The consequences you know; the whole organism will be morally poisoned. And after the organism has been poisoned, the person will become serious, and pain will come to him constantly from the outside; it will have an exterior source, for example the success of a competitor, the failure to get promotion, and the like. You see my dear, this is an old story. The story goes on about autonomy or heteronomy. I haven't said anything new, I have only ruminated on Lawrence's seriousness and finally, I have approved of it.

You will shake your head. And for two reasons at least. You will tell me that I always liked you to be merry, playful and gay. I still do. I do not know whether Lawrence is also sometimes merry, playful and gay, or never; at least he has presented himself exclusively in the position of touching the aching tooth: think of his abrupt decision to stop smoking cigars and stop drinking coffee. He was frightful. But I hope that you do not think that serious persons cannot be playful or that gaity does not befit them? If you did, you would have accepted the false image of seriousness, and together with it, also the wrong idea that seriousness befits ripe or old age. The wrong idea of seriousness raises suspicions against gaity and playfulness. I want to see you gay and playful and I also want you to be serious. One is not playful and gay in general. One is playful in something, one is happy about something, one gets pleasure out of something. This is, again, not a new idea, for the Epicureans never ceased to speak in these terms. And since your friend declared his sympathy to Epicureanism near the end of this dialogue, he will not mind if I make some friendly reference to his old gentleman-master. The real question has nothing to do with generalities. You are playful all right, but what is your game? You are happy, but what is the source of your happiness? You enjoy something, but what are the things you enjoy? I know well that the special friend of your friend, named Joachim, will warn me that in the mind of his own dear Kant such distinctions do not matter. For merriment is merriment, joy is joy, sensual is sensual; identity, this is all. But I am not a great believer in the *plein pouvoir* of the law of identity, especially not if it comes to emotions or feelings. Emotions, feelings are involvments in something. And they differ from one another at least on the count of the thing(s) a person is involved in. One can be involed in murder or in planting trees; is the joy one feels in those two cases the same kind of joy? No person with the minimum common sense (or everyday experience) would answer in the affirmative. They will tell us instead that one is the joy of an evil person whereas the other kind of joy is light and lovely, but says little about the person whose joy it is. You mentioned that your friend Laura enjoys helping others, so you can sympathize with her joy and also fancy it as an unmixed pleasant feeling. A serious person (serious in my sense) may enjoy his seriousness too; it is obvious that Lawrence immensely enjoyed writing his dialogue. He enjoyed doing this a thousand times more than going to a party with loud rock music where you cannot hear one another's voices. If I read him properly, he would be rather bored had he been obliged to go to such a party. All lovers of conversation – and Lawrence is one of them – enjoy going to places where there is a chance of having a good conversation. If one knows which things a person enjoys most one can form an idea about the character of that person. Please, do not misunderstand me. I do not think that young persons of seriousness enjoy being serious all the time. When I said that I can read people's character roughly from the things they do enjoy, I haven't had in mind serious things first and foremost. Good characters enjoy a great variety of things, and each one different things. Your cousin Andrew said when he was six years old, 'I love nature', and he was not repeating something which he had overheard (I never say 'I love nature') for he, indeed, loved nature and he still does. I see your smile, yes, of course, for me the love of nature is a serious matter; I also have the secret (unconfirmed) belief that people who, after a strenuous hike, sit down beside a little stream for hours to listen with enchantment to the sound of water cannot be morally bad. Funny, but I do not think the same about people, who after a strenuous hike, look down with pleasure from the very peak on the landscape below. Do you want an explanation? I have none. But since your smile is well taken I will stop referring to the love of nature as the source of a morally indifferent kind of joy, and will stop speaking of Andrew too. Young people enjoy exercising their body – to run, to surf, to play ball and so on. No, no, I do not mind at all if a serious young man plays unseriously. I would mind instead if he played seriously. If one plays seriously one plays only formally, essentially (again to employ metaphysical language) one does not play. What the person then enjoys is not playing but victory, not the exercise of his body or skill or mind, but success. This reminds you of Rousseau. But had I brought you up in the fashion of Emile? Did I mind if you participated in a competitive game? I didn't even mind that you liked to win. Since so many games are about winning it would be unnatural not to strive for victory once haring participated in such games. I know that children like competing; this is somehow in our genes. To fight against something that is natural is foolish. But to counter-balance it is less foolish. Let me come back to the seriousness of the game. The less serious the game, the better, for the more it will be an end-in-itself. And a person of good character does many things which are ends-in-themselves. One cannot counter-balance the unrestrained desire to win by suggesting that a child should play exclusively for the sake of playing; but one can suggest that while enjoying their victory children (and adults) should not gain additional pleasure from the defeat of others. I see your smile again, but this is your smile as a child. Of course, you loved to win, although it was not a matter of life and death to you, never that serious. You were not unhappy because others were defeated – otherwise how could you have won at all? You were, however, sad whenever you realized that the loser was unhappy and that she suffered (even if you regarded this as foolishness). One can be pleased with one's victory and simultaneously be displeased with the sadness of the loser, and in addition, also disapprove of her noisy grudging. I do not need to explain this to you. Feelings can hardly be explained, but this time they do not need to be explained because all that I have now said I once learned from you. I remember what you told me after you have won the children's table-tennis competition when you were just ten. You said, 'Granny, I will take a cake to give it to Paula, because she is so sad that she lost the game.'

Thus, in my mind youth is the time of seriousness, while later in ripe age, one can take life more lightly. But youth is the time for seriousness just for young people who become what they are, and life can be taken later more lightly by people who became what they are, substance rather than husk. Life can be taken more lightly when commitment is transformed into something one could term 'sense'. One develops the sense to follow one path rather than another, one kind of path, rather than another kind. If one has developed a 'sense', one does not need a map in one's style of life. This 'sense' is unlike the sense of direction, for one needs to have a set goal to know the direction. If one hasn't set a goal to arrive at, one can hardly speak about the direction of one's movements. It is the 'pull' one follows. But one does not obey the pull. One feels the pull. If one feels the pull one becomes curious and goes after the pull to find out its source and reason. This adventure of curiosity is guided by the 'sense'. I don't pretend to have said anything new. What I just described, or at least something similar, has been termed 'autonomy', although not moral autonomy, by a few modern thinkers. I stress that there is a 'sense' at work here, for there is a kind of lightness, a feeling of relief, a kind of harmony (or the promise of harmony, perhaps).

I know that the ideal of the so-called harmonious personality has fallen lately into bad repute, as a poor tradition in European humanism. Old-fashioned as I am, I would not reject this tradition too easily. Perhaps the problem lies in the term 'harmony'. Harmonious personalities are sometimes equated with the ideal of the 'beautiful soul' in Goethe or Hegel, at other times with the many-sided, universal individual who has developed all his talents and abilities, the universal man. The universal and universally harmonious individual is then a man, to paraphrase the young Marx, who is fishing, hunting, critiquing, writing, painting, and doing all possible things in good proportion, around the clock. The ideal is then the personality whose intellectual, spiritual and physical capacities are equally, to the same extent, developed. This is the idealized and stylized version of the Greek man, more particularly of the free Athenian citizen, of the *kalokagathos*, a Renaissance idea that had been renewed in the German culture since Winckelmann. Hegel elaborated a theory about Greek plasticity – and surely this model of the harmonious personality is plastic and not musical. Whatever you think of harmony, you must admit that the harmony of a statue and the harmony of a musical sentence are of different kind. No, I will not come up with a surprising theory of harmony, for I am bad at theorizing. When I speak of harmony, I have a very simple everyday perception of harmony in mind. For example, the landscape before me I perceive as harmonious. But if you insisted that I tell you why this is so, and whether I have in mind that the different shrubs, trees and flowers, the sky and the sun and the smell and the sounds are in a proper proportion, I would laugh, because this sounds absurd. Yet I will stick to my perception of the harmonious landscape. I do not know why; and the landscape does not know it either.

I have just said that the more substantial a person becomes, the more he develops a sense of destination, and the more lightheartedly he will proceed as if he were dancing (would Nietzsche say this?), and the more he will become (perhaps) harmonious. But when I say 'harmonious' I do not think of the kind of harmony one might associate with many-sidedness or with a structure of the right proportions. Although I love the ideal of the *kalokagathos*, as I am pleased to look at girls and boys with a beautifully proportioned body, I would not recommend you to divide your days proportionally between gymnastics, studies, bath, walking in the market-place, fighting war, doing politics and so on. You might have taken up jogging lately and be proud of combining intellectual activity with physical exercise, but aping fashions does not make anyone Greek, even if it is pleasant and refreshing. What is mere fashion now was embedded in the way of life once upon a time. Nowadays physical exercise has nothing to do with the sense of beauty. It is rather a fashion, motivated by the inability of men and women to face death. And to face sickness. It is not the spirit that fails to reconcile itself with nature, but spiritlessness.

I see, my thoughts continue to wander, although they have not wandered too far. When I said 'spirit' I also meant the face. Goethe once wisely said, I don't know where, that everyone over thirty is responsible for his or her face. A cruel or an empty face is the responsibility of the person who wears it (you wear your face, don't you see?). Look straight into a persons's face and you will see how many of his choices are written on it! There are good faces and bad faces. Good faces are open, they offer themselves to scrutiny, to be seen by the other; they turn towards the others just like a sunflower turns towards the sun to catch its rays. Bad faces, on the other hand, show a cruel or an utterly vain, wicked, but at any rate an extremely suspicious soul. They are closed faces, they avoid scrutiny. Not because the wearers of those faces are inner-directed, but because they avoid contacts. But why do I tell you all this? You surely remember, Fifi, our old and innocent game? Do you? We were sitting in a café, you and me, and we played the game of guessing the character of the passers-by from their faces. I feel a little uncomfortable about this game now. True, we played this game only on people whom we did not know, otherwise it would not have been a game. In addition we expected to see each person only once (it happened in a big city where we never lived) and we knew that we would never find out whether we had hit the jackpot or not. Still, I am afraid that there is a grain of instrumentalization, of using people unknowingly as objects, in a game of interpretation. But we all do little things that cause moral discomfort. The main thing is to be aware of it. If one does not hurt anyone, a little escapade of playfulness is hardly a vice. We practised the judgement of human character on living beings as if we were judging portraits in a gallery. Painters knew all about good and bad faces, they presented them as such, so that we can find out much about entirely unknown persons in a potrait gallery. You, Fifi, and me, we behaved like painters who cannot paint.

I am getting old, this is why I go on in circles. I almost forgotten about the harmonious person. One cannot describe a harmonious person by mixing various elements in a right proportion. And what makes the proportion right, anyway? A harmonious person resembles a harmonious landscape. When I speak of harmony I do not mean something that one can achieve on purpose, through planning, or through the realization of an ideal one previously had in mind. A harmonious landscape is not a well-kept garden. Harmony resembles the ease in following one's good sense, the lightheartdness, the dance, and also a vague feeling of self-certainty. I mean a vague, not strong feeling. A strong feeling of self-certainty is not 'more' than a vague feeling, it is something entirely different. If one acquires strong (even if never absolute) self-certainty one is already dead even if one lives for another forty years. For one continues to live only if there is an aspect of self-uncertainty in one's feeling of life (*Lebensgefühl*). The feeling of vague certainty makes one lighthearted, but this lightheartedness remains open. One is open for surprises, for the sudden appearance of paths one has never expected, lanes one can begin to tread on, although one treads on each of them without a map. Openness – sometimes called freedom – implies the 'rather this than that' (has Heidegger said something similar, speaking about Leibniz?), the sense that a direction is set, that you are in the process of becoming what you are – till death. There is nothing to worry about, yet still, the openness is there, there is always a possibility that you will fail to continue in your own direction if you take one path rather than the other. Philosophers normally describe these life-experiences in terms of freedom of the will, or freedom of choice and the like. But I am afraid that philosophical terms (or characters) like 'autonomy', 'freedom as sponta-neity', as the 'recognition of necessity', as the 'determination by law', as the 'play of imagination', as 'self-realization', as also the freedom of the 'existential choice', are all describing one single process, yet from differ-ent aspects, while they are magnifying one aspect against all the others, and finally offer the privileged aspect the throne of being the first cause or the final explanation. My experience shows that all philosophical generalizations are somehow wrong. I remember one interesting passage from the dialogue. Young Lawrence discussed psychoanalysis with his friends, and one of them (perhaps Vera) came up with the idea that everyone carries a different kind of 'soul' inside. This, so the continued, explains why some people recognize themselves in Freud rather than in Kierkegaard or Heidegger, and the reverse. Lawrence (or one of his masks) also said that there are typical, culturally representative networks of explanation that even average people employ if they want to under-stand themselves. What I have tried to express is something similar, although not exactly the same. When you take all the descriptions of experiences of movements that philosophers normally describe with the categories of freedom, together, you will see that one of them is stronger in one person than in the other, and one will be stronger at one moment, and another aspect in another moment, in the same person. There are constant fluctuations in the experience of freedom in every person, but different kinds of fluctuation in different persons. Not because each person is driven by his or her 'will to power'. After all, the movement that Nietzsche termed the 'will to power' is also one aspect of the entire movement of freedom-experience in its fluctuation, one enlarged aspect taken as an explanatory device, as the only and single and general one. The problem – that there is no single explanation – is not sincerely addressed but pushed one level along (higher or lower, as you wish) from its original place of appearance. It is tautological to say that the fluctuation of a great diversity of openings cannot be explained either by causes or by purposes. Since even if you have said only that much you have already presupposed that one must explain them either with the former or with the latter.

But what I really wanted to speak about, although I don't let myself come to the point because of my chattiness, is my own idea of harmony. What I call harmony is the coexistence of different – many, perhaps even all – kinds of openness, of freedom. I know this sounds obscure. I will try to elaborate it further. As I said, a person of absolute self-certainty is virtually dead (he is not free, neither is he harmonious), but harmony requires a vague feeling of self-certainty. The harmonious person can also be described as the lighthearted person. The lighthearted person is not an ideal to follow; one is never free in the above sense if one follows anyone. Harmony is the feeling of freedom. Maybe in more than one way. One can say that a harmonious person experiences his own freedom, but also that we can experience the freedom of a harmonious person.

I don't think that the latter is true only in cases of people. A harmonious painting is felt to be free as is also a harmonious landscape or a musical chord. I have already confessed that I know little about music, but here I am supported by Adorno's professionalism. It was Adorno who said that freedom dwells in the chord, and especially in the triad, and that it is freedom which is lost with the loss of tonality, for example in Schoenbergian serialism.

When Lawrence reads this he will be shocked. I am, I know, entirely illogical. We (men and women) feel the landscape free and the musical sentence free or another person free. But feeling ourselves free or another person or a landscape free, are qualitatively different kinds of feelings. If I feel myself free, freedom is not a matter of observation but of practice. Moreover, I do not only feel something else, I also say something else, when I tell you that I feel my own freedom and when I tell you that I feel the freedom of another person. However, this is not so simple. In the course of action, the feel of my own freedom is the feeling of (relative) self-certainty. Self-certainty is then the basic feeling that supports all the others. One experiences strong and heterogeneous feelings while acting, given that one is concentrating on something. Concentration is a forceful kind of involvement. And feeling is nothing else but being involved in something. Pure action is pure spontaneity. Spontaneity as *actum purum* is not observable for the acting person. Your Lawrence expressed something very well in his dialogue when he said, 'I am carried away, I follow my destiny.' But while you are carried away, you do not thematize your choices nor the experience of being carried away. You must stop being carried away to become aware of your freedom as freedom. When I jump or leap, I may feel joy or perhaps anxiety or enthusiasm (like your Lawrence), but I do not 'feel free'. Your self-certainty – that manifests, itself in action – becomes a matter of reflection or obervation when you stop acting. At that stage you can relate to yourself in a very similar way to relating to a flower or to a landscape, or to another person, for you are involved in yourself, as you are also involved in the landscape or in the other person.

But I do not want to ruminate about freedom in general, but rather about the balance of different kinds of freedom, about harmony. If you agree, we can all experience freedom directly in action (as relative self-certainty) but we do not 'feel' ourselves harmonious, beautiful, in action. Harmony, together with the feeling of harmony, presents itself for judgement or for observation. It would be odd even to say that we feel ourselves harmonious and beautiful after having stopped acting, given that we are never in the position of pure self-observation or self-reflection. One feels the harmony of another (a person, a landscape, a piece of music, a painting). This would perhaps sound absurd to your philosopher friend, but a person of common sense would readily accept it. True, had I left out men, had I spoken about landscape, painting, an arrangement of flowers alone, had I thrown into the discussion the famous Kantian 'free play of understanding and imagination', Lawrence could have described my position as unorthodox (Kant would have never mentioned painting in this context), yet still as something understandable in terms of philosophical thinking. But why do I include men and women here? Just because we, an older lady and a child, used to sit on the terrace of a café sixteen years ago to find out whether the passers-by had a good or a bad face?

Let me think together with you, let us find out together how far we can go in this direction. How far can we go in making guesses about the freedom of another? How far can we go about our guesses concerning the harmony (or disharmony) of the other?

I see a good face, an open face, I make some guesses about his character. I assume that he was free to have a good or a bad face – and he has a good one, so he is a free person. Why is the face of a bad person unlike the face of a good person? Why is a bad face not a free one, although the bad man was also responsible for his face? A theologian would say that he was responsible for his bad face in a far greater degree. We see the bad face as closed, hidden; unlike the sunflower it does not open itself up to scrutiny. Is it possible that I feel, I see, another person's freedom? And that I see it rather than I see my own? Is it because the other sees my face (whether good or bad) and I have no access to it?

Because if I look into my mirror I observe my face in the state of unspontaneity and never in the state of spontaneity? Can I presuppose here the manifestation of the free play of understanding and imagination? The harmony between understanding and imagination? Or, perhaps a pre-established harmony?

Joachim, your friend's friend, would raise a serious objection here. The kind of freedom that manifests itself in the free harmonious play of understanding and imagination is, he would say, the freedom of beauty, that has nothing to do with other kinds of freedom, particularly not with freedom of the will, or of choice, not even mentioning transcendental freedom. For the latter kinds of freedom are not beautiful. Choice can be related to the beautiful only through the mediation of the concept of perfection; but then one does not deal with pure beauty. I understand the objections but I don't accept them. After all, beautiful is that which we love, which we in principle love, which we erotically love. I know that this is a traditional Platonic idea, but I still believe in it: what is good is also beautiful, and what is beautiful is also good. We love the good because it is beautiful. Whether one understands beauty as the free play of imagination and understanding or as something else should be philosophy's problem. For I confess that I perceive the harmony I have just described, or rather the balance (or accord?) of freedoms that still remain open for imbalance, as the beautiful. And here I rest my case.

I just see that I have not written anything about Lawrence's work. I was too single-minded, I have filled too many pages. Yet I must stop for now, because the mail will be soon collected, and I want to post my letter soon. I promise that I will write a follow-up letter about feelings. And I also want to say something about the centre that we are supposed to hit by 'throwing' and by 'being thrown'. Next time, my dear, next time.

Love from your old Granny

Cable from Fifi to her Grandmother

Can I show your letter to Lawrence? kisses Fifi.

Fifi to her Grandmother

My dearest,

Thanks for your prompt call. I cabled because you did not answer the phone. I guessed that you were spending the whole day out in the garden and would never pick up the damned machine.

Yesterday I discussed a few passages from your letter with Lawrence. He got excited, walked up and down for a while before he began to speak; but then the words began to pour out from his mouth – as the Bible would say: like honey.

It is difficult to sum up his chain of thoughts. I haven't even understood everything, and I doubt that he did. I have noticed that one can say interesting and new things without fully understanding one's own meaning. You may call this 'intuition'. Intuition resembles the 'sense of direction'. If one has a strong sense of direction one can follow one's feelings blindly. The best things one frequently does blindly. There is a light somewhere, an open spot, and one is pulled by this light and simply goes ahead. Retrospectively one notices the crossroads, and realizes that one has chosen one among many possible paths. But while being pulled, one remains mostly unaware of having chosen because one never hesitates. This also happens with a chain of thoughts. After having arrived somewhere and stopping to recapitulate the whole chain, one will be surprised by one's own ideas and sometimes realize that one does not fully understand one's own thoughts. And still, one can have, again, the feeling that the thoughts are, nevertheless, right, and that they must (and can) be put into an elementary order. If one fails to rationalize one's insights, one had better shelve one's ideas and return to them later, or alternatively, one had better abandon them as the yield of bad intuition. At this stage the so-called law of identity plays a decisive role in thinking, namely the role of control. It is a strict master, perhaps a boring master, but a necessary one. Like the laws of grammar. Do you remember how as a child I hated grammar? I found it a nuisance, for only thoughts matter. Now I know it better, or at least otherwise, for – unfortunately or fortunately – one needs to communicate one's thoughts (although not all of them) and if one does, they need to be put into a proper order. The intuitions that we never cheked just come and go. Hannah Arendt has termed this constant fluctuation, this come-and-go, 'the life of the mind'. I find this a beautiful and telling expression, particularly because my mind – like yours – loves to wander. To return to Lawrence: I am sure that he said many things that he has not, for the time being, fully understood himself, but his thoughts were not worse because of it, neither were they less exciting.

Lawrence said, 'It is an interesting thesis [meaning your ideas], although philosophically inconsistent. Let me see: your grandmother protests against the close association between harmony and right proportion, but she reinstates the connection. Allow me a few introductory remarks. Your granny substitutes a musical concept of harmony for a plastic concept of the same. She believes that the model of musical harmony fits the description of the modern person better. But she should know that it was mainly moderns (from Winckelmann to Hegel) who attributed plasticity to the *kalokagathos*, although Plotinus was one of their predecessors. Plato, however, modelled the harmonious person on the idea of musical harmony. But let me continue to criticize your Granny's major self-delusions. For who is her harmonious human person if not an individual whose freedoms (in the plural) are constantly in the process of regaining balance after falling into imbalance? If you accept the idea of this balance you must presuppose that all the aspects of freedom, such as moral autonomy, choice, 'recognition of necessity', the open space (clearing), spontaneity, self-realization, and so on, in fact all the kinds of freedoms that were once identified as the essence of freedom, or the foundation of freedom, or the idea of freedom by a wide range of philosophers are somehow always 'there', just that one of them gets the upper hand in one process, whereas the other will get the upper hand in another. In brief, your grandmother is saying that all definitions of freedom are wrong just because all of them are right. They are wrong for two reasons. First, because they construe a fixed hierarchy where there is fluidity, and second, because they justify the ugly, the non-harmonious person. For it is the ugly, the unharmonious person who exhibits a reified character through the fixation of the relationship among all those different aspects of freedom. You see, your granny confused two entirely different things. She said something important when she tried to track down harmony or beauty. It makes sense to say that human beauty resides in a character that succeeds in her 'economy of freedoms', in a personality who constantly regains the balance of the different kinds of freedoms so that none of them should get the upper hand in a fixed hierarchy. But – and here comes my essential objection! – it is quite different to say that, look, such are the beautiful people, and to confuse beautiful people with free people. If only one single interpretation of freedom possesses a man, he can still be a free man; and also very much lovable. But enough of this.

Now comes my second – less essential – objection. Your grandmother described freedom from the standpoint of the observer. She does not quite say that in action one is unaware of one's freedom, but she terms this feeling as that of a relative 'self-certainty'; she insists that one cannot sense or feel or experience one's own harmony or beauty. We normally believe that men have a privileged access to their own experiencs, but your granny says that we have a privileged access to the other in matters of beauty or harmony. All kinds of 'otherness' are then treated as if they were similar. She could enumerate in one breath the harmony of a landscape, of a painting, of a face, or of a person. She should have added God – although she avoided it – since her concept of freedom strongly resembles Spinoza's *amor dei intellectualis*.

Your granny speaks about the standpoint of observation; so far so good. But she never makes it clear what kind of observation she has in mind. Is it the speculative attitude (such as the thinking of thought or the love of God) or the reflective judgement in the Kantian sense? In the first case God is thought as absolute freedom, thus thinking God absolutely is absolute freedom because God is absolute freedom. If you say that you love freedom, you declare the object of your love free, and become – in your dual capacity as the knower and the lover of freedom – also free. Both the lover and the beloved are free, but the lover is free because the beloved (who is freedom absolutely) is loved by him freely. You remember how I protested against your granny's predilection of identifying the harmony among freedoms (the beauty) of a man with the freedom of a man . . . But if observation is meant to be a kind of metaphysical speculation, one can susbtitute freedom and beauty, one for the other, without much ado. God is, for example, beauty; I love God – I love beauty; and I am beautiful (my soul is beautiful) since I love beauty above all. One can even go further in the direction of the reversal of the relationship: God loves me, and thus beautifies me, I am beautiful through his love.

Your granny, however, threw into the philosophical ring the Kantian concept of reflective judgement. But she has not realized that if one takes the position of reflective judgement, one will arrive at a concept of harmony that has little to do with the concept of harmony one has encountered from the position of metaphysical speculation. Kant hints at the supersensible, but does not say anything about it. The free play of understanding and imagination points at a pre-established harmony we do not know anything about, a harmony we can only guess or hope for. But the free play is there, it is located in us, in our reflective judgement, in a feeling which is not a feeling, which claims universality and necessity. But your granny presumes that harmony is there, in the landscape, in the painting, and particularly in the person whom we observe. It is not in our judgement that the harmony – the proper balance of freedoms – rests.

If you speak about the beauty of the flower then the Kantian gambit of reflective judgement (of taste) works. The harmony is elicited by the pure form of this or that flower, but it establishes itself between our faculties. Since our aesthetic judgement passed on to a painting or a person is never pure, we cannot support their 'harmony' with the model of pure reflective judgement of taste. If man is harmonious, he is harmonious in a quite different way from how a flower is. I am afraid that your granny's reference to Kant can be written down as an intermezzo. Sometimes she relapses into old metaphysics, sometimes she continues in an epistemological mood. Let me return to one of her basic tenets: we are aware of our freeom, beauty or harmony when we stop acting, when we reflect and reminisce. This is old Plato mixed with a little Hegel. But then, she also reminds me of Husserl and Schütz, of course. How wonderfully your granny's mind works, and still, hers is an untutored mind. In one minute she thinks like Plato, the next minute like Spinoza, then again, like Kant or Heidegger or Husserl – and never just as one of them, that is, consistently.

Your granny never speaks about the source of freedoms. Where is this source? If all the concepts of freedom make sense, and if all the kinds of freedom are just the single aspects of a whole 'movement' what is this 'movement'? The old lady is not a foundationalist, she does not care for the *arche*. She is just an observer and an intellecual lover of God. But I think that all her intellectual love is vested in single individuals. When your granny speaks about *amor dei intellectualis* she does not think of the divine, the unchangeable, the eternal, but of creation, of the mortal. She thinks of things and persons who will die or wane tomorrow like herself. Yet as long as she exists, these beautiful persons and those beautiful things are eternal, for she relates to them in eternal love . . . especially to you. You are in your granny's mind the model of the person who embodies all the freedoms she has mentioned, who has a good face, who is beautiful, harmonious and who deserves to be loved. I hear you saying that I am kidding, because you never thought about yourself in those terms. This makes me rethink what your granny said; maybe there is great wisdom in it. For if you do not see that her story is your story, that you are the harmonious individual who deserves to be loved (and that the landscape and the flower are serving only as analogy), then you are unaware of your beauty, and particularly of the harmony of freedoms that is so manifest in your character. And then your granny is proved right; the beauty, the harmony of a character presents itself to the other, to the observer. It is not harmony and beauty but (relative) self-certainty that a person is aware of in herself as the voice of her freedom.

But if this is so, and your granny is right, she is also wrong, or at least one-sided. For as I told you right at the start, I disagree strongly with her strong preference for harmony. So I repeat: a man can be as free as a man can only be if one aspect of freedom devours all the others in his soul. Relative self-certainty will guide him in his actions just as it is guiding a beautiful soul. The game of good or bad faces irritates me. Perhaps one can tell good faces from insignificant, empty and wicked faces. I will give it a try. But one cannot tell the face of a harmonious person from the face of a person whose soul is in the state of constant imbalance. It is even worse to identify the good face with the face of the harmonious person. Moreover, it is a kind of colour-blindness. Perhaps your granny loves only harmonious souls, but others can love, and love dearly, characters who stake everything on one single freedom, and entirely so. What would be, in this case, the judgement of the observer?

This was only a brief summary of Lawrence's long monologue, and you understand why certain thoughts of his remained obscure, at least for me. Lawrence hints at the most absurd thing: that I would be the model for your harmonious person. This is impossible. You said in your letter that seriousness befits youth, that a kind of lightheartedness develops as one proceeds in age, and this lies still far ahead of me. To be candid, I think of you, and of you alone, as the model of the harmonious personality; it is difficult to imagine you as a young girl, since I know you as being always lighthearted in your sense of the word. But enough of this. To continue, Lawrence's constant references to names, such as Husserl, Hegel and so on, have not helped me to understand him. Since I have not read those authors, I could not understand his hints. But I will read all those books soon to find out whether they have to say anything of importance to me. Still, in a few points, I found Lawrence's ruminations highly illuminating. I think that he has interpreted your vision of beauty and harmony beautifully and harmoniously. From now on, whenever I think of beautiful and harmonious persons, I will think of them as of happy characters who constantly restore the disturbed balance among the different aspects of freedom, while following their sense of direction in spite of incidentally falling into a few traps. But, contrary to Lawrence, I think I understand why you have dismissed the theory of right proportion. 'Harmony', in your interpretation, has nothing to do with many-sidedness or individual universality, for example with exercising many occupations. It does not require that one practises one's mind, body and soul to an equal extent and simultaneously. Your *kalokagathos* is a modern one. Your *kalokagathos* is a throw. Your *kalokagathos* has not received as his birthright the preliminary knowledge of a model that will help him shape his body and mind adequately. Your *kalokagathos* is open, she chooses herself, but her self-choice is not the only, exclusive manifestation of her freedom. Sometimes she obeys the moral law, other times she chooses the unavoidable, sometimes, again, she chooses one among many possibilities or paths, sometimes she speculates in the clearing of being, sometimes she just looks at a landscape and takes free pleasure in it or she just cultivates her garden, and sometimes . . . I do not continue, I only wanted to show you that I understood you. It is obvious that you did not say that only the observer is free, for this would have been sheer nonsense, you wanted to say that the beauty that ensues from the harmony of freedom presents itself to the observer. Even the word 'observer' is wrong: it presents itself rather to the other, to the other person. One's harmony of freedom is a present, a gift, to the other. I think that I understand what you mean when you speak of the intellectual love of God. It is your love, the love that takes pleasure in the beauty of others. Lawrence is right: you take pleasure in the beauty of individuals. For a landscape, a flower, a person – they are all individuals. This is why you referred to the 'goldentree of life' that is green. Concepts are grey; Lawrence, too, said something like this in his dialogue. You do not love concepts, they cannot be harmonious. This, however, makes me think. Can you love, for example beauty? Or liberty? What would such a love mean? You love harmony, beauty. But a concept, such as liberty or beauty, cannot be harmonious. Beauty is not beautiful (has Heidegger said something similar? or perhaps Plato before? Who knows?). Liberty is not free and so on.

Lawrence's brief critical remarks on our distinction between good and bad faces are, however, based on a total misunderstanding. He thinks that we attributed a harmonious personality to good faces and a disharmonious personality to bad ones. Sorry to say, you are not entirely innocent in this mistake. Since you wrote your letter to me and not to Lawrence, you took many things for granted that we both know, but Lawrence could not possibly know. I remember, how could I have possibly forgotten, how we were sitting in the café and passing judgements on the faces of the poor passers-by. We always noticed more good faces than bad ones. Perhaps this was so because I, as a child, saw people in a more favourable light, and you let me have my judgement. Because you, I know, have no strong inclination to detect only the best character traits in a person. You are just, but you are also strict in your judgements. You are never vengeful, but you rarely forget. But perhaps it takes time for you to form a proper judgement. Maybe this is why we both – not just I – detected more good than bad faces. I said that you do not forget easily, but this is not entirely true; you forget almost all things except nastiness, baseness and cruelty. I never saw you smiling at a person whom you disliked. What a detour I made! I just wanted to explain why Lawrence's interpretation of our distinction between 'good' and 'bad' faces is insensitive. The 'good face', 'bad face' game has to do with freedom on one single point. This is the attitude of openness. We always believed that a 'good face' is an open face. But it is not necessarily also a face of a beautiful or a harmonious personality. The good face is the face of a person who is morally upright, or close to that, who is reliable as a friend. If a person whose character becomes the vessel of one overriding kind (or interpretation) of freedom which can be morally upright – and surely, he can – his face will be a good one. In the 'good face', 'bad face' game one makes a judgement of the fundamental ethical character and not of the whole character, not even of the whole moral character. We presupposed the existence of a fundamental moral character when we began to play, and also that this fundamental moral character shows itself in the face. I do not recall whether the passers-by were young or old. Listening to you now, they could not be very young. I remember, how stupid of me that I had not noticed this immediately: you quoted Goethe saying that everyone over thirty is responsible for his or her face. A child is not yet responsible for her face. So we observed people above thirty, give or take a few years.

I have already made a well-deserved concession to Lawrence: a fundamentally upright character does not need to be harmonious and beautiful. But has this fundamental moral character – if there is such a thing at all – a special affinity with certain feelings and emotions? The philosophical tradition would answer this question in the affirmative. You know those answers by heart: in a moral character reason is the king, and all the feelings and emotions must obey it; or, an upright person can find pleasures in refined things alone, his desires drive him towards remote ends and not towards immediate satisfaction and so on. You wrote a few fascinating things about emotions, about moral or ethical emotions yet also morally indifferent ones, but nothing in the spirit of the philosophical tradition, neither approvingly nor disapprovingly. Do you think that one cannot generalize in matters of feelings and emotions? Are emotions strictly individual? And if yes, what can we say about them in moral terms? I noticed that here we have stepped on to slippery ground; to decide that we are going to think and speculate about single persons and single persons alone, is to step on a very slippery ground. It is rewarding to speak so, because – as I think – morality rests ulltimately on the individual person; only if one addresses the individual moral person directly and speaks about the individual as individual, can one really hit at 'the thing itself' (*die Sache selbst*). Freedom is also individual. This is what I liked in your idea of the beautiful and harmonious person. (And this is why I could easily accept Lawrence's corrections.) Only individuals can be free. Freedom is not free. Now I see how I may answer my own question. If one loves liberty one loves the condition of the freedom of individuals. What one really loves are these free individuals. But I admit, this ground remains slippery. One cannot say anything about individuals unless one speak about them directly. This is why there is more moral philosophy in Shakespeare than in all the books of moral philosophers. The morality of Hamlet or Lear or Beatrice and Benedict are strictly individual. Morality dwells in their character. Lawrence too noticed this; this is why Benedict and Beatrice play such an important role in his ethics of personality.

As I mentioned, we have already discussed Beatrice and Benedict with Lawrence, in our first encounter. But when *we* discussed Beatrice and Benedict we did *not* discuss the ethics of personality; I had no idea then that such an ethics existed. We discussed Beatrice and Benedict as living persons, at it we were discussing you. No, not quite, since Beatrice and Benedict are put into a plot. Moreover, they are not just harmonious beautiful people for us, the observers, but Shakespeare created them as harmonious people as he also created the plot. The plot is about the world that was thrown into the state of an absolute moral imbalance till its balance had been (relatively) restored by these two people's rectitude, their moral beauty. It is easy, unproblematic, and even rewarding to think about the fundamental character of literary figures, because they were created with such a character on purpose and put into the plot to show their worth or unworth. But if I speak (or even think) of the moral character of a living person (like you or Lawrence), I have a feeling of uneasiness that I never develop when I think of Shakespeare's characters. You – or Lawrence – are after all persons who can speak for themselves, whom I can ask, and who have an open life with an unfinished plot. Even at your age, you are not a character from a plot. This is why whenever I speak about you – as I also spoke about you to Lawrence in ethical terms – I develop a feeling of unease that I am somehow instru-mentalizing you, treating you as raw-material, as an example, that I'm turning you into an object. I do not use you as sheer means, of course, but as a kind of means, nevertheless. But then, if we believe that mor-ality rests ultimately, in the last instance, on the single 'exister' in Kierkegaard's words, and the only way to speak about ethics is to speak about the single exister, and yet speaking of the single exister has a touch of instrumentalization, is it true that the only relevant moral philosophy would be the moral interpretation of fundamental characters from a work of literature? The sole other alternative would be to construct fictitious persons for the sake of moral interpretation in the manner of Kierkegaard. But when we think or speak of those characters we cannot help generalizing them, or at least typifying them. When we speak of a person *A* we do not reflect upon *A* alone, but about many *As* (the type of *A*). Even Kierkegaard, who was aware of this pitfall and spoke about Abraham or Judge William or Climacus and other single 'existers', even he could not possibly have avoided this pitfall. The moment one speaks about 'the aesthetic', 'the moral', 'the religious' spheres or attitudes, one has not only single individuals but also ideal types in mind. We invent 'types' to avoid generalizations, but the 'types' are also generalizations. I am glad that I am a student of literature and not of philosophy. For no grey concept will ever do justice to the 'goldentree of life'. And all the emotions and feelings – always personal occurrences – are my best defence witnesses.

On second thoughts – and this is already my fifth second thought today – haven't we done something that should have been better avoided in our childish game of good and bad faces? If every person is just an individual, a single existing individual, absolutely unique, why have we created these two types for the sake of a joke? Are there, really, good or bad faces? Or is this guesswork just an everyday and childish version of common philosophical practices? I do not want to say that to tell good from bad faces amounts to playing the game of metaphysics, for this would be foolish, and in addition, I have no strong objections to metaphysics. I say that we did something that implied the opposite of our philosophical convictions. But, forgive me, this was a sensless statement. There are no two leaves of a tree alike, there are no two characters alike. Still we speak about 'leaf', and this makes sense, and we distinguish the oak leaf from the pine leaf and this also makes sense. I do not want to hide behind the old debate concerning the existence of universals because it is not the old debate that I continue in my soul. To tell good from bad faces is a crude typification. But we make compromises, dear Granny, we always make compromises in our thinking as in many other things. Identity thinking is also a compromise (and I was obliged to learn some grammar at last). One cannot avoid compromises. This is the price that everyone pays for living in the community of one's fellow creatures, for the urge to make oneself understood – only thus can one fly on the wings of imagination.

The word 'imagination' decided on its own to get into this letter; it flew into the text without my contribution. To reflect upon a single 'exister' requires imagination, and so does the interpretation of creatures of imagination (like Beatrice and Benedict). But to design a theory of the ethics of personality requires far greater and more forceful imagination, and one of a different kind. Here one dreams about something that is not, something that comes into existence – if it comes – through our dreams. There is no ethics of personality – there is no such ethics; perhaps it is impossible to have one. But if you read Lawrence's dialogue well, you will see *his* ethics of personality. The landscape of his ethics has been built from bricks of grey theories, but a landscape it still is, a broad and fine one – the echo of his own personality. You will see flowers there and trees that bring fruit. This is the fantasy world to which we have access, the dream that – unlike the dreams the Heraclitus spoke about – do not need to remain private.

I have no excuse for writing impressionistically. Please, read this letter as a testimony of the flow of my thoughts, as the abbreviated text of the life of (my) mind in the last ten minutes, or for a little longer. Be patient with me. The request is funny. With me, you have always been patient. So instead, I ask you: be patient with Lawrence, too.

My love (for the time being and forever), your Fifi

Mrs Sophie Meller to her Granddaughter, Fifi

My dear,

I deserve to be scolded; I have no practice in argumentation, I began to talk about good faces and harmonious personalities in one breath, forgetting the main requirement of a theoretical discussion that I should distinguish my idea from the ideas of others. It is not easy. There are no definitions here, no strict lines of division. I use my intuition when I tell a good from a bad face; I also use my intuition when I speak about a beautiful character. I also appeal to your intuition that you approximately understand my meaning. But I will now try to proceed more logically.

You are right. Twenty years ago, when we played the game of telling good from bad faces, we took it as self-evident that a 'good face' is the face of fundamentally upright and reliable person. An upright character is not necessarily a harmonious person or a beautiful character as well. It is easier to recognize a good face than to make a fair guess about the beauty of a character, for it is easier to pass an independent ethical judgement than an independent aesthetic judgement, as it is – perhaps – the most difficult thing to exercise judgement in moral aesthetics. It requires more than good judgement.

Lawrence has noticed one of my weaknesses: my reading of *Critique of Judgement* is one-sided, to say the least. I was never interested in the system; nothing can keep me as cool as a transcendental deduction. I am fascinated by the content, the message of this work, not by its author's arguments. I take from Kant what I please, among others his insight that judgement requires free play between understanding and imagination. But you see, to pass judgements like 'this rose is beautiful' is simple. Both understanding and imagination are elementary and uncomplicated here. But if I pass a judgement on one person, then on another, and then again on another – on a few entirely different characters – and say that they are beautiful, both my understanding and my imagination need to be far more complex. There are conditions of a good judgement, such as: life-experience, moral taste, refinement, especially emotional refinement. Since the harmony or the beauty of a character presents itself in her emotional world, the person who passes a judgement in moral aesthetics needs to develop an emotional wealth, an emotional density or intensity that enables her to pass such a delicate judgement. Fortunately or not, I have to turn back here to painting or landscape. You need to have practice in aesthetic judgement to develop a taste that enables you to tell good and bad paintings from one another, and even more to distinguish between more or less perfect natural and artificial landscapes. You smile, perhaps, at my old-fashioned views, for nowadays many so-called important people hold that one painting is as good as the other, and that our highly praised sense of beauty is but the manifestation of an old-European sense of hierarchy. There is no difference, so we are told, between low and high art, and beauty is a matter of subjective taste. If you accept this new way of thinking, then it will no more make sense to speak about a beautiful character at all.

Allow me – an old-fashioned woman – to carry my conviction and taste into the grave. Those convictions and tastes – as my life experience – suggest that there are beautiful characters and you can tell them from all the other ones, if not easily. To tell good faces from bad faces – the game we played together – is relatively easy; a child can do it. Lawrence was right when he remarked that not all upright persons are beautiful or harmonious characters. Now I would go a step further: I am convinced that an upright character *can* at least be, or become, a beautiful character. Being upright is the precondition of the beautiful character, although being upright does not suffice for becoming such a character. That uprightness is the condition of the beauty of character is obvious. In our game we distinguished between open faces and 'closed', suspicious faces. We assumed that a good face is an open face and vice versa. Since openness is one – and an important – aspect of freedom, one cannot intuit beauty, which is a balance of freedoms, behind a closed and suspicious face.

Good/bad is, however, a universal (empirically universal) pair of categories of value orientation: no human society, no human life is possible without making such distinctions; one always makes this distinction, one always did. In the most abstract and preliminary sense, good is what one's society (according to its customs and norms) approves of, bad is what the society (your environment) disapproves of. In this sense ethics is also an empirical universal. There is always ethics, for there are always norms and rules. Nazis had their own ethical code and so did Bolsheviks, as did everyone.

Assume that Nazis or Bolsheviks would play our game of telling good from bad faces. In a community where blind subjection to a community is 'good', the same face that we judged to be a good one would be judged 'bad' and vice versa. This is so, because an open face suggests disobedience, whereas a closed one can easily be associated with readiness for submission. This is not just my hypothesis. Next week you will go to Vienna. I recommend you to pay a visit to the exhibition 'Art and dictatorship'. Just look at the portraits. They present idealized faces, the so-called 'good' faces from the standpoint of the official ideology of the painter. They are all empty, blank, stupid, sometimes almost idiotic faces; they never look like 'good faces' to us.

You remember: an upright person can be a beautiful person. We have, obviously, already presupposed this connection in our childish game. We looked for faces that were the faces of 'upright' persons, we called them good faces. Is this connection entirely contingent or subjective? Is the whole philosophical tradition a mistake in connecting the good and the beautiful and in associating both to a kind of freedom? I will not answer this question. But I tell you that I have lived through two dictatorships, I saw many exhibitions of those pictures, and I always knew, even as a child, that they were false, wrong, untrue. And those who now visit the gallery in Vienna, and cast a glance on the products of the art of dictatorship, will see the paintings in the same light as I (and many others) saw them at the time when they were painted and officially praised. I stay by my intuition that good faces, uprightness, and the condition of a beautiful or a sublime character somehow go together. For of course, a good character can also be sublime. A sublime character is not harmonious, but Lawrence was right: he is not less attractive than a beautiful one.

You observed that my beautiful character is a 'throw', a contingent person. I loved Lawrence's dialogue because your friend has such a deep insight into the experience of contingency. A modern person's beauty and harmony is unlike the Greek *kalokagathia*. True, Plato and all the Platronists like to speak about the harmony of the soul. But contrary to Greek music which exhibited an ethos, modern music speaks entirely, or at least mainly, in the name of the 'I'. At least Adorno says so, and I believe him because I feel similarly. The ancients, among them Plato, Aristotle, the Stoics or the Epicureans, had one thing in common. They all believed that the harmony of the soul has something to do with homogeneity: the more homogeneus the soul, the more beautiful it becomes.

There is another, perhaps more important, difference between a beautiful contigent character and the Greek *kalokagathos*. But let me tell you first that something worries me in the philosophy of existential choice. Your friend, and his friend Vera, told us that in an existential choice a person transforms his or her contingency into destiny. Up to a degree I sympathize with the suggested message of this metaphor. You guess the reason for my sympathy from what I wrote in my previous letter: after great seriousness comes lightheartedness, one gains a sense of direction, and so on. This can also be described with the heavy word 'destiny'. But this destiny does not annul contingency, for our modern person remains contingent throughout his life. If you became your destiny absolutely, you could not lose the balance between your freedoms, and you would be in no need to restore the balance. In losing and regaining balance one always relates to others. I remember saying that we are always involved in something; we are involved in many things (or in people) in different ways.

These involvements are our emotions and feelings. We lose (we can lose) ourselves if we invest too much feeling in someone or something. In this case this other being or thing or cause will be our destiny. In one interpretation we are our own destiny, because we do not lose our substance, but still, we can lose ourselves. Beautiful women and men frequently lose themselves too, for self-abandon implies that we lose ourselves to someone or to something. You see my reservations against the strict formulation of the existential choice, and I am afraid that a strict formulation does not do justice to the 'goldentree of life' that is green, and remains green. Our music is silenced by death alone, and even after death this music still sounds in the souls of others who echo it.

The ancient ideal of the homogeneous soul is linked to the idea of the immortality of the soul. But the modern harmonious person is never homogeneous, she loses balance and regains it, and it is in such a way that she gets richer, that she plays her own variations on her own themes. And when she is silenced, all those around her will take over her theme in quotation marks and will sense the presence of her personality in the midst of her silence. I am a sentimentalist in saying all this. But I was thinking of your mother, who was not just a musician by profession but also a musician in character. And her melodies sound in me, and – although you were very young when she died – you will recognize those harmonies somewhere hidden in your soul.

The contingent modern person, who never entirely transforms her contingency into destiny before she dies – how wise your Vera was! – is unlike the Greek *kalokagathos*, at least as he appears in Plato's or Aristotle's or in their followers' portrayal, and also in another aspect. Speaking about harmony, the Greeks – and after them almost all philosophers – have the harmony among the various human faculties primarily in mind. Whether they call them faculties or not is of secondary importance. They all believe that we are put together from different elements, and that these different elements are also heterogeneous among each other for they are of entirely heterogeneous origin (such as matter and form, reason and senses, nature and freedom, soul, spirit and body). In addition, these elements are supposed to compose the person. In an ideal person there will be harmony among the elements, for the highest element (reason, spirit and the like) will control and imbue all the other (lower) elements. The lower elements (such as drives, emotions, feelings) must obey the dictation of the highest element. The highest element brings order into disorder, regularity into irregularity, it limits the unlimited. In this tradition harmony results from a command/obedience relationship. There is never a quartet in which all four instruments are equal to each other to create a melody and harmony together. The kind of beautiful character I have in mind, the kind of harmonious character

I think that a contingent person can become, is harmonious like a quartet. Each instrument plays its own role, offers its own tone and timbre. This is harmony without the command/obedience relationship. I am not a Nietzschean, even less a Nietzschean character than your Lawrence, who does not know me, has fancied me to be. So please, mark that I do not wish the reversal of the traditional command/obedience relationship among the 'elements' or faculties. In a quartet, one instrument after the other can assume the leading role and play the melody, or even a solo. So it happens in the modern harmonious soul: one or the other instrument can play the solo for a while, and then the other(s) will take over. Now, if you think about harmony in terms of the harmony between faculties, you cannot avoid designing the model of harmony hierarchically. But if you fancy harmony as the harmony of all the variations of freedom, then you leave the question of faculties (whether there are any such at all, what they are, what their origin is) wide open. You smile now, I can almost see. You will say, 'But Granny, this amounts to the same.' For if the insight into necessity plays the first fiddle for a while in a soul-quartet, then it is reason in the sense of ratio that gains the upper hand, and something similar happens if in our musical sentence free speculation commands. I have no objection to this interpretation. Sometimes, freedom results from good theoretical reasoning and if this freedom plays the first fiddle, reason does also. But other times free judgement or intuition or love will get the upper hand, and in such a moment theoretical reasoning only accompanies or can even be silenced. Freedom of choice, for example, can be as much a matter of intuition as of practical reasoning. But one cannot choose (and cannot be free) without taking the famous leap – and the leap, the final resolve, is not rational, although it is not irrational either. Reasoning and sudden insight, self-control and self-abandon, prudence and creativity – all of them are freedoms. One cannot cut reason from emotion and feelings except artificially; consequently most philosophers preferred that artificial move. This is why your Lawrence observed that philosophers suspected colour, they loathed colour; they were writing and thinking only in black and white. Even if they payed lip service to musical harmony, their essential model of harmony was the harmony of a statue – of an unpainted statue. Only plastic harmony can be fancied in black and white. The harmonious and beautiful person, who is contingent, and in the deepest sense remains contingent – is a person of colour, for she thinks in colour as she lives in colour.

You have surely noticed, because you are a good observer, that although I defended our game of telling good and bad faces, I have never suggested thinking in terms of a beautiful/ugly dichotomy in the context of a judgement of character. It would be artificial, and too philosophical for my taste, to continue the discussion of the beautiful character with the discussion of its opposite: the ugly character. I do not think that it would make much sense to dissect the ugly character, for I doubt whether 'ugly character' is a good description of characters that are not beautiful. There are shallow characters – I mentioned them in my previous letter – I called them persons who resemble 'husks'. But to say that 'husk' people are ugly or unharmonious is misleading. A husk-like person can be a bad character, although he is not always bad. Some authors, mainly Marcuse, I think, termed such persons 'one-dimensional men'. It is a good description. Yet others termed them 'other-directed men', this is also a good description. A one dimensional man cannot be either harmonious or unharmonious, because he is entirely flat. And in the case of the other-directed person one cannot repeat the old question and ask whether only one of his faculties command him, or many, or none, because he stands under no command of his own faculties, be they rational or sensual, for he obeys the commands of something (someone) who is entirely exterior. One wonders even whether one dimensional or other-directed people can be called 'bad' characters. In fact they are no characters at all. For example, Elizabeth Bennett from Jane Austen's novel is a beautiful character; her younger sisters are entirely other-directed, yet they are not ugly characters; they are characterless (although in a good novel characterless people are also characterized).

I hesitate between the two expressions: 'to be a character' and 'to have a character'. A contingent *kalokagathos* 'is' a character. But the more other-directed a person becomes, the more I am inclined to say that he 'has' a character, as if he owned a character. Someone owns a character if he gets (receives, borrows, steals, purchases) his character from someone else, and puts on an act accordingly. One is a character if one is what one is, just oneself, idiosyncratic, unique. Beautiful characters are like this.

Alas, you will say, why do we speak about people who 'have' a good face? Surely, one cannot say that a person *is* a good face. The character *is*, the face shows something of what you are. It is in this sense that you *have* it, not in the sense that you received it. Unfortunately, language does not do justice to the nuances of our experience, yet we cannot think these nuances without employing language as a crutch. But if we want to speak about all those things that Lawrence summarizes as 'an ethics of personality', we must bend language, but only in language can one go beyond langue – at least in public. If you were here, sitting beside me, we could say something important about the 'ethics of personality' beyond language and without language. Great beauty is in doing exactly this. It is also a great beauty to live in language, but another kind of beauty. Particularly for men and women who are poets. Poets are the luckiest people, for they can live paradoxically (in going beyond language in language). If a good witch were to grant one of my wishes, I would wish that beautiful characters were all poets – but this is not to be.

It is late. These are the rare moments of silence when you can hear from afar the train's passing. These are also the last years on this earth when you can still hear the silence.

Kiss you – my best greetings to Lawrence, yours, Granny

Fifi to her Grandmother

Dearest,

Your letter was too short for my liking. Just when it began, it stopped. And it was also too open-ended. I think that you have failed in knotting together all the threads you have spun. I expected you would. Later, I will ask you a few questions. But first I must report an unusual effect: your letter made Lawrence positively angry. After reading it, he began to walk up and down, full of indignation. I will sum up the contents of his monologue as I did last time, but I cannot describe his anger – you should have seen him! Thus Lawrence spoke:

'Your granny is a classicist and classicism is not as innocent an ideal as it seems. It is a form of the terror that universalism exercises against the individual's uniqueness, his birthright. Your grandmother speaks about the existential choice, but she does not understand it. First of all, there is her predilection for the harmony of freedoms. She has not given up on this, has she? She has admitted – grudgingly – that not all upright persons are harmonious characters. But she side-stepped the other issue, namely that extremely unharmonious men can be just as free as harmonious characters – they are sometimes more free than all the rest together. She repeats and repeats her main hobby-horse that no kind of freedom should have the upper hand over another, for if it had, the person's character would be as reified as a statue, or as the embodiment of a fixed hierarchy (excuse me, it is your granny who employs such awful similes). But this is wrong, or at least oversimplified. For in the life of modern men the existential choice of ourselves – the leap – is the fundamental freedom, for it is the condition of all the other freedoms. Without such a choice we will remain a mere husk – in your granny's expression. Freedom is our foundation, our foundation is freedom. But the foundation is not placed on top of a fixed hierarchy of freedoms. On the contrary, the leap itself warrants that there is no fixed hierarchy. To express myself better, it warrants that there will be no fixed hierarchy in the sense of traditional metaphysics. For the leap warrants that – whether there will be a hierarchy or there will be none – the self-choice of the person will be the root, the reason, the intuition according to which a man will develop a self-determined hierarchy for his freedom or keep his freedoms in balance unhierarchically. This is why your granny's classicism is terroristic. She wants to prescribe to people who choose themselves, what they should choose within themselves and how. But if we were following her recommendation we could not choose ourselves at all, but a kind of Goethe or granny or Fifi in ourselves – all what we are not. I repeat, your granny has not the faintest idea about the character of the existential choice. Choosing yourself – must I repeat it? – is also to choose your complexes, your infirmities, your unconscious, and also your parents, your age, your childhood and so on – you choose yourself fully. One person who chooses herself fully and begins to become what she is, will be a beautiful person. But another character, who also chooses himself existentially, cannot become a beautiful person, because simply he is not one. If he became beautiful in your granny's sense he would become someone else than what he is – an existential *malheur*, a complete failure, and in the last instance, instead of being free he would be rather unfree. Your grandmother's concession is no concession at all; she concedes – I've already said this – that not all upright men are harmonious characters. But there are men and women who choose themselves existentially under the category of difference. They are, perhaps, not even upright, but since they choose themselves, they acquire their fundamental freedom. Whether they will become harmonious or not is as much an open question as in the case of men and women who choose themselves under the category of the universal; since the former as much as the latter become what they are, and not someone else. You will remember that in my dialogue I experimented with the idea of distinguishing between two different hierarchies of character: one is the hierarchy of greatness, the other that of decency. One can be at the top of both, but this happens rarely. Your granny's classicistic ideal is not the ideal of greatness. Among the well-known great personalities Goethe alone fits the bill entirely. You remember our Nietzsche classes. Our teacher chose Nietzsche rather than Goethe as the exempification of the ethics of personality precisely because Goethe's classicism is too exceptional, atypical, a rare bird in our times. You would come to a very similar result if you took into consideration only the men and women who chose themselves under the category of the universal – as decent persons. We are torn, split, suffering beings – sick animals, as Nietzsche would say – and provided that we become ourselves in freedom, how could we become harmonious? I am, unlike your granny, not doctrinaire; I repeat, there are harmonious characters in your grandmother's sense, and they are unconditionally lovable. But not everyone can become like them freely; and if someone wants to become someone that he is not, he will become – I repeat – unfree rather than free. A moral aesthetics, if modelled on the beautiful character, would be a thin, or a rather narrow and one-sided aesthetics, a classicist moral aesthetics. Your granny herself mentioned a different character-type that could be admitted to her pantheon: the sublime character. Typically for your granny, she just mentioned the sublime character, but had nothing to say about him. Let me speak about him.

The sublime character is blessed by nature by over-sensitivity, a strong inclination for suffering, an internal psychological imbalance. While choosing himself he chooses all of the above; thus he becomes melancholic. He chooses himself as a person who is at war with himself and the world – he chooses himself as such. If he chooses himself as an upright person he becomes what he is, an upright man who is at war with himself and the world. One single choice, one single commitment, one single freedom dominates his character – the freedom of self-choice. All the other kinds of freedom may vanish or be pushed into the background. This is not a 'hierarchy' of the reified kind, but a unique and very personal way for the melancholic man to live up to the choice of his own self. Sublime people do not have a happy life, neither do they have a long one. They can end their lives by suicide, as Walter Benjamin did. They are also men of forceful imagination; they not only sense, but also imagine, dangers that threaten them from the outside as well as from the inside. They constantly fend off the dangers; this is why they are upright. But they fend them off in constant wars that tear them apart. The beautiful character protects herself by an invisible screen; the menacing forces of the world hardly infiltrate it; in contrast, the sublime character leaves himself unprotected; he instead reinforces, aggravates, enlarges the menaces of the world by an inbuilt psychological power-plant. This is why he suffers. Being supersensitive, tense and generous to the extreme, the sublime character is always great, heavy and significant. He is as lovable as the beautiful character; perhaps even more. Don't you think so, Fifi?'

Thus spoke Lawrence.

Now I come to my far more modest points.

Your criticism of the philosophy of the existential choice was not entirely just. Both Lawrence and his heroine, Vera, presented the existential choice (under the category of the universal) as the model to establish the moral centre of the circle in the souls of modern men and women. But Lawrence never said, neither did his heroine Vera, that decent people actually hit the centre of the circle. They approximate to it. When you now emphasize openness and say that no one ever entirely becomes her destiny, you are not refuting Lawrence's philosophy. You show instead that people normally do not hit the centre, although they should. I have the strange feeling that you and Lawrence criticize each other for the same mistake. You accuse Lawrence of dogmatism because he allegedly speaks only of pure types and neglects all the approximations, whereas he accuses you of dogmatism, because you (allegedly) stake everything on the beautiful character and put the sublime character on the sidelines. Both of you defend difference and uniqueness against pure types and generalizations. You two are very much alike even if you do not notice it.

Second (should I have said 'first' first?), your remarks on emotions remain obscure. I think I understand what you mean by involvement. I also understand your reference to a philosophy with, or without, colour. You did not mean that emotions 'put colour' into life, for emotions cannot be compared with 'makeup'. Without emotions there is no human life and human face at all; there is nothing one could apply the makeup to. Still, I do not see how the relation between emotional life and the beautiful character develops, although I see that there is an essential relationship. Is a harmonious character also emotionally harmonious? Lawrence added to my difficulties. How would you describe the emotional life of a sublime character?

Third, despite your sceptical treatment of the metaphysical tradition, in the discussion of one major issue you remain a hundred per cent true to this tradition. For example, the relation between aesthetic and moral beauty. When once upon a time young Plato fell in love with his teacher Socrates, he could not hide (not even from himself) the fact that his teacher was ugly. To love the ugly was out of the question; the Greeks loved beauty alone. Thus Plato invented the distinction between the beauty of the body and the beauty of the soul. Socrates' body was ugly, but – lo and behold – inside the ugly exterior was hidden the most beautiful interior! Your beautiful character looks like Socrates. Why don't we abandon the old metaphysical tradition? Why don't we say simply that love has nothing to do with beauty at all? Is there any connection between beauty in a strict aesthetic sense, and beauty in an ethical sense?

Fourth, if there is beauty in the ethical sense that differs from beauty in the aesthetic sense, do you ascribe to the beautiful character a particular way of life or conduct of life? Can this particular way of life, or conduct of life, be termed 'an aesthetic way of life'? Further: is an aesthetic kind of life possible in the world without silence, in a world where the remote sound of a passing train cannot be heard, where only ornithologists pay attention to the songs of birds??

I cannot keep on with my counting . . . fifth, what has love to do with moral aesthetics? I ask this in general, although you have not yet answered my previous questions: can one love an abstraction? How are those abstractions related to the single things and individuals we love, or we are supposed to love?

Finally, dear Granny, you have not reflected at all on Lawrence's manuscript. You haven't said anything so far that would have eased my anxiety (am I too egocentric??).

Please, Granny, answer me soon, and also continue to write during peaceful and quiet nights. Your granddaughter, who is surrounded by noisy cars, the stink of gasoline, and the loud voices of passers-by who walk fast and disappear into the anonymous crowd so that I cannot any more look at their faces to guess whether they are good or bad – you granddaughter really needs your advice.

Love (thousand and one kisses exactly) Fifi

Mrs Sophie Meller to her Granddaughter, Fifi

Dear Fifi,

I haven't forgotten your anxiety or your worries, my dear, but I confess that I do not yet see why Lawrence's dialogue had such a disquieting effect on you. Now that I have finished reading it, I have not stopped wondering why. Lawrence wrote a book on philosophy. The book offers no solution, it does not give an apodictic answer to the questions discussed by the three interlocutors. Is it this that makes you worried? But why? It is rather reassuring that a young man like your Lawrence does not pretend to know answers where there are none, that he instead questions, and questions from all sides, many of the 'final' answers of yesteryear. He is a fine thinker, and philosophy is, after all, about thinking. My favourite works in philosophy are the dialogues by Plato that are attributed to his youth: while reading them I can think more freely, because they do not put fixed ideas in my head. The dialogue written by Lawrence reminded me remotely of young Plato (although only in this respect); I agreed at one time with Lawrence, at another with Joachim, and then with Vera, because none of them was completely right or completely wrong; or rather, one was right in one matter and the other was rather right in another. This did not worry me, but rather appealed to me; moreover, it pleased and amused me. What else did you expect? Did you expect me to scold 'contemporary youth' for its loss of certainties, its moral laxity or its alleged relativism? I hardly think so. I still remember when I was your age, and my grandma used to say that the young in her day were more dutiful and had better morale, than my irresponsible, loud, impolite friends, how ridiculous she seemed to me in her self-righteous solemnity. I am afraid that if you listened to the older generations, the whole history of the human race – particularily in modern times – would appear as a story of constant decline. I sincerely do not believe that my generation was better than yours. I do not know anyone among my old friends, who, as a youth, would have written such an open-ended, sincere dialogue as your Lawrence did. The boys of my time were more sure of the truth of their convictions and their ideas, they believed they knew exactly what was right and what was wrong, and they produced the answers before they raised the questions. Some of them had high and sublime ideals, they were unconventional and they challenged the crowd, but they believed in the truth and the rightness of one single cause or idea even more, and more ardently and absolutely, than the rest. It was not easy to have an open-ended conversation with them, particularly if you were a girl. They agreed in one point, all of them: girls should not intervene in the serious conversation of boys. Or at least they should not criticize the boys too loudly. You see, I like Lawrence because he is different, although I liked some of the boys of my youth too: a few of the conventional ones for their simple rectitude, and a few of the unconventional ones for their blind enthusiasm.

My dear, I saw what has happened to this generation, and how many of those once lovely boys have failed the moral examination; but you must admit that the headmaster – the history of the twentieth century – made the standard too high. Very few of those brilliant young men stood their ground; yes, some of them even failed miserably. They were not better than Lawrence and his friend, yet they were not worse either; it was just that the stakes were too high.

Still, it is pleasing to see Lawrence, a young man who still continues to think of ethics, yet leaves many questions open, a young man who is in no need of certainties, but who is still passionately committed to philosophy and to the 'thing itself'. Your Lawrence is not just innocent, innocuous, but it is very unlikely that he could become guilty of crimes similar to those of the youth of my generation. You would reply that he has not yet stood his historical examination, and that you have the presentiment that he and his friends would not fare better than the previous generation if the chips were down. But I wish you would not stretch your imagination in this direction. Future is the space for hope, it is an open space. Should I, the old girl who sees no future, tell you not to prejudge possibilities? True, I must confess, I am happy that I am soon going to die. I confess that I would not like to live in the world of the future. I love mine. Or do I? I hated mine when I was your age, but this was another age. But now, at least in my part of the world, the darkest clouds are gone; for a moment the blue of the sky can be seen. Now that I am writing this letter, it can still be seen. I expect new clouds to gather. In all probability they will not be as dark as the clouds of my youth, they will perhaps be less threatening. Still, it is good to die during the intermission. This is why I do not want to ponder any more much about the future.

If you tell me, for example, that in all probability no great music will ever again be composed, I can answer: how do you know? But I can also offer a more sincere answer: I do not care. Future generations will still have what we had, our Bach, Mozart, Beethoven have already presented the world with inexhaustible gifts. They, and all the others like them, can make life meaningful and rich for all people in all times to come, if they turn to them with love. I can say the same about philosophy; I am not interested in the future of philosophy. I have my Plato, my Aristotle, my Kant; so do you. So what if no new original philosophy is born in the future? We can still think with the ancients, as we can go on thinking philosophically about everything that is worthy of being thought about – and everything *is* worthy of being thought about . . .

I see I have an easy task. I am not a philosopher. I write letters, not books. Letter writing has its privileges; for one, you can do what philosophers cannot: think about questions that matter as if you were the first person ever to think about them. If you write a letter you do no need to refer to the real or imaginary sources of your ideas. Sometimes you paraphrase an author, sometimes not, sometimes you remember the texts you have once read, sometimes you do not. No footnote is needed. Letter writing has an additional advantage: you address one person and one person alone, you address a person whom you know, mostly a person whom you love too. Some philosophers used this form because they saw its advantages particularily Kierkegaard, one of Lawrence's favourites. True, the letter form can also be misused. But only by a philosopher. And finally, everything can be misused.

I am sorry, I still can not fathom why Lawrence's manuscript worried you so much. I still think that it was perhaps the dialogue form that made you uneasy. Are you thinking that the dialogue form is just an elegant way to avoid answering the most pressing questions? True, in a dialogue many different convictions can seem convincing, and perhaps convincing to the same degree; the author may hide himself behind his masks. And he can do this without relapsing into cheap relativism. He simply lets the readers/hearers make up their own minds and choose: either/or. Do you think that this is wrong? That one has to take sides openly and absolutely? That the philosopher should not just present the either/or but that he should himself make a choice: that he himself, as a philosopher, should leap?

I do not think that this is a moral issue. Lawrence made one thing clear and I agree: your choice can be morally right, and equally right, whichever of the three representative philosophical avenues you enter at the crossroads. Your choice has something to do with your psychology or biography. Yes, this is it, now I understand you! You are not worried because there is something wrong philosophically in the dialogue but because something disturbs you in Lawrence himself, psychologically or humanly. Lawrence's dialogue on the ethics of personality made you anxious – about Lawrence's personality. Is this the case?

An ethics of personality is a risky endeavour. Not for the philosopher as a philosopher, but for the actors who are committed to it. An ethics of personality is risky because its practice requires too much from the single individual, perhaps more than what a single individual is capable of bearing. A general ethics or moral philosophy, for example the Kantian, is not risky at all. As your friend says, such an ethics offers a reliable crutch. And as he also says, sometimes even men and women driven by *amor fati* will rely on such a crutch. But what makes me worried – for, on second thoughts, I am also a little worried – there is nothing in your

Lawrence's philosophy that would tell us why people would seek (and find) such a crutch. In the mind of a lay person, like myself, the ethics of personality is immensely demanding: it stabilizes uncertainties and it still requires a heightened sense of responsibility. Not everyone can carry such a heavy weight. For a bad weight – lifter, the stabilization of uncertainties goes with the decrease in the sense of responsibility. On the other hand, one cannot walk solely on a crutch . . .

Tomorrow I will continue.

Now (on Wednesday) I come to your questions. I will not refer to anyone, for it makes no difference – in a letter – whether I say something for the first time or for the millionth time. Everything that is said here is said both for the first and for the last time.

As a former schoolteacher (once a teacher always a teacher!) I am not unfamiliar with the practice of answering questions point by point. But I already disliked the practice in my teaching days. True, I was teaching history and German literature, and I felt this method to be particularly unsuited for making my own subject-matter enjoyable and understood. You are the schoolteacher now, even if you don't want to be one, and I am the student who answers the questions point by point. Then let me begin.

I haven't directly criticized the concept of the existential choice. Or at least this was not on my mind. I understand that a perfect choice of oneself as a good person is the choice of a centre, and when one begins to become what one is, one approximates to this self-chosen centre. And one person will approximate to it more closely than another. But I saw, and I still see, that although the theory admits the probability that some people will end up closer to their centre than others, it does not address itself seriously to this experience. Philosophically this may be all right. Moral philosophies speak always about the norm, that is, about the centre, as they also assume that people do not hit the centre. If they speak about empirical, real people at all, they just enumerate the reasons why they (most of them) fail to land even close to the centre.

It seems as if this question would be entirely unanswerable in the framework of an existence-philosophy. After all, everyone chooses his own centre, and by hitting this very centre all those who choose themselves as good can be good in their own way. There must be as many ways to approximate to the centre as there are people who choose that centre. One cannot say that someone has failed to approximate to her centre because she did not listen to reason or to her best instinct, and so on. This explains Lawrence's silence, but silence is not always an answer.

I began my ruminations at the point where Lawrence stopped. Actually I said to myself: I and my granddaughter, we always did the same that Lawrence did. We distinguished good faces from bad faces. We had no theory, we just did it. Lawrence said, either/or; either you become what you are (in approximation) or you lose yourself, you will be an absolute failure. You and I, however, were aware that not all faces can be identified strictly as good or bad ones, and certainly not under the age of thirty.

The face is a result, or rather the expression of the result, but not necessarily the mirror image of an existential success or failure. The empty face, the blank face – not necessarily the bad face – can be ascribed, perhaps, to an existential failure, although I have some doubts. Empty and blank faces are normally those of people who have never chosen themselves existentially. And after all, where does a so-called existential failure begin to be an existential failure, that is, when does a person cease to become what he is? When does one stop becoming that which one has chosen oneself to be?

It seems as if it were easy to point out existential failures whenever the existential choice has been performed, in the vocabulary of Lawrence's teacher, under the category of difference. If you cease to become a writer you are no more a writer. But in case of the choice of decency this is not so simple. I cannot explain anything philosophically, but in my life-experience as a teacher I have learned that there is not only a continuum in approximation but also a continuum in the opposite direction. Before one loses oneself entirely one always has the chance to regain oneself. And I think that one can lose oneself entirely only at the moment of one's death. At least I would not like to speak about anyone as a total existential failure. As a teacher I do not like it. I always told my students when they did something morally wrong that it was wrong; I never tolerated moral misconduct or even ambiguity; everything less than a sincere judgement is, in my view, not a sign of liberalism but a sign of indifference. But I would have never said to any of my students that I considered her an existential failure, that she had passed the line of no return, that she would never become what she had chosen herself to be, or that she had lost the capacity to choose herself as a decent human being altogether.

If it comes to the existential choice under the category of difference, then you can tell someone (tactfully, yes, but still) that she will not become what she has chosen herself to be, for example, that she will never be a playwright or painter, or a concert pianist. You ask me why? Just because this is simply so. It is the matter of sincerity to tell a person this – tactfully, of course, to make the pain less painful – to throw a life-hire to the person who, perhaps, does not yet know that she will be drowning, but who is actually drowning. Here, one is not passing a moral judgement, because it is not a moral failure to realize that one's talents are not up to one's resolve, but there is a moral element in passing such a judgement, for – in my mind – there is a kind of moral shortcoming if one avoids passing this judgement or postpones it. And perhaps there is also an aesthetic shortcoming.

It might be difficult to divide the ethical from the aesthetic element in a judgement like this. But I propose to disregard or to dismiss all kinds of pragmatic motivations. You may say, 'Granny, now it is your turn to neglect empirical men and women.' Because 'empirical' men and women are, normally, pragmatically motivated. For example, you will tell someone that he is not (and never will become) a concert pianist, in order to tell him that he will not make his living as a concert pianist, so he needs to find a good profession to support his family. Let me answer your (possible) objection. Even this kind of pragmatic advice includes an ethical element.

It is true that sometimes pragmatic considerations are entirely void of ethical or aesthetic motivation; they can even be bluntly amoral and entirely tasteless. But I will still neglect all pragmatic considerations void of ethical and aesthetic aspects. This will be easy. I just need to continue doing what we were both doing when we were making guesses about good and bad faces: I have to take the position of an observer. But contrary to our game of good and bad faces, the observer is here in the possession of information and she is simultaneously involved: she knows the other and cares for the other. She cares for the other for the other's sake or for the sake of a third party (be it taste or idea), but certainly not for her own sake, nor for the sake of people she identifies herself with. That is, neither interest nor the conviction of an 'I', or of a 'we', can be the reference point of the judgement. We know well how to pass such judgements, because we, as naïve readers and listeners, (and who is not also a naïve reader and listener?) pass judgements on the characters in novels or dramas in such a way all the time. These judgements contain an aesthetic element. For example, we pass a judgement not just on Goethe's Werther, but also on the characters of Lotte and Werther. Lotte we recognize as a beautiful character, Werther as a sublime character. But both of our judgements (of Werther and of Lotte) are also aesthetic, and not only ethical. More precisely, they are eminently aesthetic.

You see for yourself that neither indifference nor the absence of passionate involvement characterize the standpoint of this kind of observation, of an aesthetic attitude par excellence. We are involved in the character, in his or her emotions, vicissitudes and fate.

I know that here I have stepped on slippery ground. I cannot interfere with the life of a novelistic character; I cannot give her advice. There is reciprocity (in a hermeneutical sense) but never in a practical sense. It can be similar in real life. I can enjoy a beautiful human character when I see one; I can watch her from afar; she may never be in need of advice, and I might never be in the situation to advise her. My next-door neigbour is just like Lotte, for example; I take pleasure in seeing her surrounded by her little brothers and sisters. But my responsibility to my neighbour entails that I suspend the position of observer at any moment when interference (help or advice) is required. This is why I wrote to you right at the beginning of our correspondence about Lawrence's book, that the harmonious-beautiful (free) personality manifests herself for the observer. In passing aesthetic judgement on the other in real life, the readiness to switch from the attitude of the observer to the attitude of the actor needs to be omnipresent. Actually, this is the decisive moral aspect to the attitude of a real-life spectator. And we should not forget, that if we switch from the attitude of the observer to the attitude of the actor, it will be of no moral relevance whether the person who cries for our help is a beautiful personality or not (e.g. whether my beautiful neighbour Lotte or one of her little sisters – whose character is not developed, or perhaps is ugly – cries). But if we failed to take aesthetic pleasure in our neigbour's moral beauty, our human experience would be impoverished.

How much I would like to speak of beauty! How delightful it would be to ruminate on the old metaphysical question whether it is beauty that we love, or whether love makes that which we love beautiful! But I promised to keep my intellectual *wanderlust* in check and to stick to Lawrence's text.

Fortunately, his ethics of personality itself makes the quest for the beautiful one of the central themes. The first Lawrence (who died at the age of twenty-three in 1911, and who re-entered life in the first Joachim's dialogue, re-entering, together with the new Joachim, very recently in the new (our) Lawrence's dialogue), once waged a little private war against the aesthetization of life. The ethics of personality was then in vogue for the second time, and became attached to the project of the aesthetization of life. I think that the ethics of personality of the new (our) Lawrence will bravely withstand the attacks of the (first) Lawrence. (Our) Lawrence's ethics of personality does not imply the aesthetization of life, although the protagonist of his ethics is also an aesthetic 'objectivation' – if I am allowed to use this ugly and fairly inadequate word. For what else is the approximation of the self-chosen centre if not our old acquaintance 'self-perfection', but self-perfection without the imposed model of the 'perfect'? And what is self-perfection without an imposed model of perfection if not the work of art of the genius (and not only in Kant's theory!)? Is not every individual who becomes what he is (what he chose himself to be) a work of art (as perfect as it can only be), an inimitable, unique, single and absolute work of art? Is such a person not similar to the 'tragic' hero of Lukács's *Metaphysics of Tragedy*, to the Platonist beyond Platonism, to the individual who is – as individual – the ideal itself, and the ideal's sole representation? True, Lawrence's person-alities are not tragic, or at least they do not need to be. Although Lawrence's latest outburst in favour of the sublime character awoke my suspicion that perhaps he still identifies the tragic hero with the authentic character of an ethics of personality . . .

The character (in terms of an ethics of personality) becomes what she is – to become what you are is, in itself, an aesthetic quality. It contains the elements of self-perfection, even if it is far from perfect. Above all: the character pleases. It pleases us (the observers). Beautiful characters also enjoy themselves, for all joy entails self-enjoyment. But I would hardly say that they please themselves, for they are not narcissistic; rather, they find pleasure in the other(s). What is, however, the most important thing is that those beautiful characters do not conduct an 'aesthetic life' for they choose others (just as they choose themselves) *as they are*; they do not pre-fabricate them, they do not stage them, since they do not set the stage. Life is not an artwork for them, neither do they regard themselves as works of art; their likeness to the works of art appears – as I repeat it for the thousandth time – to the involved and loving observer.

I postponed, and postponed, reacting to Lawrence's angry outburst. There was some truth in his outburst. I am a 'classicist'. Since I chose myself, I also chose the 'classicist' in me; I became what I also am a classicist. This is no mitigating circumstance in philosophy. Although philosophy is, in the last instance, autobiography, it is such only in the last instance, and philosophers are not supposed to present their self-portrait; they must place themselves in the position of the others and think with an 'enlarged mind', as Kant once put it. I am, however, not a philosopher, but an old schoolteacher and a grandmother; I have the privilege of being able to portray myself. Still, I did not do it. My taste is classical, but the portrait of the 'beautiful person' I draw is not my self-portrait. Still, I agree, I neglected the sublime character; I have not even tried to paint his portrait, perhaps because he is a too complex personality and I am a bad portrait artist. But perhaps, because I understood Lawrence as well as he understands himself. I did not want the tragic personality to occupy the centre stage in the show of modern moral/aesthetic characters. The archetype of the beautiful person is a woman; the archetype of the sublime person is a man. As a woman I defended the archetype of the beautiful character; as a man Lawrence defended the archetype of the sublime character. But if we really turn our faces towards each other and do not just pay cheap lip service to alterity, then it is I who should make the strongest case for the sublime character (man's modern archetype) and Lawrence who should make the strongest case for the beautiful character (woman's modern archetype). But after tomorrow, perhaps, there will be no beautiful women or sublime men left; it is too late to reverse the roles.

Since every beginning is hypothetical, for it is the beginning of an end, and thus the beginning depends on the end, few things can be said about the difference between the beautiful and the sublime character in psychological terms. The hypothetical dovetailing of the two kinds of a priori (the genetic and the social) leaves tensions behind. When the person chooses himself, he also chooses those tensions. It is very likely that the character of the tensions which are thus re-chosen has something to do with the pychological makeup of the moral character, whether it will be beautiful or sublime.

Yet the beautiful and the sublime characters have something in common: both of them re-choose their tensions in positive terms: they both love their tensions; Lawrence would speak of *amor fati*. Tensions (between the two kinds of a priori) can also be re-chosen, so to speak, negatively: you choose them as your own, but you do not love them. If this happens, your character will be upright, but neither beautiful nor sublime; you will be not an aesthetic character in those traditional terms. Perhaps we need to invent new terms to describe them aesthetically. Your Joachim is, for example, neither beautiful nor sublime. But he is upright in the most subtle way.

Lawrence speaks only about the tensions of the sublime character. But the balanced, the beautiful personality grows primarily from the existential choice of original tensions. Adorno says that beauty is the *Homoestase der Tension* and Hegel at one point says that beauty is *dynamisches Gleichgewicht*. There is no more merit in becoming beautiful than in becoming sublime or just (seemingly unaesthetically) righteous or subtle. Yet a beautiful character is the most pleasant company for others; and becoming a beautiful character is a blessing for the beautiful character herself. Never believe that a beautiful character does not suffer; she suffers deeply, although not loudly; but she suffers from something real; she has little imagination if it comes to the worst; thus she does not suffer from never-embodied spectres.

There is something I have not told you as yet (and if I did, I have forgotten it): the beauty of the character has nothing to do with centring. If someone chooses herself as a decent person, goodness will be her centre; this is what she will approximate to. But the harmony of freedoms is not a centre to approximate. It cannot be chosen either. When you choose yourself (existentially) you also choose the possibiliy of becoming beautiful or sublime, but this remains a possibility and not even a probability. The identity of goodness and beauty is a metaphysical idea. One can – in the Platonic tradition – equate the Idea of Beauty and the Idea of the Good, but then one makes the attribute 'beautiful' void of its aesthetic content and connotations. For in terms of the metaphysical idea, the objects and sources of sensual perception, reflective feelings and emotions included, occupy the lowest stage of the hierarchy of the beautiful or are excluded from this domain entirely. Thus I can only repeat that if goodness is in the centre of the soul, there is the possibility of being beautiful and sublime.

But what about the reverse relation? Can one choose oneself as evil existentially and secure thereby the possibility of being and becoming beautiful or sublime? The problem is more serious than it seems, but since – thank God – your teacher spoke about it in her lectures on Nietzsche and *Parsifal*, a course that both you and Lawrence attended, I am at liberty to add some *ad hoc* remarks. I think that no one has ever chosen himself as evil existentially. Shakespeare seems to attribute this kind of choice to Richard III. But if Gloucester chose himself as evil existentially (as he declared in his first monologue), his choice certainly did not come off and he failed, for at the end he hated himself for his wickedness. But there is evil in the world. Evil does not pertain to the existential choice of evil. However, an existential choice under the category of difference can become the source of evil. Yet if the existential choice of ourselves is actually the source of evil, the character cannot become beautiful or sublime. What is the daemonic then? Is the attraction of the evil daemon similar to the attraction of the beautiful? I do not understand and perhaps I never will.

I am sorry, but I must turn back to a neglected issue. True, one does not choose beauty as the centre of one's life, one does not choose oneself existentially as 'beautiful' (or as sublime). But the beautiful character is still not a birthday present. Beauty is something that one normally cultivates. The cultivation of beauty entails, among other things, the cultivation of emotions, especially of emotional intensity and density in our relations with others, and also the cultivation of taste and refinement and the gay *Lebensgefühl*. A character can be beautiful whether she is conscious or unconscious about it; she is usually unconscious about it. One cultivates one's own character-beauty unconsciously: through cultivating beautiful things, through creating beauty around oneself, through transforming – perhaps again entirely unconsciously – one's environment to match one's personality. I liked what Lawrence said about taste and about caring for beautiful things. What he ommitted to add was that one can create a beautiful environment around oneself irrespective of one's character. In olden times (in the times of my grandmother) very conventional persons could do it, just by following their traditions, whether aristocratic, bourgeois or gentry. Sometimes there was just a light touch of individuality in all the beauty that people surrounded themselves with. If you are born in a tasteful Elizabethan mansion in England, you have a fair chance of learning in your infancy how to tell beautiful from ugly in a shrub or in a flowerbed, or in a piece of furniture or in a painting. Now that elegant traditions are dying, both elegance and the sense of beauty will become individual achievements. But, alas, the individual – as I understand him or her – is the exception, and the beautiful individual the exception among exceptions. The individual has an environment, the others just surroundings. Surroundings can be pleasing to the eye but they are unrelated to the personality whose surroundings they are. Surroundings manifest fashion instead of tradition, wealth (or poverty) instead of care (or the lack thereof) . . . But you see, I have done something I promised to avoid: I have compared the times of my youth to the times of my old age: don't take it seriously. I must be exhausted. Let me continue tomorrow.

My dearest, I am arriving slowly at your second (or third?) question. The term 'one-dimensional man' catches the representative feature of men who cease to represent anything at all. Sheerly formal conventions, the leftovers of a tradition, are spiritless yet still representative. Hegel spoke about their 'positivity'. To speak a Hegelian language – it does not suit me, so I do it only for abbreviation's sake – this positivity needs to be negated. By negating positivity the contingent person becomes aware of her contingency. The negation of negation is then the restoration of the unity of spirit and form, a kind of harmony, yet this time by force of the resolve of an individuality who has chosen herself existentially. It is this achievement that I (or perhaps Hegel already?) call harmony. There is another alternative: to rely on a merely formal and positive external guidance, which, after being negated by the subjective spirit, has lost its representative character. Such are customs without past (and without future), customs that are embedded in the absolute present tense. Whatever becomes fashionable is serving as a point of guidance. Other-directed people are guided by customs that are not authentic customs, by forms that were never abandoned by the living spirit because they have never ever been inhabited by the spirit: fashions. To follow fashions is easy. One observes what others do and does the same thing, without reflecting, thinking, without asking questions whether the thing itself is right or wrong. The observations of the one-dimensional man are pragmatic in kind: he observes in order to imitate the behaviour observed that already is, on its part, the imitation of the behaviour of others: the shadow of the shadow. Imitation is not alien to the ethical tradition. I have learned from Joachim (in Lawrence's dialogue) that we imitate the perfectly moral person who occupies, allegorically speaking, the moral centre. But since the imitation of fashion waives moral considerations, conscience shrinks, subjectivity becomes superfluous and increasingly shallow. Interest is vested in finding out what others are doing, in order to keep pace with the crowd, and do exactly the things that are expected by the crowd. Since emotional richness depends on the multiplicity of involvements, on the continuity of reflection and self-reflection that accompanies these involvements, an other-directed person loses his depth. Literarily, he becomes two-dimensional, not one-dimensional, but since Marcuse wrote an interesting book about this phenomenon and baptized it 'one-dimensional man' I like to use his telling metaphor.

After I reread a few sentences penned down yesterday, I was grasped by something that resembled sadness. Am I really seeing things in a dim light because I am old or do I have a premonition of real disasters? It occurs me that perhaps the beautiful contingent person has appeared among us only for one historical moment – that she is the exception, not only in the sense that beautiful individuals are normally rare, but also in the sense that soon there will be no single one left. The liberation from mere plasticity was the condition of the modern miracle: beauty became incarnated in simple, everyday, yet in their everydayness exceptional, individuals. Will other-directed persons, who are neither plastic, nor musical, given that they are one-dimensional, sweep away beauty once and for all? I have not forgotten Nietzsche's words, which your teacher quoted with some gusto: it is perhaps easier to dance in chains. I keep thinking about it.

I keep thinking about the parallel between the art form and the beautiful character. Art forms have also liberated themselves, they have got rid of their chains; at the historical moment of liberation (that has lasted for about three centuries) great, three-dimensional, and individual archetypical artworks have been created out of nothing. But from liberation grand freedom was born and the tradition was quickly exploited so that now every tree is free to bear any fruits, for the difference between the trees (the genres) was annulled. However, they all bear small fruits, very much like one another, and they are hardly edible. The denizens of the art world are constantly chasing novelty, yet nothing new happens any more under sun of the world of art.

I am sorry, I am repeating myself. In a former letter I tried to console you with pointing at our wonderful companions, all the works of art that remain with us, from now to eternity. I have not entirely convinced myself. For if the same thing happened to characters as happened to works of art, if the beautiful character – the musical beauty in Adorno's interpretation – (and also the sublime character) dwelled among us just for one single historical moment, only to disappear and to be replaced by the one-dimensional man, the 'eternity' of our artwork-companions would be shortlived. Works of art are inexhaustible in meaning, if men and women visit them for their meaning; they are lovable, if men and women love them for what they are, and only three-dimensional men and women seek meaning in works of art and love them for that what they are. Without beautiful and sublime characters, I am afraid, there will be no interpretandum, for there is no interpretandum without interpreters.

Fifi dear, I have just noticed that I disregarded your third and fourth question and jumped, too soon, to the fifth. Yes, you are right, both the beautiful and the sublime character have to do something with a way of life. They conduct their lives in a way that their lives match their character. Yet since the form of life of every beautiful person and of every sublime person is unique, very few things can be said about their life-conduct in general. Still, since you asked, I answer. I cannot help falling back on a few generalities, and angering Lawrence once again, for I will speak only about beautiful characters.

I will first mention a few representative beautiful characters: Jane Austen, George Sand, Rosa Luxemburg, Hannah Arendt. They are all women of course, for as I said, most beautiful characters are women while most sublime characters are men (although I once knew a man who was the most beautiful character of them all). There is another problem with my examples: they are all well-known women, although I insisted that the beauty of character appears in everyday life and has nothing to do with fame or creative excellence. But I could not help referring to them, for had I instead mentioned my aunt Sissi – a very beautiful personality! – you couldn't have done anything with the example for you did not know her personally. And Lawrence – to whom you will show this letter – has not even heard of her. We must make a compromise. The well-known figures will also show clearly what I have in mind.

Jane Austen, George Sand, Rosa Luxemburg, Hannah Arendt . . . None of these women can be said to be 'happy' in an ordinary sense. They were all exiles, either in fact, or in a metaphorical sense; they all had a difficult life. None of them lived out their life in full – Rosa Luxemburg was assassinated. Still, they were beautiful – and they were happy! They were not suffering from the malaise of insecurity, they were noble characters, they constantly kept their freedoms in balance. All these four women surrounded themselves with beauty, they loved beauty, as they also loved good conversation and good company. They were loyal friends and they also cultivated friendships, emotional attachments and sentiments. Naturally, they also loved the beauties of nature. They were women of emotional density and richness.

Yes, those beautiful characters were not happy in an ordinary sense, but they were happy in an ancient Greek sense. Not in a Stoic, but in an Aristotelian, or perhaps even in an Epicurean sense. In his dialogue, Lawrence defended Epicureanism. Why hasn't it occurred to him that his sublime characters have nothing to do with his Epicurean ideals, whereas my beautiful characters are living up, or at least can live up, to the ideals of this venerable tradition?

But this is all wrong! I should throw out this letter and start again. Although my beautiful characters are not happy in an ordinary sense, neither are they happy in an ancient Greek sense. They are unlike the Stoics (they would not feel happy inside the infamous bull of Phalaris) but their happiness is not of an Aristotelian or Epicurean kind either. Gaity, love of life and cheerfulness are not Aristotelian virtues, they are not even emotional dispositions of ethical or intellectual virtues. An Epicurean kind of happiness demands that one turn away from one's sufferings and disregard them, but a modern happy person's happiness includes suffering. Life is good if it is lived to the full.

No one stands higher than a good person. Lawrence (or Joachim) quoted Kant: a good person's good will shines as a jewel. A good person is the living Utopia. Nothing is more Utopian than a good person. Reverence is due to the good person – and he receives our reverence.

A beautiful character is not a 'more' in goodness or perfection that is somehow added to a good character. *A beautiful character represents a non-Utopian element in the decent character.* The good person is worthy of happiness; the beautiful person is the good person who is actually happy (in a non-vulgar sense). She approximates to the good (this is her centre); her beauty is grace – the gift of grace; but she also cultivates this gift.

Beautiful characters are the good chacters who have received what they are worthy of – happiness. This is why the sight of the beautiful character is the promise of happiness (*la promesse du bonheur*). *The beautiful character is the only promise of happiness in a godforsaken world.*

She promises happiness because she is happy (although not in an ordinary sense): she thus embodies the possibility of the unity of goodness and happiness. Moreover, she does not just promise happiness, she can also make us happy, if only for a brief moment. She makes happy the disinterested (although never dispassionate, never indifferent) spectator.

I have still a duty left: to satisfy Lawrence and to do him justice. I once again neglected the sublime character, although only for a very personal reason: no one can sing his praise so eloquently than Lawrence, so I don't even try. The sublime character is not the promise of happiness – he is never happy. He can be favoured by fortune with talents, riches, loving friends; still he will never be happy, because he will look at the world with gloomy eyes and the world will look back at him as a miserable dwelling place. But the high tension of a melancholic character, his quest for an absolute, his despair in anything less than absolute, is also a promise, at least in our world. The sublime person is the promise of grandeur. Once upon a time, for example in Hamlet's time, melancholic characters could be princes; they could act grandly, they represented grandeur. Now, melancholic characters are left without a task, and they normally release their internal tensions in the wrong places, or they despair because they cannot release them.

Our century has seen many leaders of fake and phoney grandeur. As a result, 'greatness' as such is depreciated and has become suspect, and rightly so. But still, the conclusion that mediocricity is preferable to grandeur is shamelessly false. The fact that there are no more tragedies does not annul the greatness of the tragic character. Melancholic characters are potential tragic characters – tragic characters without tragic situations. They are not always decent people in a very strict sense, but they put decency on the highest pedestal – as Hamlet put Horatio.

Sublime characters promise things of vital import, albeit only negatively: on the one hand, they strip from fake grandeur its borrowed glory; on the other hand, they represent the potential for tragedy in the absence of tragedy.

I noticed Lawrence's hesitation between two interpretations of grandeur; once he associated grandeur with the choice of ourselves under the category of difference, another time, however, with the existential choice under the category of the universal. I associate grandeur exclusively with the sublime, and discuss the sublime as one character-type resulting from the existential choice of goodness. Heightened creativity can also be described in terms of greatness, but I think that although the art of a great artist is great art, great art in itself doesn't bestow the virtue of grandeur on the artist himself.

I wanted to end my letter here, but I can't because I still owe you an explanation. It is a long tradition of popular (and less popular) philosophy to associate women's character with beauty and men's character with the sublime. Kant, for one, in the second chapter of one of the charming works of his youth, spoke about the 'sublime and the beautiful among men and women' in a similar spirit. Kant admits that the beautiful character is gay, whereas the sublime is melancholic, yet he places the beautiful (female) character below the rank of the sublime character. However, speaking of an ethics of personality, Kant's description of the beautiful character fits our bill almost perfectly. This I can quote because I used to read this passage to my students in class. Kant writes, Women 'werden das Böse vermeiden, nicht weil es unrecht, aber weil es hässlich ist, und tugendhafte Handlungen bedeuten bei ihnen solche, die sittlich schön sein. Nichts von Sollen, nichts von Müssen, nichts von Schuldigkeit . . .' Not bad, not bad at all. One could even reverse the signs in the spirit of an ethics of personality and say that the 'female', the beautiful character, is superior to the 'male', the sublime character. But I would not do it. For there is no way to compare the beautiful and the sublime. And please, take care: the promise of happiness embodied in the beautiful character has absolutely nothing to do with the traditional images of the 'saviour woman'. No single woman has 'saved' any single melancholic man without having lost herself in the process. So, take care.

I stop here, my dear. I need to be in a better mood to continue.

Your Granny

Fifi to her Grandmother

My dearest,

You asked my about my worries, and here you are – I have spoiled your good spirits – my gloom made you gloomy. I believed that you will cheer me up: it is my turn to cheer you up. Yet instead of cheering you up, I must still press you to answer all my unanswered questions . . . And I have to add a new one to them. First, you appreciated Vera's description of happiness in Lawrence's rendering; happy is a person who never finds out whether he chose himself under the category of the universal or of difference. Happy then is a person who remains decent throughout his whole life and also develops his talents in full. You may remember, Lawrence himself was not satisfied with this answer, for he insisted that one does not wait for happiness till the end of one's days – but you liked this formula, you approved of it. And now it seems as if you began to speak about happiness in an entirely different sense. You just said that harmonious (beautiful) people are the promise of happiness. You added that they are actually happy although not in an everyday and banausic sense. But what their happiness consists of, you have not spelled out. If happiness were an entirely subjective experience your silence would be justified; one cannot say anything about a merely contingent, subjective sensation. But you associated happiness with beauty, with something that is not merely a subjective experience. Let me press you again: what is happiness? What aligns happiness with the love of beauty, with enjoyment, with being pleased, or with the play of imagination? What does it mean that the beautiful character, the promise of happiness, or happiness itself, is 'grace'? What is grace? Does it stand simply for the 'undeserved'?

All the answers you still owe me are somehow related to this matter. I understand that you don't want to speak about emotions in general, as I also understand that the emotional world of a beautiful person is rich and deep (or intense?) and so on, but still, you mentioned love many times, as in love of beauty, love of nature and the like, but not just as love *simpliciter*. Is love included in the promise of happiness? You mentioned – on the side – the dilemma of certain Platonists (what we love is beautiful – it is beauty that we love). It was easy for them to resolve the issue: the beautiful soul loves all things of beauty – both are beautiful because they both participate in the beauty of the highest, simplest one, Beauty itself. But do we love only things of beauty? And does only the love of beauty belong to the promise of happiness? or to happiness put simply? I will even repeat my oddest question: can one love abstractions, like liberty, beauty, love?

In the sign of liberty, beauty and especially of love,

yours, Fifi

Mrs Sophie Meller to her Granddaughter, Fifi

Dearest Fifi,

I deserve your reproach for interrupting my letter without answering many important questions. I manœuvered myself into a bad mood, but you have nothing to do with it. Soon the bad mood was gone. I put on a record, almost randomly, but I did it with a lucky hand. Glenn Gould played Beethoven's Bagatelles. It is not my favourite set of piano pieces, but lo and behold, I heard something extraordinary, indescribable; next month, when you come, we shall listen to it together. Suddenly, I felt something one could call 'felicity'; I loved the world, my times, and everything; I suddenly became a ridiculous sentimentalist. Have no worries because of me, dear.

You are right: I approved Vera's understanding of happiness more than Lawrence did. But 'happiness' is such a lousy, polysemous word, it refers to such different, such heteronomous experiences, that I never suspected that someone could mistake Vera's suggestion for a definition. A few weeks ago, an old friend of mine, Professor Horius (you perhaps remember the tall bald gentleman with his cigars) sent me a draft of a lecture he is going to deliver soon at a conference in Vienna. The lecture is about happiness and good life. It is a prosaic lecture, quite dry, and slightly didactic. But I learned a few things from it.

Professor Horius distinguishes between three philosophical conceptions of happiness. They are: the subjective conception, the objective conception, and combinations of the two. The elaboration of the three conceptions is very complex, there are many twists and turns. I will simplify things. First, one can describe happiness as a subjective experience: everyone knows best what makes him happy or unhappy, no one can know it better than the person who experiences it. One cannot argue about happiness. Two persons may have the same, get the same, lose the same; one of them will says that he is happy, the other that he is unhappy – there is no impartial judge or assessor in this matter. Second, there can be a generally accepted description of the constituents and the conditions of a person's happiness. They can be generally accepted by all, by many, or just by a few; but if someone is a member of the group that subscribes to such a definition he exposes his own experience of happiness or unhappiness to an objective scrutiny. Then an impartial judge can tell him that he is happy or unhappy (irrespective of his subjective experience). Third, the two conceptions can be combined. Professor Horius discussed many of such combinations, and especially the Hegelian kind. When I approved of Vera's recommendation perhaps more than Lawrence did, I had an objective conception of happiness in mind, the kind of objective description the attributes of which are accepted by a few people. This time, they are accepted by people who are aware of having made an existential choice, and who are also aware of the risks that such a choice implies. Vera addressed Lawrence, she addressed a person who had already accepted the philosophy of existence and who was aware of having made an existential choice. She addressed a member of an invisible community. The criterion of happiness that Vera spoke about is an objective criterion that is to be shared by this invisible community.

As you notice, an objective criterion also includes references to subjective experiences, at least in a negative sense. For a decent person who is simultaneously committed to a particular destiny, the most terrible experience imaginable is to stand before the choice between decency on the one hand, and the commitment made under the category of difference (for example to become a philosopher in Lawrence's case) on the other hand. A person is happy – or, if you speak of the criterion only in its objective sense, lucky – if he never stands on this crossroad, if life (luck? grace?) spares him the most devastating experience which, had he gone through it, would have accompanied him from then on as a dark shadow until death. Even the grace of beauty fades in such a trial. A person who goes through such a trial cannot remain (even if she once was) a beautiful (happy) character. Although he can remain (or become) a sublime character.

Let me return to the different kinds of happiness. Vera's story of happiness is objective, although it has a subjective aspect (the absence of a terrible experience). This is why she can say that no one is really happy before death. One can find many other, and broader, or more positive, objective criteria of happiness. In the pre-modern world all men and women accepted objective criteria of happiness, but nowadays merely objective criteria shape the perception of the other-directed, the one-dimensional men alone. Professor Horius discussed them briefly. To have money, to live in a big house, to marry a wealthy man, to have an envied and lucrative job – all those instances are objective criteria of happiness. But you understand that I do not find it worthwhile to explore their path.

You know how I think: beautiful individuals, harmonious people are happy. I wrote about this to Professor Horius, telling him that he neglected this objective type. It is an objective description, I continued, for I can describe to you (Professor Horius) objectively which kind of person is harmonious and which is not; and impartial observers of beautiful characters will in all probability agree with me and understand me. Professor Horius answered shortly. He appreciated my point but he also said that I had not employed the term 'objective' properly. For I created, in his mind, a seemingly objective criterion from a common (or seemingly common) subjective experience. The harmony I spoke of, the free play of imagination, is a subjective experience of the observer, whereas happiness is the subjective experience of the actor. The harmony between the two experiences is contingent, or if it is 'pre-established' we cannot know it. For empirically, he added, characters who do feel unhappy can appear beautiful to the observer. Professor Horius added that I could make a good case only if I referred to the transcendent sources of grace.

I am not a philosopher and I have no arguments to offer, but I still think that Professor. Horius is wrong. For if I can immagine the community of existential thinkers I can also imagine the community (invisible community) of those who judge characters (also) aesthetically, and who agree that a 'beautiful character' is a decent person who constantly develops a variety of her freedoms musically-harmoniously and who thus has a happy constitution. For the members of this (invisible) community, love of beauty gives momentary happiness (and this is the promise of happiness). It is this (invisible) community that bridges the paradox: our love makes the beautiful beautiful – it is beauty whom we love – the prestablished harmony.

Tragic fate (the sight of the sublime character) also elevates us. When tragic fate shakes you, particularly the tragic fate of a living person and not of a fictitious being, you are shaken from head to toe, but one cannot say that you are pleased or that you enjoy what you see, even less that you become happy through this experience. Literature, fiction in general, is entirely different. I have no time to write about it, although I confess something. When I was a child my father used to take me to the theatre, and particularly to the opera; he was a great lover of opera. After seeing a play that ended in tragedy, blood and death, I returned home in the best of moods, very cheerfully, whereas comedy made me sad, so much so that I was close to tears. Why this happened to me I never understood, and still don't, since when it came to the tragic fate of a living being, I never felt glee. Generally, we feel it wrong to be happy on the occasion of a real life catastrophe, and this is why we do not feel happy. Fiction liberates us from ethical responsibility, so we can feel glee without guilt, but this does not yet explain why we actually feel it. Is this topsy-turvy experience perhaps a kind of counter-balance to the external impulse, a life instinct to restore our emotional health? But perhaps my experience is entirely subjective and merely personally psychological. Please disregard it if so.

Am I on a side-track again? Love, of course – you asked me questions about love. There are as many kinds of love as experiences of happiness. Who has ever counted them? I love good books, music, my trees, my dogs and cats; I love the sunshine, and the snowfall; I love the breeze; I love walking; I love my house. I love good conversation. I love to have people around me; I love solitude; I love to drink a glass of wine; I love my old students; I love a few friends; I love you my dear as I love Johnny. As you know, I was eighty-five last week. And I still love my David who died fifty-five years ago at the age of thirty-two, and who left me three small children to love.

When I now speak of love I do not mean charity. Charity is a virtue; being charitable is a matter of goodness. The kind of love I speak about stands closer to happiness. It is a pleasent emotion. It enhances life, our feeling of life (*Lebensgefühl*). Perhaps Spinoza said something similar when he spoke about the soul's transition to a state of higher perfection. The kind of love I have in mind makes us strong and cheerful. Cheerfulness and strength belong together. If you wake up in the morning with love in your heart you begin your day in good spirits; it will be a good day, dense and fruitful.

Yes, there are also other kinds of love. I read in a book by an American (I do not remember his name) that there are two types of love: D-Love and B-love, the love of dependency (or deficiency?) and the love of (or for?) being. The kind of love I have in mind is the love of (for) a being: Being. I read in a book (by someone else) that love is an emotional disposition rather than an emotion. If one is in love, for example, one is disposed to be in different emotional states depending on the situation. For example, when his beloved does not requite his love, a man will be saddened; when his beloved is seriously ill he will be gripped by panic; when his beloved is successful, he will be glad; and so on. I think that this is a good description of the dynamics of many kinds of love. For example, I love trees, so when I noticed that pollution destroyed one of my favourite pines, it saddened me. In this sense, almost all kinds of love (although not all of them) can be described as emotional dispositions. The difference between D-love and B-love is, perhaps, that they are different dispositions; to refer to them with the same word ('love') is just one sign of the poverty of our vocabulary.

Now I remember that the psychologist who differentiated between the two types of love (his name began with an M) also made mention of a primary, all-encompassing disposition for all kinds of love-of-being: the capacity to be involved in the other for its Being, that is, for its being-what (how) it (he or she) is. I would say, to return to my hobby-horse, that this general disposition for loving all kinds of beings with B-love can also be termed the sense of beauty. It is Spinoza's shortcoming, as with all rationalists, that although he knows that love enhances strength and increases freedom, he forgets about beauty. In case of B-love the *relation* is beautiful. If you are predisposed to love everything that (whom) you love with B-love (love of their being), you and the things (people) you love will be kept in balance (or in harmony) in the relationship. I mean thereby that you do not feel yourself subjected to the beloved, you are not dependent on him, her or it, yet you are not in the position of domination either; you do not master them. The balance is the balance of symmetry. Love ranges from the simplest to the most sublime, and symmetry assumes different forms and modes in due course. But there is a grain of 'symmetry' in the most primitive kinds of love. For example, I love a fine glass of wine; the idea is not that I consume wine, that I swallow it, for this has nothing to do with loving wine. The idea of 'loving wine' entails that you taste it, that you distinguish between less and more 'beautiful' wines, moreover that you preserve the taste of the good wine in the memory of your palate. This kind of love is sensual, and in this sense erotic. All kinds of love are in one or the other sense erotic. D-love, the love springing from deficiency or dependency is not always erotic (I doubt whether it is erotic at all). Please don't misunderstand me: I have not forgotten my Plato, I know that Eros is the child of Penia as much as the child of Poros. But Love (as the love-of-being) is an emotional disposition, and the feelings of absence, of lack, are emotional occurrences of this disposition. There is no desire without absence or lack, and there is no love without desire. D-love is, in my mind, non-erotic, because dependency is fundamental to this emotional disposition, not just to its emotional occurrences; it is Penia without Poros.

Thus all kinds of B-love are erotic, and all kinds of B-love contain beauty. The symmetrical relationship is beautiful because there is a balance between the lover and the beloved. Sublime characters sometimes destroy that (whom) they love, but then they also destroy themselves. The relation that was once symmetrical ceases to be symmetrical and thereby beautiful, moreover, it ceases to be a relation, at least in a positive sense. But Lawrence may think otherwise . . .

I said that B-love (love of the being) is a beautiful disposition (relation), but it is also the love of beauty. The love of beauty in this sense is not the love of beautiful bodily forms. You may smile: now comes the lecture on the so-called spiritual love, the love for the beautiful soul, old stuff. But I will not have any part of it. Because this old stuff does not describe my experiences in matters of love. I believe that to make a strong distinction between the love of the body and that of the soul is a dubious metaphysical tradition, and that it is somehow connected to the old-fashioned theory of faculties. Since I do not believe in faculties, since I am talking about the balance between freedoms and not about the mastery of the emotions by reason or vice versa, I do not see any descriptive merit in the juxtaposition of love of body and love of soul. To see what I mean, one does not need to go as far as the love men and women have for one another. One can start with simple things. I do love my dog. My dog will not win a beauty contest, he will not even receive a modest prize. But I love my dog. My dog is beautiful. I love him to be as free as a dog can be; I try to give him very few commands, yet I do not subject myself to his whims either. I think that our relation is beautiful, it is as symmetrical as a woman–dog relation can be. I love the little wooden statue on my desk; I received it from you; do you remember? You brought it from Fiji. It is a lovely statue, it is beautiful. Tell me, is it the body or the soul of this little statue that I love? Have I compared this statue with others to find out whether it is more or less beautiful than they are? This does not make sense at all, and you know it. You love Judit, although Judit, just like my dog, will not win a beauty contest. (Excuse my bad taste, this was not meant as a comparison!) Do you love her because of something? Because of her body, her spirit, her soul? I remember when you last came home, and you noticed Judit approaching from afar, her figure was almost indistinguishable, but you recognized her. How you ran towards her with open arms! You certainly love her colouring, her gait, her mannerisms, her voice, just like her common goodness, her humour and much else. You simply love her. And this is it. But this is not all that I wanted to say. Do you love beauty in loving Judit? Your love to her is a beautiful love; it is also the love of beauty.

This is why I appreciate what Kierkegaard (or his character, Judge William) wrote about marital love; and I also appreciate that a young man like Lawrence can appreciate it. Love for another human being is the essential aesthetic aspect of the ethical. Surely this is true only about B-love (the love for being), but then D-love (deficiency love) is neither aesthetic nor ethical; it is psychological. D-love can enhance hatred, weaken the character, and it is always morally suspect. Moral aesthetics embraces B-love, because B-love is both beautiful and ethical. D-love is neither, although, I admit, it can be intense. Intense, but not tragic. Tragic love is B-love, a kind of B-love that is destroyed by fate or destiny. The love of the sublime character is also B-love, though it is (or may be) sometimes destructive and self-destructive like Hamlet's love. I would like to follow this path, but unfortunately it would lead me, again, too far.

All my self-discipline has not been of great help so far. I wanted to speak about happiness, with reference to my old friend Professor Horius's paper. But perhaps Professor Horius can also be a little helpful in our discussion on love, although, as I said, he is a dry person and his writings reveal his dryness only too obviously. Still, he is a man capable of emotions. His emotions are not deep, but he is faithful. He is a very faithful friend. I think he is a beautiful character after all.

So can we distinguish between three different philosophical conceptions of love as he distinguished (in his Vienna lectures) between three different conceptions of happiness? One can say, first: love is entirely subjective. One person loves this, the other that. One cannot argue about love. I cannot tell you that you love the wrong tree or the wrong person, that you vest your feelings into the wrong object, that you love something or someone that (who) is unlovable and hateful. Love is then described as a merely personal (non-social) need, moreover as an unrationalizable need.

There are no true and false needs, and it is arbitrary to distinguish beween real and unreal needs. For if someone says 'I need this', another cannot retort, 'No, you don't really need it, I know better', for this would be ridiculous. The person needs what he needs. In this sense, all needs should be recognized as real and as true. Subjective love (need) is true if it is truely subjective. But certainly, the recognition of a need does not necessarily call for its satisfaction. One can answer a person who declares his needs, 'I recognize your need, it is real, but I cannot satisfy it: I do not want to, since my needs are different', or you can give other reasons. Among the other reasons, however, you can also include the criticism of the need that calls for satisfaction. The child says, 'I need a bar of chocolate', the parent answers, 'You cannot have one, because I have no money', or 'because you will upset your stomach'. In the first case I have no satisfier, in the second case I criticize the need itself.

When you speak about love in subjective terms alone, you will say that every love is real if it is felt, or true if it is truly felt. But you can answer to a claim of love or to a declaration of love in the same way as you answer to a declaration of need in general: 'I cannot satisfy you, for I do not love you', or, 'The man whom you love is a well-known scoundrel. Please, listen to the opinion of other people for a moment; this love will destoy you.'

One can also have an objective conception of love. One can then say that to love someone means to satisfy some objective criteria of love. For example a father loves his child if he plays with the child, hugs him, teaches him, listens to his wishes, sends him to good schools, give him money to spend, etc. If he does not do most of these things or none of them, one can justly say that he does not really love his child; he only says that he loves him (he loves him merely subjectively).

Normally, of course, one ends up with a third position, a mixture of some subjective and some objective criteria.

I don't know whether I mentioned to you that Professor Horius paid me a visit last week. After a long walk in the woods we sat down for coffee, and had a good conversation. I told him the same thing I have just mentioned you, namely that only B-love can be, for D-love (dependency or deficiency love) must be merely subjective, since it is neither ethical nor aesthetic, but psychological. I told the story of a friend of my youth, a very sweet woman, who was beaten by her husband every day, yet she loved him (so she said) all the same. I tried to make her change her feelings by showing how undeserving her beloved was. This did not help. Then I tried to criticize her own love as blind and crazy. This did not help either. That D-love is immune against all criticism – so I concluded – shows how subjective this kind of love is. Professor Horius objected. He said that psychologists would explain to me that D-love is in fact objective and can easily be typified. They would enumerate the criteria, the symptoms, and also the possible motivations or causes of such a love. And then, Professor Horius added, 'Only B-love can really be subjective, because only a relatively free subject can develop subjective emotions, only this kind of subject has *Innerlichkeit*. (Professor Horius likes to insert German words into his narratives.) But apart from our controversy, we agreed that D-love cannot be beautiful, for unfreedom is a deformity of the character or the soul.

After the departure of my old friend I began to have second thoughts. Too many beautiful things had been said about B-love. As if instances of B-love – subjective and beautiful – could stand beyond, and in no need of, moral criticism! What if you love a person for-its-being-sake, without being dependent on him – if you simply let-him-be and surround him with a kind of *amor intellectualis*, and this person happens to be a scoundrel? What if the person whom you love for his own sake demands from you moral sacrifices, for example, that you lie or cheat for his sake? Of course you can answer, and you should answer if you are a decent person, 'This need of yours I cannot satisfy', but then he will tell you that you do not really love him for-his-own-sake and absolutely, because you prize your moral integrity more than, for example, his pride. And then you, perhaps, will not answer the way you should, but instead yield to his wishes with the final gesture of love. Being-in-love is madness, amatory madness as Plato said, and madness carries you towards extremes, be it love of the B-love kind or D-love.

True, high characters do not fall in love just with anyone who crosses their path. Although Titania was enamoured of an ass, this was fairly decent ass. This why her story was grotesque or comic, whereas falling in love with evil would not fit into a comic play. At any rate: fundamentally decent persons very rarely fall in love with an absolute scoundrel. But they frequently fall in love with people who have chosen themselves under the category of difference and since *amor fati* transcends ethical standards, the demand for moral sacrifice may arise. The decent-beautiful person can also fall in love with the sublime person, and as you might have had opportunity to observe, not only their psychologies, but also their moral standards are different from those of beautiful persons.

The many wonderful things I said of B-love remain true about all kinds of B-love – except amatory madness or infatuation. But then, most of the wonderful manifestations of love present themselves in the state of 'amatory madness' in a far more heightened way than in all other kinds of B-love. In a post-metaphysical world we cannot get things straight anymore. As you said, how wonderful it was to believe in the One Single Simple Beauty mirrored in both the beauty of our soul and the external beauty that our soul beholds – to be confident that similar recognizes similar, beauty recognizes beauty, spirit recognizes spirit in Eros *extaticos*!

Love is good if the beloved is worthy to be loved. Who is worthy to be loved? Who is worthy to be loved by a decent person? And by a beautiful-decent person? You can answer: everything is worthy to be loved, every living being is worthy to be loved, every human person is worthy to be loved. Or you can add the follow-up question (which you did);

what is worthy to be loved? Are abstractions (like beauty or freedom) worthy to be loved? What do we mean when we say that we love (or do not love) an abstraction? Loving an abstraction means to love various things, or states, or states of mind, or institutions, or persons, or else what or whom we associate – in our life (or life experience) with those abstractions. Love, as always, is an emotional disposition here – but it is not erotic. The erotic requires (or implies) sensual pleasure or the sublimation of sensual pleasure, enjoyment in a personal experience of a concrete thing, practice or event. My love of freedom is non-erotic, but my experience of yearning for liberation in servitude and my experience of the moment of liberation can be described also as love-of-freedom and as the fulfilment-of-that-love in erotic terms, even if we rarely describe them in erotic terms.

But I want to speak instead of the love for single beings and persons. Within this circle everything and everyone is worthy of love – but worthy of love in the sense of benevolence or charity; these are virtues of Jewish-Christian origin. But love that includes an erotic element cannot be described, or not entirely described, as a 'virtue'. You may say that there is also an aspect of 'charity' in my love for my dog or my apple tree. This may be true, but charity is not the sole component here, not even the main one. My love for my dog and my apple tree has a sensual aspect: I enjoy their being, I love to look at them and to touch them. The sublimated kinds of love (be it the love of a single person, animal, thing or of the results of my activity) preserve the memory of the sensual. Sometimes language too preserves the connections, like the Greek word *theoria* was associated with seeing (sight) so is the German *Begriff* (concept) associated with grasping. We have a 'taste' for art and beauty.

The arts employ just sight and hearing as their media, but smell, touch and taste are inexhaustible resources for allegories and metaphors employed to describe sublimated erotic attraction. In Cusanus for example the fragrance of flowers serve as the allegory for the attraction of God. Love increases by touch and manifests itself in touch in the love of humans to humans; one touches animal-warmths in human warmth too; still, love is never entirely unsublimated; charity can also manifest itself in touch. It is a matter of course that the opposite of B-love, which is violence and not hatred, also manifests itself in touch (and in the sublimation of touch by verbal abuse and blackmail).

I have to stop writing about matters which are beyond our topic – and beyond my head. I wanted simply to find out whether the theory of my old friend Professor Horius about happines can be applied to love or not. I now think that love (like happiness) is neither merely subjective nor merely objective. If love were only subjective, we could not criticize anyone (or ourselves) in matters of love for moral reasons and for reasons of taste; but we do it, and it makes sense to do it, especially, although not exclusively, in the cases of D-love. If love were only objective we could give reasons why we love X and not Y – something we can never do (or which we can offer a number of heterogeneous reasons, which amounts to the same). All seeming explanations in matters of love are interpretations, and the interpretandum stands here higher than the interpreter (self-interpreter). We just love X because we love him and not someone else – period.

Thus love (like happiness) is both subjective and objective, that is to say, the emotional disposition manifests itself both in subjective and objective judgements. Both judgements manifest the same emotional disposition of the same person; they are the same judgement on the level of the emotional disposition, but they are separate judgements on the level of emotional occurrences. They are emotional judgements, non-rational judgements, but not irrational judgements. Is an emotional judgement of this kind a reflective judgement in Kant's sense? Yes and no. Yes, because it reflects upon the single (upon a 'this') and it does it without any concept. And no, because emotive and cognitive interpretations can also inhere in the judgement.

Can we say then that certain persons are worthy of being loved (having in mind erotic love, not charity) whereas certain others are not, or certain individuals are worthy of the love of X and certain other individuals are not? What makes a person worthy of love? And worthy of being loved by someone?

The lover does not ask this question, for if she asked it, she would no longer – or not yet – be a lover. Or: does a person really ask this question before he or she falls in love? There is nothing 'before' falling in love. As long as you ask the question, you are not in love; if you are in love you do not ask the question. My life experiences suggest something else and more: if you ask this particular question you will never fall in love. For falling in love is also a leap – a leap over an abyss. You can fall into the abyss, but if you ask this question you will never leap. Finally, I think that the question whether someone is worthy of my love is a question unworthy of a lover. But it is not unworthy of the spectator.

I am beginning to think that the love of the contingent individuum, the erotic love of the modern individuum, is entirely personality-dependent. It seems as if modern love could be described as the manifestation of the ethics of personality alone. Moreover, it seems as if love were the crowning achievement of this ethics. After all, in *Either-Or* Kierkegaard wrote about nothing but love, and Lawrence began his ruminations by following Nietzsche's *amor fati* . . . But, unfortunately, this is philosophy and philosophy is above my head.

My love, my dearest, your Granny

Fifi to her Grandmother

My dearest Granny,

Once again I showed your letter to Lawrence, and once again he expressed his disagreement, or rather his discontent. I will give a true report of his mild rhetorical outburst a little later. But this time I want to speak first, because I want to sum up your ideas as I understood them.

D-love is the love felt by the inauthentic person, of the person who has not chosen himself/herself at all. Surely, a person who has not chosen himself existentially is also capable of B-love, but his B-love will remain contingent just as his D-love is contingent. By 'contingency' I do not mean in this context that the lover cannot justify why he loves A rather than B, but I mean, rather, does his love (the object of his love) call for justification at all? Thus the problem here is not contingency but the incapacity to accept contingency as something final – as something that becomes destined through the relationship itself. An authentic person never asks the question 'Why did I fall in love with A rather than B?' because whether he fell in love with A or B he will never regret it, his love will be a part of his life. An inauthentic person's D-love (authentic persons do not love with D-love), the love of dependency and deficiency, always calls for explanation. Dependency is an alien power; it is external to the character; one has to explain why one succumbs to an alien power. The inauthentic person will then ask, 'Why did I fall in love with this person in particular? Why has this terrible experience, this addiction, befallen me, exactly?' And if the lover asks himself these questions, the observer surely asks similar ones and he will also provide the explanations. Your friend, Professor Horius will tell you that these explanations include so-called 'objective' descriptions. For example the psychologist will tell you that X has developed dependency love for Y because as a child he was unloved by his mother. True, no explanation is final – unless you are a vulgar analyst – but explanation follows upon explanation, for D-love is considered as something out of order, a kind of sickness, or mishap. This is interesting, for many instances of infatuation, or amatory madness, as you put it after Plato, are cases of D-love.

Men and women who love others for their being without being dependent on the beloved, and without seeking remedies for their deficiencies in being loved by them, are normally those men and women who have chosen themselves existentially (under the category of difference or universality, or both). Their love cannot be explained, for it has *no cause* at all. Of course, if someone seeks causes he can always find some, but no causes will explain authentic love. It holds true for B-love, and B-love alone, that love is open for interpretation but not for explanation, and that it is in no need for justification for it is self-justificatory. For the love of the decent person is inbuilt (it becomes inbuilt) in the 'projection' which this personality really is. Choosing oneself includes the choice of our loves too, and this is not a temporal occurrence; we choose in ourselves our past, present and future loves, all of them (if we have more than one love) we choose (to speak with Leibniz) with the complete idea of our individual substance. The individual substance as free substance permits, allows, furthers B-love in general, and all instances of B-love develop, or reveal, or enhance the substance itself.

But (and here comes the 'but') the story which you told – and I here repeat – is morally suspect. Since the story is about existential choice in general, it is also the story of men and women who choose themselves under the category of difference. The moral of this choice is simple: remain true to yourself, that is, to your choice of your self. If remaining true to one's choice requires the doing of evil, one does evil. And if it is required to love the evil, one will love the evil. You wrote in your letter and you convinced me that one does not choose oneself (existentially) as evil, but you have not denied (for you know better) that the love of evil can become embedded in the destiny of a person who has chosen himself under the category of difference. One can love evil for evil's sake, or not? Can one do evil for evil's sake and enjoy doing it, or not? This love (since it is B-love) does not call for explanation or justification. It cannot be explained or justified, unless – as naïve psychologists sometimes do – we treat them as if they were cases of D-love, cases of sickness and so on. You would say that if someone loves evil with B-love, he does not love the evil *because* he is evil; but if you say so, you begin doing something which you should not, namely to explain. True, people who choose themselves under the category of the universal are normally resistant in face of the attraction of the daemonic. But this is not the case with those who choose themselves under the category of difference; should I refer to Mann's Adrian Leverkühn, as an example? To sum it up: I think that you treat evil too lightheartedly, that you do not take the daemonic really seriously. Because evil can be beautiful, is this why?

Should I put your thesis in the following way: B-love does not call for justification, it cannot be explained; but it can be ethically criticized, that is, not the love itself, but the acts that follow from it, can be ethically criticized. An authentic person is (relatively) autonomous, he has the capacity to make promises, whether he chooses himself under the category of the universal or of difference; he is a subject responsible for his acts, for he is responsible for himself. In contrast, D-love calls for explanation. Certainly, D-love – as an emotional disposition – is as little open to criticism as B-love, but unlike B-love it can also be treated as a pathological phenomenon, therapeutically. Yet the person who loves with D-love is also open to ethical criticism. True, he is not a (relatively) autonomous subject for he lacks the capacity to make promises, and has – at least on this level – diminished responsibility, but he still remains responsible for not having chosen himself, responsible for not being (becoming) authentic. Would you agree? Entirely, partially, not at all?

You will understand why I tried to disentangle a few motives from your letter before giving you a brief report on what Lawrence said. This time he was not really angry; he looked rather sad as if he were grieving or as if he recalled the content of your letter with nostalgia and disbelief. 'I see', he said, 'that your granny was ready to make concessions by adding few realistic features to her dream-image. It was an honest gesture on her part to admit that every single occurrence of love is entirely unique and inexplicable. But then she stepped back immediately, so much so that she accepted Maslow's pedestrian distinction between B-love and D-love; from the infinite kinds of love she kept just two kinds. Just like Spinoza, who, having solemnly declared that God is endowed with infinite attributes, continues discussing only two, and in a way that no philosophical space even remains for a third one. For about the unique, about the infinite, you cannot say a thing, but about the 'two' you can speak at great length – and this is exactly what your grandmother did.

She believes that one cannot speak about anything at all without first making a distinction; thus she makes a distinction between D-love and B-love. But, as happens to almost all of us, she becomes the captive of her own distinction. She does not notice nuances. Instead of thinking in terms of infinite diversity, she continues to make further distinctions, making allowances for exceptions, for irregular cases and for admixtures. But in the case of love, distinction resembles the evil touch; it destroys beauty, including the beauty of the ugly. Better to speak about love without making any distinctions'.

'It is the greatest thing in great love', Lawrence continued, 'that it causes great suffering. As long as you suffer you are alive. Walter Benjamin once said wisely that love, suffering and death are the three eternal sources of meaning. Among them, I would add, suffering is the greatest. You suffer from death, from the death of your beloved ones and from the premonition of your own, as you also suffer from the death of gods, from the premonition of the death of your culture and of your world. But you suffer most from love. Oh, Nietzsche, Nietzsche, how much wiser were you than Solon – so close but also so remote!

You are close, my brother – your eyes are full of tears, yet your vision is not blurred. You understood how to make yourself unhappy and how to live with your dissonances towards madness and death – bravely. I do not mind how many cruel and dangerous things you hold us, for the logic of your heart means more to me than the logic of your reason. Fifi's grandmother knows little of the logic of the heart, for she does not even see the difference between reason's and heart's logic. It is here, only here, that she fails to make a distinction: She is a woman. It is beautiful to be a woman, to be unable (or unwilling?) to make this sole, this necessary, distinction. Perhaps this absence is the source of the beauty of their characters.

My brother Kierkegaard, my brother Nietzsche, so close but so remote! The death of your culture that you have anticipated is now accomplished. The vocabulary of emotional expression has shrunk to the bare minimum of 'I love you', 'I love you too', the vobaculary of erotic experience has fared even worse; it shrank below the bare minimum to a sheer 'I come' and 'O yes'. No one understands you any more.

Fifi's grandmother knows as much about our times as I do. Why would she otherwise pick up the master words from the vocabulary of the once 'new', and now defunct, left, such as 'other-directed' or 'one-dimensional' man? But if she knows why does she still continue to design her images of the beautiful character, harmonious, happy and free? She sees what she sees but she refuses to take notice. Grudgingly, she admits the sublime character to her paradise. But what does she know about the sublime character? She admits that no character – not even the beautiful – is entirely transparent, not even to the lover – but this is a weak admission. Sublime individuals are secrets, not just for others but for themselves too. A secret cannot be known, but it needs to be respected. Fifi, your grandmother does not feel any respect for the secret of the sublime character. She has empathy for suffering but no respect. She is anxious about the daemonic but does not pay respect to it. She has respect for Eros but she refuses to respect Thanatos. Yet Eros without Thanatos is banal.

You see now, Fifi, that I cannot say anything about your granny's letter. We are different. There is no mediation. I think that we have to give up on each other.'

Dear Granny, this is what he said: 'There is no mediation'. Should I understand this sentence as a gesture – the gesture of rejection? Or does the sentence mean that Eros cannot employ Hermes in his service? That love has to resign the hope of interpretation altogether? Or perhaps Lawrence has only meant that the love of the sublime person is beyond understanding and interpretability? Or did he mean that the interpretation of love is unethical? Or that the interpretation of the love of a sublime person is unethical? But surely, one cannot resign the attempt to interpret (to try to understand) the emotional world of a sublime person, his relations to others, whether beloved or not beloved? And surely we cannot resign the hope (the faint hope) of understanding a person whom we love? Can we resign redemption? I have not forgotten your warning: I know that I cannot will to save him for if I did I would lose myself; still, can we resign redemption?

It was an answer to this question that I tried to convey you at the beginning of this letter. I said that B-love cannot be explained and that it does not call for justification. And I also said that a person who has chosen himself existentially, loves with B-love alone. But perhaps Lawrence is right, and we do not need to make this distinction at all. Or we need to make it as spectators but not as lovers. Or perhaps some lovers need to make it too, but not us – not Fifi and Lawrence, for it is impossible for us to make it. How can I distinguish between the unquenchable thirst for him – call it deficiency or dependency – and the reflectively passionate adoration, the wonderous respect that fills me as I turn towards him to enjoy his being, his ipseity? Poros and Penia are not just the parents of love; they are love, they are interlocked in one single emotion (or emotional disposition as you termed it). And this is why one suffers from love. Why have we forgotten something that we once all knew? Why do we philosophize? Just to turn our faces away from our fellow creatures and ponder their shadows on the empty sky?

Granny, I give up on understanding Lawrence. It does not matter to me whether he loves with D-love or B-love; what matters is whether he loves me at all. Interpretation is the game of curiosity, a touch that arrives at the wrong place in the wrong time, for there is never a right place and a right time. Granny, I love him. But I am also afraid of him. How can one live with someone who rejects the thing he calls 'mediation'? I desire a common life with a man who makes himself as transparent to me as he is to himself, a man who expects reciprocity. What should I do? What is the right thing for me to do? For I desire to embrace him – but what then?

Fifi

Mrs Sophie Meller to her Granddaughter, Fifi

My dearest,

Here, we arrive at the crossroads. I predict that this time you will not show my letter to Lawrence. So much for your rejection of secrecy.

Is Lawrence your man or is he not – this is the question; that you love and desire him is not the question. Still, your alternatives are not ethical. I cannot give you any real advice. You may say that your happiness is at stake. But the consequences of such a choice cannot be forseen, although some consequences can be guessed far ahead: for example, whether you would suffer much or little in a relationship.

Lawrence was right, I do not respect suffering as such, for I rather respect an ethical sense of gaiety and I do not think that suffering is a 'deeper' feeling than gaiety. Yet even if I had some reliable premonitions about the kind of suffering you would undergo, this still would not offer ethical reasons for me to give you any advice. But . . . my love for you makes me cross the limits that I would never cross otherwise – I will describe my premonitions, frankly.

A beautiful character and a sublime character are ill-suited to one another. Both psychologically and ethically ill-suited. He is not made for gaiety, you are not made for melancholy; he loves to go to extremes, you love measure and harmony. He loves outbursts, you love tensions re-solved. I could go on. One thing is certain: whether Lawrence accepts you or not, your choice will cause you much suffering, although I cannot foresee whether you will suffer more intensely if your love is rejected or if it is accepted. And you must know in advance what I know from lifelong experience (perhaps I have said it already?) that beautiful characters, like you my dear, do not suffer less, or less deeply or intensely than sublime characters do. The difference is, that contrary to sublime characters, they keep themselves open to the experience of joy, that they are more happy than the rest even while suffering. 'More' is the wrong expression here, because it suggests that there is something to quantify. But a beautiful person's sense of joy and happiness, for merriment and enjoyment is different from the similar experiences of other kinds of men and women, because it flows from her character, it inheres in her *amor fati*.

You are not afraid of suffering – why should you be? But if you want to have a common life, as you wrote, you had better stay away from Lawrence. You want to understand him, but he does not tolerate inter-ferences into his secret chambers. Like Bartok's Bluebeard he is jealous of his castle; and this is what I call psychological incompatibility.

But Lawrence is right: I cannot really distuinguish between the logic of reason and the logic of the heart. I admit that if you follow the logic of your heart, this will be also the logic of your reason.

I am now close to taking back my advice. (For I advised you despite my reluctance to do so!) I realize only now how little I know about Lawrence. I know only that he exaggerates. He always exaggerates. He also exaggerates in things which have nothing to do with his 'secrets'. Just recall what he said about the world. He is right that not only Schubert and Goethe, but also Kierkegaard and Nietzsche, belong to a bygone world. But the famous 'tower' of Goethe is still open to us; there are niches in this world where we can still live a good life. It is not necessary to live in necessity; should I tell Lawrence this? Emotional impoverishment, banausic gestures, *ressentiment* are the order of the day; but we are at liberty to stay in a circle of friends, and have a rich life, rich in emotions, taste and experience. A noble and beautiful life. Not a harmonious life, if we invite our sublime friends into our esoteric circle . . . but we shall still invite them my dear!

After all, melancholic characters are the tragic characters of a non-tragic age; their interior fuel, passion or pathos that cannot carry them towards violent deeds, will at least get some sympathetic appreciation from friends who have preserved their sense of grandeur in a world without grandeur. I see now, once again, how good a judge of character your Lawrence is: although I do not respect suffering, my empathy still goes out to the sublime sufferers. They lost more than we did. They deserve that we lend them a hand. Am I again, as you said, chasing shadows on an empty sky?

My dear, whether you declare your love to Lawrence or do not declare your love to him, you will regret neither.

You decide. I am with you, my dearest, whatever you do.

Granny

Fifi to her Grandmother

Dearest Granny,

Despite your expectations I did show your letter to Lawrence. I understood that you put me on trial – or was it a trial only because I understood it to be so? I subjected myself to the trial voluntarily, bravely, didn't I?

Lawrence read the letter to the very end, slowly, waited a moment and then said, 'Our professor has written four volumes on ethics and on the philosophy of morals. But you see Fifi, one cannot say anything about morality, anything beyond empty generalities, that could give even an approximate account of one single decent gesture of one single decent person. The love of wisdom, of goodness and of beauty is as unique and as inimitable as the love of a friend or of a woman. Do we understand the beloved? Will the beloved understand? In the end you will say the same as you have said in the beginning: the source of morality is transcendent; one cannot explain it and one cannot explain it away. One labours to understand morality with love; Love's Labour's Lost. Still there are good men and women who do not labour, and here we go again: Love's Labour's Lost.'

And then I said, 'I could love you.' You might ask why I didn't say simply, 'I love you.' Not just because Lawrence exemplified exactly the statement 'the bare minimum of emotional expression' typical of the emotional impoverishment of our days, for after all, the meaning of a sentence is carried by the speaker at least as much as by the sentence itself. I chose to say, 'I could love you' because it means something else, perhaps something more, than the simple 'I love you.' It means, 'I promise you to love you well.' You will smile and say that this is a fragile promise, because it says something about a future that depends on another person's acts, moreover, on another person's expectations. But my promise has nothing to do with the future tense, for it is not meant as a temporal, but as an eternal promise. Once loving – always loving. I learned this from you Granny, and I kept it in my remembrance.

And Lawrence answered, 'Let us pay a visit to your granny together.' That is: he has not answered, or has he?

So we shall arrive next Wednesday on the 6.20 train from Budapest. Only fifty-five hours left.

I even count the minutes, as I once did before Christmas. What present I will receive after these fifty-five hours have elapsed, I do not know, but it will be beautiful beyond imagination.

Yours, happy as always, Fifi

Postscript: Lawrence said, 'Love's Labour's Lost.' But how can you know that love's labour is lost before you try hard to perform love's labour? 'Love's Labour's Lost', said Lawrence, as if he were summing up the results of an ethics of personality.

There are philosophers – maybe, for I am not sure – who can immediately jump into an ethics of personality without performing love's patient and sometimes boring labour on a general ethics and on a philosophy of morals first. But the person who chooses herself existentially as good and brave needs a crutch first, and only after a shorter or longer use of the crutch can she throw her crutch away. Some will never throw their crutches away. All these crutches are carved with love's labour.

Yesterday evening I went, as always, to my Shakespeare class. My head was spinning: Lawrence's sentence 'Love's Labour's Lost' has fully occupied my mind, because of Lawrence and because of Shakespeare. I felt the urge to talk to someone about it. After class, I was walked home by my classmate Youri, a good listener and a good friend. I told him everything that I told you, except the personal angle. He agreed with me in matters of ethics of personality, moral philosophy and general ethics, and advised me to re-read the last sentences of Wittgenstein's *Tractatus Logico-Philosophicus*. At home I picked up the book from the shelf, and there I found something that I wanted to say, in a concise and beautiful formulation. I don't think that you own Wittgenstein's *Tractatus*, so I quote it:

'Meine Sätze erlautern dadurch, dass sie der, welcher mich versteht, am Ende als unsinnig erkennt, wenn er durch sie – auf ihnen-über sie hinausgestiegen ist. (Er muss sozusagen die Leiter wegwerfen, nachdem er auf ihr aufgestiegen is.) Er muss diese Sätze überwinden, dann sieht er die Welt richtig. Wovon man nicht sprechen kann, darüber muss man schweigen.'[185]

The ladder metaphor reminds me of Johannes Climacus. The crutch metaphor is less ambitious; this is why I like it better. Throwing a crutch away is not such a final gesture as throwing the ladder away. One can still pick up this crutch or another one, but if a ladder is thrown away, one is entirely enveloped in one's silence. I want to stay in the company of my fellows, of Youri, of Joachim, Vera, Judit – in the company of Lawrence, and of you, my dear Granny. Is love's labour ever lost?

Forever yours – and no more postscripts,

see you on Wednesday, Fifi

Notes

These lectures are based on my course on Nietzsche's ethics in the spring semester 1993. The course, delivered in fourteen lectures, covered a much broader field.

1 Nietzsche, vol. 6, *Ecce Homo*. All Nietzsche quotations are given in German (with the exception of *On the Genealogy of Morals*) from Friedrich Nietzsche, *Sämtliche Werke: Kritische Studienausgabe*, in 15 vols de Gruyter, 1967–77, Duenndruckausgabe, 1980, Munich, Berlin, New York. True to the critical edition, I keep Nietzsche's orthography.

2 I have described the three possible approaches to ethics in the Introduction to my *General Ethics*. I analyse the existential choice in *Philosophy of Morals*. Both are published by Blackwell Publishers, Oxford, in 1988 and 1990 respectively.

3 Sören Kierkegaard, *Either-Or*, Princeton University Press, Guildford, NJ, 1987.

4 Nietzsche, vol. 6, *Ecce Homo*, Foreword, I.

5 I described the possibility of a dual existential choice in the first chapter of my *Philosophy of Morals*. Since I am dealing here with the ideal type of an ethics of personality alone, I ignore this possibility.

6 Nietzsche, vol. 6, *Ecce Homo*; *Also sprach Zarathustra*, par. 3.

7 Nietzsche uses this expression frequently, for example in vol. 5, *On the Genealogy of Morals*, essay two.

8 Shaw's interest in the portrayal of an ethics of personality will be discussed later.

9 As we shall see later, the two major 'seducers', Socrates and Wagner, will sometimes be almost identified.

10 Lukács, Gyorgy Naplo-Tagebuch (1910–11), Lukács diary, Akademiai Kiado, Budapest, 1981.

11 Hannah Arendt liked this Goethian aphorism; she was also inclined to accept an ethics of personality rather than any other kind.

12 In Franz Rosenzweig, *The Star of Redemption*, Routledge and Kegan Paul, London, 1971.

13 Nietzsche said very different things about Dionysus. His Dionysus in *The Birth of the Tragedy* is a different one than the Dionysus of the Dionysus dithyrambs or Dionysus-the-philosopher, who figures in several later writings. Yet Goethe is certainly one of the models.

14 He told me that the notes for this book had been confiscated by the GPU (State Political Administration, the former name of the Soviet secret police) on the occasion of his arrest.

15 Needless to say, no absurdity remains unsaid for long.

16 Marx refers to the break between the 'philosophy hitherto' and philosophy of praxis (that changes the world) in his 11th thesis on Feuerbach. Nietzsche refers to Dionysus, the philosopher, and to his radical atheism and anti-Christianity (and immoralism) as frequently as to the new enlightenment.

17 See for detailed discussion A. Heller, 'The place of ethics in Marxism' in F. Fehér and A. Heller, *Grandeur and Twilight of Radical Universalism*, Transaction, New Brunswick, NJ and London, 1991.

18 In almost all his studies of 1918–19, but particularly in 'Bolshevism as a moral problem' and 'Tactics and ethics'.

19 Nietzsche, vol. 6, *Ecce Homo*. His life consists of his works.

20 Nietzsche writes 'Sie [the experimental philosophy] will vielmehr bis zum Umgekehrten hindurch-bis zu einem dionysischen Jasagen zur Welt, wie sie ist, ohne Abzug, Ausnahme und Auswahl – sie will den ewigen Kreislauf – dieselben Dinge, dieselbe Logik und Unlogik der Knoten. Hoechster Zustand, den ein Philosoph erreichen kann; dionysisch zum Dasein stehn; meine Formel dafuer ist amor fati . . .' '[The experimental philosophy] will, rather, arrive at the opposite – at the Dionysian 'saying yes' to the world as it is, without subtraction, exception or selection – it wills the eternal circling – the same things, the same logic and illogic of the knots. The highest state a philosopher can reach; standing for Being in a Dionysian way; my formula for this is *amor fati* . . .'), spring-summer 1888, 16 (Note 32), in Nietzsche, vol. 13, Nachgelassene Fragmente.

21 Nietzsche generally uses the term *'Wahrhaftigkeit'* (truthfulness) and *'wahrhaftig'* (truthful).

22 For example, vol. 13, Nachgelassene Fragmente, 11 (Note 149), 11 (Note 332), 13 (Note 3), 14 (Note 9).

23 Nietzsche, vol. 1, 'Die Philosophie im tragischen Zeitalter der Griechen'.

24 Nietzsche preferred Diogenes Laertius.

25 This is why (in essay three of *Genealogy*,) Nietzsche's first answer to the question 'What is the meaning of the ascetic ideals to the artist?' is a blunt 'Nothing'. We do not know Homer, but one thing we can know: he was unlike Achilles or Odysseus.

26 Nietzsche, vol. 6, *Der Fall Wagner*, par. 7.

27 Generally, Nietzsche refers to himself (and in *Beyond Good and Evil* to the 'free spirits' also) as an 'immoralist', as the shorthand version of 'immoralist moralist'.

28 Several prominent figures in contemporary academic Nietzsche research tried to 'elevate' Nietzsche to the rank of academic philosophy. E.g. Deleuze frequently emphasizes that certain statements of Nietzsche are only seemingly inconsistent, verily everything 'Clicks': Nietzsche is

consistent. Yet if Nietzsche is consistent, his consistency is of another kind than the consistency of system-building philosophers. On his part, he defied the traditional criteria of consistency, and did his best to avoid it. Nietzsche's consistency lies in his personality, in his 'perspective', or rather in the synthesis of his many perspectives. This accounts for the unsystematic character of his works and also for many of his logical inconsistencies.

29 I could never discover the reasons for his preferences. It must have been just a matter of taste.

30 Nietzsche holds Saint Paul responsible for the moral degeneration of European culture. Paul invented all the hypocritical features of Christianity. Sometimes Nietzsche places Augustine beside Paul.

31 Whenever he praises Machiavell Nietzsche always has the author of *Il Principe* in mind, and never the author of *Discorsi*. The way Machiavell ponders over the interrelationship between Virtus and Fortuna particularly appealed to Nietzsche.

32 This attitude is termed (also by Nietzsche) heroic pessimism.

33 See particularily in Book Five of *Die Froehliche Wissenschaft* and in two representative passages of *Also sprach Zarathustra*, Nietzsche, vols 3 and 4 respectively.

34 This is a reference to Heidegger's famous essay in *Holzwege*: 'Nietzsche's word, "God is dead" '. Heine spoke frequently about the dying or the death of the Jewish-Christian God. In his brilliant book, favoured by Nietzsche, *Religion and Philosophy in Germany*, Heine credits Kant with having killed deism.

35 Nietzsche's main argument against utilitarianism can be summed up as follows: when they reduce everything to the utility of a thing, they identify the genesis, meaning, function and telos of this thing (phenomenon). Paul Rée's 'genealogy' is also criticized by Nietzsche in this spirit. His is a vulgar procedure, for it fails to grasp the shifts and the reversals of meanings, overdeterminations, and the whole complexity of spiritual life. That, in spite of his protest against crude reductionism, Nietzsche himself will be guilty of a more complex kind of reductionism, in reducing every striving to our affects, and finally, to the will to power, cannot be discussed within this framework. Actually, no radical philosopher of the nineteenth century, with the possible exception of Kierkegaard, could entirely avoid the pitfalls of reductionism. The concept (not the expression) of disenchantment of the world stems from Nietzsche.

LECTURE TWO

36 I do not have in mind the Kierkegaardian absolute paradox here (the Eternal Truth enters historically) but the paradoxicality of his concept of truth (Truth is subjectivity) together with its ramifications. Since the Christian leap of faith is not the sole existential leap, Nietzsche could have presented his paradox as such without resigning his anti-Christian philosophical passion.

37 So Nietzsche's remark in *Ecce Homo*, that he has not spoken about Wagner at all, but only about himself, is an extreme exaggeration.

38   See, e.g., Bartok's *Cantata Profana*. In general, Nietzsche rejects what he
      calls artistic decadence from the perspective of a more streamlined version
      of modernism, that has not yet made its appearance in his time. In aesthet-
      ics, Nietzsche's prophecies are good predictions. True, Van Gogh and
      Cézanne were Nietzsche's contemporaries, and, in principle, Nietzsche
      could have known Cézanne, but he did not know him. The two artistic
      genres (literature and music) that stood at the centrepoint of Nietzsche's
      aesthetic interest, developed avant-garde modernist tendencies far later
      than did the fine arts, particularily the pioneering painting.
39   *Ecce Homo* (*Menschliches*, par. 3), Nietzsche, vol. 6.
40   Ibid., par. 4.
41   Ibid., par. 5.
42   Thomas Mann, in his novel *Doctor Faustus*, uses this motive, yet attributes
      the (in)famous signature to Adrian Leverkuehn, who was modelled mainly
      on Nietzsche (and not Wagner).
43   Nietzsche refers here to the final sentences of the Introduction to *Ecce
      Homo*, Nietzsche, vol. 6.
44   Ibid., and *Also sprach Zarathustra*, par. 1.
45   Ibid.
46   Here, I use the term 'symbol' in Nietzsche's sense, namely as 'representative
      manifestation', not in the sense of a semblance or resemblance, or as a
      quasi-metaphor.
47   Nietzsche, vol. 12, *Nachgelassene Fragmente*, summer 1886–autumn
      1887, 5(Note 40).
48   Ibid., 5(Note 41)
49   The already-mentioned work by Deleuze is full of such attempts. In
      addition, he comes up with the (in my mind entirely absurd) idea, that
      On the Geneology of Morals should be read as the refutation of
      Kant's dialectic in *Critique of Pure Reason*. Nietzsche, in all probability,
      never even read Kant in the original (he normally refers to neo-Kantian
      versions and interpretations), and whenever he abuses dialectics, which
      he frequently does, he has the dialectics of Socrates/Plato mainly in
      mind.
50   Whether Nietzsche had syphilis or not, no one knows. But what one can
      know is that he manœuvred himself into a philosophical situation (and
      philosophy was his entire life) where madness was the only escape left. Just
      as Kierkegaard, after his attacks on Christendom, had no other choice left
      for himself than crossing the line between Christianity and atheism, or die,
      instead collapsed and died.
      One could object to my interpretation that even at the end of his
      reinterpretation of *Genealogy* (where he calls it the most uncanny work he
      has ever written) Nietzsche returns to the position according to which
      Zarathustra is the counter-ideal to Parsifal. There are always moves in both
      directions. But there is no hope (creed) that would guarantee certainty in
      Nietzsche's mind.
51   *Beyond Good and Evil*, par. 47 and par. 240, Nietzsche, vol. 5.
52   *Der Fall Wagner*, Postscript, Nietzsche, vol. 6.
53   This also happened in *Beyond Good and Evil*, where Nietzsche identified
      Wagner with Kundry, as though Kundry was a man, not a woman.

54 Ibid., Epilogue.
55 *Götzendämmerung*, Preface, Nietzsche, vol. 6.
56 *Ecce Homo*: 'Unglaublich! Wagner is fromm geworden', *Menschliches, Allzumenschliches*, par. 5, Nietzsche, vol. 6.
57 *Der Antichrist*, par. 32, Nietzsche, vol. 6.
58 This is not the right occasion to speak about Nietzsche's ambivalent relation to Dostoevsky. Among others, Nietzsche paid attention to the Mishkin figure in his *The Idiot*: 'Ich kenne nur einen Psychologen, der in der Welt gelebt hat, wo das Christentum möglich ist, wo ein Christus jeden Augenblick entstehen kann... Das ist Dostoewsky. Er hat Christus errathen: – und instinktiv ist er vor allem behütet geblieben diesen Typus sich mit der Vulgarität Renans vorzustellen... Und in Paris glaubt man, dass Renan an zu vielen finesses leidet!... Aber kann man ärger fehlgreifen, als wenn man aus Christus, der ein Idiot war, ein Genie macht?' (vol. 13, Nachgelassene Fragmente, spring 1888, 15(9)) ('I know of only a single psychologist who lived in a world where Christianity was possible, where a Christ could emerge at any minute. He is Dostoevsky. He found out Christ, and he was protected from understanding this type by the vulgarity of a Renan. And they believe in Paris that Renan suffers from too much finesse! But can one make a greater blunder than that of making a genius of Christ, who was a fool?'). Sometimes Nietzsche simply refers to Christ, as the 'Idiot'. Obviously, he connected the Dostoevsky portrayal of Mishkin with Wagner's Parsifal as the *reine Thor*. We should speak rather of an association than of a comparison. The comparison in any event would have been insupportable, given that Parsifal is not a good man as long as he remains a fool. Moreover, he will not be a 'good man', but a Redeemer, through empathy-given knowledge; whereas Mishkin is and remains a fool precisely as the prototype of the 'good man'.
59 *On the Genealogy of Morals*, essay three, Nietzsche, vol. 6.
60 T. W. Adorno and M. Horkheimer, *Dialectic of Enlightenment*.
61 See Frederick Love, *Young Nietzsche and the Wagnerian Experience*, University of North Carolina Press, Chapel Hill, NC, 1963.
62 Oedipus in *Oedipus at Colonus* must have been too Christian for Nietzsche; he disregarded the last drama of Sophocles completely.
63 Nietzsche writes, 'Pilatus die einzige honnete Person, sein dedain vor diesem Juden-Geschwaetz von "Wahrheit", als ob solch Volk mitreden durfte, wenn es sich um Wahrheit handelt' Nietzsche, vol. 12, Nachgelassene Fragmente, autumn 1887, 9(88) (63). Nietzsche expresses himself in a similar vein in *Antichrist*, par. 46, Nietzsche, vol. 6.
64 *Ecce Homo: Der Fall Wagner*, par. 1, Nietzsche, vol. 6.
65 *Nietzsche contra Wagner*, foreword, Nietzsche, vol. 6.
66 *Nietzsche contra Wagner*: 'Wie ich von Wagner loskam', par. 1, Nietzsche, vol. 6.
67 It is difficult to explain why Nietzsche exempted Maupassant from the guilt of being a decadent Frenchman.
68 Nietzsche seems to prefer the original ending: the glorious Siegfried and Brünhilde singing the hymn of free love. Thank God, Wagner – like Nietzsche – had his own love of fate – and could not bring himself to destroy one of his works for the sake of ideology.

69 Pessimism is also a branch or kind of nihilism, particularily of 'passive' nihilism. There is also another type of pessimism: tragic, or heroic. Heroic pessimism is related to total nihilism that is due to result in the overcoming of nihilism (possibly in the future). Nietzsche sometimes describes himself in terms of heroic pessimism and total nihilism. He also says that he is a decadent, yet *also the opposite of a decadent*. As a historicist, Nietzsche inserted himself into his nineteenth-century world, but as a person who viewed this world from a unique perspective, who practised (in his life and philosophy) a new kind of ethics, and (in so far as it was possible) became 'untimely', he run ahead of his time. Nietzsche's most radical opponents share much with him. Wagner as decadent, nihilist and pessimist of an elegant kind (a genius) should be attacked, but the insignificant little workers, the *Herdentiere*, need only to be mentioned in a group and not attacked in person. There are, of course, exceptions even here; a for example, Nietzsche viciously attacked Dühring, who was indeed a *Herdentier* and an insignificant (although rancorous) person.

70 Letter of 1868 (letter 591), in Nietzsche, *Sämtliche Briefe*, 2 vols, Gruyter Verlag Munich, 1980.

71 Nietzsche, vol. 12, autumn 1887, 10 (111–13).

72 There is also a philosophical taste. Had I the opportunity to analyse the randomly mentioned books as they deserve to be analysed, I could make a good case for my taste. Unfortunately, I cannot touch upon even the most important aspects of Nietzsche's anti-metaphysics in this limited project.

73 *Jenseits von Gut und Böse*, par. 205, Nietzsche, vol. 5.

74 Ibid.

LECTURE THREE

75 *Der Fall Wagner*, Nietzsche, vol. 6.

76 Ibid. Nietzsche has in mind Wagner's book on Beethoven, *Beethoven*, E. W. Fritzsch, Leipzig, published in 1870.

77 See Love, *Young Nietzsche and the Wagnerian Experience*.

78 See Hegel, *Encyclopaedie*, Part III, Philosophy of Mind, 3: 'The absolute spirit', par. 560. Or see Hegel's *Lectures on Aesthetics* Introduction.

79 Marx formed the same opinion about Schiller. He contrasted Shakespeare to Schiller, whereas for Nietzsche Shakespeare was just a half-barbarian. For him only Greek tragedy (before Euripides) counts as the real thing.

80 English translation by Lionel Salter, 1970.

81 Letter to Mathilde Wesendonck, 29–30 May 1859.

82 Nietzsche is never tired of Disentangling tragedy and pessimism. A real tragedy, as a manifestation of Dionysian genre, says 'yes' to life.

83 G. Lukács, in his outstanding sketch of the non-tragic drama, points out that the hero of a non-tragic drama must be either a wise man or a saint. He discusses only wise men.

84 All these are references to the Nietzschean understanding of 'good men'.

85 The centrality of compassion in ethics is also Schopenhauerian. It is Schopenhauer who writes that morals are based on the spontaneous recognition that the other is ourselves. The combination of *Mitleid*-ethics and

pessimism, with emphasis on Buddhism, is, however, not this time on Wagner's agenda.

86 Sándor Ferenczy expressed a similar idea in psychoanalytical terms: 'Ohne Mitleid keine Heilung' (without compassion, no healing).

87 Goethe, J. W.: *Gedichte*, in *Werke*, west-Östlicher Divan.

88 I dismiss the vulgar interpretation, namely, that Amfortas contracted veneral disease. For in this case syphilis also stands for something else; it has a symbolic meaning. I begin right with the symbolic meaning.

89 Nietzsche, vol. 13, spring 1888 (15).

90 Nietzsche, vol. 13, spring 1888, 15(15).

91 Nietzsche, vol. 13, 15(17).

LECTURE FOUR

92 Nietzsche, *On the Genealogy of Morals*, par. 1. All English quotations translated by Walter Kaufmann.

93 Ibid., par. 2.

94 Ibid., par. 3.

95 Ibid., par. 5.

96 Ibid., par. 6.

97 Ibid., par. 7.

98 Ibid., par. 7.

99 The philosophical inclinations and interests of Gottfried Keller and Wagner were very similar for a considerable amount of time. Nietzsche shared the enthusiasm for Wilhem Meister, which is another exemple of *amor fati*.

100 There are two kinds of Kundry, the evil and the repentant, yet they both are also one. Kundry, as a temptress to the good, and Kundry, as temptress to the evil, equally conjure up the figure of Parsifal's mother.

101 *On the Genealogy of Morals*, par. 8.

102 This too is paradoxical, as is almost everything in Nietzsche. Obviously Wagner would not have recognized his project in Nietzsche's presentation, and not just because of his anti-Semitism, but because he had a very different conception of Christianity, even in his strictly atheistic and communist period.

103 Nietzsche dismisses Rousseau's understanding of the 'noble savage', of course.

104 *On the Genealogy of Morals*, par. 13.

105 Ibid., par. 14.

106 Ibid., par. 14.

107 Ibid., par. 16.

108 I prefer my translation 'the capacity to make promises' to the 'right to make promises' of Kaufmann.

109 This reminds us inevitably of Freud. There are motives also in *Parsifal* (e.g. of Oedipal character) that will recall similar associations.

110 *On the Genealogy of Morals*, par. 1.

111 Nietzsche operates with different concepts of rationality in a very sensible way. Rationality is (here I agree with him) a practical category; it refers to

action. The concepts Nietzsche applies here (in dealing with elementary practical facts of life) are not metaphysico-ontological. For example, Nietzsche does not 'believe' in ontological causality (belief is, in his mind, an act of will) neither does he presuppose it as a kind of cognitive a priori; he rather agrees with Hume that thinking causally helps us to act rationally, to anticipate, and also to have the right to make promises. For the critique of traditional metaphysico-ontological concepts see especially (in addition to *On the Genealogy of Morals*): *Beyond Good and Evil* and *The Twilight of the Gods*.

112 *On the Genealogy of Morals*, par. 2.

113 Ibid., par. 3.

114 Nietzsche once describes man as 'the wounded animal' in essay three. This may be a reference to Parsifal's pain.

115 This is the stage when guilt is not yet fused with bad conscience, not yet internalized, not yet linked to pain. It is rather a contractual (or quasi-contractual) obligation. Whoever fails to repay his debt is guilty that is, he remains in debt, and will be (must be) punished. I retold this story with several modifications in my essay 'The power of shame', in Agnes Heller, *The Power of Shame*, Routledge and Kegan Paul, London, 1989.

116 *On the Genealogy of Morals*, par. 7.

117 Ibid., par. 16.

118 Ibid., par. 18 and 19. Bad conscience is here already described as an illness – but, Nietzsche adds, as illness, just as pregnancy is an illness.

119 Ibid., par. 22.

120 Nietzshce frequently uses olfactory metaphors, e.g. he says that he can 'smell' things that are 'in the air'. In discussing morality, and particularily Christian morality, he frequently exclaims 'bad air!'. His favourite poet (beside Goethe), namely Heine, writes in one of his poems 'dass der Rabbi und der Mönch-dass sie alle beide stinken'.

121 This is recurring theme of Wagner. Siegfried, the fearless, experiences fear when confronted with the awakening Brünhilde. In *Parsifal* too, dread (*Bange*) arises in the encounter with the seductress. But here the conditions of anxiety are more complex, all of them having to do with knowledge (*Erkenntnis*).

122 Sören Kierkegaard, *The Concept of Anxiety*, Princeton University Press, Princeton, NJ, 1980, p. 42.

123 Presented, among other places, in *Der Fall Wagner*.

124 *On the Genealogy of Morals*, par. 24.

125 Ibid., III, par. 1.

126 Ibid., par. 2–5 discuss Wagner and his *Parsifal* as well as the relation of the artist to his works. Since we have spoken about these themes already, we will omit them here.

127 Ibid., par. 6.

128 Ibid., par. 8.

129 Ibid., par. 10.

130 Ibid., par. 10.

131 For Nietzsche's critique of the essence/apppearance distinction see *Jenseits von Gut und Böse* and *Götzendämmerung*.

132　In the second act we came across the simile of pregnancy, when Nietzsche mentioned the illness of men of conscience, and added that this is an illness just as pregnancy is an illness. Yet there is another branch of 'sickness' discussed right afterwards, which is entirely barren.

133　*On the Genealogy of Morals*, par. 10.

134　Ibid., par. 11 and 12.

135　Ibid., par. 13.

136　Ibid., par. 14.

137　Ibid., par. 23.

138　The Zarathustra quote preceeds par. 1 of essay three in *Genealogy*.

139　Ibid., par. 23 of essay three.

140　Ibid., par. 24.

141　Ibid., par. 27. Not just this sentence, but the whole chain of thought is remarkably very Hegelian. That Nietzsche rejected Hegel's philosophy is well known. Yet I do not think that he ever read Hegels's *Phenomenology*.

142　Ibid., par. 27.

143　Some contemporary interpreters of *Parsifal*, see in it a pagan myth rather than a Christian mystery-play.

144　Ibid., par. 28.

145　Ibid., par. 28.

146　Ibid., par. 28.

147　*On the Genealogy of Morals*, par. 28.

148　Hegel says that the word 'perhaps' has no place in philosophy. Yet it has a place in Nietzsche's philosophy.

149　Pascal, *Pensées*, Series II (The wager).

150　Nietzsche, vol. 13, spring 1888 15(30) 2. The quoted lines terminate a lenghthy discourse on (against) decadence. The 'us' of the quotation refers to those who, like Nietzsche, are decadents yet, also simultaneously the opposites of the decadents.

151　The similarity between Leibniz's and Nietzsche's perspectivism was pointed out by Heidegger, in *Holzwege*: 'Nietzsche's word, "God is dead"', Klostermann, Frankfurt, 1952.

152　Lukács, in *History and Class Consciousness*, went to great pains to rescue the absolute standpoint without resigning perspectivism. But then he had to reintroduce the concept of a 'privileged standpoint' into his narrative, substituting the proletariat's attributed consciousness for God's absolute consciousness.

153　Lucien Goldmann applied the Pascalian idea of the wager in a similar manner, in his *Le Dieu caché*.

154　*On the Genealogy of Morals*, par. 23.

155　Lukács, *A Regeny Elmicere Mapueto* (*The Historical Novel*), Gondoled, Budapest, 1975.

156　*Ecce Homo*, par. 8.

157　Many will disagree with this sentence. After all, it is common knowledge in some philosophical circles that Nietzsche fully deconstructed the subject. The topic is too complex to be discussed here fully. Let me quote two, seemingly contradictory, sentences to make my point briefly. Both are taken from Nietzsche's notebooks, spring 1887, from vol. 12 of the *Studienausgabe*; both were committed to paper during the years that we here more closely scrutinize. First see 7(60): '"Es ist alles subjektiv" sagt ihr: aber schon das ist *Auslegung*, das "Subjekt" ist nichts Gegebenes, sondern etwas Hinzu-Erdichtetes, Dahinter-Gegebenes, Dahinter-Gestecktes . . .' ('Everything is subjective, you say; but his is already an *interpretation*. The subject is not something given, but something practically added or given behind, put behind . . .'). Then see 9(106) '*Das Subjekt is allein beweisbar; Hypothese, dass es nur Subjekte giebt* – dass Objekt nur eine Art Wirkung von Subjekt auf Subjekt ist . . . *ein Modus des Subjekts* (emphasis by Nietzsche). (Only the subject can be confirmed. The hypothesis that only subjects exist, that the object is nothing but a kind of influence exercised by a subject on the other subject . . . One modus or subject.) 'We do not speak here about an ontological subject, less about a transcendental subject, but about will to power, the driving energy, affect, life that drives us as it drives also others; yet it drives us in different directions and towards different kinds of knowledge.'

158 Hegel was sometimes accused, with no justification, with having done something similar. He recognized destiny in history (in the march of the world-spirit) and would have never identified Schicksal with himself.

159 Nietzsche, vol. 13, spring 1888, 15(120).

160 Ibid.

161 '*Jenseits von Gut und Böse*', par. 203, Nietzsche, vol. 5.

162 As mounted by Hegel before him, but without Nietzsche's knowledge.

163 Nietzsche, vol. 13, spring 1888, 15(114).

164 See note 66.

165 Scheler in his book on ethical formalism (*Formalismus in der Ethik und die materiale Wertethik*) learned much from Nietzsche. Let me add that in his concept of 'stages' Kierkegaard too solved the conflict between merely formal and merely substantive approaches by a kind of typology.

166 Nietzsche refers either to Diotima's account in *Symposium*, or to Socrates' account from *Politeia*. True, Nietzsche sometimes observes, for Plato, that metaphysics is the way to preserve artistocratic values and ideals in a decadent age.

167 See note 40, second lecture.

168 About the latter see *Jenseits von Gut und Böse*, par. 260. On the topic of Christian love see also par. 269.

169 Nietzsche, vol. 13, Spring 1888 (92).

170 The discussion of the active/reactive differentiation is the best part of Deleuze's book on Nietzsche. The distinction is a theme that follows Nietzsche throughout his whole life; it occupies an eminent place in 'Vom Nutzen und Nachtheil der Historie fuer das Leben' from *Unzeitgemaesse Betrachtungen* (*Untimely Meditations*), Nietzsche, vol. 1.

171 Ibid., par. 263. At this point we should recall Wagner's letter to Baudelaire, and Nietzsche's comment on it.

172 Ibid., par. 287.

173 Nietzsche, vol. 13, spring 1888. It is obvious that Nietzsche wanted to reopen the case in his planned book *The Will to Power*.

174 Nietzsche had a deep aversion for Stoicism, regarding it as one of the forerunners of Christian ethics. His relation to Epicureanism is more complex.

175 Actually, the Nietzschean aesthetization of ethics was directly taken over

by some leading figures of Nazi Germany, Hitler included.

176 *Ecce Homo*: 'Zur Genealogie der Moral', Nietzsche, vol. 6.

LECTURE FIVE

177 Nietzsche's emotional swings also need to be noted. While he speaks about himself as about a historical turning point, he also notes that his attacks against Christian morality (and morality in general) do not harm morality at all; it has remained untouched by them.

178 *Jenseits von Gut und Böse*, par. 230, Nietzsche, vol. 5.

179 To avoid misunderstanding: there is nothing 'aesthetic' in the categorical imperative. But the upright man (of *The Doctrine of Virtues*) has already aquired an aesthetic dimension that was being prepared ever since *The Critique of Judgement*.

180 *On the Genealogy of Morals*, essay three, par. 23.

181 *On the Genealogy of Morals*, essay two, par. 2.

182 Nietzsche, vol. 6, Dionysus-Dithyramben.

183 *On the Genealogy of Morals*, essay one.

184 Dostoevsky's hero, Raskolnikow, bows deeply before the suffering of humankind. I have discussed this 'moral gesture' in my study 'The power of shame' in similar terms to those that I now use to discuss Parsifal's empathy, in *The Power of Shame*, Routledge, London, 1985.

LETTERS CONCERNING MORAL AESTHETICS

185 'My propositions are elucidatory in this way: he who understands me finally recognizes them as nonsensical, when he has climbed out through them, on them, over them. (He must so to speak throw away the ladder, after he has climbed up on it.)' Ludwig Wittgenstein, *Tractatus Logico-Philosophicus*, trans C. K. Ogden, Routledge & Kegan Paul, London, 1922.

Index

a priori, 51, 52, 204, 207, 209; cognitive, 305; genetic, 204, 205, 206, 208, 211, 270; immoral, immoralist, 51; social or socio-cultural, 204, 205, 206, 208, 211, 270

absolute, 87, 112, 113, 300; God as, 136

absolute spirit, 166, 185, 206, 211

Adorno, Theodor, 32, 240, 254, 274

aestheticization, 81–3; of ethics, 307; of life, 269

aesthetics, 147, 260, 262; moral, 81–2, 251, 260

affect, 45, 59, 72, 81, 88, 307; of shame, 52

amor fati, 7, 13, 17, 33, 39, 44, 60, 74, 114, 115, 124, 128, 131, 143, 144, 147, 156, 159, 164, 170, 191, 201, 218, 265, 271, 286, 288, 294, 304

Antichrist, 31, 36, 62, 90

anti-Semitism, 34–5, 304

anxiety, 58, 195, 198, 241, 305

arché, 21, 120, 173

Arendt, Hannah, 121, 167, 170, 173, 204, 244, 274, 275, 298

aristocracy: cultural, 21; intellectual and emotional, 125; traditional, 81

Aristotle, 13, 100, 102, 135, 178, 183, 193, 194, 200, 206, 227, 254, 255, 264, 275; distinction between practical and theoretical thinking, 112; his ethics, 135; his metaphysics, 135; *Nicomachean Ethics*, 100, 135

ascetic ideal, ideals, 22, 27, 37, 62, 63, 64, 66, 67, 68, 69, 75, 87, 88, 90, 92, 149

ascetic priest, 44, 61, 62, 63, 64, 65, 67, 76, 89, 143, 213

atheism, 39, 66, 299, 301

Augustine, 102, 300

Austen, Jane, 257, 274, 275

authenticity, 27, 72, 125, 137, 161, 162, 165

autonomy, 47, 86, 91, 98, 178, 198, 199, 209, 212, 213, 234, 237 239; moral, 133, 237

avant-garde, 301; modernist, 23, 28, 29; music, 35

bad conscience, 52, 55, 57, 59, 60, 90, 110, 305

Baudelaire, Charles, 34, 156, 307

beautiful, the, 7, 108, 119, 242, 271

beauty, 108, 242, 244, 245, 246, 247, 248, 252, 253, 254, 262, 269, 272, 274, 275, 276, 278, 280, 281, 286, 291, 292, 296; aesthetic, 262; cultivation of, 272; moral, 250, 272; taste for, 287

becoming, 81, 148, 174, 217, 239; becoming-what-you-are, 130

Beethoven, Ludwig van, 14, 27, 29, 30, 42, 156, 264, 279

being, 51, 141; and becoming, 81; clearing of, 247; fact of, 177–8; love of, 283–4

Benjamin, Walter, 7, 261, 291

Bestimmung, 81

biography, 103, 104, 158

castes: aristocratic, 53; high and low, 22; society of, 72

categorical imperative, 4, 30, 51, 85, 105, 106, 107, 108, 109, 111, 114, 116,

categorical imperative (*cont'd*):
117, 125, 127, 130, 132, 135, 137,
146, 192, 193, 198, 223, 225, 307;
absoluteness of, 113

causality, 56, 147; concept of, 147;
natural, 121; ontological, 305

cause, causes, 7, 12, 21, 163; and effect,
54; sufficient, 146

certainty, 27, 57, 112, 140; Absolute
Certainty, 120; self-certainty, 239, 240,
241, 245, 246, 247

Christ, 5, 14, 31, 41, 302; Jesus Christ,
53; pagan, 84

Christianity, 5, 22, 27, 31, 33, 40, 49, 53,
61, 66, 234, 300, 301, 302, 304; anti-
Christianity, 299

classicism, 259, 260

communication: direct, 97; indirect, 7, 97,
98, 123, 129

compassion (*Mitleid*), 45, 47, 51, 55, 60,
61, 62, 90

conscience, 29, 52, 54, 55, 56, 59, 60, 87,
88, 90, 104, 127, 168, 170, 184, 273,
305; active and reactive, 79; bad, 52,
55, 57, 59, 60; emergence of, 56;
European, 106

consciousness, 5, 208; of contingency, 5;
of human finitude, 5; self-, 208; social,
16; solitary, 88

consequentialism, 157, 168

contingency, 3, 5, 13, 40, 56, 70, 73, 75,
112, 119, 128, 144, 171, 208, 254,
255, 273, 289; absolute, 205;
consciousness of, 5; cosmic, 208; of
history, 75; human condition of, 53;
world of, 75

contingent existence, 13

creativity, 143, 207, 256, 277

culture, 181, 182, 185, 206, 291;
aristocratic, 80; decadent, 41, 42;
European, 51; high, 183; morbid, 58; of
truth, 45; sick, 64; spiritual, 45;
warrior, 81

Dasein, 144, 178, 200

death, 15, 41, 54, 59, 105, 143, 144, 227,
238, 239, 255, 291; of God, 48, 61, 66,
104, 106, 135, 208, 218, 227

decadence, 22, 35, 36, 42, 43, 46, 55, 61,
69, 90

decency, 12, 83, 126, 132, 155, 169, 172,
223, 260, 267, 280

decision, 3, 5, 6, 15; final, 16; moral, 116

Deleuze, 299, 301, 307

democracy, 16, 84, 183, 184, 185, 199;
communitarian, 185; liberal, 185, 187

Derrida, Jacques, 3, 5, 6, 105

Descartes, René, 153

destiny, 7, 13, 33, 39, 40, 43, 44, 45, 46,
47, 52, 59, 61, 62, 63, 67, 72, 73, 75,
89, 90, 97, 101, 126, 128, 134, 143,
144, 150, 151, 153, 154, 155, 160,
164, 170, 171, 178, 191, 201, 205,
208, 213, 217, 241, 254, 255, 284,
290, 307; ethical, 90; fulfilment of, 52;
history's, 73; love of, 7; towards, 59

determination, 12, 140, 145, 147; by law,
239; causal, 121; self-determination,
146, 147

difference, 13, 29, 149, 152, 153, 154,
155, 159, 160, 165, 168, 169, 176,
177, 179, 189, 207, 233, 260, 261,
267, 272, 277, 278, 280, 285, 290,
294

Diogenes Laetertius, 196, 299

Dionysus, 15, 32, 33, 36, 56, 89, 299

Dostoevsky, Fyodor, 5, 13, 14, 302, 308

duty, duties, 100, 101, 105, 108, 129

education, 52; moral, 53, 54, 55, 56;
novel of, 52

ego, 99, 164, 200, 201

Eichmann, 100, 105, 121, 122

either/or, 41, 134, 188, 201, 265, 266

enlightenment, 16, 45, 66; man of, 52;
radical, 9

Epicureanism, 195, 216, 217, 235, 275,
307

Epicurus, 215, 235

epistemology, Kant's, 111, 112

equality, 46, 113, 183, 184; formal, 113;
ideals of, 84; political, 86

Eros, 174, 283, 286, 292

essence, 78; bipolarity with appearance,
64

eternal recurrence of the same, 17, 26, 62,
90, 124

eternity, 101, 102, 218, 274

ethics, 2, 3, 4, 5, 6, 11, 13, 15, 17, 19,
36, 84–5, 95, 96, 100, 103, 105, 113,
115, 117, 122, 125, 128, 148, 156,
157, 158, 159, 168, 169, 174, 209,
214, 253, 264; aestheticization of, 307;
Aristotle's, 135; Christian, 5; of the
consciousness of human finitude and of
contingency, 5; contemporary, 4;
Epicurean, 213; of existence, 134;
formal, 75; general, 2, 6, 11; Jewish-

Christian, 20; Kantian, 4, 114; modern, 2, 6; new, 85; Nietzsche's, 11; of personality, 3, 4; pure, 4; of responsibility, 4, 5; source of, 128; traditional, 3, 16

ethics of personality, aesthetic conception and formal conception of, 125; substantive definition and formal definition of, 82, 89–90

ethos, 95, 254; of personality, 61; practical, 137

eudaimonia, 77

Euripides, 303

evil, 21, 29, 45, 47, 52, 53, 54, 55, 75, 90, 107, 108, 114, 122, 132, 133, 137, 164, 198, 227, 272, 290, 304; base-evil, 46; modern, 48; radical, 109; radicalization of, 21, 22

existence, 13, 71, 142; contingent, 13

existential choice, 11, 12, 130, 132, 133, 134, 135, 147, 148, 150, 152, 153, 154, 155, 156, 157, 159, 160, 171, 172, 174, 176, 178, 179, 180, 188, 205, 208, 232, 233, 234, 239, 254, 255, 259, 260, 261, 266, 267, 271, 272, 277, 280, 290

exister, 51, 98, 133, 136, 137, 142, 143, 144, 148, 150, 152, 163, 169, 173, 174, 178, 200, 218, 250, 251

fate, 13, 17, 39, 40, 44, 51, 59, 101, 104, 118, 123, 128, 130, 137, 143, 144, 165, 170, 188, 268, 281, 284, 302; love of, 13, 59, 128, 134, 137, 156, 160

Feuerbach, 35, 39, 66, 151, 299

finitude, 5; fact of, 177, 178, 186; human, 5

Flaubert, Gustave, 35

free spirit, spirits, 21, 22, 32, 37

freedom, 13, 21, 36, 40, 47, 87, 111, 117, 118, 127, 183, 186, 195, 208, 209, 225, 239, 240, 241, 242, 244, 245, 246, 247, 249, 253, 254, 255, 256, 259, 260, 274, 275; absolute, 245; actuality of, 58; of choice, 242, 256, 261; consciousness of, 87; essence of, 244; feeling of, 240; foundation of, 244; harmony of, 248; idea of, 244; instinct of, 117, 118; law of, 132; love of, 287; moral, 121; possibility of, 58; traditional, 91, 111; transcendental, 118, 127, 132, 133, 134, 191, 218, 242; of will, 64, 239, 242

Freud, Sigmund, 16, 198, 200, 201, 206, 239

genealogy, of 'bad conscience', 57; of morals, 51, 84, 95; Nietzsche's, 52, 56; of responsibility-taking, 57; Wagner's, 52, 54

genius, 12, 29, 34, 207; moral, 14

God, 17, 22, 31, 32, 44, 49, 57, 61, 66, 67, 71, 72, 102, 104, 108, 135, 136, 137, 144, 146, 177, 185, 223, 227, 245, 248, 287, 291, 306; as absolute, 136; absolute consciousness of, 307; Christian, 22, 66; death of, 47, 61, 62, 66, 104, 106, 135, 208; existence of, 70, 71; as God-Man, 108; of Israel, 210; love of, 145, 245, 248; as pure spirit, 142

God is dead, 22, 48, 78, 102, 135

gods, 65, 185

Goethe, J.W. von, 3, 8, 13, 14, 15, 32, 33, 46, 56, 85, 124, 141, 143, 237, 238, 249, 259, 260, 268, 295, 298, 305

good, the, 17, 19, 21, 24, 29, 43, 46, 51, 53, 54, 108, 110, 120, 126, 131, 133, 195, 242, 276; and bad, 52, 53, 55, 79, 104; and evil, 52, 53, 89, 104, 107, 114, 132, 133, 137, 138, 164, 210, 227; idea of the Good, 120

'good life', the, 2, 217, 218

goodness, 12, 14, 79, 86, 108, 120, 121, 130, 132, 169, 271, 276, 277, 295; source of, 128, 132

Goodness–Truth–Beauty, 108

grace, 137, 156, 157, 276, 278, 281; divine, 140

Grail, the, 40, 42, 43, 46, 48, 52, 54, 60, 62, 66, 67, 68, 89, 90–1, 154; Holy, 41, 44, 60

guilt, 29, 55, 57, 59, 60, 61, 110, 195, 197, 305; Christian theme of, 65; feeling of, 52; recognition of, 60

happiness, 37, 99, 100, 101, 217, 228, 276–83, 287

harmony, 237, 239, 240, 244, 245, 246, 247, 252, 255, 256, 259, 273, 280, 281, 282, 294; between faculties, 256; of freedom, 248; between understanding and imagination, 242; of the other, 241; pre-established, 245

Hegel, Georg, 39, 75, 86, 99, 102, 111, 119, 128, 129, 141, 142, 166, 183, 206, 211, 227, 237, 244, 246, 271, 273, 279, 303, 306, 307; his critique of

Hegel (*cont'd*):
Kant, 99; *Phenomenology of Spirit*, 99,
141, 185, 206, 306; *Philosophy of
Right*, 99, 227
Heidegger, Martin, 8, 113, 141, 144, 183,
204, 239, 246, 247, 248, 300, 306
Heine, Heinrich, 102, 300, 305
Heraclitus, 57, 146, 251
herd, the, 34, 65; opinion of the, 81–2
hermeneutics, 142, 199; ethical, 122; of
existence, 182; of experience, 196;
moral, 122
heteronomy, 84, 86, 217, 234
hierarchy, 215, 244, 253, 259, 260, 261;
of duties, 105; of greatness, 116; moral,
116; of ranking, 79; of values, 79, 115
historicism, 96, 102, 104, 112, 116; anti-
historicism, 78; radical, 78
historicity, 112, 178
history, 74, 75, 96, 104, 119, 140, 174,
266; contingency of, 75; destiny of, 73;
mythologized, 56
Hitler, Adolf, 75, 76, 83, 89, 307; as
artwork, 82
homo noumenon, 109, 110, 113
homo phenomenon, 109, 110, 113, 117
Horkheimer, 32
humankind, 4, 16, 33, 69, 75, 99, 113
humanism, 32, 203; European, 237
Hume, David, 146, 305
Husserl, Edmund, 246, 247

Ibsen, Henrik, 13, 24, 47
id, 200, 201
idea, ideas, 7, 11; avant-garde, 29; of
Beauty and of the Good, 271; moral,
54; Platonic, 243
ideal, ideals, 3, 66, 69, 70, 71, 87–8, 102,
155, 185, 239; aesthetic, 81, 84;
Dionysian, 105; of equality, 84; ethical,
81; new, 53; regulative, 6, 15; *see also*
ascetic ideal
imagination, 59, 207, 251; play of, 239,
241, 245, 280
individual, the, 22, 81, 98, 101, 117, 118,
130, 176, 249, 269; autonomous, 87,
90; emancipated, 87; free, 88;
harmonious, 237; his or her perfection
and completion, 88; the sovereign, 56,
87, 88, 90; the universal, 237
individuality, 158, 272, 273
instinct, 24, 56, 57, 59, 81, 85, 96, 97,
98, 114, 121, 122, 123, 126, 134, 143,
150, 152, 164, 167, 201; of esteem, 80;

of freedom, 117, 118; good, 24; moral,
118, 197; and reason, 82, 122, 125
instrumentalization, 90, 105, 238, 250;
Kantian formula of non-
instrumentalization, 122, 125
ipseity, 99, 113, 117, 133, 181, 199, 218,
293

Jesus, 31, 32, 33, 37; Jesus Christ, 53; *see
also* Christ
judgement, 121, 126, 256, 267; aesthetic,
211, 252, 269; moral, 115, 117, 122,
123; reflective, 121, 245, 246, 288
justice, 4, 55, 100, 114, 115, 157, 169,
276; virtue of, 55

kalokagathos, *kalokagathia*, 237, 244,
247, 254, 255, 257
Kant, Immanuel, 4, 20, 29, 72, 75, 85,
86, 90, 99, 100–1, 102, 103–7, 108–9,
111, 113, 115, 117–19, 121, 127,
130–1, 132, 134, 137, 145, 146, 151,
153, 155, 156, 158, 163, 165, 166,
167, 168, 169, 182, 186, 187, 191,
192, 195, 196–8, 199, 200, 201, 206,
207, 209, 210, 211, 212, 214, 217,
235, 241, 246, 252, 264, 269, 275,
277, 288; *Critique of Judgement*, 121,
141, 172, 175, 187, 252, 308; *Critique
of Practical Reason*, 104, 111, 142,
301; *Critique of Pure Practical Reason*,
104, 111, 142, 301; *Critique of Pure
Reason*, 111, 141; his epistemology,
111, 112; *Groundwork*, 111, 130;
Metaphysics of Morals, 100, 121, 127;
his moral law, 120; his moral
philosophy, 99, 103, 107, 108, 111,
112, 123; his practical philosophy, 111
Kantianism, 99, 119, 121, 123
Kierkegaard, Sören, 7, 12, 15, 16, 22, 51,
58, 97, 113, 129, 130, 132, 133, 134,
136, 143, 144, 145, 146, 148, 157,
169, 172, 173, 176, 180, 185, 192,
195, 198, 209, 217, 234, 239, 250,
265, 284, 292, 295, 298, 300, 301,
307; as anti-Cartesian, 136; *The
Concept of Anxiety*, 195; *Concluding
Unscientific Postscript*, 180; *Either-Or*,
288, 298
knowledge, 3, 6, 36, 53, 56, 58, 59, 60,
61, 62, 89, 110, 112, 113, 119, 120,
121, 127, 128, 132, 134, 135, 148,
164, 173, 305; destiny towards, 59;
modern, 135; philosophy of, 112; pre-

knowledge, 30; rational, 127; scientific, 135; of the source, 128
Kuhn, Franz, 112

law, 3, 4, 5, 107, 108, 119, 152, 209; absolute, 4; divine, 90; as fact, 111; of freedom, 132; human, 112; moral, 5, 91, 99, 104, 105, 106, 107, 111, 112, 113, 114, 115, 116, 117, 118, 119, 120, 121, 122, 123, 127, 128, 132, 135, 149, 155, 167, 172, 175, 186, 191, 192, 198, 218; of nature, 112, 121, 235, 236; obedience to, 127; reverence for, 98; universal, 5, 99, 121
Lebensgefühl (feeling of life), 239, 272, 282
Leibniz, Gottfried, 70, 71, 72, 112, 113, 177, 178, 204, 239, 290, 306
Lessing, 180
Levinas, 92
liberation, 274, 287; in forgetting, 107
life, 17, 18, 20, 27, 32, 43, 47, 51, 57, 59, 63, 71, 98, 103, 104, 113, 125, 129, 158, 236, 282, 307; degenerating, 64; enemy of, 64; good, 2; love of, 275; Nietzsche's, 25; personal, 24; philosopher's, 18; philosophical, 24; preservation of, 64; 'yes' to, 57
logic, 291; of the heart, 295; of the modern era, 113; of reason, 295
love, 7, 46, 47, 58, 63, 79, 115, 123, 134, 174, 247, 256, 262, 269, 284, 286, 287, 288, 289, 290, 291, 293, 294, 295, 297; erotic, 175–6, 179; of fate, 13, 125, 156; gospel of, 53; self-love, 109, 110, 133; sensual, 47, 61; sexual, 61, 62; subjective, 285; tragic, 285
Lukács, Gyorgy 2, 3, 14, 15, 16, 72, 124, 185, 269, 298, 303, 306
Luther, Martin, 35, 65
Luxembourg, Rosa, 274, 275

Machiavelli, Niccolo, 20, 76, 300
Mann, Thomas, 27, 290, 301
Marcuse, Herbert, 257, 273
Marx, Karl, 3, 16, 96, 237, 299, 303
mask, masks, 11, 22, 30, 63, 265
maxims, 4, 105, 108, 109, 116, 121; moral, 112, 162, 163, 164; universal, 88
metaphysics, 31, 44, 84, 87, 102, 120, 141, 145, 182, 183, 195, 204, 208, 210, 246, 251, 307; anti-metaphysics, 303; Aristotle's, 135; Dionysian, 57;

end of, 135; need of, 210; Platonic, 78; of suffering, 57; traditional, 177, 195, 259; Truth of, 66
Mishima, Yukio, 124, 144, 151
Mitleid, 45, 90; *Mitleid*-ethics, 303
modernity, 18, 40, 105, 106, 137, 169, 184, 209
Montaigne, Michel de, 20
morality, 4, 15, 19, 20, 31, 51, 58, 66, 71, 73, 75, 80, 84, 88, 90, 91, 95, 99, 100, 104, 106, 107, 111, 115, 116, 118, 119, 120, 121, 127, 128, 132, 133, 155, 157, 158, 164, 170, 191, 193, 195, 209, 210, 249, 290; Christian, 20, 39, 305, 308; of custom, 87; determination of, 128; Jewish-Christian-Kantian, 58; Kantian, 48; master, 80; new, 21; pagan, 39; sceptical, 39; secular-humanist, 39; slave morality, 80; source, sources of, 128, 210; of sympathy, 90; traditional Jewish-Christian, 67
morals, 20, 22, 51, 83, 84, 87–8, 108, 111, 115, 120; Christian, 19; genealogy of, 51; philosophy of, 2, 6, 11, 12, 75; source of, 128
music, 26, 27, 34, 35, 36, 38, 44, 240, 255; avant-garde, 35; and drama, 50, 51; 'French', 35; pure, 38
myth: of Cain and Abel, 23; of the prodigal son, 23
mythology, mythologies, 33, 36, 208; Christian, 31; historical, 21; Nietzsche's, 78; Wagnerian, 31

Napoleon Bonaparte, 13, 14, 32, 33, 45, 48, 56, 71, 85
natality, 204, 205, 208
nature, 61, 119, 121, 127, 132, 144, 185, 191, 206, 238, 255; external, 121; law of, 121, 235, 236; teleology of, 119
necessity, 56, 70, 73, 101, 102, 111, 119, 128, 144, 218, 239, 244, 245; world of, 75
Nicholas of Cusa, 108, 109
Nietzsche, Friedrich, *passim*; *Antichrist*, 31, 32; *Beyond Good And Evil*, 20, 30, 37, 80, 299, 301, 305; *Birth of Tragedy*, 23, 32, 57, 299; his break with Wagner, 39; *Case of Wagner*, 30, 31, 299; *Dawn*, 39; *Ecce Homo*, 12, 18, 22, 24, 26, 30, 32, 33, 34, 61, 298, 299, 300, 301, 302; his ethics, 11; as European, 85; his genealogy, 52, 56;

Nietzsche (*cont'd*):
 Human, All Too Human, 24, 25; as
  immoralist, 19; his life, 25; as
  metaphysician, 87; his mythology, 78;
  Nietzsche Contra Wagner, 33, 39; as
  nihilist, 87; *On the Genealogy of*
  Morals, 23, 26, 27, 28, 29, 30, 36, 37,
  39, 50, 53, 54, 55, 65, 69, 71, 79, 298,
  299, 301; his Parsifal, 68; his
  personality, 30; his relationship with
  Wagner, 25, 26, 37; his self, 25; *Thus*
  Spoke Zarathustra, 26, 28, 84, 300,
  301; his truth, 51; *Twilight of the Idols*,
  31, 37, 305; *Untimely Meditations*, 23,
  307; *Will to Power*, 23, 25, 29, 307
nihilism, 15, 18, 22, 35, 43, 51, 87, 90,
  107, 112, 191, 302; absolute, 106;
  active, 66; passive, 66, 113, 302;
  philosophy of, 22; total, 303
nobility, 30, 79, 80, 81, 100, 125, 181,
  187
norm, norms, 3, 4, 5, 7, 12, 15, 125, 169,
  253; ethical, 5; of virtue, 6
nothing, 90, 208, 210
nothingness, 49, 58, 62, 90, 209; will to,
  67, 69
noumenon, 98, 119, 133, 196; noumenal
  nature, 218

Oedipus, 32, 33, 62, 92, 200, 202, 302
openness, 209, 239, 240, 242, 253
order, of rank, 75, 77, 78, 79, 85, 86;
  sacred, 52
orientative principle, 5, 6, 7; moral, 6
Other, the, 3, 4, 5, 7, 12, 43, 45, 153,
  168; suffering, 91
other, the, 99; as bad, 53; harmony/
  disharmony of, 241; identification with,
  61
overman, overmen, 22, 44, 45, 72, 76, 78,
  81, 82, 89

Parsifal, 26, 30, 32, 36, 37, 39, 40, 41,
  44, 45, 47, 48, 49, 51, 52, 53, 54, 55,
  56, 57, 58, 59, 60, 61, 62, 64, 66, 67,
  68, 69, 75, 76, 77, 84, 89, 90, 92, 111,
  119, 124, 143, 272; *Anti-Parsifal*, 49,
  50, 51, 58, 61, 62, 63, 65, 67, 87, 89,
  301, 302, 304, 305, 308; Jewish-
  Christian, 58; *see also* Wagner
Pascal, Blaise, 70, 306
pathos, 39, 45, 47, 295; moral, 84
personality, personalities, 15, 16, 17, 18,
  20, 27, 30, 33, 45, 47, 51, 85, 96, 98,

115, 161, 179, 180, 181, 182, 183,
  211, 255; beautiful, 271; essential, 234;
  ethical, 213; ethics of, 3, 4; ethos of,
  61; harmonious, 237, 247, 248; human,
  98; idiosyncratic, 95; great, 14;
  Nietzsche's, 30; rank order of, 86;
  sublime, 86; theory of, 2, 103; unique,
  16; virtue of, 212
perspective, 19, 60, 62, 71, 73, 87, 113
perspectivism, 70, 72, 97, 112, 113, 136,
  215, 300, 306; personal, 74; radical,
  71
pessimism, 22, 36, 42, 43, 90, 302, 303;
  evil, 235; heroic, 91, 300, 302–3;
  symptoms of, 51
pharmakon, 51, 105, 125
phenomenon, 119, 133, 196
philosophy, 6, 16, 18, 22, 63, 64, 84, 97,
  98, 101, 123, 128, 132, 140, 143, 147,
  152, 215, 233, 264; anti-moral, 21,
  104; critical, 103; of existence, 178,
  191; existence-philosophy, 266;
  existential moral, 12; Kant's, 195;
  Kantian, 75, 190; of knowledge, 112;
  metaphysical 'wrapping' of, 64;
  modern, 12; German, 102; moral, 1, 4,
  5, 11, 12, 19, 21, 22, 99, 101–2, 103,
  104, 106–7, 108, 109, 110, 111, 112,
  113, 114, 116, 119, 121, 123, 125,
  126, 127, 130, 132, 191, 192, 193,
  194, 195, 196, 250; of morals, 2, 6, 11,
  12, 75, 297; of nihilism, 22; post-
  Kantian, 113; practical, 110, 111, 112,
  127; of practice, 16; radical, 16, 22, 69,
  71, 72; speculative, 142; traditional,
  141; transcendental, 194
phronesis, 100
Plato, 13, 18, 20, 36, 37, 77, 78, 83, 102,
  105, 120, 121, 175, 176, 179, 184,
  187, 193, 194, 200, 202, 244, 246,
  248, 254, 255, 262, 263, 264, 269,
  283, 301, 307; *Gorgias*, 120; *Republic*,
  120, 307; *Symposium*, 203, 307
Plotinus, 244
pragmatism, 150
praxis, 87, 89; totality of, 88
principle, principles, 4, 5, 47, 87;
  foundational, 21; orientative, 5, 6, 7;
  orientative moral, 6
psyche, 62, 193, 194, 195, 211
psychoanalysis, 199, 200, 202, 239
psychology, 152, 193, 194, 195, 198, 209,
  265; cognitive, 206; existential, 195,
  201; Freudian, 201; moral, 81, 195

Rangordnung, 83, 84, 85, 86, 88
rationalism, 116, 118, 119, 121; hyper-rationalism, 133
rationality, 111, 120, 304; enlightened, 53; limits of, 112; of practical reason, 121
Rawls, 186
reason, reasons, 7, 12, 21, 59, 81, 83, 96, 97, 99, 110, 118, 119, 121, 123, 125, 128, 133, 141, 152, 163, 164, 165, 166, 170, 184, 195, 237, 255, 256, 291; fact of, 111, 177; and instinct, 122, 150, 152; life's reason, 81; limits of, 112; practical, 1, 72, 81, 97, 110, 111, 113, 121, 256; sufficient, 146; theoretical, 1, 113
redemption, 5, 28, 32, 42, 44, 45, 58, 62, 67, 68, 77, 78, 90, 298, 302; Christian theme of, 65
Redlichkeit (uprightness), 48, 50, 85
relativism, 112, 137, 191, 263, 265; moral, 113
religiosity, 42, 43
Renaissance, 116, 238
repetition, 208; existential, 209; of the human condition, 209; of the same, 205
responsibility, 3, 4, 5, 7, 19, 54, 55, 56, 59, 61, 125, 290; ethics of, 4, 5; men of, 60; personal, 3; prospective, 60; responsibility-taking, 57, retrospective, 60; will to, 64
ressentiment, 34, 43, 46, 51, 65, 74, 76, 183, 186, 187, 215, 229, 295
Robespierre, Maximilien, 102
Rosenzweig, Franz, 14, 15, 298
Rousseau, Jean Jacques, 118, 236, 304

Sand, George, 35, 274, 275
Sartre, Jean-Paul, 21
scepticism, 20, 137
Scheler, 307
Schiller, J.C.F. von, 40, 86, 303
Schopenhauer, Artur, 30, 35, 42, 51, 57, 66, 90, 303
sciences, 112; modern, 66, 84; natural, 22, 112, 207
seduction, 46, 49, 51, 53, 60, 62; to Christendom, 49; Oedipal nature of, 62
self, selves, 24, 30; Nietzsche's 25; phenomenal, 98
self-creation, 12, 77, 78
sensuality, 47, 63, 76, 84
sexuality, 61, 63
Shakespeare, William, 114, 115, 116, 172,

216, 250, 272, 297, 303; *Macbeth*, 114; his tragedies, 115
Shaw, George Bernard, 13, 17, 226
sickness, 51, 55, 58, 61, 238
sin, 42, 47, 59, 60; Christian theme of, 65
singularity, 98, 128, 130, 185, 203
Sittlichkeit (morality), 15, 99, 135, 196; Christian, 135; Jewish, 135
Socrates, 18, 36, 37, 78, 120, 159, 173, 184, 262, 301, 307
Sophocles, 64, 302
Spinoza, Baruch, 102, 226, 245, 246, 282, 291
Stoicism, 196, 216, 217, 307
subject: Kantian, 169; Kierkegaardian, 169; its identity with object, 94; transcendental, 307; universal, 95; world-historical, 74
subjectivism, 136, 191
subjectivity, 99, 273
sublimation, 287; of desire, 63; spiritual, 63
substance, 167, 234, 235; individual, 290
suffering, 21, 25, 57, 61, 66, 67, 69, 85, 87, 88, 156, 157, 165, 175, 209, 234, 291, 294; human, 92; meaning of, 86, 87; metaphysics of, 57; senseless, 57; source of, 61; with-the-other, 57
super-ego, 200, 201

taste, 86; aesthetic, 82; classicistic, 29; culinary, 82, 83; for decency, 82; ethical, 83; good, 85
teleology, 205; of nature, 119
thing-itself, the (*die Sache selbst*), 249, 264
time, 63, 183, 184; pure, 142
totality, 71, 72, 87, 89; epistemological, 72; metaphysical, 86; metaphysical concept of, 88; of praxis, 88
tragedy, 36, 38, 39, 276, 303; Shakespeare's, 114, 115
transcendental anthropology, 159, 160, 165
transcendental deduction, 120
transformation, 61; of Parsifal, 56
transvaluation: of all old values, 48; of all values, 19, 21, 31, 72; of eternal values, 74; of values, 14, 21, 53, 79; *see also* value
truth, 7, 20, 21, 32, 33, 60, 66, 68, 72, 84, 87, 89, 90, 106, 108, 136, 140, 167, 175, 176, 191, 192, 193, 210, 232; absolute, 215; culture of, 45; eternal, 193; historical, 73, 74;

truth (*cont'd*):
  Nietzsche's, 51; of-a-person, 73;
  plurality of, 210; relative, 136;
  subjective, 136; supreme, 108; value of,
  66; will to, 66; as a woman, 136
Truth, 40, 41, 42, 44, 46, 47, 66, 70, 71,
  72, 73, 87, 89, 137, 219, 263; ancient,
  48; of Christian God, 66; Grail as, 67;
  metaphysical, 67; metaphysical concept
  of, 73; of metaphysics, 66; as
  unconcealment, 41; uncovering of, 40
truthfulness, 19, 125, 162; virtue of, 66

unconcealment, 40, 67; Truth as, 41
unconscious, the, 148, 198, 199
understanding, 60, 252, 292; free play of,
  241, 242, 245
uniqueness, 83, 117, 130, 203;
  individual's, 259; universal, 203, 261
universal, the, 12, 13, 22, 98, 99, 117,
  128, 148, 149, 150, 151, 153, 154,
  156, 157, 161, 169, 172, 176, 177,
  189, 233, 237, 251, 253, 260, 261,
  277, 278, 278, 290
universalism, 84, 129, 176, 200, 257
universality, 13, 72, 85, 99, 101, 111,
  118, 119, 128, 130, 149, 168, 169,
  174, 180, 207, 245, 289; individual,
  247
utilitarianism, 22, 52, 300

value, values, 12, 15, 28, 45, 46, 49, 51,
  69, 71, 72, 79, 82, 85, 90, 91, 115,
  125; aesthetic, 35; eternal, 49, 74;
  ethical, 35; hierarchy of, 79, 115;
  historicist, 82; Jewish, 53; Jewish and
  Christian, 79; moral, 21, 101; of
  Parsifal, 31; reversal of, 22; Roman, 47;

of slaves, 79; substantive, 90;
  traditional, 21, 23, 46; traditional
  system of, 72; of truth, 66; of western
  culture, 84; *see also* transvaluation
virtue, virtues, 4, 45, 76, 83, 85, 90, 100,
  108, 125, 287; Aristotelian, 275; ideal
  of, 70; of justice, 55; norms of, 6; of
  personality, 212; of truthfulness, 66;
  substantive, 90
Voltaire, 126, 127, 137

Wagner, Richard, 18, 19, 23–8, 30, 32–
  40, 42–52, 54–8, 61–3, 65–9, 78, 84,
  89, 90, 92, 95, 150, 301, 302–5, 307;
  as artist, 25; his genealogy, 52, 54;
  Götterdämmerung, 36, 42; *Der Grüne
  Heinrich*, 52; *Meistersinger*, 30, 36, 42;
  Nietzsche's break with, 39; *Parsifal*, 25–
  8, 30–1, 33–6, 38–40, 42–3, 45–8, 50–
  2, 54–8, 61–2, 65–6, 84, 89, 116, 125,
  305–6; his relationship with Nietzsche,
  25, 26; *The Ring*, 36; *Tannhäuser*, 36,
  42, 43, 47, 140; *Tristan*, 42
Weber, Max, 4, 18, 118, 147
will, 55, 62, 67, 74, 86, 87, 90, 110; free,
  87, 110; freedom of, 64, 239, 242;
  good, 128, 131; human, 62; memory of
  the, 56; to nothingness, 67, 69; pure,
  111; to responsibility, 64; of the spirit,
  64; to truth, 66
will to power, 30, 39, 45, 63, 69, 72, 81,
  87, 88, 90, 164, 207, 240, 307
Wittgenstein, 2, 141; 148, 194, 297;
  Tractatus Logico-Philosophicus, 2, 297

Zarathustra, 19, 26, 27, 44, 45, 47, 57,
  65, 67, 67, 78, 84, 88, 89, 219, 301,
  306; *see also* Wagner